Ius Gentium: Comparative Perspectives on Law and Justice

Volume 119

Ius Gentium is a book series which discusses the central questions of law and justice from a comparative perspective. The books in this series collect the contrasting and overlapping perspectives of lawyers, judges, philosophers and scholars of law from the world's many different jurisdictions for the purposes of comparison, harmonisation, and the progressive development of law and legal institutions. Each volume makes a new comparative study of an important area of law. This book series continues the work of the well-known journal of the same name and provides the basis for a better understanding of all areas of legal science.

The *Ius Gentium* series provides a valuable resource for lawyers, judges, legislators, scholars, and both graduate students and researchers in globalisation, comparative law, legal theory and legal practice. The series has a special focus on the development of international legal standards and transnational legal cooperation.

Shai Farber

The Amicus Curiae Phenomenon

Theory, Causes and the Significance of Third Party Interventions

Springer

Shai Farber
Department of Criminology
Max Stern Yezreel Valley College (YVC)
Emek Yezreel, Israel

ISSN 1534-6781 ISSN 2214-9902 (electronic)
Ius Gentium: Comparative Perspectives on Law and Justice
ISBN 978-3-031-67224-8 ISBN 978-3-031-67225-5 (eBook)
https://doi.org/10.1007/978-3-031-67225-5

This Springer imprint is published by the registered company Springer Nature Switzerland AG
The registered company address is: Gewerbestrasse 11, 6330 Cham, Switzerland

Acknowledgment

The origins of this book go back to 2010 when I started researching the *Amicus Curiae* as part of my master's and Ph.D. studies at university. The book was eventually written over a period of about 3 years. Whenever it felt like I had completed the task, I read the draft carefully and realized there was room for more precision and further improvements. I would find myself engrossed once more in working on the book—trying to write it differently. This happened three times, resulting in three different versions. Each version focused on different aspects of the amicus phenomenon, emphasizing different elements of the enormous influence third parties have on the law, society, and our daily lives. Only when I finally felt that, not only from an analytical perspective but also from an intuitive point of view, that the focus and emphases were correctly balanced did I complete the version before you. It is far from perfect and could still be better, but the book does examine and describe a dominant phenomenon that affects our lives. After I finished writing the final version of the book, I realized that some of the questions and issues raised by the book are also my own dilemmas as a person, citizen, lawyer, social activist, and academic.

The subject of Amicus has occupied me for most of my academic life. My involvement with this topic goes beyond my academic interests. Over the years, as part of several positions I held in academia and practice, I became a shadow advisor to many organizations (rights organizations, commercial companies, and law firms) when they considered joining as amici for standing proceedings. Many of these cases involved applying in practice-specific legal information that could affect the proceedings in court. I very much enjoy connecting academic theory with practical experience.

The book before you is ambitious. It seeks to encompass how the "*Amicus Curiae Phenomenon*" works in most countries where the procedure exists as a significant part of the legal institutions. The book reviews and examines Amicus Curiae in continental law, used mainly in Europe, Asia, Latin America, and in common law institutions. This is indeed a challenging and ambitious task, complicated by the fact that many of the sources I relied on for the book were written in different languages: English, French, Spanish, German, Arabic, Hebrew, and others.

Reflecting on completing this academic book, I am grateful to the many people who have accompanied me on this profound and transformative journey. Writing a book of this kind is not an individual effort but a collective effort, and I owe a debt of gratitude to all those who took part in its creation.

I will not acknowledge individually the contributions of my friends and colleagues who accompanied me on this intellectual journey but express my deepest gratitude here to all of them. Their intellectual camaraderie, stimulating discussions, and willingness to offer constructive feedback shaped my thoughts and strengthened my arguments. Their academic and personal support has been an invaluable source of strength.

The book has many partners who helped, gave advice, checked a footnote, focused on a line of reasoning, thought differently, or read a document in its original language and translated it for me. I want to thank, therefore, Nir Kedar, Einat Buch, Shira Gelb, Ilan Friedgot, Adriana Lizardo, Roni Eigle, Matan Goldblatt, and Snir Ahiad Yehezkel.

I would also like to thank the following people for their help in preparing this book: Springer, for their careful attention to detail and for their invaluable suggestions. Staff at the publishing house for their professionalism and dedication. Anonymous reviewers for helpful feedback.

I also express my gratitude to the Max Stern Yezreel Valley College for their generous financial support in covering various expenses associated with the production of this book.

Above all, I would like to thank my dear family.

Thank you for your patience and understanding to my wife, Michal, and our daughters, Gili, Roni, and Ori, who have witnessed the late nights, countless hours of solitude, and sacrifices to pursue knowledge. I love you.

Finally, I extend my heartfelt appreciation to the readers of the book. I am grateful to you for your engagement with this work, knowing that your exploration of the ideas presented within these pages brings purpose and meaning to my academic endeavors. I hope this book sparks new conversations, inspires further inquiry, and contributes to the knowledge in our field.

For all those who have journeyed with me, whether near or far, your presence has had an indelible impact on the creation of this book.

Even though this book seems to end a journey, it begins a new one. Hopefully, this book will be a valuable resource for those whom this topic is interesting. I am grateful for the opportunity to share my research with the world and hope it will positively contribute to the field.

2024

Shai Farber

About the Book

This book discusses how the legal practice known as the "Friend of the Court" (henceforth: **Amicus Curiae**) has developed into a central phenomenon in modern society, having a profound influence on the law and the way in which litigation is conducted in the courts. The Amicus Curiae allows one or more third parties, known as "amici," not formally involved in an ongoing legal procedure, to present information they have assembled to a court by submitting an "amicus brief." The amicus brief may include the opinions of experts, but it does not have to cover all relevant data appertaining to the proceedings in question, so may be regarded as supporting the point of view of the amici. Third parties submitting amicus briefs can be non-governmental public organizations such as human rights or "green" organizations or other organizations concerned with the rights of religious, LGBT, or women's groups. These third parties can also be corporations, professional unions (for example, bar associations or accountants), and politicians who seek to influence a particular issue held in the courts.

The author terms the rapid adoption of Amicus Curiae in countries around the world, together with the increase in its use, the "**Amicus Curiae Phenomenon**." The book describes and analyzes the dimensions and impact of this phenomenon, within which, in a short period of time, countries using Common law have increased their use of Amicus Curiae while European countries and developing countries in Africa, Asia, and Latin America, together with many international institutions, have adopted its use for the first time. Over the last three decades, there has also been a significant increase in the scope of the use of Amicus Curiae and the variety of courts that accept this procedure. The book examines the Amicus Curiae Phenomenon based on several criteria, with its general conclusion being that using the Amicus Curiae has a real impact on the work of the courts, on law, and on society.

In order to demonstrate the centrality of the "Amicus Curiae Phenomenon" in society and its significance as a procedure influencing the work of the courts, the book raises and discusses numerous examples from various countries around the world using different legal systems. The variety of courts within which amicus briefs are submitted and the diversity of amici submitting these briefs are highlighted throughout.

The first dimension of the "Amicus Curiae Phenomenon" to be described, and to some extent quantified, is the rapid growth in numbers of countries and institutions using the Amicus Curiae practice. Within a relatively short time of about 30 years, dozens of countries around the world that had previously not recognized the amicus practice adopted its use. This has included countries in Latin America (such as Brazil, Argentina, Venezuela, and Peru), Africa (Rwanda, Ethiopia, and Namibia), Asia (such as South Korea or Thailand), and Europe (such as Spain, Sweden, Austria, the Czech Republic, and Belgium), as well as most of the international institutions in the world (such as the World Trade Organization or the European Court of Human Rights) which have, one after the other, adopted the practice of using Amicus Curiae or significantly increased its use. Along with the initial adoption of this practice in these countries, the use of Amicus Curiae also gradually intensified in most common law countries (the United States, Canada, Australia, England, South Africa, New Zealand, Ireland, and many others). It is important to note that, in contrast to earlier times, the Amicus Curiae practice is now accepted in countries using continental law, as well as in those practicing common law judicial systems.

A second notable feature of the "Amicus Curiae Phenomenon" is that the number of legal topics in which Amicus Curiae briefs are submitted to the courts has grown and their characteristics have diversified. In the past, many amici became involved in cases dealing with issues of widespread public interest. Today, requests to submit an amicus brief may relate to most fields of law: tort, family, high-tech and technology, labor, corporations, environmental quality, antitrust, insurance, constitutional, criminal, taxes, and intellectual property.

A third aspect of the "Amicus Curiae Phenomenon" is the diversification of the types of judicial courts to which the amicus briefs are submitted. In the past, amici mainly joined proceedings in High Courts such as the Supreme Court or the Constitutional Court. By contrast, various amici have recently joined all possible types of judicial tribunals, including Family Courts, International Trade and Investment Dispute Settlement, Disciplinary Tribunals, Labor Courts, Statutory Commissions, and Military Courts. Sometimes, it is even possible to find amici in Small Claims Court proceedings. Almost every judicial court will have experienced an instance of amici who have tried to present their position on a particular subject.

An interesting aspect of the "Amicus Curiae Phenomenon," the fourth feature discussed at length in the book which has also attracted attention in the media, is the significant increase in the number of amicus briefs submitted in "mega-cases." These are cases with great interest for the public; for example, same-sex marriage, surrogacy agreements, investigations conducted under torture, affirmative action, modern slavery, deporting immigrants, wiretapping, the right to abortion, health insurance, and many others. Sometimes, a single file is joined by hundreds of amici who represent thousands of different interest groups.

A fifth and final feature discussed in the book is the significant increase in the type and variety of entities that use amicus briefs to influence the courts' rulings. The amici submitting Amicus Curiae briefs do not all share one defining characteristic. As mentioned above, various entities and organizations of different natures may apply to present their position through submitting an amicus brief. These include private individuals, governmental and non-governmental public organizations, such as Human Rights organizations, "green" organizations, labor organizations and women's groups, corporations (gas, oil, or bank companies), professional unions (for example, bar associations or accountants), and politicians.

The "Amicus Curiae Phenomenon" is thus characterized by the rapid expansion in the use of Amicus Curiae, its adoption in many countries, its application to a diverse range of issues within various types of courts, with Amicus briefs submitted by many differing groups and individuals who do not share any one common denominator. The "Amicus Curiae Phenomenon" is also accompanied by the development of processes and perceptions "external" to the Amicus Curiae practice itself, with these including: (1) Increased awareness of Amicus Curiae and extensive coverage in the media, popular literature, blogs, internet search engines, and content-sharing sites; (2) A rise in the number of published academic articles dealing with the amicus practice and its effect on the decision-making procedures of the courts; (3) The establishment of clinics training students to submit briefs as an amicus on diverse subjects in countries around the world, mainly within law schools, but also in university departments of public policy and criminology etc.; (4) The creation of a new field of specialization for lawyers entitled "Amicus Coordinator," whose role is to coordinate and regulate all amicus briefs submitted to support a particular position, aiming to avoid repetition while ensuring coverage of all aspects; (5) Aspects in the architectural planning and construction of new courtrooms with unique seating reserved for amici, even though they are not formal parties to the proceedings.

The "Amicus Curiae Phenomenon" surrounding the submission of increasing numbers of amicus briefs is one of the significant changes that has increasingly characterized the court's work from around the turn of the millennium, also profoundly impacting upon the relationship between the court and society. Formally, the amicus is a secondary player to the original litigants. However, in practice, their centrality, power, and importance to the court's decision-making processes are significant—often more so than the influence of the official litigators. In some proceedings, qualitatively and quantitatively, most information presented to the courts is given by an amicus or by several amici and not by the formal parties.

The book's main thesis links the "Amicus Curiae Phenomenon" and the rise of third parties in modern law to changes in the judicial system, to changes in the perception of the court's role in society and to changes in the courts' work methods. During the last three decades, there has been an ongoing significant increase in the involvement of the judicial system in society. This development exists in many countries with different legal traditions and types of governance. An increase in the centrality of the courts exists in both common law countries and those countries using continental law. Judicial systems have become increasingly aware of the social role of amici and of society's dependence on Amicus Curiae. In this framework, there is a growing reliance on courts and various legal procedures to regulate and handle many issues, not all of which have been previously discussed in judicial courts.

It is this growing involvement of the courts in society that lies at the heart of the "Amicus Curiae Phenomenon." As a result of the significant involvement of courts in the public sphere, substantive and procedural changes are taking place in the court's work. The content and style of the courts' work are undergoing significant changes, with many legal discussions turning from being "classic" legal disputes, such as who has a legal right, into broader discussions that raise topical, value, and economic issues, concerning the general public. Part of this transition also involves an increased volume and diversity of the legal sources discussed in judicial proceedings. Judgments may now be decided based on information and doctrines from extra-legal fields of opinion, such as sociology, economics, philosophy, criminology, and psychology.

Another change taking place in the courts has been brought about by the introduction of new working methods into legal hearings, which now cover issues not previously dealt with by the courts. For example, "rolling proceedings" are conducted under the supervision of the courts. In addition, more flexible causes and remedies have been created. Regarding the participants in proceedings, it is possible to identify more "multi-player" legal procedures—the formal parties alongside the professional experts, representatives of skilled professions, non-governmental organizations, and diverse interest groups. The greater involvement of courts in society has various causes and consequences. It is proposed in the book's discussions that one of the main consequences of this change, which is also one of the significant causes of the change, is that courts worldwide have adopted, included, or intensified the use of the Amicus Curiae.

The courts adopted and increased their use of Amicus Curiae for two main reasons that are intertwined with each other that are summarized here.

The first reason is that in order to fulfill their current judicial role and deal with modern law's diverse and complex content, courts need extensive, detailed information, including perspectives that differ from those of the formal parties involved in the discussion. Sometimes indeed, the courts need exactly that information which formal parties to the proceedings either cannot present or wish to avoid presenting because it harms their interests. When courts see their work as something that influences and shapes society, and not only as a solution to individual conflicts, they become aware of the diverse interests involved, and their obligation to take into account the consequences of their choices on the wider community. This in turn increases the courts' dependence on amici who supply additional information and perspectives, consequentially enhancing the importance of the Amicus Curiae practice, also extending the range of courts accepting the essence of the Amicus Curiae. The change in judicial policy requires openness to receiving social information and different viewpoints from those groups within the general public who may be affected by court rulings. Sometimes, courts receive amicus briefs from amici, even if they do not present new information or add to the perspectives of the formal parties. However, the courts accept the vital importance of accepting these briefs as a means for transmitting a message to those groups submitting them. The acceptance of the briefs enables them to serve as a conduit for sharing information about the public lobby and interest groups behind the issue. The Amicus Curiae briefs reflect the identities of those entities that will most likely continue to remain active in the public, legal, media, and political arenas if their positions are not accepted. Therefore, courts attach importance to the brief submitted by amici, even if they do not formally add essential information. The briefs take on a fundamental meaning because the amici are the "barometer" of society and their identities as well as their briefs provide information about the overall implications of the issue.

The second reason is that the Amicus Curiae is a procedural practice that allows more significant involvement of members of the public in the court's decision-making processes and in shaping the policies that influence their lives and environment. At the same time, while the court needs different parties who submit the Amicus Curiae briefs, the amici themselves also want to influence their lives and well-being by submitting briefs. The amicus practice improves the quality of the judicial decision and helps reduce judicial errors which may occur when they are based on partial information or fail to take into account a missing social perspective. Furthermore, as amici, the participation of groups in the public is a viable way to shape decisions that affect their well-being. Through the amicus procedure, the court has become accessible to additional parts of the population who previously did not come into the courts or were not entitled to enter the court gates.

Modern societal perceptions accept that the law reflects social attitudes, political compromises, and moral principles and actively shapes society, communities, and individuals. In order to become active parts of these crucial legal processes, non-governmental organizations (such as "green" organizations or labor unions) see the submission of amicus briefs as an effective tool, sometimes the only one, to promote their goals. For some organizations, the amicus procedure is a proper tool for political and value struggles and an additional platform through which they may influence the shapers of public opinion and the decision-makers within various authorities. This tool exists alongside other familiar tools, such as petitions, lobbying in parliament, protest demonstrations, and advertising in the media.

One further development that has been underway in recent years, which has had an impact on the "Amicus Curiae Phenomenon" is the increase in the number of lawyers worldwide, who then go on to play a significant role in influencing processes. This in turn means there is also an increase in the number of lawyers engaged in promoting various public goals who use the Amicus Curiae, because it is a successful tool for achieving these goals. Furthermore, the economic aspects related to the legal arrangements of the amicus procedure encourage its use, because writing a brief and submitting it to court involves relatively low costs (no court fees, no procedural costs) and low economic risks (no fear of cost ruling).

As a result of the processes described above, both the court and the public are interested in adopting and increasing the use of amicus briefs. From the public's point of view, Amicus Curiae increases democratic participation in the judicial process and ensures that courts take diverse social and public interests into account. From the court's point of view, amici provide valuable information about broad interests and needs, contributing to the legitimacy and acceptance of their rulings.

Even in cases where the position presented by the amicus was not accepted, it submission may have been valuable for the procedure.

Institutional, social, and democratic processes explain to a certain degree why the interests of members of the public are served by the existence of Amicus Curiae in many countries in America, Europe, Asia, and Africa. This has also occurred at the same time that diverse interest groups have begun to try and shape society through active participation in the judicial process. However, there are also legal, social, political, and economic processes that have created a need on the side of the courts for assistance from third parties. There are some global processes, but also local processes that have taken place in each country, each with its own unique circumstances. This assistance is not only in obtaining various types of information that the formal parties may not present for whatever reason, but also in understanding the overall implications of each judicial decision on a broader circle of individuals, both in the present and in the future.

The "Amicus Curiae Phenomenon" may be seen as the revival of the legal process as an inclusive social process in which many parties in addition to the formal parties, including experts and professional advisors, are involved. Understanding the "Amicus Curiae Phenomenon" is important to the legal profession in general, as well as to those interested in societal structure and change. The wide-ranging processes associated with the Amicus Curiae practice generate profound changes in many fields of law field as well as in the procedures involved in the courts' work. These changes have contributed to the perception that the judicial process often becomes a multidimensional procedure in which many parties participate, with the numbers of amici or third parties sometimes extending to even tens or hundreds of groups or different individuals. From a formalistic point of view, Amicus Curiae is only a legal practice, yet a more profound observation reveals a deeper layer reflecting changes in the courts' broad worldview regarding their role in society.

Contents

Chapter 1
Introduction

1.1 The Goals of the Book and Its Hypotheses

One of the most significant changes in recent years in the work of the courts worldwide is the emergence of the Amicus Curiae institution. The Amicus Curiae (Friend of the Court) is a legal procedure that allows a third party ("friend" or "amicus") not formally involved in an ongoing legal proceeding to present his point of view to the court by submitting an amicus brief. These "friends" or "amici" may include human rights organizations, green organizations, companies with economic interests, private people, or politicians.

This book aims to describe and present an in-depth analysis from a comparative point of view, the phenomenon the author calls the "Amicus Curiae Phenomenon" or "amicus phenomenon." The extent of this phenomenon is expressed by the widespread adoption of the amicus procedure in the courts of many countries, using different litigation systems, in a recent period, both in the Western World and other areas, as will be demonstrated in the book. Indeed, after examining the dimensions of the phenomenon, it will be possible to contend that the emergence of the Amicus Curiae institution is one of the most significant changes in recent years in the work of courts worldwide.

The amici have similar characteristics in all the countries and international institutions that use the procedure, with some variations depending on guidelines laid down in some national or institutional courts. However, there may generally be several shared purposes for submitting amicus briefs, that may be stipulated by the courts as a requirement for accepting an amicus brief, such as adding legal or factual claims not raised by the formal parties to the procedure or presenting arguments differently or more convincingly than the formal parties.

In some cases, the amici provide information (economic, environmental, security, historical, geographical, philosophical, or religious) that is not in the possession of the formal parties or that the parties do not wish to present to the courts because this harms their interests. In other cases, the amici repeat arguments presented by one of

S. Farber, *The Amicus Curiae Phenomenon*, Ius Gentium: Comparative Perspectives on Law and Justice 119, https://doi.org/10.1007/978-3-031-67225-5_1

the formal parties (usually in a different way that emphasizes certain aspects in the area of expertise of the amici), express their support for these positions, and try to convince the courts to accept the position of the formal party they support.[1]

There has recently been a significant increase in the scope of amicus, the number of courts that accept this method, and the legal fields in which amicus is used to influence the judicial decision-making process. The author defines several criteria according to which the "Amicus Curiae Phenomenon" is identified, described, and examined in this book:

The first criterion used in identifying the amicus phenomenon as a significant global phenomenon is that several different judicial systems adopted this legal practice fundamentally related to the management of the legal process within a short period of time. As part of fulfilling this criterion, it is observed that the adoption of the legal procedure (Amicus Curiae) was accepted by various courts in several countries that follow different legal methods: common law, continental law, and judicial institutions of international law. The book also describes and presents how the amicus practice has been adopted in several countries that did not recognize this practice up to the mid-nineties of the twentieth century (sometimes even a little earlier).

In a relatively short time, state courts (at almost all levels, from the high courts of that country to small claims courts), as well as a significant number of the international institutions in the world (such as the International Court of Justice and the European and South American Human Rights Courts), adopted the Amicus Curiae into their internal procedures. The author examines the interesting developments in the adoption of the amicus practice in continental law countries (Romano-Germanic). In these countries' systems (European, Latin American, or Asian countries), there had previously been a significant opposition to the intervention of parties who are not formal parties in the legal process. However, many of these countries have also adopted the amicus practice in the last two decades,[2] including most European and Latin American countries.[3] Out of those countries practicing continental law, the amicus phenomenon occurs mainly in Europe and Latin America but also in certain African countries (such as Uganda, Ethiopia, and Namibia) and parts of Asia (such as South Korea and Thailand).

The widespread adoption of Amicus Curiae legal practices by many judicial systems has led to the fact that today, in contrast to the mid-nineties of the last century, almost all common-law countries (Anglo-American), continental law countries (Romano-German), and international law institutions use the representation mechanism of amicus. As part of examining this criterion, it is demonstrated that the amicus phenomenon is not a one-off or local practice but one that exists on a large scale in many countries and organizations worldwide.

---

[1] For a different explanation see, Angell (1967); Bellhouse and Lavers (2004), p. 187; Anderson (2015); For the American amicus see, Krislov (1963), pp. 694–721.

[2] Dainow (1966) and McCormick (1997); Also, in general, Martínez-Torrón (1998).

[3] Bazán (2009), pp. 301, 310–312; Kochevar (2013).

The author's second criterion for identifying and describing the "Amicus Curiae phenomenon" is the extent to which the amicus procedure is used in different courts within countries. According to the data, when there is an increase and expansion in the scope of courts utilizing amicus practice compared to the number of ongoing procedures, the scale tends to identify it as a phenomenon of great weight. It must be emphasized that the importance of amici in the proceedings in which they are involved is reflected in more than just the relative numbers of proceedings within which they present briefs. Nevertheless, the increase in numbers of amicus briefs submitted does indicate the change that this practice brings to the work of the courts and how other legal agents operate. Within this criterion, the collected data shows a significant increase in the use of amicus in several judicial systems—state courts and international tribunals.

The author shows that, except for some specific years, there has been a consistent and steady increase in the use of the amicus practice in common law countries, primarily the United States, Canada, and England. For example, between 2015 and 2016, approximately 92% of all cases heard in the United States Supreme Court were joined by amici,[4] and between 2019–2020, about 97% of all cases discussed in court were joined by amici.[5] Several decades earlier, the participation rate of amici was only a few percent.[6]

In the United States, for example, the data shows a change in the trend regarding the use of Amicus Curiae starting in the 1980s. In the period between 1920 and 1966, amicus briefs were submitted in less than 10% of the cases discussed in the American Supreme Court.[7] From 1966 onwards, the sharp rise in the submission of amicus briefs began, with amicus briefs submitted in 54% of the cases examined between 1966 and 1975. In the ten year period starting from 1975, there was a further rise, with amicus briefs were submitted in 73% of the cases in the period between 1975 and 1985. Between 1985 and 1995, this rise continued, with about 85% of the cases discussed having been accompanied by amicus briefs. Between 2011 and

---

[4]Franze and Anderson (2016), https://www.apks.com/~/media/files/perspectives/publications/2016/09/in-unusual-term-big-year-for-amicus-curiae-at-the-supreme-court.pdf.

[5]Franze and Anderson (2020), https://www.arnoldporter.com/-/media/files/perspectives/publications/2020/11/amicuscuriae-at-the-supreme-court.pdf.

[6]Franze and Anderson (2015), http://www.nationallawjournal.com/supremecourtbrief/id=1202735095655, During these years, an average of 12 amici memoranda were submitted in each case discussed at the Supreme Court representing hundreds of different organizations and entities. Also see Collins Jr (2008).

[7]One of the pioneering studies conducted in the United States was written by Nathan Hakman. He noted that in the middle of the 1920s century, the participation of the AMICI in the Supreme Court increased significantly. Despite the increase in the participation rate of non-governmental organizations in the judicial system, their influence on the Supreme Court was negligible and was apparently created due to the "folklore of various theories in political science." Hakman concluded his words and claimed that interest groups are organized appear to play a relatively minor role in Supreme Court decision-making; See, Hakman (1966).

2014, amici joined in 96% of all cases discussed in the Supreme Court.[8] In the period of 2014 and 2015, about 98% of all cases discussed in court were joined by amici,[9] and in the years 2015–2016, amici joined in approximately 92% of all cases that were discussed in court.[10] In the years 2019 and 2020, about 97% of all cases discussed in court were joined by amici.[11]

The third criterion used for testing the extent of the "amicus phenomenon" examines the range of subjects into which this legal practice "penetrates" and is adopted into the law. The wide spread of the amicus procedure in many different branches of law that has been observed, confirms the fulfilment of this criterion. The analysis will show that the proceedings in which amici joined to submit briefs in recent years deal not only with issues related to Human Rights and constitutional issues but that amici are involved as a tool to influence the decision-making process in the courts in almost all existing areas of law—torts, insurance, family, high-tech and technology, cyber law, labor, corporate, environmental, criminal, taxes, and intellectual property.

The fourth criterion to be examined in order to ascertain the extent and universality of the "amicus phenomenon" is diversification of the types of judicial courts and judicial or quasi-judicial tribunals in which the amicus practice has recently been absorbed. Establishing this criterion can be satisfactorily achieved by showing that starting in the 1990s, the types of judicial courts to which the amici brief are submitted have expanded and diversified. While previously, amici mainly joined proceedings in high courts such as the Supreme Court of a particular country or the Constitutional Court, in the recent period, it is possible to see amici joining almost all types of existing tribunals such as peace courts, labor law courts, family courts, commercial arbitrations, disciplinary courts, statutory commissions, and military courts (and in some cases—even small claims courts).[12]

The fifth criterion through which the phenomenon is assessed is the test of the use of this legal procedure in cases of high public interest, which include broad general implications (henceforth: *mega cases*). Cases within which hundreds or even thousands of different interest groups (such as environmental, consumer, civil rights, and religious groups) express their opinion on fundamental issues through the amicus practice, demonstrate that it the practice has considerable weight in shaping the law. It must be assumed that the desire of politicians, government organizations, academics, or other groups to participate in proceedings as amici, by submitting an amicus brief, shows the importance of the practice and demonstrates its potential for

[8] Kearney and Merrill (2000), pp. 743–855. From the middle of the twentieth century to the end of the century, about half of the cases heard in the Supreme Court included amicus briefs.

[9] Franze and Anderson (2020).

[10] Franze and Anderson (2016).

[11] Franze and Anderson (2020).

[12] See the matter of small claims 8518-03-09 Narozini v. Kovner (11/24/2009). In this case, the "Association of Cat Lovers in Israel" requested to join the lawsuit conducted in the Small Claims Court as Amicus Curiae.

influencing the law. These proceedings in which multiple amici submit briefs in order to participate in and possibly influence the court's deliberations are of great public importance. Examples of topics discussed in these high profile "mega-cases" include: same-sex marriage,[13] climate change,[14] election propaganda,[15] the right to bear weapons,[16] protection against discrimination because of sexual or gender identity,[17] or the right to abortion.[18]

As part of this test, the increase in the number of amici who join "mega-cases" in various judicial systems is examined. As mentioned, these cases that are in the public and political discourse include broad general issues, with additional examples being: surrogacy agreements, affirmative action, interrogation under torture, and wiretapping.

One prominent example is found in a case dealing with health care reform in the United States (Patient Protection and Affordable Care Act (promoted by President Obama. In one case 136 briefs were submitted on behalf of hundreds of different interest groups, with these briefs being spread over thousands of pages.[19] There are many other examples of the high interest "mega-cases" which were joined by hundreds of amici. In a case dealing with equal rights in marriage in 2012, 156 briefs were submitted by various amici.[20] In another case that dealt with same-sex marriage in 2015, 147 briefs were submitted representing thousands of non-governmental organizations and different interest groups (women's organizations, religious organizations, etc.).[21] In a case brought to the court in 2016 dealing with affirmative action, 85 requests were submitted by amici groups representing hundreds of interest groups in order to express their positions.[22] Not all of these "mega-cases occurred in the United States. In Canada, for example, 63 Amicus Curiae briefs were submitted in a case that dealt with the constitutionality of the prohibition of physician-assisted

[13] Obergefell v. Hodges, 576 U.S. 644. (2015).

[14] Massachusetts v. EPA, 549 U.S. 497 (2007).

[15] Citizens United v. FEC, 558 U.S. 310 (2010).

[16] District of Columbia v. Heller, 554 U.S. 570 (2008).

[17] Bostock v. Clayton Cty., 140 S. Ct. 1731 (2020).

[18] Thomas E. Dobbs, State Health Officer of the Mississippi Department of Health, et al. v. Jackson Women's Health Organization, et al. 2022.

[19] Nat'l Fed'n of Indep. Bus. v. Sebelius, 132 S. Ct. 2566 (2012). For example, the Supreme Court cited information presented to it by many amici, including a memo that described the history of healthcare reforms. One of the memos presented a study conducted at Harvard Medical School which showed that over 45,000 Americans die each year because they do not have health insurance.

[20] United States v. Windsor, 133 S.Ct. 2675 (2013).

[21] Obergefell v. Hodges, 135 S. Ct. 2584 (2015). In the case of Obergefell v. Hodges (2015), the American Philosophical Association filed an Amicus Curiae brief arguing that the right to same-sex marriage is a fundamental right protected by the Constitution. The brief cited philosophical arguments about the nature of marriage and the right to equal protection.

[22] Fisher v. Univ. of Tex. at Austin, 136 S.Ct. 2198 (2016) Supreme Court of the United States; Obergefell v. Hodges, 576 U.S. 644. (2015). See. Supreme Court of the United States, www.supremecourt.gov/docket/docketfiles/html/public/14-556.ZIP. See: Bergman et al. (2014), pp. 82–97. doi: 10.1093/jleo/ewt024.

death.[23] Similarly, dozens of briefs from different organizations were submitted in the case of *Atala Riffo* et al. *v. Chile*, argued in 2021 at the Inter-American Court of Human Rights.[24]

The importance of examining the participation of various interest groups as amici in "mega cases" stems from the fact that these judgments contribute to the design of new legal and public policies. In some cases, the participation of amici in the process even helps to form new worldviews and creates a new version of collective memory. For example, some judges reject outright, or without significant discussion, most of the petitions and appeals they discuss; while other judges rule on most of the cases that were not dismissed in a way that may be considered formalistic and narrow. These two types of judges still discuss the cases brought before them but, as a result of amicus submissions, now do so in depth. This significantly changes the legal rule and even creates a different legal culture.

The sixth criterion for examining the "Amicus Curiae Phenomenon" and identifying its significance around the world is the test of the groups and organizations that have begun to use the amicus practice to influence court rulings.[25] As more entities start to use the amicus practice, this practice will gain even greater importance. The data shows that the variety of entities that use the amicus practice to influence the courts' rulings has dramatically increased. This contrasts with the practice in the past when the type of entities submitting amicus briefs was relatively limited. Today, it is possible to name human rights organizations, "green" organizations, religious organizations, women's organizations, government organizations, parties, and members of parliament,[26] consumer organizations, labor organizations, corporations, and private individuals who extensively use the Amicus Curiae practice.[27] In the past, only a few of the legal guilds used amicus briefs as a tool to promote specific interests. By contrast, today, the type and variety of entities utilizing the Amicus Curiae to influence court rulings have significantly increased. It is not only a formal legal tool but also a tool used by members of the general public, even by

[23] Carter v. Canada (AG) (2015). See also: R. v. Jordan (2016): 57 amicus briefs. Tsilhqot'in Nation v. British Columbia (2014): 56 amicus briefs.

[24] Atala Riffo and Daughters v. Chile (Spanish: Atala Riffo y Niñas vs. Chile).

[25] Kelleher and Yackee (2006), pp. 629–643.

[26] For example, Senator Sheldon Whitehouse has submitted multiple amicus briefs to the U.-S. Supreme Court on various issues, including campaign finance, climate change, and voting rights. In the case of Sebelius v. Hobby Lobby Stores, Inc. (2014), Senator Cruz joined an amicus brief supporting the plaintiffs who challenged the Affordable Care Act's contraceptive coverage mandate. In the case of R (Miller) v. Secretary of State for Exiting the European Union (2017), several UK MPs submitted amicus briefs to the UK Supreme Court about the Brexit process. See: UK Supreme Court—Case Page for R (Miller) v. Secretary of State for Exiting the European Union.

[27] For example, In the case of R. v. K.R.J. (2016), Jody Wilson-Raybould, who was then a private individual (but later became Canada's Minister of Justice and Attorney General), submitted an amicus brief to the Supreme Court of Canada regarding the interpretation of section 276 of the Criminal Code relating to the admissibility of evidence in sexual assault trials. See Supreme Court of Canada—Case Information for R. v. K.R.J.

non-lawyers. This stems from the "concern" of ordinary citizens who wish to influence their lives by joining an ongoing legal process.[28]

In recent years, there have been many uses of the practice of the Amicus Curiae, both in minor and extensive issues, intending to influence the way of life and the well-being of the various interest groups. For example, in a ruling dealing with affirmative action in university admissions in the United States, over 60 amicus briefs were attached.[29] Among the presenters of the briefs were presidents of leading United States universities, student organizations, the Society of Sociologists, the National Organization for Women, the Bar Association, conservative research institutes, the American Jewish Committee, the National Association for the Advancement of Colored People, former United States President Gerald Ford, serving and retired senators, 29 retired United States Army generals, and various commercial companies including Microsoft and Coca-Cola.

United States Supreme Court Judge Ruth Bader-Ginsburg stated that one of the briefs that influenced her while writing her ruling was submitted by an amicus who was a retired military officer, who noted the expected negative impact on the military if there is no proper diversity among the officers.[30]

The seventh criterion for identifying the amicus phenomenon as a central and widespread phenomenon today is the systemic need to unify the rules about all legal amicus practices and regulate them in a uniform and coherent legislative framework. The basis for this criterion stems from the thought that the very need to regulate an issue indicates its importance. After all, if the many legal systems or legislators conclude that creating a uniform set of rules for using Amicus Curiae is necessary, then this very need indicates its importance. The requirements for creating the rules may arise from the formal parties to court proceedings, but may also be based on an academic review that stems from experience gained over the years. The need to create a uniform set of rules arises also, among other things, from the current demand for harmony concerning the use of Amicus Curiae. The primary meaning of this criterion is that if it is met, it depicts a situation wherein the amicus procedure is essential in the court's work.[31]

Another criterion that the book uses to test the prevalence and importance of the Amicus Curiae phenomenon is the extent to which there are citations or mentions of the information presented in briefs by the amici by the courts.[32] The fact that the

[28] See, for example, a brief from a San Francisco citizen to the California Supreme Court on same-sex marriage: Amicus Curiae Brief for Divine Queen Mariette Do-Nguyen, Lockyer v. City & County of San Francisco, 95 P.3d 459 (Cal. 2004) (No. S122923). See, For example, Citizens United v. Federal Election Commission. In this case, which dealt with campaign finance regulations, numerous private individuals filed amicus briefs expressing their opinions on the issue. See Abrams, Floyd. Amicus brief on behalf of a group of constitutional scholars supporting the petitioner—Citizens United v. Federal Election Commission, 558 U.S. 310 (2015).

[29] Grutter v. Bollinger, 539 U.S. 306 (2003).

[30] Simard (2008), pp. 669. (referring to Grutter v. Bollinger, 539 U.S. 306 (2003).

[31] In general, regarding globalization of procedural law, Della Cananea (2003), pp. 563—578.

[32] Simard (2008), p. 669.

courts quote, mention, or refer in some way to the information brought by amici helps to establish the hypothesis that the courts were influenced in some way by the brief submitted to them. However, it is not possible to determine precisely to what extent.[33] For example, in the case *Obergefell v. Hodges*, which took place in 2015, the majority opinion cited "more than 100 amici" as support for its determination that there had been sufficient public debate over the issue of same-sex marriage.[34]

It should be noted that this citation criterion should be used with caution for several reasons that will now be detailed. First, research shows that judges sometimes cite briefs from amici on both sides to present an equally objective picture of the situation. Sometimes, judges also quote amici in their judgment to show that the position of the amici and the position of the formal litigants are the same. On the other hand, sometimes, judges allow amici to argue orally and, therefore, do not find it necessary to refer to their words in the judgment. Also, there are cases where judges are not interested in citing specific briefs due to the public image of these organizations and the fear of expressing public support implicitly for their actions.[35]

That is, the citations of amici, or the lack of these citations, in the judgments can have additional explanations other than influencing the decision.[36] It is possible to disagree on the degree of influence of an amicus brief on the court. Still, its citation or mention shows that the court took the brief into account in some way among its other considerations.[37] Either way, the reference to the information presented by amici shows that it is a valuable tool in the court's decision-making process. It is essential to know that the databases concerning certain countries (such as the United States or Canada) are relatively well-established and extensive. For them, all criteria will be examined. In addition, some countries have well-established judicial traditions regarding including third parties in ongoing proceedings. Naturally, more research has been done in these countries, making the information more accessible and comprehensive.

On the other hand, in other countries, especially countries that belong to the continental legal system—the sources of information are more limited. As will be

---

[33] For example, Collins Jr et al. (2015), pp. 917; Collins Jr (2004), pp. 807–832. The authors analyze a large dataset of Supreme Court cases and investigate the relationship between amicus participation and justices' voting behavior. They examine the influence of amicus briefs on the likelihood of judges citing specific issues and explore the persuasive power of amicus briefs in shaping the Court's decisions.

[34] Franze and Anderson (2015).

[35] Larsen and Devins (2016); Mauro (2016) https://www.law.com/supremecourtbrief/almID/1202752957056; Feldman (2016) https://empiricalscotus.com/2016/05/11/the-most-effective-friends-of-the-court; Lynch (2004), pp. 33, 46–56.

[36] See Blake (2019), pp. 216, 252, at 252 ("Rather than letting scientific knowledge mitigate Justice's ideological proclivities, the data indicate Justices on both ends of the spectrum resort to scientific arguments to bolster their underlying worldviews"), 248 ("it is likely that amicus briefs... provide the Court with relevant social science research they can choose to cite").

[37] See, for example, US Supreme Court Chief Judge John Roberts' response to a former White House counsel's amicus brief regarding the alleged corruption of the governor of Virginia: Coyle M (2016) http://www.law.com/supremecourtbrief/almID/1202756102813; see also, Kane (2017).

expanded upon later, the importance of Amicus Curiae in continental law is mainly in the absorption of the practice of Amicus Curiae. The very adoption of the amicus practice in continental law is not self-evident since the continental legal system gives its judges broad procedural tools for obtaining many types of information required for the procedure. When these tools are fulfilled, they eliminate the necessity of the amicus to present information to the courts.

In addition to the criteria mentioned above that were designed to test the influence and extent of the amicus phenomenon, the book uses additional auxiliary tests to assess the centrality and importance of the Amicus Curiae phenomenon. These other tests deal with the direct and indirect consequences and outcomes of using the amicus in legal practice. For example, following tribunals' widespread use of amicus worldwide, educational frameworks and clinics have recently been opened that train students to submit briefs as amici on various topics.[38] There are also videos on internet and various content-sharing sites that instruct citizens on how to write practical amicus briefs.[39] Many articles in academic journals, statements by clinics or lawyers' offices, and many legal blogs have been devoted to documenting and analyzing how the amicus practice is used and the influence that the amicus has on court rulings.[40] Retired judges are also interviewed in the media or write about their

---

[38]For example, *Civil Rights Amicus Brief Project*, Seattle Univ. Sch. of Law (2016), www.law.seattleu.edu/centers-and-institutes/korematsu-center/litigation/the-civil-rights-amicus-brief-project; For example, in Fisher v. Univ. of Tex. at Austin, 136 S.Ct. 2198 (2016) Supreme Court of the United States several university legal clinics filed amicus briefs. For instance, the Supreme Court Litigation Clinic at Stanford Law School submitted a brief on behalf of a group of leading social scientists supporting the University of Texas at Austin's admissions policy. See: Stanford Law School Supreme Court Litigation Clinic. Fisher v. University of Texas at Austin. Stanford Law School, www.law.stanford.edu/stanford-law-school-supreme-court-litigation-clinic/fisher-v-university-texas-austin. In United States v. Windsor (2013): The Supreme Court Clinic at Yale Law School filed an amicus brief in this case involving the Defense of Marriage Act (DOMA), United States v. Windsor, 133 S.Ct. 2675 (2013). The clinic's brief argued for the unconstitutionality of DOMA, supporting Edith Windsor's challenge to the law. See: Yale Law School Supreme Court Clinic. "United States v. Windsor." Yale Law School, www.law.yale.edu/student-life/student-journals-organizations/student-organizations/supreme-court-clinic/supreme-court-cases. This phenomenon has also permeated the legal clinics in Israel. for example, AA 11152/04 Anonymous v. Migdal Insurance Company Ltd. (4.4.2005), The Clinic for Combating Trafficking in Women of the Hebrew University requested to join the proceedings as an Amicus Curiae to challenge the compensation component of an escort institute.

[39]The use of videos on the Internet to raise public awareness and influence issues in legal proceedings has been very popular in recent years and you can find thousands of videos on these issues, for example: ZACHM0, *Amicus Curiae*, YouTube (May 12, 2013), https://www.youtube.com/watch?v=q98HAE2Tk-c.

[40]Also, in the journal called "Amicus Curiae" which has been published since 1997 and published by the Law School of the University of London, many articles and position papers are published that suggest ways to advance various issues through the submission of "amici" memoranda. Of course, no empirical research has been conducted examining the scope of articles on the subject, but a review of various databases (such as: google scholar HEIN ON LINE or Lexis-Nexis) indicates an increasing trend in writing articles on the subject since the late nineties. In addition, in recent years, academic publications have begun about friendship and the participation of third parties in

understanding about briefs from amici submitted to them and explain what types of information brought to them by amici had a particular impact on them.

Another additional test is related to amici's influence on lawyers' work. Not only do lawyers use amicus as a central tool for promoting the interests of their clients, but the Amicus Curiae has created a new field in the legal profession. These are third parties who seek to influence a case pending in the courts. Often, they hire a lawyer with the title "amicus coordinator" to coordinate and regulate all the amicus briefs submitted to support their position. One of the main requirements in most of the judicial courts in the world concerning receiving an amicus brief is that the amicus brief must be update the courts and not repeat the information already presented to them.[41]

The role of the amicus coordinator is to manage and supervise the variety of arguments raised by each organization and ensure that the arguments in the various briefs are not repeated for them to be accepted by the courts. In other words, an amicus coordinator is a coalition chairman who oversees all the coalition members (the amici) so that a unified front with a public and significant effect is presented to the courts that will meet the legal requirements of the courts.[42]

The book will show that the amicus and other practices, such as the "intervenor,"[43] change the nature of litigation in the courts. From the point of view of the participants in the procedure, a gradual transition is taking place from a judicial procedure that includes the formal parties (the official litigants: plaintiff-defendant; petitioner-respondent; state-accused) to a multi-dimensional and general procedure that consists of a large number of "players"—the formal parties and along with dozens and even hundreds of amici, including various rights organizations, commercial companies, professional professions (such as the Bar Association), private individuals[44] and different interest groups.

---

proceedings in most Latin American countries as well (for more, see the chapter dealing with continental law).

[41] Sup. Ct. R. 37.1.

[42] The concept of the Amicus Coordinator exists mainly in mega-cases, in which dozens of memoranda are filed. For example, in the procedure that dealt with the right to abortion. In the discussion of Webster v. Reproductive Health Servs., 492 U.S. 490 (1989) Dozens of memoranda were submitted representing over 420 different organizations from across the political spectrum in the United States, which represented 5469 interest groups and individuals: liberals, African-Americans, the Civil Rights Association, organizations that specialize in medical ethics, the umbrella organization of Churches in the United States, women's organizations, the association of doctors, the association of deans of medical schools in the United States.

[43] Similar to an amicus, the "intervenor" is a third party to a proceeding that seeks to influence an ongoing legal proceeding. However, unlike an amicus, the "intervenor" is usually a third party that has a direct interest in the case and may sometimes become a formal party to the proceeding.

[44] For example, Citizens United v. Federal Election Commission (2010): In this case, which dealt with campaign finance regulations, numerous private individuals filed amicus briefs expressing their opinions on the issue. See Abrams, Floyd. Amicus brief on behalf of a group of constitutional scholars supporting the petitioner. Citizens United v. Federal Election Commission, 558 U.S. 310. (2015).

The change from a two-dimensional procedure to a multi-dimensional procedure in legal proceedings expresses a perception that the subject of the topic discussed in court, even if it is not a clear public interest, is not necessarily the exclusive property of two parties to the concrete conflict. It can also be related to other parties in society who wish to be partners in the decision-making processes that affect or may affect their lives.[45]

To a large extent, this is a revival of the concept of the traditional legal process as an overall social process involving many factors that are not necessarily directly related to the particular dispute, similar to the trials held in the past in the "Town Square," and not just as a dispute between two formal parties. Amicus Curiae is not only a legal practice carried out between the walls of the courts by a closed guild of jurists. It is a popular social tool intended to serve society by allowing it to present its various positions in court. The law does not belong only to the formal parties and the conflict between them, but it affects the whole of society. Therefore, everyone can express their position in any procedure affecting their lives and well-being. The public is entitled to represent its position in legal proceedings concerning it. In many respects, the public's participation in issues that affect them through the submission of an amicus brief strengthens the democratization of the judicial mechanism and ensures that the courts take diverse social interests into account.[46]

The development of amicus and its use by various interest groups has led to the revision of the judicial procedure. Today, in multiple courts around the world, it is almost self-evident that the judicial process takes place with various third parties—governmental and non-governmental public organizations, companies, professional professions, ordinary citizens, college students, and even high school students expressing their position and viewpoints in procedures that have broad consequences.[47] The judicial procedure is changing, and it no longer includes two parties and a judge but many "players." In many litigations on issues of a public nature, the classic procedure of two parties becomes the "exception." By contrast, the new procedure, in which many amici participate, becomes routine and expected.

The amicus has caused, among other things, a new perception about legal procedures on a significant issue in which there were only formal parties and a judge who decide the issue. This type of legal procedure now belongs, to a certain extent, to the "old" world of litigation. The "new world" of legal litigation includes many amici, usually many times more than the formal parties, who try to influence the court's decision-making processes. In light of this development, in some places in the world, such as the Supreme Court in Canada, unique seating areas have been

[45] Omari Scott Simmons (2009), Box-Steffensmeier et al. (2013) and Collins Jr et al. (2015).

[46] Garcia (2008). There are parts of society, for whom the judicial process is sometimes seen as an undemocratic process, being managed by expert jurists (judges).

[47] For example, high school students filed a brief with the Michigan Supreme Court: Montemurri (2014).

built inside the courtrooms for amici, who are not a formal part of the proceedings but, as mentioned, become central and significant players in the proceedings.[48]

How did a legal practice created hundreds of years ago (according to one approach in Roman law and another approach—in the common law of the Middle Ages)[49] gain such significant momentum and become so popular and widespread in recent years? What caused this worldwide phenomenon in common-law, continental, and international law in the last three decades? Why does it occur on such a large scale, and how can it be explained? What does this phenomenon mean, and what does it teach us about modern law and the role of the modern judicial system?

1.2 The Book's Main Ideas

The main idea behind this book is to explain and give meaning to the legal, social, and intellectual processes and factors that led to the rise of the "Amicus Curiae" in the industrialized world. Starting from the 1980s and 1990s of the twentieth century, the Amicus Curiae became more widespread, essential, and central in the legal field. It, therefore, has had far-reaching effects on society, modern law, and the work of the courts.

The book's central thesis links the Amicus Curiae to the changes in the judicial system, its perception of its role, and its work style. Since the 1980s and 1990s, there has been a significant and continuous increase in the involvement of the judicial system in society. This upward trend exists in many countries which practice different legal traditions and even have varying methods of governance.[50] State and international courts have become more aware of their social role and society's demands. Accordingly—they are deeply involved in society.

As part of deepening role judicial systems in society, there is a growing reliance on the courts and legal procedures for regulating and handling a wide range of issues. Most of these issues, which come before the court today, were not previously discussed in the courts. Different courts are called upon to resolve the various problems—religious freedoms, equal rights, telecommunications and media, public policy related to criminal justice, discrimination, ethics, health, welfare, foreign relations, education, family, immigration, and environmental quality. Among

[48] Guidelines for Canadian Courthouse Facilities that provide insights into the design considerations for courtrooms in Canada: https://cjc-ccm.gc.ca/en. For example, some international courts, such as the International Criminal Court (ICC) and the International Court of Justice (ICJ), have designated public seating areas in their courtrooms. These areas allow members of the public, including third parties, to observe court proceedings.

[49] For more on the history of the Amicus Curiae, see the second chapter of this book. Also see: Crema (2019)and Angell (1967).

[50] Mazmanyan (2015), p. 200); The Judicialization of Politics in Latin America (Sieder R. et al. eds.,); The Judicialization of Politics in Asia (Björn Dressel ed., 2012); Hunt (2013).

these, there are several issues that, in the past, should have been discussed in the courts but were discussed only in a relatively limited manner.[51]

The tendency to rely on judicial systems in various fields even brings today's courts to deal with political issues and core disputes of societies and regimes. This is reflected by the courts' need to intervene in macroeconomic planning, national dilemmas, and constitutive issues at the level of society's national and collective identity. In this way, judicial systems become the main forum, and in some cases the exclusive venue, for clarifying constitutional, economic, political, and social issues. Almost any issue in the public sphere may receive a legal expression and be discussed in some judicial systems.

The result of these processes is the transformation of judicial systems in the world into an integral and essential participant in the determination of the national identity and policy of many countries. The increasing reliance on the judicial system occurs not only at the state level but also at the supra-state level. Establishing international panels and courts, such as the European Court of Human Rights, that have broad and sometimes exclusive powers to deal with Human Rights, environmental quality, governmental issues, and monetary issues demonstrates the growing influence of this reliance.[52]

As a result of the deep involvement of the courts in the public sphere, several substantive and procedural changes are taking place designed to assist them.[53] In terms of content, there is a gradual transition from a "classic" legal conflict, which deals with who has a legal right, to public and multi-participant discussions that reflect the topical, value, and economic issues that concern the public. These discussions are conducted using information and opinions from fields of knowledge and sources that are not necessarily legal.[54] In terms of the form of the debate, new work methods are being adopted, such as active negotiations or mediation attempts

---

[51] Hirschl (2006), p. 721, (hereinafter - **Hirschl, *The New Constitutionalism***); The Global Expansion of Judicial Power (C. Neal Tate & Torbjörn Vallinder eds., 1995); Hirschl (2004); Gardbaum (2001), p. 707.

[52] Slaughter (2000), p. 1103. She argues that globalization is not just an economic phenomenon, but also a legal one. She points to the increasing number of cases in which national courts are interacting with each other and with international courts and argues that this trend is leading to the creation of a global legal system.

[53] It is important to note that significant judicial involvement does not necessarily indicate social changes, for example see Schultz (1998) and Rosenberg (1998).

[54] The diversity of the interdisciplinary content of the judicial system is related to several developments known as "law and...". They are of course related to the development of the "sociological approach to law" which called for an understanding of the overall social environment in which the law operates, as well as the concept that the law and the judicial system are influenced by social interests. The change in the sources of law is also related to other trends, such as the rise of the "law and economy" movement, within which the judicial function was given the content of solving problems according to economic principles. In addition, this change is also related to the "law and psychology" phenomenon, in which the interrelationships between the law, the judiciary and the decision-making mechanism of the judicial system and psychological research are examined. For example, see: Brooks-Gordon and Freeman (2006); Posner (2006), p. 1049; Kronman (1988), p. 335; Ward (1995); Posner (1986), p. 1351.

led by the courts and their management, a balance between different rights and interests, adoption of new causes and remedies, such as the "relative nullity" requirement, flexibility of remedies, and conducting proceedings outside the court but under its supervision.

As far as the participants in legal proceedings are concerned, there has recently been a fascinating transition from proceedings that include individual "actors" to proceedings involving a large number of "actors"—which include the formal parties together with professional experts, representatives of skilled professions (such as the Bar Association or the Chamber of Accountants), non-governmental organizations and diverse interest groups.[55] One of the main consequences of these changes, which is simultaneously a cause of them, is the adoption of Amicus Curiae in courts worldwide. The purpose of this practice is to assist the courts in their role due to two factors that are mutually intertwined:

First, from the point of view of the courts, the dynamic social reality requires adjustments in the work of the courts and access to ever increasing amounts of information from numerous disciplines. The Amicus Curiae is a practice that helps to bridge these gaps. To successfully fulfill the modern judicial role while dealing with modern law's diverse and complex contents, the courts need rich and broad information and access to different perspectives. This information is not necessarily provided by the formal parties in the discussion, partly as they may not be cognizant of it. The courts therefore need external information that is relevant to the specific occurrence under discussion in the litigation but not necessarily held by the formal parties. This information may also be essential for formulating appropriate legal policy. Often, the formal parties may be aware of some information needed, but may wish to refrain from presenting it to the court because it harms their interests or because they cannot adequately present it to the court.[56] It is precisely the purpose of the Amicus Curiae to supply this missing information.

In modern times, the appreciation of the fact that the information presented to the court by the formal parties never presents a complete and coherent picture of the situation has become even more acute. Therefore, the courts need different types of information from third parties.[57] Briefs submitted by amici add factual, legal, technical, theological, historical and social information not necessarily presented

[55] See a detailed discussion on the subject in the third part of the book.

[56] See Glamis v. USA, Quechan Indian Nation Application for Leave to File a Non-Party Submission, 19 August 2005, pp. 3–4. Glamis had been authorized to utilize mining rights it owned to mine gold on federal land located near designated Native American territory in South-East California by way of open pit mining. It claimed that the United States breached its NAFTA Chapter 11 obligations by wrongfully delaying the consideration of the mining project. The tribe stated that its goal was to ensure that the tribunal would fully consider the 'sensitive and serious nature of indigenous sacred areas' and that it would address issues such as the value of the area's cultural and environmental resources, the authorization process for the mine, the regulatory framework for mining, as well as the legal framework for the protection of indigenous sacred places under national and international law.

[57] Smith (1998), at 24, 26 (hereinafter - **Smith, *Sometimes Troubled Relationship***); Garcia (2008) see *supra* note 46.

by the formal parties. Sometimes, the amici also seek to present a different perspective from that of the formal parties to the dispute discussed in the court.[58]

Since the courts have increased their involvement in shaping society and dealing with new and dynamic areas of law, they need different amici to help them fulfill the role of the modern judiciary. These will mostly be academics from various fields,[59] public and non-governmental organizations such as human rights organizations, environmental protection organizations, or professionals.

The extensive involvement of the courts in the public, economic, and social questions results not only in the fact that they need additional information beyond that of the parties directly involved but also in the fact that they are more aware of the consequences of their rulings. They now acknowledge that every judicial decision has far-reaching implications for the interests of parties other than those formally involved in the litigation proceedings. When the courts see their role as one that affects the design of the public and private space of the citizen and not only one that finds a solution to individual disputes, their awareness of the broad general consequences of their choices intensifies and increases. This judicial approach requires openness to receiving social perspectives and different points of view from other parties who are not a direct part of the formal proceedings yet may be affected by court rulings.

Therefore, the extensive use of Amicus Curiae clarifies to us that modern law cannot be satisfied with the existing legal tools. A court that is involved in shaping society needs different amici to help it understand not only different types of information that the formal parties do not present but also the social implications of the courts' decisions. The possible consequences can be expressed, for example, in interpersonal relationships or quality of life or have a political,[60] security,[61] ecological,[62] or cultural significance—such as changing norms, values, and beliefs that shape the consciousness of the individuals and the society in which they live.[63] The judicial issues that the court discusses are broader than the circle of individuals

[58]For example, in Zivotofsky v. Kerry, 135 S.Ct. 2076, 2091 (2015), which dealt with the president's foreign policy authority, the United States Supreme Court held that the memos submitted to it were "of considerable assistance to the Court."

[59]See Fallon Jr (2012), pp. 225–226 (citing survey of Justices and their clerks), 228 (referring to "distinctively scholarly expertise and perspective" and "an implied warranty of scholarly integrity").

[60]See, for example, Mclauchlan (2005). See, for example, the memoranda submitted in the judgment Citizens United v. Federal Election Commission or Citizens United v. FEC for short or Barnovich National Committee v. Democratic National Committee (2021).

[61]See, for example, the memos submitted by amici in Heller (2008). District of Columbia v. Heller, 554 U.S. 570 (2008).

[62]See, for example, the briefs filed by various amicus briefs in Massachusetts v. Environmental Protection Agency (2007).

[63]See, for example, the amicus briefs in Bostock v. Clayton County.

directly involved.[64] The courts are aware that their attitude to the issues brought before them is prospective as much as retrospective, and the amici help in this.

In addition, the briefs of the amici constitute, for some judges, a sort of "social barometer" that indicates the public's position on the issue discussed before them. The role of the amici is not limited to presenting social perspectives and legal information or an ideological stance that helps the courts internalize and understand the broad picture of the issue before them. The presence of the amici, as incorporated interest groups, may pressure the judges to accept the position that the interest group promotes. This approach of a kind of "broadcasting" to the court on the part of interest groups about the desired result "from their point of view" is based on the assumption that judges tend not to stray too far from the public consensus, that they are attentive to the public's positions, and that they give considerable importance to the positions of interest groups.[65]

That is, the information about the broad implications of the court's ruling is more comprehensive than just the formal content of the brief. The emphasis is placed on the actual submission of the brief and the interest groups behind the submission. Since judges also tend to consider public opinion, especially in cases with public resonance, they refer to the amicus briefs presented to them as a kind of "barometer" that helps them understand the expected consequences of their decision.[66] Through the amici briefs, the judges "feel the public pulse" because the amici reflect a more comprehensive range of opinions than the formal parties.[67]

The second cause behind the Amicus Curiae is a social factor. The amicus is a procedural practice that allows greater public involvement in the court's decision-making processes. Through the amici, groups in society can shape the policies that affect their lives and their environment. In other words, while the courts need amici to obtain broad perspectives on the issues before them, the amici are also interested in being able to access the courts in order to influence their own lives and well-being by submitting amicus briefs.

Not only does the amicus practice improve the quality of judicial decisions and help reduce judicial errors based on partial information, but the participation of different public groups as amici is also a viable way to shape the decisions that affect their own well-being. The idea underlying this is that the law reflects not only social

[64] For example, in the case of Comptroller of Treasury of Md. v. Wynne, 135 S. Ct. 1787 (2015), the United States Supreme Court quoted from several amicus briefs submitted to it while emphasizing the memo's contribution to understanding the broad economic implications of Maryland's tax laws.

[65] Collins Jr (2004), pp. 807–832 (Examining the influence); Songer and Sheehan (1993), pp. 339–354.

[66] Garcia (2008) see *supra* note 46. Garcia contends that while some limits on amicus participation are necessary for the proper functioning of the judicial system, these limits should be minimal in light of the democratic and constitutional values at stake.

[67] Salzman et al. (2011), pp. 294–295; Collins Jr (2004), pp. 807–832 (***Examining the Influence***); Collins Jr (2018), pp. 219–237.

attitudes, political compromises, or moral principles but also is an active participant in shaping society and the lives of individuals and communities.[68]

The social cause of the Amicus Curiae rests on three layers that complement each other: the first social layer is an increase in the power and influence of non-governmental public organizations.[69] At the same time that the judicial systems need to receive social information and different perspectives, interest groups in society, led by many non-governmental organizations, see the submission of an amicus brief as a potential for advancing their goals, which allows them to express their point of view in the legal arena. Due to the increased power of the law and the courts in public life, non-governmental organizations see amicus as an effective, sometimes exclusive, tool for promoting their cause.[70]

In the eyes of some of the non-governmental organizations, the Amicus Curiae is seen as the formal end of a political or value struggle and as another platform through which it is possible to influence the shapers of public opinion and decision-makers—alongside tools such as petitions, lobbying in parliament, protest demonstrations, and advertising in the media.[71] The entry of social organizations into the legal arena and their active participation as Amicus Curiae has resulted in a significant change in the form of discussion, legal thinking, and the public nature of litigation in the courts. As the book shows, today, there is almost no procedure in which a significant public policy is discussed without many amici, primarily non-governmental public organizations, expressing their position.

The second social layer contributing to the increased use of Amicus Curiae is strengthening the legal profession from a social point of view and the increase in the number of lawyers worldwide. The growing number of lawyers in the world, and in particular the rise in the number of lawyers engaged in promoting various public goals ("Cause Lawyering" or "Public Interest Lawyering"),[72] also contributes significantly to the Amicus Curiae phenomenon. From those lawyers' point of view, using amicus is one of the most successful forms of law for promoting social

[68] For examples in which the law "succeeded" in promoting fundamental social changes in historical contexts, see: Berman (1983) and Ackerman (1998) We the People: Transformations; Engel (1998) How does law matter in the constitution of legal consciousness?; Levitsky (2015), pp. 382–398.

[69] Reimann (2006), pp. 45–67; Hodson (2011); Charnovitz (1997), pp. 281–282.

[70] Charnovitz (1997). The article also examines key issues arising from the expanding involvement of NGOs, cataloging the pros and cons of an active NGO role, discussing various functions that NGOs fulfill, and listing ten techniques of NGO participation.

[71] For a description of the role of the amicus as attracting "attention" through the media that accompany the public litigation, see O'Connor and Epstein (1981–1982). This is doubly true when the court did quote from the brief submitted to it by the organization. In these cases, the members of the organization feel that the court has legitimized their action and that their presence as an organization in the court is important and justified.

[72] In other contexts of social law, it is also referred to as "Progressive Lawyering." Diamond (2000). For more see: Sarat and Scheingold (1998).

change.[73] Many lawyers promoting various public goals find the amicus a suitable and effective tool for forwarding those causes they wish to promote.

The third social layer on which the Amicus Curiae phenomenon rests is the low economic cost of the legal procedures that incentivize using Amicus Curiae. Writing an amicus brief and submitting it to the court involves relatively low outlays since there are no court fees or procedural charges. Also, the briefs are sometimes composed by students or citizens at meager costs. These are low economic risks, so there is no fear of ruling expenses against the amici.

As a result of the two processes described earlier, the court and the public are interested in increasing the use of Amicus Curiae. From the public's point of view, amicus increases democratic participation in the judicial process, which is perceived to some extent as an undemocratic process managed by legal experts. In this way, it is possible to ensure that the courts consider diverse social and public interests. Regarding the courts, the amicus provides the court with important information about broad interests and needs and contributes to the legitimacy and acceptance of their rulings. On the one hand, through amicus, public participation in the decision-making processes is expanded, and thus, the institutional legitimacy of the system is strengthened. On the other hand, the amicus brings a more prominent public commitment to the ruling by being part of the procedure—even if its position was not accepted.

1.3 The Research Questions Discussed in the Book

A discussion of the Amicus Curiae phenomenon raises questions both on the descriptive level and on the normative level, as follows:

1. How has the practice of Amicus Curiae developed until the present day, in which ways and why?
2. What are the existing prototypes of the amicus?
3. What is the difference between the amicus and other intervention practices of third parties in modern law, such as the "intervenor"?
4. How did a legal institution that has existed in law for hundreds of years become so popular and prevalent in recent decades—in common law, continental law, and international law?
5. What is the Amicus Curiae, how can it be characterized, and in what ways is it reflected in modern law?
6. Why does the Amicus Curiae occur in these dimensions, and how can this be explained?
7. What does the Amicus Curiae mean in terms of developing new forms of court discussion?

[73] Hilbink (2004), pp. 657–698; Sarat and Scheingold (2006).

8. What does the Amicus Curiae teach us about modern law and the work of the courts and society?

The current legal literature does not adequately describe the Amicus Curiae at its various levels, which transverses countries, international institutions, and legal methods. The literature also lacks sufficient attention to the factors influencing the formation of the Amicus Curiae and its influence on the design of modern law and the work of the courts. At best, there are limited descriptions describing specific changes in local law, mainly in the United States, without reference to all the aspects of the Amicus Curiae phenomenon as the author described above.

The existing literature does not explain, let alone analyze, the significant phenomenon the author explains, particularly its contribution to formative changes that have occurred in modern law and the work of the courts, with an emphasis on the development of new forms of discussion. No essay in the existing literature describes the depth of the Amicus Curiae phenomenon or analyzes the causes behind its formation, its meaning, and its contribution to the design of modern law in general and the modern judicial system in particular in recent decades. This book tries to fill this scientific void. It describes in-depth and extensively the Amicus Curiae phenomenon as it occurs in the world today, together with the various legal methods involved. The book also compares the amicus phenomenon with other legal institutions that have begun to take shape in recent decades. The book describes the contribution of the amicus to the design of legal norms and new judicial practices and offers a comprehensive explanation for all aspects of the Amicus Curiae.

The ideas appearing in this book contribute to the development of scientific research and are innovative in various subjects:

1. The book offers, for the first time, a systematic description of the development of the amicus in the Western world—from Roman law to the present day. In this way, it offers extensive reading and new insights regarding the Amicus Curiae in a broad historical and intellectual view.
2. In addition, the book offers, for the first time, a systematic description of the Amicus Curiae phenomenon as a legal and social phenomenon in the modern law of the Western world, taking place in several legal methods simultaneously.
3. Also, the book offers a comprehensive explanation of the causes shaping the development of the Amicus Curiae practice, the depth and breadth of the phenomenon, its meaning, and its influence on the design of modern law. It explains the contribution of the amicus to the creation of new legal norms and new judicial practices in recent decades.
4. The book explores the mutual effects between the amicus practice and other changes and innovations in the courts. In this way, it explains the idea that the Amicus Curiae embodies and the meaning and implications of this concept.
5. The book demonstrates how the amicus practice gives the judicial system a new capacity, ideas, and tools that have brought about a change in form, substance, and content.

1.4 The Book's Research Methods

This book's primary research method is based on theoretical-comparative legal analysis. In the appropriate cases, the work is based on an interdisciplinary and integrative approach and uses findings from tangential disciplines such as political science, sociology, economics, and communication.[74] These interdisciplinary discussions seek to enrich the work and contribute to broadening the canvas and the analysis. It will be emphasized that the interdisciplinary studies presented in the work will serve the legal analysis and the research questions posed and will not stand as an end in themselves. The book is based on a "weak interdisciplinary" approach. Within it are insights, concepts, perspectives, and methods from different fields of knowledge that enrich and improve legal knowledge while "crossing borders" between the territories of other disciplines.[75]

1. *The theoretical legal research*—the research will focus on analyzing and discussing the Amicus Curiae in common law, continental, and international law, the causes of the formation of this phenomenon, and its normative significance for the law, the judicial system, and society. The book is based on an analysis of primary sources—legislation, case law, rules of various courts, treaties and international reports, decisions of international arbitrations, and secondary sources, such as academic literature. The theoretical analysis will be at the heart of this work. Methodologically, to identify the Amicus Curiae as a significant phenomenon in the legal field, several criteria were defined as described above, according to which the existence of the Amicus Curiae phenomenon is examined:
    1. Adoption of legal practice related to managing the legal process by several judicial systems.
    2. Increasing the use of legal procedures in judicial systems at an increasing rate.
    3. Diversity in the range of legal issues and branches of law in which the Amicus Curiae spreads.
    4. Growth and diversification of the types of judicial courts into which new legal practice penetrates.
    5. An increase in the use of the procedure used in proceedings of high public interest, known as "mega cases".
    6. The type, variety, and nature of the bodies that began to use new legal practices to influence court rulings.

[74] In the general context see: McConville (2017) Research methods for law. Edinburgh University Press. The book covers the principal research traditions and is designed to serve as a handbook for research methods courses. It also appeals to students of related disciplines who have an interest in legal issues, including those from criminology, sociology, psychology, government, politics, and social administration.

[75] See Vick (2004), pp. 163–193; Baron (1999), pp. 1059–1085; van Hoecke (2011); Siems (2009), pp. 5–17. [identifies four different types of interdisciplinary legal research: one basic and three advanced types. His new taxonomy is helpful for identifying the benefits and difficulties of different types of interdisciplinary legal research].

7. The systemic need for grouping and regulating the rules relating to legal practice in a unified and coherent framework.
8. The citation or mention of the information presented by the amici to the courts.[76]

As mentioned above, along with these criteria, additional auxiliary tests will be used that help characterize the phenomenon of the amicus. These include the opening of clinics that train students to submit briefs as amici; Creating a new field of specialization in the work of the lawyers—a lawyer with the title "coordinator of the submission of amicus brief;" and planning and building courtrooms with unique seating for amici, even though they are not official parties to the proceedings.

It will be noted that the book examines the Amicus Curiae in the conventional common law, continental, and international law systems. However, its primary focus will be discussing various aspects of the amicus in common law countries. These countries generally have a long-standing tradition of including third parties in ongoing legal proceedings. In addition, several academic sources deal with various aspects of amicus in these countries. On the other hand, compared to the countries that belong to the continental system, the origins of information are relatively limited.[77]

As mentioned above, the book also discusses the adoption and acceptance of amicus in continental law. As the reader will discover, the importance of the amicus practice in continental law, as mentioned, is in its very absorption into the system. Adopting the Amicus Curiae in continental law, regardless of the number of amici appearing in the proceedings or other criteria related to the Amicus Curiae, is not self-evident. The reason is that, as a rule, the continental legal system provides its judges with inquisitorial procedural tools for obtaining many types of information required for the procedure, which fulfill the role of the amicus to a certain extent and seemingly eliminate its necessity in this legal system.[78]

For example, beyond the fact that the court in the inquisitorial system intervenes more, it is also entitled to invite expert witnesses and other parties to argue before it on its own initiative. In addition, the state authorities also have more options to intervene in the legal process in these countries. Therefore, the very introduction of

[76] As mentioned, the fact that the courts cite, mention, or refer in some way to the information presented by amici, helps establish the hypothesis that the courts were influenced in some way by the briefs submitted to them, although it is not possible to determine precisely to what extent. In relation to many countries (such as the United States or Canada), the databases are relatively well-established and broad and for them all the criteria will be examined, while about other countries, an effort will be made to examine as much of the criteria as possible, according to the limitations of the study.

[77] McCormick (1997). McCormick's article explores how Habermas' theory can bridge the gap between Anglo-American and Continental legal traditions, providing a comprehensive understanding of law and its role in modern society.

[78] Jolowicz (2003), pp. 281–295. [Jolowicz argues that a truly inquisitorial procedure can only be found in specific situations, and that both systems have elements of the other. The article provides a comparative analysis of the two models, examining their principles, fairness, and efficiency].

the Amicus Curiae to this legal system and the continuous and increasing use in countries that have adopted the amicus, such as Colombia, Argentina, Uruguay, and Peru, show the importance of the phenomenon in this part of the world as well.

2. *Comparative research*—conducting comparative research regarding amicus in the countries and methods in which the Anglo-American legal system practices and the continental legal countries in Europe and Latin America.[79] Also, a comparative examination will be made of the arrangements developed in various international institutions, such as the World Trade Organization, and of international courts, such as the European Court of Human Rights or the Latin American Court of Human Rights. The comparative law discussions throughout the book will help map, identify, and describe the global Amicus Curiae and provide a broad legal and intellectual perspective to illuminate how different legal methods deal with the challenges that the Amicus Curiae poses.[80]

1.5 The Structure of the Book

The book has three main parts. The first part of the work deals with the historical, social, and cultural background of the Amicus Curiae; different definitions of amicus; the prototypes of the amicus; other mechanisms of representation of third parties; the distinction between the Amicus Curiae and other types of interventions by third parties, in the development of the "classic amicus" to the "modern amicus" and the criticisms voiced about these developments.

The work's second part will outline one of the crucial developments of the modern judicial procedure in recent decades, which the author calls "the Amicus Curiae Phenomenon." It will deal with its description and scope. This section of the book will show how the Amicus Curiae became common and significant in countries using different judicial systems worldwide, including Israel. The comparative information that will be examined in this chapter, both at the local level, at the state level, and at the supra-state level, will allow analysis and discussion of the causes of the formation of the phenomenon and its effect on the design of modern law and modern justice systems.

As we know, each local culture reacts to a global phenomenon differently. Between the local culture and global phenomena, there are mutual relations where,

[79] See also in general: Martínez-Torrón (1998). [He demonstrates that the Anglo-American legal tradition has more elements in common with Continental law than is frequently believed. By examining the historical and institutional contexts of England's court system, Martínez-Torrón highlights the shared roots and similarities between the two legal traditions, providing a comprehensive understanding of their interconnectedness.

[80] See also in general: Damaška (1974). [He argues that the two systems are complementary and can be combined to create a more effective system of justice]. Damaška's book has been influential in the field of comparative law, and it has helped to shape the debate about the best way to organize a system of justice.

for the most part, the global phenomenon is absorbed in the local culture with specific changes and in a way that affects additional practices in the local culture. Thus, the author will show how the comparative context of the amicus illuminates the local context of the amicus and how the local context contributes to an understanding of the global context of the phenomenon.[81] The organization of this section is as follows: In the first part, the author will outline and examine the arrangements practiced in some leading countries in the (Anglo-American) common law system where the amicus and other forms of intervention by third parties exist. In the second part, the author will examine the absorption of the amicus in international law, particularly in international judicial systems and institutions, to settle international disputes. In the third part, the author will describe the development of the Amicus Curiae in the continental legal system in European and Latin American countries. The reason for this order in describing the developments of the amicus in the world, as will be explained later, is that the development of the Amicus Curiae in the continental legal system is primarily based on the development of the amicus in international law.

The third part of the work discusses the Amicus Curiae and the questions it raises, including what caused it to gain momentum throughout the Western world in recent decades. Why does it occur in these dimensions, and how can it be explained? What does it mean, and what does it teach us about modern law and the role of the modern judicial system? The thesis of the book links the Amicus Curiae to the changes that have taken place in recent decades in the justice systems in the world and the perception of their role and work style. The work reveals how the legal and social processes that plagued the judicial systems in the last three decades are the intellectual ground for understanding the Amicus Curiae. These processes will provide an understanding of the factors that led to the Amicus Curiae phenomenon, and at the same time, they will illustrate the contribution of the amicus to the design of new

[81] It is common to call the meeting point between the global phenomenon and the local reality as "glocalization." Ritzer (2003), pp. 193–209. George Ritzer argues that the traditional view of globalization as a one-way process of Westernization is no longer accurate. He proposes two new concepts to better understand the complex and contradictory nature of globalization: glocalization and grobalization. Glocalization refers to the process by which global forces are adapted to local conditions. Also see in general: Roudometof (2016). Roudometof defines glocalization as "the process through which global forces are adapted to local conditions and vice versa." He argues that glocalization is a more accurate way to understand the complex and dynamic nature of globalization than traditional views that see globalization as a one-way process of Westernization. Roudometof argues that glocalization is a complex and dynamic process that is constantly evolving. He also argues that glocalization is not a monolithic process, and that it can take different forms in different contexts. In general, see also: Shapiro (1993), pp. 37–64. Shapiro argues that the globalization of law is having several important effects. First, it is leading to the development of a global legal order. This global legal order is not a single, unified system, but rather a complex network of overlapping and competing legal regimes. Second, the globalization of law is challenging the sovereignty of states. As states become more integrated into the global economy and as they are subject to the jurisdiction of international organizations, they are losing some of their control over their own legal systems. Third, the globalization of law is raising new questions about the relationship between law and justice.

forms of discussion and a modern working style of judicial systems throughout the Western world.

References

Ackerman B (1998) We the people: transformations

Anderson HA (2015) Frenemies of the court: the many faces of amicus curiae. Univ Rich Law Rev 49:361

Angell E (1967) The amicus curiae: American development of English institutions. Int Comp Law Q 16:1017

Baron JB (1999) Law, literature, and the problems of interdisciplinarity. Yale Law J 108(5): 1059–1085

Bazán V (2009) En Torno al amicus curiae. Revista Oficial del Poder Judicial 3:301, 310–301, 312

Bellhouse J, Lavers L (2004) The modem amicus curiae: a role in arbitration? Civ Just Q 23:187

Bergman D et al (2014) The supreme court database. J Law Econ Organ 30(1):82–97

Berman HJ (1983) Law and revolution

Blake WD (2019) Don't confuse me with the facts: the use and misuse of social science on the United States supreme court. Maryland Law Rev 79:216, 252, at 252, 248

Box-Steffensmeier JM, Christenson DP, Hitt MP (2013) Quality over quantity: amici influence and judicial decision making. Am Polit Sci Rev 107(3):1–15

Brief from a San Francisco citizen to the California Supreme Court on same-sex marriage, Divine Queen Mariette Do-Nguyen Lockyer v. City & County of San Francisco, 95 P.3d 459 (Cal. 2004) (No. S122923)

Brooks-Gordon B, Freeman M (2006) Law and psychology

Charnovitz S (1997) Two centuries of participation: NGOs and international governance. Mich J Int Law 18:281–282

Collins PM Jr (2004) Friends of the court: examining the influence of amicus curiae participation in United States supreme court litigation. Law Soc Rev 38(4):807–832

Collins PM Jr (2008) Friends of the Supreme Court: Interest groups and judicial decision making

Collins PM Jr (2018) The use of amicus briefs. Ann Rev Law Soc Sci 14:219–237

Collins PM Jr, Corley PC, Hamner J (2015) Influence of amicus curiae briefs on U.S. Supreme Court opinion content. Law Soc Rev 49:917

Crema L (2019) The common law (and not roman) origins of Amicus Curiae in international law–debunking a fake news item. *Global Jurist* 20(1):0038

Dainow J (1966) The civil law and the common law: some points of comparison. Am J Comp Law 15

Damaška M (1974) The rule of law in comparative perspective. The inquisitorial system and the adversarial system: a comparative study by Mirjan Damaška

Della Cananea G (2003) Beyond the state: the Europeanization and globalization of procedural administrative law. Eur Public Law 9(4):563–578

Diamond M (2000) Community lawyering: revisiting the old neighborhood. Colum Hum Rights Law Rev 32:67

Engel, DM (1998) How does law matter in the constitution of legal consciousness?

Fallon RH Jr (2012) Scholars' briefs and the vocation of a law professor. J Legal Analysis 4:223–269

Feldman A (2016) The most effective friends of the Court, Empirical SCOTUS. https://empiricalscotus.com/2016/05/11/the-most-effective-friends-of-the-court

Franze AJ, Anderson RR (2015) *Record breaking term for Amicus Curiae in Supreme Court Reflects New Norm,* Natl Law J. http://www.nationallawjournal.com/supremecourtbrief/id=1202735095655

Franze AJ, Anderson RR (2016) In unusual term, big year for Amicus Curiae at the Supreme Court, Natl Law J https://www.apks.com/~/media/files/perspectives/publications/2016/09/in-unusual-term-big-year-for-amicus-curiae-at-the-supreme-court.pdf
Franze AJ, Anderson RR (2020) Amicus Curiae at the Supreme Court: last term and the decade in review, Natl Law J. https://www.arnoldporter.com/-/media/files/perspectives/publications/2020/11/amicuscuriae-at-the-supreme-court.pdf
Garcia RJ (2008) A democratic theory of amicus advocacy. Fla St Univ Law Rev 35
Gardbaum S (2001) The new commonwealth model of constitutionalism. Am J CompLaw 49:707
Hakman N (1966) Lobbying the supreme court—an appraisal of political science. Folklore. Fordham Law Rev 35:15. 50
Hilbink TM (2004) You know the type...: categories of cause lawyering. Law Soc Inq 29(3): 657–698
Hirschl R (2004) Towards Juristocracy: the origins and consequences of the New Constitutionalism
Hirschl R (2006) The new constitutionalism and the judicialization of pure politics worldwide. Fordham Law Rev 75:721
Hodson L (2011) NGOs and the struggle for Human Rights in Europe
Hunt S (2013) The judicialization of politics in Canada and the United States (Bowling Green State Univ., Honors Projects, Paper 39)
Jolowicz JA (2003) Adversarial and inquisitorial models of civil procedure. Int Comp Law Q 52(2): 281–295
Kane JB (2017) Lobbying justice(s)? Exploring the nature of amici influence in state supreme court decision making. State Politics Policy Q 17:251
Kearney JD, Merrill TW (2000) The influence of amicus curiae briefs on the supreme court. Univ Pa Law Rev 148:743–855
Kelleher CA, Yackee SW (2006) Who's whispering in your ear? The influence of third parties over state agency decisions. Polit Res Q 59(4):629–643
Kochevar S (2013) Comment, Amici curiae in civil law jurisdictions. Yale Law J 122:1653
Krislov S (1963) The amicus curiae brief: from friendship to advocacy. Yale Law J 72:694–721
Kronman A (1988) Jurisprudential responses to legal realism. Cornell Law Rev 73:335
Larsen AO, Devins N (2016) The amicus machine. Va Law Rev 102:1901
Levitsky, SR (2015). Law and social movements: old debates and new directions. The Handbook of Law and Society. pp. 382–398
Lynch KJ (2004) Best friends? Supreme court law clerks on effective amicus curiae briefs. J Law Policy 20:33, 46–33, 56
Martínez-Torrón J (1998) Comparative studies in continental and Anglo-American legal history: Anglo-American law and canon law: canonical roots of the common law tradition, vol 18. Duncker & Humblot, Berlin
Mauro T (2016) Bolstered by briefs, liberal justices lash out during contraceptive debate, Natl Law J, Mar. 23 https://www.law.com/supremecourtbrief/almID/1202752957056
Mazmanyan A (2015) Judicialization of politics: the post-soviet way. Int J Const Law 13:200
McConville M (ed) (2017) Research methods for law. Edinburgh University Press, Edinburgh
McCormick JP (1997) Habermas' discourse theory of law: bridging Anglo-American and continental legal traditions. Modern Law Rev:60
Mclauchlan JS (2005) Congressional participation as Amicus Curiae before the U.S. Supreme Court American Legal Institutions
Montemurri P (2014) Ann Arbor Teen's legal brief: juvenile lifers deserve a 2nd chance. Detroit Free Press, Detroit, p 1
O'Connor K, Epstein L (1981–1982) Amicus curiae participation in U.S. Supreme Court litigation: an appraisal of Hakman's "folklore,". Law Soc Rev 16:311
Omari Scott Simmons (2009) Picking friends from the crowd: amicus participation as political symbolism. Conn Law Rev 42:185, 190
Posner RA (1986) Law and literature: a relation reargued. Va Law Rev 72:1351
Posner RA (2006) The role of the judge in the twenty-first century. Boston Univ Law Rev 86:1049

Reimann KD (2006) A view from the top: international politics, norms and the worldwide growth of NGOs. Int Stud Q 50:45–67
Ritzer G (2003) Rethinking globalization: Glocalization/grobalization and something/nothing. Sociol Theory 21(3):193–209
Rosenberg G (1998) Knowledge and desire: Thinking about courts and social change. Leveraging the Law: Using courts to achieve social change
Roudometof V (2016) Glocalization: a critical introduction. Routledge, Milton Park
Salzman R, Williams CJ, Calvin BT (2011) The determinants of the number of amicus briefs filed before the U.S. Supreme Court, 1953–2001. Just Sys J 32:293, 294–293, 295
Sarat AD, Scheingold SA (1998) Cause lawyering and the reproduction of professional authority: an introduction. In: Sarat A, Scheingold S (eds) Cause lawyering: political commitments and professional responsibilities, vol 3
Sarat A, Scheingold S (2006) Cause lawyers and social movements. Stanford University Press, Stanford
Schultz DA (1998) Leveraging the law: using the courts to achieve social change
Shapiro M (1993) The globalization of law. Indiana J Global Legal Stud 1(1):37–64
Siems MM (2009) The taxonomy of interdisciplinary legal research: finding the way out of the desert. J Commonwealth Law Legal Education 7(1):5–17
Simard LS (2008) An empirical study of amici curiae in Federal Court: a fine balance of access, efficiency, and Adversarialism. Rev Litig 27:669. (referring to Grutter v. Bollinger, 539 U.S. 306 (2003)
Slaughter AM (2000) Judicial Globalization. Va J Int Law 40:1103
Smith PM (1998) The sometimes-troubled relationship between courts and their "Friends," Litigation, Summer, at 24, 26
Songer, Donald R., and Reginald S. Sheehan. "Interest group success in the courts: Amicus participation in the Supreme Court." Polit Res Q 46.2 (1993): 339-354
The Global Expansion of Judicial Power (C. Neal Tate & Torbjörn Vallinder eds., 1995)
The Judicialization of Politics in Asia (Björn Dressel ed., 2012)
The Judicialization of Politics in Latin America. (Sieder R. et al. eds.,)
van Hoecke M (ed) (2011) Methodologies of legal research: which kind of method for what kind of discipline? Bloomsbury Publishing
Vick DW (2004) Interdisciplinarity and the discipline of law. J Law Soc 31(2):163–193
Ward I (1995) Law and literature: possibilities and perspectives. Cambridge University Press, Cambridge

Part I
"Amicus Curiae": Background, Typology, and Definitions

Introduction

The literal translation from Latin of the concept "Amicus Curiae" is—"friend of the court" (Amicus—friend; Curiae—of the court). The Amicus Curiae is a legal institution by which a third party who is not formally involved in ongoing legal proceedings but has some interest in it may present his point of view to the court by submitting an Amicus Brief. Amicus has various applications that may be used separately or simultaneously: 1. Adding legal or factual arguments not presented to the courts by the formal parties; 2. Presenting those arguments already submitted to the courts differently or from a broader perspective; 3. Providing different types of information (for example, economic or environmental) when the formal parties do not have access to this information or they do not wish to present it;[1] 4. Submitting a brief in which an attempt is made to convince the courts to accept the position of the formal party they support.[2]

The roles of Amicus Curiae differ in all countries and legal systems where the procedure exists. Even within the same type of legal system, there is a difference (sometimes a significant difference) between the countries that follow particular legal systems in using the amicus and the legal possibilities it confers. In the United States, for example, amicus is used as a third party acting as a kind of lobbyist who

[1] Steger D (2002) Amicus Curiae: participant or friend? – The WTO and NAFTA experience, in: Bogdandy A von et al., (Eds.), European integration and international co-ordination – studies in transnational economic law in honour of Claus-Dieter Ehlermann, The Hague, pp. 419, 447. See also R. Howse et al., Written submission of non-party amici curiae in EC-Seals, 11 February (2013), para. 13 ('The preliminary submissions in this brief are aimed at correcting the misleading and incomplete manner in which Canada has characterized the objectives of the measures at issue in this dispute. . .').

[2] Bellhouse J and Lavers L (2004) The Modem Amicus Curiae: A Role in Arbitration? 23 Civ. Just. Q. 187; Krislov S (1963) The Amicus Curiae Brief: From Friendship to Advocacy, 72 Yale L.J. pp. 694–721; Kearney JD and Merrill TW (2000) The Influence of Amicus Curiae Briefs on the Supreme Court, U. Pa. L. Rev.148: 743-855.

supports the position presented by one of the formal litigants who tries to convince the court to adopt this position. This is usually a non-governmental organization or an interest group (for example, environmental organizations, the umbrella organization of churches, women's organizations, or labor organizations) that seeks to present a position that supports one of the parties in the conflict before the court. This support is intended to advance the interests of the organization itself.

On the other hand, in other Anglo-American countries which belong to the common law system (such as England, Australia, or Canada), the amicus is considered a third party of a more neutral and restrained nature which is invited by the courts to submit a brief to them that will help them in their work.[3]

The increasing use of amicus as a type of lobbyist by various interest groups (mainly non-governmental organizations),[4] in a way that has political overtones, arouses a certain resentment and causes many to wonder whether the name "Amicus Curiae" which translates as "friend of the court" indeed corresponds to reality.[5] Some argue that the name Amicus Curiae (in other words, a true friend of the court) today is fiction, a nostalgic or romantic memory, and nothing more. Because the amicus is a "friend" of one of the formal parties he supports, he is not a "true friend" of the court. The goal of the lobbying amici is to advance their doctrine and influence the courts' decision-making processes in the issues brought before them.[6]

One of the questions discussed in this context is whether it is possible to continue to call it "Amicus Curiae." Is a party undertaking this function of amicus really a

[3]Tams CJ (2016) Bridging Comparative and International Law: Amicus Curiae Participation Procedure in the United Kingdom and the European Court of Human Rights. European Journal of International Law, 26(4), 851–875. [The article offers a theory of the internationalization of law and the emergence of internationalized legal transplants, drawing on a study of the Amicus Curiae participation procedure's internationalization from the United Kingdom to the European Court of Human Rights].

[4]"Interest groups" refers to the definitions accepted in the literature that state that interest groups are organizations that enjoy independence from the government and political parties that try to influence public policy. What distinguishes interest groups from political parties is that they strive for the narrowest goal of influence only, without coming to power. Generally, the motivations to join interest groups are divided into three: material (such as: joining the group gives a financial advantage); social (such as: a desire to meet with people with similar tendencies) or purposeful (such as: joining a group to promote human rights). For more information regarding methods of operation and the division of interest groups according to their organization or characteristics. for example, see: Thomas CS and Hrebnar RJ (2008) Understanding interest groups, lobbying and lobbyists in developing democracies. J. Public Affairs 8, 1–2; First World Interest Groups: A Comparative Perspective; Thomas CS (2004); Berry JM and Wilcox C (2018) The interest group society. Routledge. Routledge (2012); Berry, JM. (2015) Lobbying for the people: The political behavior of public interest groups. Princeton University Press.

[5]John Bellhouse and Anthony Lavers (2004) The Modern Amicus Curiae: A Role in Arbitration? 23 Civ. Just. Q. 187.

[6]An article that argues that the Amicus Curiae has evolved from its original role as an impartial "friend of the court" and that anyone can claim to be a factual expert due to the easy availability of factual information on the internet, see: Larsen AO (2014) The Trouble with Amicus Facts, Va. L. Rev, 100:1757–1818.

friend of the court, in the way someone fulfilling this role was in the past (apparently), who came to assist the court in its work, or is this person/organization a friend of one of the litigants?[7] On the other hand, maybe things were always the same? Even if the amicus supports a formal side, and even if this is done openly and blatantly—the courts still get a broader picture or different points of view and perspectives about the issue before them, and thus, they benefit from the procedure. The lack of clarity about the exact name of the amicus led, for example, the Supreme Court of England to change its rules in 2011 so that the title of the amicus proceedings is no longer "Amicus Curiae" but "Court's Advocate." In this way, the English judicial system sought to emphasize and clarify that the English "amicus" is not a friend of a party to the proceedings but only of the court.[8]

It is not easy to precisely define the concept of the Amicus Curiae because its roles have changed throughout history, sometimes beyond recognition, according to the historical, legal, and social circumstances that prevailed in the judicial systems that used it. Christina Murray claimed it might be easier to define the amicus negatively rather than positively.[9] Moreover, in many countries, legal institutions fulfill purposes similar to those of the amicus. A prominent example is a legal practice called "Intervenor." Like an amicus, the intervenor is a third party seeking to influence ongoing legal proceedings. However, unlike the amicus, the intervenor has a direct and tangible interest in the case, and sometimes, he may even become a formal party to the proceedings.[10]

In addition to the intervenor, some legal institutions have similarities to amicus, such as: (a) an Expert witness on behalf of the court who is appointed to assist the court upon the court's invitation;[11] (b) Pro-bono lawyers are sometimes appointed by the courts as "Officers of the Court" to fulfill various legal tasks, such as representing incompetent parties;[12] (c) The Litigating Amicus is a hybrid between an amicus and a formal party. The Litigating Amicus (sometimes referred to as "Amicus Plus") has powers similar to a formal litigant (such as: questioning

[7] Ibid, among other things, they argued that the common interpretation of the term "Amicus Curiae," "friend of the court," is misleading and should be avoided.

[8] Supreme Court Rules 2009, SI 2009/1603, r 35; Harlow C (2002) Public Law and Popular Justice. Mod. Law Rev. 65:1.

[9] Murray C (1994) Litigating in the Public Interest: Intervention and the Amicus Curiae. S. Afr. J. Hum. Rts. 10:240, 242.

[10] Collins, Jr. PM, and McCarthy LA (2017) Friends and Interveners: Interest Group Litigation in a Comparative Context, J.L. & Courts 5.1, pp. 55–80. [By comparing the role of Amicus Curiae in various legal systems, the article provides insights into the similarities and differences in interest group litigation across different jurisdictions].

[11] Champagne A, Shuman A, and Whitaker E. (1991) An empirical examination of the use of expert witnesses in American courts. Jurimetrics J. 31.4, pp. 375–392; Mnookin, JL. (2007) Expert evidence, partisanship, and epistemic competence. Brook. Law Rev. 73:1009–1033.

[12] Granfield R (2007) The meaning of pro bono: Institutional variations in professional obligations among lawyers. Law & Society Review 41.1, pp. 113–146.

witnesses or oral argument). However, on the other hand, he is not exposed to court costs if he loses the procedure.[13] The Federal Court of the Sixth Circuit in the United States decried the litigating amicus as a legal mutant.[14] Anyway, this representation of the mechanism is relatively rare.[15]

Since in different judicial systems, those institutions which express various forms of participation of third parties in ongoing proceedings may be mixed together, often without a formal distinction between them, it is necessary to clarify the concept of amicus.[16] In the coming pages, we will examine different definitions and interpretations of the Amicus Curiae.

[13] See, for example, Liberty Res., Inc. v. Phil. House. Auth., 395 F. Supp. 2d 206, 209–210 (E.D. Pa. 2005). In this case, the court denied an "intervention" request but granted "enhanced powers" to the amicus. For more information about the development of the "disputing amicus" see: Lowman, MK (1992) Comment, The Litigating Amicus Curiae: When Does the Party Begin After the Friends Leave? Am. U. Law. Rev, 41:1243, 1245. [Lowman also explores the limits and constraints on Amicus Curiae participation, arguing for a balance between allowing Amicus Curiae to contribute valuable information and preventing them from unduly influencing the outcome of litigation].

[14] United States v. Michigan, 940 F.2d 143, 164 (6th Cir. 1991). Most of the time, the "disputing amicus" was the Attorney General of the United States and his powers were increased similar to those of a formal party, at the request of the court, and for the Attorney General to assist the court in its work.

[15] Id. At 382 ("The term seems to have died away").

[16] For the distinction between the Amicus Curiae and an expert witness, see below the first title, paragraph 5 (starting on page 40). For the distinction between the amicus and the "intervenor" see below the first title, paragraph 6 (starting on page 42).

Chapter 2
"Amicus Curiae"—Definitions and Interpretations

The dictionary definitions of Amicus Curiae are not uniform and do not establish a coherent understanding of the term. The "Modern Dictionary for the Legal Profession" defines the amicus as follows: "Individuals or groups who are not formal parties in the litigation process but are nevertheless allowed to present their position on the issues in the case pending in court, by way of submitting a written brief or by presenting the argument orally."[1] The legal dictionary "Law Lexicon" defines Amicus Curiae as follows: "Someone who, on his initiative, or by court's invitation, provides information to the court on a legal issue, and this when the court is satisfied with the issue or when the court is wrong about the issue. The amicus presents facts or other important information to help make a proper ruling in the case that the court is discussing."[2]

"Mellinkoff's Dictionary of American Legal Usage" defines the amicus as follows: "Someone who is not a formal party to the proceedings but usually has a preference in favor of one of the formal litigants who is authorized to present his position before the court."[3] On the other hand, the definition that appears in "West's Encyclopedia of American Law" is: "A person with a direct interest or a clear position regarding a legal proceeding who is not a formal party to the proceeding, may apply to the court with a request to submit an alleged brief on behalf of a party, But in fact to offer his views to the court."[4]

Even among the various countries that have adopted the Amicus Curiae in their legal system, there needs to be more clarity about the definition of amicus and its role within the legal system. For example, the court in Australia defines the amicus as follows: "one who is engaged in legal practice or a person with another occupation

[1] Beyer and Redden (2001).

[2] Aiyar (1997) (referring to 1 Edward Coke, Institutes of the Lawes of England 178 (London: J. Flesher, 1622).

[3] Mellinkoff (1992).

[4] West's Encyclopedia of American Law (2008).

S. Farber, *The Amicus Curiae Phenomenon*, Ius Gentium: Comparative Perspectives on Law and Justice 119, https://doi.org/10.1007/978-3-031-67225-5_2

who has the appropriate qualifications to assist the court."[5] The Ontario Supreme Court defined amicus as "an observer from the side who informs the court about a particular legal matter."[6] In England, the Court of Appeals determined that the role of the amicus is "to assist the trial by presenting the law without bias."[7] In Malaysia, the Supreme Court ruled that the amicus is "one who is invited to a legal proceeding by the court to assist the court, and he does not volunteer on his initiative to assist the court."[8] And in South Africa, it was determined that "the Amicus does not aspire to take over the management of the legal process."[9]

These and many more contradictory definitions show a need for more agreement regarding the role of the amici and their powers. The lack of understanding or dispute regarding the definition is not only found in legal definitions but also in practice since different countries act de facto according to different definitions.

The author believes that the difficulty in finding an accurate and agreed-upon definition for the concept of Amicus Curiae can be explained by two main factors: First, the characteristics of the amicus have undergone significant changes during the last hundreds of years according to the historical, legal, and social circumstances that prevailed in those countries where the amicus was recognized. Therefore, some definitions do not correspond to the situation "in the field." These definitions were copied and transferred to more updated dictionaries and adopted in jurisprudence, sometimes without referring to the social and legal changes in this practice. Second, many times, it is possible to find a lack of care on the part of judicial systems in making a precise distinction between different legal institutions, such as the "intervenor," "expert witness," or "court officer," and the "Amicus Curiae." The lack of legal distinction in various judgments often needs to be clarified.

The ambiguous interpretations given to amicus by various courts around the world (sometimes, there is a contradiction between the definition of parallel courts in the same country), the different dictionary definitions, which are often contradictory, together with an inappropriate regulation (regulation) have often led to a situation of ambiguity and lack of clarity regarding the role of the amicus.[10] For example, one can find cases where "expert witnesses" who appeared in professional

---

[5] *PW & CA* (1988) 12 Fam LR 467.

[6] Grice v. R. [1957] O.W.N. 527 (S.C.).

[7] Allen v. Sir Alfred McAlpine & Sons Ltd. [1968] 2 QB 229 (CA) 266.

[8] Hamid bin Hassan v. Returning Officer, Karak, [1979] 2 M.L.J. 183.

[9] *Grimshaw v. Mica Mines Ltd.* 1912 TPD 450.

[10] At times, this ambiguity and lack of clarity led to strange results. For example, in 1830, a lawyer who was the permanent representative of two parties was involved in a legal process of bankruptcy in which one party regularly represented by him was sued by another party who was also regularly represented by him. This lawyer did not know to which of his clients the duty of representation applies and how he should manage his steps and therefore requested the court's decision. The English judge who heard the case believed that he had no legal authority to recommend to the lawyer which of the two clients he should represent. However, to overcome the legal hurdle, the judge appointed himself as Amicus Curiae and in this capacity provided a legal recommendation to the lawyer, see: Krislov (1963), pp. 694–721.

matters in court are asked to appear at the appeals court as amici (and were rejected)[11] or a judge who asked to join as Amicus Curiae in an appeal against her ruling to protect her good name (the request was denied).[12]

Even if we assume that it is natural that there will be deep disagreements amongst the amicus definitions, these definitions still need to answer many questions. For example: Does the court invite the amici, or are they allowed to invite themselves to the court to present their positions? Is the amici legally trained, or can the amici also be legally uneducated? Do the amici assist the court neutrally, or do they unilaterally side with a particular formal litigant? This book will try to answer these questions in the coming pages by mapping the prototypes of Amicus.

2.1 The Prototypes of the "Amicus Curiae"

There are several prototypes of amici in judicial systems throughout the Western world. In general, on one side of the spectrum stands the "neutral amicus" who comes to assist the court without any personal interest. Sometimes, this amicus is referred to by the following names: "the Roman amicus," "the ancient amicus," "the decent amicus," or "the classic amicus." On the other side of the spectrum is the "lobbyist amicus," who seeks to participate in an ongoing legal process to advance his agenda in court. This amicus is sometimes called "the modern amicus" or "the political amicus." In the middle, between these extremes, there are other models of amici.

2.1.1 The Classic Amicus Curiae

This prototype of the amicus is manifested when the court needs information or other assistance not provided by the formal parties to the procedure, either since they wish to refrain from assisting the court by offering information in their possession as it may be detrimental to their case, or due to their inability to do so as they do not have the professional knowledge required to interpret the data or have access to various interpretations and viewpoints regarding the information. In such a case, the court may ask a third party, external to the procedure and independent, usually an expert lawyer, to advise the court independently or to objectively present to the court the legal issue that the court is discussing. This amicus aims to assist the court by providing advice (sometimes legal advice but not necessarily) or a professional opinion on an issue addressed in court. Sometimes, the court needs to broaden its horizons and broaden its knowledge of the issue it is discussing. The official parties

[11] Witty v. Planning & Zoning Comm'n of Hartland, 784 A.2d 1011, 1018 (Conn. App. Ct. 2001).
[12] Ligon v. City of New York, 736 F.3d 166, 168–169 (2d Cir. 2013).

may not be interested in assisting in the matter because the law the court wishes to develop may harm their interests or because they may be afraid that the information the court requests will lead to a ruling that will damage them.

The "Classic Amicus" does not represent the proceeding's formal parties or other interests. He also has no utilitarian interest of his own. His sole purpose is to help the court rule in the best possible way. Different judicial systems make use of this type of amicus in the following cases:

(a) When the matter under discussion in the court involves issues that impact upon the public interest from a social, constitutional, political, economic, or ecological point of view. In these cases, where the court wishes to receive broad information about all the interests at stake and to understand how its ruling affects groups other than the formal litigants, it may invite a third party to complete said information to the court.[13] Sometimes, this amicus is called "the lawyer of the court." In the United States, for example, this type of amicus is used to justify rulings of a lower court when the two formal parties do not agree on the reasoning of the ruling.[14]
(b) When an issue that arises during the discussion does not necessarily directly concern the formal parties, yet the court wishes to develop a legal rule.[15] The apparent problem with this type of "amicus" is that it seems that the court does not serve as an altogether "neutral party," as expected in the adversarial method, and it takes a position even when the parties are represented by their own attorneys. On the other hand, these appointments of amici can be seen as the desire of the court to get the whole picture when the formal parties do not share this desire.

2.1.2 *The "Bystander Amicus"*

Another prototype of the amicus is called "Bystander Amicus" or "Intervening Good Samaritan Amicus."[16] The main difference in this amicus compared to the classic

---

[13] For a description of this process, see for example: Collins Jr. et al. (2018), (Influence of), [The authors use plagiarism detection software to assess the extent to which the justices incorporate language from amicus briefs into their opinions. Their findings indicate that the justices are influenced by amicus briefs primarily based on the extent to which these briefs contribute to their ability to make effective law and policy].

[14] Goldman (2011), pp. 907, 909–11; Shaw (2015), p. 1533; Solimine (2013). See for example Prof. Paul Cassel's invitation on the case of Nat'l Fed'n of Indep. Bus. v. Sebelius, 132 S.Ct. 608 (2011)—(inviting a lawyer to argue about the correctness of the judgment of the Court of Appeals).

[15] Angell, E See *supra* note 1; Mohan (2010), pp. 352–374.

[16] "The Good Samaritan" is a concept that describes an expression of helping others without recompense, which originates from the "Parable of the Good Samaritan," which appears in the New Testament, the Gospel according to Luke 10.

model is that the bystander amicus offers assistance, or a viewpoint not presented to the court by the formal parties on his initiative. The development of the "bystander amicus" lies in the fact that in the past, every person who had information essential to an ongoing proceeding was entitled to share this information with the court and was not required to request an initiative from the court to do so. A classic example of this amicus is an issue that arose in 1293 in England regarding the interpretation of a deed, in which the Amicus Curiae informed the court on his own initiative that he knew a precedent that could help the court rule on the matter.[17]

Usually, this amicus is a person or organization that does not support either party to the formal proceedings. These types of amici wish to present their positions on their own initiative because the issue is important to them and because they want to influence the court. The use of this type of amicus, certainly in the United States, is rare. For example, in the case of *Hobby Lobby Stores, Inc. v. Sebelius* (in the matter of the relationship between corporate law and religious freedom),[18] out of 84 briefs of different amici that supported one of the formal parties, two briefs were submitted by private individuals who presented an independent position, without support for any party.[19]

2.1.3 The "Supporting Amicus"

The third model is the "Supportive Amicus." This prototype is divided into three categories. The first category becomes involved in cases where the court appoints an amicus to represent an unrepresented litigant. The common law tradition is that there is a strong interest in ensuring fairness in representation, mainly when legal aid is hard to come by. Beyond the fact that the provision of legal assistance by lawyers through the amicus is intended to allow the accused to exhaust his rights, the courts may also appoint amici because the management of the criminal proceedings when the accused is not represented is more complicated and complex from a legal point of

[17]YB 21 Edw. 1, p. 149, Easter (1293), another example is The Massachusetts Digest: Being a Digest of the Decisions of the Supreme Judicial Court of Massachusetts, Volume 2 (1823), by Samuel Putnam. In 1811, it became clear to the Massachusetts Supreme Court that one of the jurors in a criminal trial was also the complainant against the defendant. A lawyer who was present in the courtroom named Joseph Story (who was later appointed to the Supreme Court) asked to submit on his own initiative as Amicus Curiae that in his opinion the court should disqualify the juror. He noted that there is a similar precedent that occurred in the state of Virginia, where the Supreme Court dismissed juries for this reason. The Massachusetts Supreme Court rejected this claim, which is firmly rooted in the rules of natural justice. Contrary to what seems clear to us today, the court ruled that the fact that the juror knows the accused from prior acquaintance will help the court in clarifying the truth. He stated that this familiarity will help the jurors to understand the true nature of the accused and that this familiarity makes him a better juror than other jurors.

[18]723 F.3d 1114 (10th Cir. 2013).

[19]*Amicus History: Hobby Lobby Supreme Court Amicus Briefs Among Record Levels*, Becket: Religious Liberty For All. http://www.becketfund.org/hobbylobbyamicus.

view. When a defendant is not represented, the fear arises that the acceptance of the state's position in court will not result from its position being right but from its superior ability to conduct the proceedings.

Therefore, some courts appoint a defense attorney as amicus in appropriate cases. This appointment is made mainly in proceedings where there is no obligation of representation according to the law. In cases where there is a duty of representation by an authority, and the court insists on appointing a defense attorney, it sometimes calls the defense attorney appointed by it an amicus. For example, the Supreme Court of South Dakota appointed a lawyer for a defendant sentenced to death as Amicus Curiae to raise any possible defense on behalf of the defendant after realizing that the defendant's defense attorney had been instructed not to do so.[20]

The second category of the "Supportive Amicus" is when a third party not related to one of the formal litigants has a personal and direct interest in the outcome of the judgment, and he wishes to join the procedure and thereby influence his affairs. A classic example of this is the *Coxe* case from 1736 in England, where an Amicus Curiae assisted the court by informing the court of a conspiracy hatched by one of the parties against his opponent. If this plot had come to fruition, the amicus himself would have been harmed, and therefore, this case can be seen as the precedent for third-party intervention in common law when that party's interest is at stake.[21] As will be clarified later, this type of amicus is the beginning of a significant change in the modern role of the amicus, through which the mechanism of the classic Amicus Curiae took on entirely new and different dimensions.

The third category of "Supportive Amicus" is that of state attorneys who present the broad public interest to the courts in an Amicus Curiae role when, generally, there is no legal obligation to do so. When there is a legal obligation to appoint a lawyer or for the state to appear (such as: in cases of adoption of children), it is not a voluntary matter but a statutory matter. An example of the category can be seen in the case *Rondel v. Worsley*, in which the Solicitor General of England was invited to present the state's position before the Court of Appeal as Amicus Curiae in an issue that dealt with the professional liability of lawyers.[22]

---

[20] State v. Robert, 820 N.W.2d 136, 140–141 & n.7 (S.D. 2012), the Supreme Court mentioned: "This Court is aware of society's interest in the constitutional imposition of the death penalty.... This interest exists independent of the State's interest in punishing [defendant] for his crimes."

[21] Coxe v. Phillips (1736) 95 Eng. Rep. 152; 1 Cas. t. Hard. 237. The case, from the year 1736, dealt with a financial fraud committed by Ms. Phillips against a claimant whose name is unknown. Lord Hardwicke pointed out that when there is a fear of collusion between two formal parties in a legal proceeding, there is no obstacle for an external third party to submit the application as an amicus.

[22] Similarly, in the judgment Morelle Ld. v. Wakeling [1955] 2 QB 379 (CA) The Solicitor General of England was invited by the court to present the state's position in a dispute between two private litigants where the judgment concerned the interests of the state. In Hong Kong courts appoint amici in ex parte civil applications, such as corporate liquidations. In these cases, there is no obligation for the state representative to be present at the hearing and when he appears, he serves as Amicus Curiae. For example, in Re S. China Strategic Ltd., [1997] H.K.L.R.D. 131 (C.F.I.), discussed a question of contractual sanction for a debt forgiveness arrangement. In this case, the court appointed the representative of the Ministry of Justice as amicus and he assisted the court with important

Unlike the classic amicus, which is generally used as the "Lawyer of the Court," this amicus is not invited to the court to present a position but to assist the court in a more principled way by presenting the public interest.[23] This category includes, as a rule, cases in which representatives of the Attorney General or the Ministry of Justice join ongoing legal proceedings (not by a legal obligation to do so) after a dispute between two formal parties, the court requests to know the position of the "state" in the matter.

2.1.4 *The Modern Amicus*

The fourth prototype of the amicus is the "Political Amicus," which is also called the "Modern Amicus" or the "Lobbyist Amicus."[24] This model is characterized by the fact that the amicus has a solid and clear interest, but not necessarily a personal one, in the outcome of the judicial process or in the law that will be adopted, and he seeks to present his position to influence the courts' decisions. The standard methods of action of this amicus are the presentation of the main arguments of the formal side in a different way or presenting arguments that the formal parties did not assert, adding other arguments and emphasizing them, expressing explicit support for the justice of one of the parties, and trying to convince the court to accept his position. This amicus is not a formal party in the proceedings, and his rights and obligations are not the same as the rights of the formal litigants. However, his desire is clear: he wants to express a position in a way that will influence the judgment and the decision-making process of the court.[25]

As will be clarified later, sometimes the argument appearing in the "lobbyist amicus" brief does not bring significantly new information for the court, but the judges nevertheless accept these briefs. This is because the briefs "update" them about the public lobby behind a specific party and the bodies and interest groups working on the matter in the legal, media, and political arena.[26] The social arguments

factual information. For more examples from Hong Kong see Re Carrian Holdings Ltd. (In Liq.), [1990] 1 H.K.C. 320 (C.F.I.); Re Grandeur Constr. Co., ex parte Law Hoi Chuen, [1987] 3 H.K.C. 480 (C.F.I.).

[23] Thompson and Wachtell (2009), pp. 237, 242. (Demonstration of how the United States Supreme Court uses the United States Attorney General as Amicus Curiae).

[24] The origin of the term is in the entrance hall (lobby) of the House of Commons in Great Britain, where people can approach members of parliament and present their arguments. The term "lobbyist amicus" took shape in the US. Fowler V. Harper & Edwin D. Etherington, Lobbyists Before the Court, 101 U. PA. L. REV. 1172 (1953).

[25] Collins Jr (2007), pp. 55–70; Larsen and Devins (2016); Collins Jr., (2018), pp. 219–237.

[26] O'Connor and Epstein (1981). [The authors then examine the types of organizations that file amicus briefs in the Supreme Court. They find that the most common types of organizations are interest groups, law firms, and government agencies. Interest groups are the most frequent filers of amicus briefs, and they tend to file briefs on behalf of their members or on behalf of a particular cause].

presented by amici also influence the decision-making procedures of the courts; not infrequently, the courts are influenced by the interest groups that stand behind the submitted brief or at least present themselves as attentive to their positions, even if they did not accept them in practice. Sometimes, the amicus briefs are intended to convey a broad message to the legislature, the judiciary, and the general public rather than to obtain an "immediate achievement" in the trial itself.[27]

A significant and comprehensive use of the "Modern Amicus" is currently made in the United States. For example, a study found that in 2014 and 2015, about 98% of all cases discussed in court included amici,[28] and in 2015 and 2016, about 92% of all cases discussed in court were joined by amici.[29] This trend continued, with about 97% percent of all cases discussed in court in 2019 and 2020 being joined by amici.[30]

The number of briefs submitted in "mega cases" (public cases of high public interest and great weight) has also increased significantly in recent decades.[31] According to various estimates, dozens of amici will join each case that will be heard in the United States Supreme Court in the coming years.[32] The Amicus Curiae in the United States is not just a tool used by lawyers but a "people's" democratic tool used in public service. In the eyes of many, it is the primary and most effective tool of interest groups that participate in legal proceedings to promote their position in this arena.[33]

Over the last few decades, tens of thousands of different amici—companies, organizations, ordinary people, and politicians representing wider groups behind them joined legal proceedings and tried to influence the court's decision-making process.[34] In the eyes of various interest groups and particular non-governmental organizations, the Amicus Curiae are seen as the formal end of a value struggle and as another stage where it is possible to influence the shapers of public opinion and

---

[27] Collins Jr (2004), pp. 828; O'Connor and Epstein (1981).

[28] Franze and Anderson (2015).

[29] Franze and Anderson (2015).

[30] Franze and Anderson (2020) Amicus Curiae at the Supreme Court: Last Term and the Decade inReview,NAT'Ll.j.,November18.2020, https://www.arnoldporter.com/-/media/files/perspectives/publications/2020/11/amicuscuriae-at-the-supreme-court.pdf.

[31] While between the years 1946–1955, ten amicus briefs were submitted in only three cases discussed at the United States Supreme Court, between the years 1986–1995, over 120 cases discussed at the Supreme Court contained at least ten briefs in each case. Between the years 1985–1995, in more than twenty cases more than twenty memoranda were submitted in the case ("mega cases").

[32] Collins (2008).

[33] Caldeira and Wright (1990), pp. 782–806. [The authors find that organized interests are the most active participants in Amicus Curiae briefs and that their participation has increased over time]. Hansford (2004), pp. 170–197.

[34] Mclauchlan (2005).

the decision-makers in the various authorities, alongside petitions, protest demonstrations, and advertising in the media.[35]

Although various interest groups had already used amicus briefs in the United States in the twentieth century, non-governmental public organizations, particularly advocacy and human rights organizations, have recently led to widespread public attention and a significant development in the "Modern Amicus."[36] Critically important cases conducted in the twentieth century in the United States resulted in the submission of thousands of briefs from hundreds of different rights organizations and a significant increase in the use of Amicus Curiae. Throughout the twentieth century, there was a constant increase in the number of amicus briefs submitted by non-governmental organizations to the courts. Among them: the American Civil Rights Association (ACLU), the American Association for the Advancement of Black Rights (NAACP), the American Jewish Congress (AJC), the National Organization for Women (NOW), and the American Federation for Labor Rights (AFL).

For example, in the *Smith* case, the court determined, based on amicus briefs submitted to it, that non-white citizens may vote in local elections.[37] In the Sweatt matter, the court accepted memos from dozens of non-governmental organizations and prohibited racial discrimination in law schools.[38] To avoid self-incrimination, many briefs were submitted by human rights organizations.[39]

In general, in the 1960s, the Supreme Court, headed by Judge Earl Warren (Earl Warren), was very much involved in establishing civil rights protection, particularly in criminal procedure. Thus, various social groups and non-governmental organizations began to try and influence the court's decision-making process. Indeed, this policy results in many non-governmental organizations directly shaping United States law by submitting amicus briefs. For example, in the *Aguillard* case, which

---

[35] Ibid and also, Box-Steffensmeier et al. (2013) [They find that amici curiae briefs from repeat players in the Court and those with a reputation for telling the truth are more persuasive to the Court]; Collins et al. (2015).

[36] The first case of the use of Amicus Curiae by a human rights organization was on the subject of the deportation of the Asian population from New York at the beginning of the twentieth century. In the case Ah How v. United States, 193 U.S. 65 (1904), the Supreme Court was asked to approve the deportation of a person of Chinese descent. The rights organization "New York Chinese Charitable and Benevolent Association" submitted an amicus brief in which it claimed that the deportation of citizens of Chinese origin is discriminatory, unequal, and contrary to the American Constitution.

[37] Smith v. Allwright, 321 U.S. 649 (1944).

[38] Sweatt v. Painter, 339 U.S. 629 (1950).

[39] Miranda v. Arizona, 384 U.S. 436 (1966). Another famous decision that is an outgrowth of information presented by amici is the case of Escobedo v. Illinois, 378 U.S. 478 (1964), in which a brief was submitted on behalf of the Civil Rights Association as Amicus Curiae. The Supreme Court ruled, based on the association's brief, that the Sixth Amendment gives suspects the right to consult with a lawyer during a police investigation. Harris (2000). [The article examines the role of Amicus Curiae briefs in American jurisprudence and argues that while they can be helpful in providing the Court with additional information, they can also be used to advance the interests of particular groups or individuals].

dealt with the constitutionality of religious studies in public schools, the Supreme Court accepted an amicus brief compiled by a coalition of 72 Nobel laureates, 17 social science researchers, and seven recognized scientific organizations. Following the information presented to the court by the amici, it was ruled that teaching the "religion of creation" in public schools is contrary to the United States Constitution because it promotes a particular religion.[40]

Additionally, following the attempts of various interest groups to influence the court's decision-making processes through the "modern amicus," identifying the amicus as the judge's good friend who assists him in his work became dimmed. As time passed and the flow of requests from non-governmental organizations to become amici increased, the Amicus Curiae ceased to be a neutral institution, indifferent to the litigants who helped the court avoid mistakes or clarify the law objectively. The tone "changed," and the amici became active participants, sometimes the harshest and loudest participants in the legal process.

The United States courts were aware of this trend. They began to see amici curiae as potential litigants, allies of one of the parties, or semi-formal representatives of interests that were not represented. "Friendship" in the classical sense—died out. Samuel Krislov called this process: "From Friendship to Advocacy," that is, a continuous process of transitioning the way Amicus Curiae is used from a neutral side that comes to help the court avoid mistakes (or neutral by definition) to an interested and lobbyist side that favors the formal side.[41]

Looking at the Amicus Curiae as potential litigants led the United States Supreme Court (and accordingly, as will be explained, other courts in the world) to tighten its rules on the subject and to establish regulation. For example, in 1990, after over 78 briefs were submitted by dozens of amici in a case dealing with the right to abortion (the *Webster* case), the Supreme Court revised its rules on Amicus Curiae.[42] As part of the new rules, the court emphasized to the amici (existing and potential) that only memos that have the purpose of bringing fresh and relevant information

---

[40] Edwards v. Aguillard, 482 U.S. 578 (1987).

[41] The description according to which, starting in the middle of the twentieth century, there was a significant change in the American Amicus Curiae is the dominant research paradigm and many scholars from different research disciplines (mainly law, but also political science and history), have adopted this thesis. American historian Stuart Banner disagrees with this description. In summary, his conclusions are as follows: First, there has never been a "pure" period in the practice of American litigation where the amicus was solely a neutral body that came to assist the court. Second, there was no transition from "friendship to advocacy" but both elements existed simultaneously when, from the mid-nineteenth century, there were more supportive amici than neutral amici. Thirdly, the increase that occurred in the nineteenth century in the number of the supporting amici at the expense of the neutral amici lies in the difference of the litigation in the courts: a transition from a spontaneous oral argument to a written argument. Since the lawyers did not need to be present in the courtrooms to keep up to date with the rulings, they preferred to read and keep up to date with the legal precedents in their office and therefore did not spontaneously help in cases that were not theirs. See: Banner (2003), pp. 1790–1890.

[42] Webster v. Reproductive Health Servs., 492 U.S. 490 (1989).

will be accepted, while briefs that do not comply with this rule: "simply burden the court and are not welcome."

Several years later, the rules were tightened again. It was established that the Amicus Curiae was required to state whether he was financially supported by a formal party to the proceedings or whether a formal party assisted in writing the brief. Also, the amicus must indicate the funding sources for writing the brief to remove the fear of improper connections. The origin of these requirements is the desire of the judges who read the briefs to correctly and more accurately evaluate the brief brought before them.[43] Another possible explanation for these rules is that the official litigants may manipulate the court by inviting many amici to support their position. The courts may get the mistaken impression that when many public organizations join in favor of a particular litigant—then public opinion is supportive of it. However, these amici were, in fact, "invited" by one of the litigants to create a "sympathetic atmosphere."[44]

Be that as it may, the "modern" Amicus Curiae choice to advance a specific agenda is mainly in a direction opposite to the "classic amicus." This distance is so significant that it sometimes blurs the difference between a "modern amicus" and a formal party. Today, there are judicial systems in which the rights of the Amicus Curiae are so broad that the difference between him and a formal party is negligible. This type of amici, a subset of the "Modern Amicus," is called "Litigating Amicus" in the United States. Although these amici are third parties and are not a formal part of the proceedings, they are allowed to argue orally before the court, question witnesses of the other side, and present to the court evidence on their behalf.[45]

2.2 Amicus Curiae and the Intervenor

Alongside the amicus practice, another common mechanism for the participation of third parties through which their position is presented to the courts is called "intervention," whereby an intervenor is the third party. The basic idea behind this practice is that a ruling by the court on a specific matter may affect the rights or interests of people not involved in the procedure. The intervenors are concerned with ensuring that their interests or the interests of the general public will be appropriately represented. The courts are generally interested in receiving all the essential, legal,

[43] Similar procedural rules have been adopted by various judicial systems—in South Africa, Australia, Canada, and international courts. See for example: Md. R. 8-511(b)(1)(E); Minn. R. Civ. App. P. 129.03; N.D. R. App. P. 29(c)(4); Tex. R. App. P. 11; W. Va. R. App. P. 30(e)(5); For the ICSID arbitration panel, see, Biwater Gauff (Tanz.) Ltd. v. United Republic of Tanzania, ICSID Case No. ARB/05/22, Award, ¶ 359 (July 24, 2008), Procedural Order No. 5.

[44] Sup. Ct. R. 37.6.

[45] For other examples, Lowman (1992), p. 1246.

or factual information to best decide the case before them.[46] The courts' approach is that joining "intervenors," if they meet the conditions for applying and providing new information, may improve their work and increase the chance of a complete and correct decision.[47]

In general, third parties seek to "intervene" in legal proceedings in several situations: First, if the "intervenor" is a formal litigant in a proceeding in which issues identical or similar to the issue in which he seeks to intervene are discussed. The intervenor aims to influence a particular case to affect his similar interest in another case. Second, if the "intervenor" represents a group of people who have a direct bearing on the legal issues that arise in the procedure in which he seeks to intervene. For example, as part of a proceeding between a municipality and a developer regarding real estate development rights, various bodies (such as the neighborhood committee or an urban experimenter) can request to be "intervenors" and present to the court the overall consequences of the matter on their community, on parking shortages, or lack of places in schools.

Third, if the "intervenor" fears that the expected court ruling may affect his other interests. In rare cases, courts allow third parties to join the proceedings as "intervenors" even though they do not fully comply with the required terms but are still interested in hearing their position. These "intervenors" are sometimes called "Near Intervenors." For example, an Indian tribe in the United States was refused to join as an "intervenor" in a proceeding that dealt with a conflict between two casino owners because it did not meet the above conditions. However, the tribe was authorized to submit a written brief only without their other procedural rights and this because of "the tribe's involvement in the events that led to the conflict."[48]

Unlike the tests for receiving an amicus brief (which will be examined in depth in the second part of this study), the principle guiding considerations regarding the requests of third parties to join as "intervenors" are, in essence: first, will the arguments of the "intervenor" help the court decide the case (hereinafter: **the "proposed contribution" test**). Second, are the arguments of the "intervenor" different from those of the formal parties.[49] Third, the importance of

[46] Collins Jr. and McCarthy (2017), Alarie and Green (2010) and Lester (1988). [The chapter discusses the role of Amicus Curiae briefs in the European Court of Human Rights and their use as a means of providing the Court with additional information and perspectives. The author notes that while amicus briefs can be helpful, they can also be used to advance the interests of particular groups or individuals, and that the Court should be cautious in relying on them].

[47] See Callaghan (2020), p. 33.

[48] NGV Gaming, Ltd. v. Upstream Point Molate, LLC, 355 F. Supp. 2d 1061, 1068 (N.D. Cal. 2005).

[49] According to Canadian Supreme Court Judge John Sopinka: "Third party intervention will be welcomed if the applicant provides the court with new information or a new perspective on a constitutional matter or an important public issue." Reference re Workers' Comp. Act, 1983 (Nfld.) (Application to Intervene), [1989] 2.S.C.R. 335, 340 (citing Brian Crane, Third Party Practice And Advocacy In The Supreme Court 1.1.05 (1983)). In addition, there are additional legal procedures such as the time for submission of the brief, and financial guarantees to be paid to the original disputants if they are harmed as a result of the intervention.

the case.[50] Fourth, the potential harm to the rights of the formal parties due to the joining of the intervenor.[51] Fifth, the type of proceedings and the practices used in the proceedings.[52]

Against the background of these definitions, it is easy to distinguish between the amicus and the intervenor. Unlike the amicus, who usually has no personal interest in the proceedings' results, the intervenor is a third party with a direct or genuine interest in the results. Often, his intervention is expressed through the submission of a written position. However, he may argue verbally or become a formal party on all the meanings attached, per the court's discretion and the law's provisions. Jillian Welch claimed that: "An intervenor is the statutory equivalent of the common law amicus."[53] She believes that in many countries, there is not a clear enough distinction between the intervenor and the amicus since their attributes and rights are determined through the court's discretion, which varies from case to case, often without sufficient reasoning.

The difference between the intervenor and the formal litigators is that the concrete decision that is the subject of the discussion is crucial for the formal litigants as it affects them directly. On the other hand, many times, the legal precedent that will be established in the case is just as important for an intervenor because these proceedings may affect identical, similar, or future proceedings in which they are or maybe a formal party.[54] To a large extent, the practice of the intervention of a third party is an exception to the tradition of adversarial law, according to which legal proceedings should be decided through the legal arguments of the formal parties to the proceedings. As will be explained later, since it is an exception to the prevailing norm, intervenors (as well as amici curiae) are required to obtain the court's approval before joining the ongoing proceedings.

From the point of view of third parties who wish to influence an ongoing legal proceeding, the amicus and the intervenor are on a continuum where the amicus (except for "the American amicus") is usually a more objective third party who comes to help develop legal principles or to fulfill functions more in the procedure. As a rule, the amicus is invited by the court. On the other hand, the intervenor often has a direct interest in the procedure. After accepting the intervenor's request, he may even become a formal party with extensive legal rights. Due to the prominent involvement of the intervenor in the procedure, he may be exposed to court costs.

On the other hand, an amicus will always be limited to presenting an argument (usually written and sometimes oral argument)[55] within the limits of the dispute

[50] *Nat'l Austl. Bank v Hokit* (1996) 39 NSWLR 377, 381; *US Tobacco Co v. Minister for Consumer Affairs* (1988) 20 FCR 520.

[51] The procedure in the case of Hokit, Murray (1994), p. 242; Campbell (1998) pp. 225, 256.

[52] Metcalfe (2009), pp.18–26. See mainly the discussion on the comparative law.

[53] Welch (1985), p. 204.

[54] Brodie (2000); Brodie, Friends of the Court (Preferencing third parties over others confirms the fact that the Canadian Supreme Court is a political actor).

[55] For an interesting analysis of the oral argument aspect see: Gleason and Ivy (2021), pp. 416–433.

established by the parties. He will not be exposed to financial sanctions except in exceptional and sporadic cases.[56]

A ruling that demonstrates the (sometimes elusive) distinction between the amicus and the intervenor is found in the Auckland Area Health Board judgment in which the High Court of New Zealand discussed the question of whether cutting off the ventilation support system of a patient with Guillain-Barre disease should be declared his murder. The Attorney General requested to join the proceedings as Amicus Curiae, but the court refused him. The court stated that the Attorney General would be recognized as an intervenor in the proceedings, not an amicus. The court added that when the applicant to join, a case wishes to present legal arguments when he has a direct interest in the proceedings, he will be defined as an intervenor and not as an amicus.[57] In the *Peel* case, which dealt with a law to reduce public activity on Sundays, the Court of Appeals in Ontario (Canada) determined that since the targeted law did not directly affect the applicant, it did not meet the "direct interest" requirement. Therefore, the applicant could serve as an Amicus Curiae, not an intervenor.[58]

In specific issues, Canadian courts are assisted by amici curiae, usually approached by the courts, and by intervenors who come to the courts on their own initiative. One of the prominent judgments on the subject is Reference re Secession of Quebec, in which the Canadian Supreme Court ruled that the Province of Quebec may not withdraw from the Canadian Federation unilaterally.[59] In this case, the court used legal, historical, economic, and social information regarding the consequences of withdrawal from Canada presented by intervenors and amici. Another example is the procedure of Reference Re Certain Titles to Land in Ontario, which deals with constitutional Real Estate transactions in Ontario.[60] Several third parties appeared before the court, some as amici and others as intervenors.[61]

Another example of the distinction, which is not always easy to identify, between the Amicus Curiae and the intervenor can be found in a ruling that dealt with a

[56] In some countries where there are representation mechanisms of amici curiae "and interveners" there is a statutory or jurisprudential distinction between the two practices. For example, in the province of Ontario (Rules of Civil Procedure, R.R.O. 1990, Reg. 194), rule 13 is divided into two categories - a request to join an "intervenor" as an additional litigant and a request to intervene as Amicus Curiae ("Leave to Intervene as Friend of the Court"). In relation to amicus, it is established in the Civil Procedure Rules as follows: "Any person, after receiving the permission of the court, or if the court has invited him, and without being a formal party to the proceedings, may be an Amicus Curiae to assist the court by way of presenting an argument." The Nova Scotia Civil Procedure Rules (Nova Scotia Civil Procedure Rules, N.S. Gaz., Nov. 19, 2008, r 35.10, 90.19) also make a distinction between joining as an "intervenor" versus joining as an amicus when an intervener is allowed to join the proceedings If his personal and direct interest is at stake.

[57] *Auckland Area Health Bd. v. Attorney-General* [1993] 1 NZLR 235 (HC) at 240.

[58] Peel v. Great Atl. & Pac. Co. of Can. Ltd. (1990), 74 O.R. 2d 164 (C.A.).

[59] Reference re Secession of Quebec [1998] 2 S.C.R. 217.

[60] Reference Re Certain Titles to Land in Ontario, [1973] 2 O.R. 613 (C.A.).

[61] For more see Brooke (2007); Chan (2009); Murray (1994), p. 244; Clark (2005).

dispute between the United States government and the state of Michigan regarding prisoners' incarceration conditions. The Court of Appeals for the Sixth Circuit rejected the prisoners' request to join the proceedings as intervenors but allowed them to submit a written position as Amicus Curiae.[62] Similarly, the court in New York ruled that in a municipal dispute that dealt with natural gas mining, a group of residents would be recognized as amici and not as intervenors, "Although members of the citizens' group submitted affidavits identifying effects that hydrofracking may have on their daily lives, these claimed impacts were largely speculative and failed to demonstrate a substantial interest in the outcome of the action different from other residents of the Town."[63]

2.3 Amicus Curiae and Expert Witness

Similar to the distinctions between the Amicus Curiae and other third parties, it is vital to make this distinction also regarding the "expert witness." The expert witness is also a third party who provides information to the court, but his role and essence differ from that of the amicus. An expert witness is a witness brought to court to present his expertise on a specific subject discussed in the legal process. The expert court witnesses commonly are doctors in various fields (orthopedics, gynecology, surgeons, etc.) and engineers in multiple areas (building, noise, machinery, electricity, etc.). The difference is that, unlike an ordinary witness whose testimony deals with the facts as known to him, the expert witness presents to the court the meaning of the facts presented to the court. There are different arrangements regarding the bringing of expert witnesses: sometimes, each litigant can bring their own expert witness, and in other cases, the expert witness is invited by the court.[64]

Usually, expert witnesses are used in proceedings that involve specific professional knowledge for which the court does not have the tools or the expertise to decide on the matter without this external expertise (such as a doctor, engineer, real estate appraiser, architect, accountant, economist, or handwriting expert).[65] In most cases, the expert witness's testimony is submitted to the court in writing, and the opposing party has the right to submit a counter-opinion. Similar to ordinary testimony, the parties are usually allowed to question an expert about his opinion. The court often appoints a "neutral" expert, with or without the parties' consent. Such an expert is referred to as a "court-appointed expert." An expert whose opinion

---

[62] United States v. Michigan, 940 F.2d 143, 164 (sixth Cir. 1991). In the case itself, the court even allowed increased powers to these amici.

[63] Norse Energy Corp. USA v. Town of Dryden, 964 N.Y.S.2d 714, 718 (N.Y. App. Div. 2013).

[64] Champagne et al. (1992); Saks (2003), pp. 235–244.

[65] For more see Saks (1990). The author notes that the law's policies for the use of expertise shift from stage to stage as litigation progresses, or differ between categories of legal cases, or with a party's use of an expert, and that the role of the expert should be reshaped accordingly.

is required to decide between conflicting opinions is referred to as a "decisive expert," and if he is appointed with the parties' consent, his opinion replaces their opposing opinions.

Given this distinction, it is easy to distinguish between the Amicus Curiae practice and the expert witness. For several reasons, the information presented by amici is fundamentally different from the information presented to the courts by expert witnesses. First, the expert witness's purpose is quite different from the amicus' role. While the role of the expert witness is to discuss the meaning of the specific facts presented to the court from a professional perspective (such as a doctor or ballistics expert), the role of the Amicus Curiae (such as a human rights organization or women's organizations) is to represent from the public perspective an interest or an opinion that deserves to be heard before the court, especially when it is a public issue that affects large groups other than the formal litigants.[66]

Second, in most areas where the courts are interested in obtaining social information and different perspectives, not all "expert witnesses" can be used, mainly from the procedural aspect of not complying with the customary legal procedures regarding bringing expert testimony.[67] Also, not all amici who wish to present their position meet the criteria for recognizing the knowledge they bring with them as reaching the level of expertise acceptable in the courts.[68] Unlike expert testimony, the expertise of the Amicus Curiae is not tested in the procedure, including by way of an investigation in court, and it is certainly not a condition for submitting a brief as exists in expert testimony.[69] Amici can present their position without relying on academic information. Even if they present academic knowledge, it is not obligated to be tested and undergo a scientific evaluation process. Nor is it required that the scientific community recognize the theory and expertise presented by the amici. By contrast, this requirement does exist for the testimonies of experts.[70]

---

[66] Along with these, there are exceptional cases in which United States appeals courts ask experts in certain fields to submit their position as amici and not as expert testimony. The rules of the Court of Appeals for the Federal Circuit in the United States allow inviting "expert amici" from a closed list. FED. CIR. R 29(b): The clerk will maintain a list of bar associations and other organizations to be invited to file Amicus Curiae briefs when the court directs. Bar associations and other organizations will be placed on the list if they request. The request must be renewed annually not later than October 1. See also FED. R. APP. P. 21(b)(4). See for example the memo of retired judge Lewis A Kaplan as Amicus Curiae in Stein v. KPMG, LLP, 486 F.3d 753 (2d Cir. 2007).

[67] Mcdorman (2010).

[68] See in this context also Larsen (2014), p. 1800 ("many of these amicus briefs are also 'mismatched' from author to subject matter— meaning that a group who is not an expert on the factual subject submits factual authorities to the Court anyway").

[69] For a critical article challenging the presentation of the information by amici, see Larsen (2014).

[70] The guiding ruling given in this case is Daubert v. Merrell Dow Pharmaceuticals, Inc., 509 U.S. 579 (1993). The United States Supreme Court established a series of criteria for recognizing scientific knowledge as such reaching the level of expertise. It was determined that scientific knowledge, as opposed to a scientific degree, can form the basis of expert testimony before the court only when certain conditions are met. See Bernstein (2008), p. 451. The Rules of

2.4 Additional Representation Mechanisms of Third Parties

Alongside the representation mechanism of the Amicus Curiae, there are several mechanisms of representation for third parties who wish to present their position to the courts. The common denominator of these representation mechanisms is that third parties can express their interests in the courts through different practices. Of course, there is significant variation between these third-party representation mechanisms. For example, class action differs from the other mechanisms of third parties since class action is a representation mechanism for the parties not before the court. As will be described in the third chapter, the Amicus Curiae practice integrates with other mechanisms of representation of third parties in the judicial process (such as the "class action" or the "intervenor") and, to some extent, changes the nature of litigation in the courts.

2.4.1 The Class Action

Another representation mechanism of third parties in administrative, civil, and consumer issues is the institution of class action.[71] In general, a class action is a civil lawsuit in which a single person sues on behalf of a group. The class action is based on cases where there are many victims or plaintiffs, but each of them suffered minor damages, so it is not worthwhile for each individual to file a lawsuit due to the costs and hassle involved. The class action allows the class plaintiff, who is part of the group of victims, to sue on behalf of the entire group and receive special increased compensation for having taken on the effort of representing the groups and himself.[72] In addition, this saves litigation expenses and administrative costs because many claims are grouped into one procedure.[73]

Class action is an unusual procedure in legal proceedings. It allows the plaintiff and his attorney to file a lawsuit on behalf of a group of plaintiffs without express

---

Evidence in the Federal Courts (FED. R. EVID. 702) adopted the rule and stated that any expert testimony should include the following three elements:

(b) the testimony is based on sufficient facts or data;

(c) the testimony is the product of reliable principles and methods; and

(d) the expert has reliably applied the principles and methods to the facts of the case.

See also Solomon and Hackett (1996), p. 131.

[71] The roots of the class action are found in an English procedure from the seventeenth century called "bill of peace." This procedure allowed courts of justice to allow a claim by or against a group of interested parties if two conditions were met. First, the number of interested parties was too large to allow all of them to be joined in one lawsuit. Second, each of the representatives had a common interest in the subject of the lawsuit. Marcus (2012), pp. 1953–1980, 587–595; Fiss (1996), p. 21.

[72] Hensler (2009).

[73] Klement (2002).

authorization for this representation. Moreover, the class action results are binding on the represented plaintiffs as a court action, even though they did not participate in the proceedings, and their representation is made by the court's decision approving the class action.[74]

A class action has distinct advantages in achieving its goals, but alongside them, disadvantages arise from how it is managed.[75] Therefore, there is significant variation in the legal methods they have adopted, and in ways of regulating the procedure.[76]

Class action and Amicus Curiae are both legal practices through which third parties can influence their world in ongoing legal proceedings. Furthermore, in some instances, it is possible to find different amici who appear in class action proceedings (for example, consumer organizations that seek to oppose a consumer compromise settlement). The differences are mainly found in the type of procedure involved, as class actions usually deal with civil-commercial issues (but not only). In addition, the tests for joining as a representative plaintiff often differ from those for joining as Amicus Curiae. Finally, the procedures in class action proceedings (the group, attorney's fees, etc.) are often regulated as a derivative of the proceedings.

2.4.2 Particular Arrangements in Legislation That Give Status to Third Parties

Representation mechanisms of third parties are also found in particular legislative arrangements that give expression to various public organizations in procedures of public interest. There are two main types of these representation mechanisms. First, the legislation allows third parties to express their position as formal parties in the procedure. The second type is legislation that gives public organizations the authority to represent their position as third parties without taking a formal part in the procedure.

For example, in the United States, there are Federal Rules of Civil Procedure, with Rule 24 governing intervention, which allows third parties to join ongoing litigation if they have a claim or defense that shares a common question of law or fact with the main case.[77] In addition, Rule 29 provides Guidelines for filing briefs as Amicus Curiae in federal appellate courts.[78]

In Canada, for example, the Canadian Constitution Act, 1982: Article 24(1) of the Charter of Rights and Freedoms establishes the status of individuals and

[74] Ibid.

[75] Ibid.

[76] Ibid.

[77] Fed. R. Civ. P. 24.

[78] Fed. R. Civ. P. 29.

organizations to seek remedies for violations of their constitutional rights.[79] Likewise, the rules of civil procedure in any province or territory in Canada may provide provisions for intervention and compliance in civil litigation.

The Civil Procedure Rules Part 19 of the Civil Procedure Rules governs the role of interested parties in legal proceedings in England and Wales.[80]

In Israel, for example, section 6 of the Law for the Prevention of Environmental Hazards (Civil Claims), 1992–5572 gives standing to specific associations to file a claim under the law. It enables the representative workers' organization, the commission, or "an organization engaged in promoting the rights of people with disabilities" to approach the courts regarding workers.[81]

A second set of representation mechanisms allow third parties to express their position without being formal parties. In Israel, section 13 of the Equal Opportunities at Work Law, 1988 (under the title "Right to intervene in lawsuits") authorizes women's organizations to "speak out in the way they see fit."[82] These representation mechanisms allow non-governmental public bodies to express their position without taking a formal part in the proceedings and without being exposed to the risks that apply to formal parties.

The practice of the Amicus Curiae differs from these arrangements because the amicus significantly expands the possibilities of different bodies to express their position—both in terms of the types of proceedings and the types of courts. Amicus is not limited to a closed list of legislative texts or defined issues. On the other hand, the disadvantage of the amicus compared to these particular arrangements is that they usually grant to non-governmental organizations or other groups broader powers than those given to amici (such as the right to oral argument, cross-examination; on the other hand, they entail legal obligations and potential exposure to expenses Court).

2.4.3 The Presence of Representatives of the Government's Legal Advisor

Another third-party representation mechanism separate from the formal hearing is the presence of representatives of the legal advisor to the government (Attorney General/Solicitor General). In general, most countries of the world allow a representative of the Attorney General to appear in an ongoing legal hearing, even if he is not a formal party, if a public interest is affected or involved, or may be affected or

[79] CAN. CONST. Art. 24(1).

[80] Civil Procedure Rules, Part 19.

[81] Ibid, Section 6 of the Law for the Prevention of Environmental Hazards (Civil Claims), 1992–5572.

[82] Ibid, Section 13 of the law states: "In lawsuits due to the violation of this law, the labor court may allow the organization dealing with women's rights to make its case heard in any way it deems fit."

involved, in a particular procedure.[83] Many times, the courts are the ones who ask the representatives of the Attorney General to appear in a legal proceeding to express the state's position.

For example, in the United States and Canada, the Attorney General can intervene in proceedings according to needs and interests.

In the United States, various sections of the United States Code, such as Title 28 (Judiciary and Legal Procedure)[84] and Title 5 (Government Organization and Employees),[85] provide legal authority and guidance for the role and responsibilities of the Department of Justice and the Attorney General. Also, federal rules of civil procedure, such as Rule 24, allow government bodies' intervention,[86] including the Ministry of Justice, in civil litigation when their interests are involved. The United States operates according to a common law system that has a tradition of supporting the participation of government representatives in ongoing legal proceedings. This is due to the calculation of legal precedent and judicial decisions in the design of the law.

Canada's Attorney General or Ministry of Justice representatives can participate in legal proceedings to represent the government's interests.[87] The common law tradition in Canada recognizes the role of the Attorney General or the Ministry of Justice in representing the government's interests in legal proceedings.

As will be detailed in the second part of this book, in many countries (such as the United States, Canada, and Australia), the status of the Attorney General in Amicus Curiae is regulated by legislation and representatives of the Attorney General, as well as representatives of other government bodies, are authorized to submit an amicus brief on behalf of the state even without the approval of the court.[88] In the context of the use of Amicus Curiae practice, an inherent deliberative advantage is granted to the representatives of the Attorney General (and representatives of official state bodies) over non-state bodies.

An excellent example of the government's legal advisor's standing as an amicus can be seen in *Rondel v. Worsley*, in which the Solicitor General of England was invited to present the country's position before the Court of Appeal as Amicus

---

[83] In general, the powers of the general prosecutors of the countries of the continent are also very broad. See for example Zweigert and Kötz (1998).

[84] U.S. CODE: Title 28.

[85] U.S. CODE: Title 5.

[86] Fed. R. Civ. P. 24.

[87] Canadian Charter of Rights and Freedoms, s. 12.

[88] Furthermore, studies have shown that the most cited memo in the United States Supreme Court is the State Attorney's memo. Sometimes, his memo is referred to as the "king of the citation-frequency hill." Between 2010–2015, in eighty percent of the cases in which the United States government appeared as Amicus Curiae in the Supreme Court proceedings, the Attorney General's brief was cited in the judgment. Franze and Anderson (2015).

Curiae.[89] The Solicitor General was invited to assist the court in a more principled way by presenting the public interest.[90] As will be detailed in the second part, in countries that grant great power to the Attorney General to join ongoing legal proceedings, relatively limited use is made of amicus on the part of the state representatives since the law mentioned above allows full representation, with all powers.

2.4.4 *The Public Petition*

Another prominent representation mechanism of third parties seeking to influence issues discussed in court is the institution of the "public petition." As a general rule, a public petitioner is a person or organization that applies to the court for a general public purpose. Sometimes, the public petitioner is faced in legal systems with the limitation of not having legal standing (or by its Latin name Locus Standi), which limits the ability of the public petitioner to raise issues before the court. Legal standing is a threshold condition for filing a legal claim. According to the situation, the claimant must be harmed by the injustice against which he is filing the claim.[91] This practice is mainly used in common law in matters of principle in the context of proceedings against the government because, in many cases, violations of the government's law do not have specific victims but consequences for the broad public.[92]

---

[89][1967] 1 QB 443 (CA). Similarly, in the judgment Morelle Ld. v. Wakeling [1955] 2 QB 379 (CA) The Solicitor General of England was invited by the court to present the state's position in a dispute between two private litigants where the judgment concerned the interests of the state. In Hong Kong courts appoint amici in ex parte civil applications, such as corporate liquidations. In these cases, there is no obligation for the state representative to be present at the hearing and when he appears, he serves as Amicus Curiae. For example, in Re S. China Strategic Ltd., [China Strategic Ltd 1997] discussed a question of contractual sanction for a debt forgiveness arrangement. In this regard, the court appointed the representative of the Ministry of Justice as Amicus Curiae, and he assisted the court with important factual information. For more examples from Hong Kong see Re Carrian Holdings Ltd. (In Liq.), [1990] 1 H.K.C. 320 (C.F.I.);; Re Grandeur Constr. Co., ex parte Law Hoi Chuen, [1987] 3 H.K.C. 480 (C.F.I.).

[90]Thompson and Wachtell (2009), pp. 237, 242. (demonstrating how the United States Supreme Court uses the United States Attorney General as Amicus Curiae).

[91]The requirement for legal standing is intended, in the view of its supporters, to prevent the court from being flooded with lawsuits that are intended to seek general justice and not to correct an individual injustice. In addition, it was argued by its supporters, that this approach was designed to achieve justice and effectiveness in the petitions.

[92]The origin of the term is in the tort law of the British common law tradition, where the plaintiff is required to prove that he was directly damaged by the action of the defendant for which he went to court. Over time, as a result of the growth of the modern state and its increasing influence on many aspects of the citizen's life, the use of the term was extended to the fields of public law as well Fletcher (1988), pp. 229–291.

The institution of public petitions is more common in common law countries than in the continental law countries. As a general rule, in countries where the continental legal tradition practices do not recognize the institution of the public petitioner if public petitions receive any recognition, it is limited to issues such as the quality of the environment or infringement of competition laws.[93]

In recent years, we have witnessed drastic changes in the laws of standing. These changes allow third parties (such as human rights organizations) to petition directly against the authority's decision.

For example, in a series of critical rulings, the Canadian court ruled that when it comes to general legislation aimed at the general public, a public petition must be allowed out of concern that without it, the examination of minor matters will be prevented.[94] Starting in 2012, in the well-known *SWUAV* case, the Canadian court significantly softened the tests of the legal standing and opened its doors to the public petitioner.[95]

Similarly, in England, the birthplace of the doctrine of legal standing, the concept was initially discussed only in case law, which expressed contradictory trends. For a long time, the discussion of the right to legal standing and its conditions was tied to the relief the petitioner requested in each case.[96] Over the years, the English court adopted a relatively liberal interpretation of "interest" that justified granting legal standing. It even allowed third-sector organizations to represent general interests before it.[97] The Human Rights Act should be added to the model of standing, enacted in 1998 to incorporate the European Convention on Human Rights into English law. This adoption has since allowed any British citizen to petition in a British court against any violation of the right enshrined in the treaty by the government.[98]

Even so, in Israel, until the 1980s, the traditional approach of the court was that a condition for standing in the Supreme Court was the existence of a personal, real, and direct interest of the petitioner in the subject matter. The concept that prevailed was that the person who submits his petition to the court should show, before the clarification of the allegations, that he has a direct interest in the subject matter of the

[93] Eliantionio et al. (2012). https://doi.org/10.2861/10624. See also Fletcher WA.

[94] Thorson v. Attorney General of Canada, 1974 CanLII 6 (SCC), [1975] 1 SCR 138. Nova Scotia Board of Censors v. McNeil, [1976] 2 S.C.R. 265.

[95] Canada (Attorney General) v. Downtown Eastside Sex Workers United Against Violence Society, 2012 SCC 45 (CanLII), [2012] 2 SCR 524.

[96] Loveland (2009), pp. 543–544.

[97] Eliantionio et al. (2012), pp. 60–63.

[98] Eliantionio et al. (2012), pp. 65–67. They show that since the Human Rights Act legislation adopted the Convention, in practice, into common law, there is a question regarding the relationship between the limited right to stand by virtue of Article 34 of the Convention and the broader right to stand defined in the Courts Senior Act. It is not clear whether the provisions of the Convention on the subject of a Convention constitute a negative arrangement that prevents those entitled to compliance according to the English test from submitting petitions for infringement of their rights enumerated in the Convention.

petition.[99] This approach was abandoned, and it was determined in its place that to gain legal standing status, the petitioner does not need to indicate an interest as stated. However, his status will be recognized even when his petition raises a problem of a distinct constitutional nature. This problem has a direct bearing on the existence of the rule of law, as it indicates an actual violation of a person's fundamental freedoms or when the object of the petition is an act of corruption by the government.[100]

The distinction between the public petitioner and the Amicus Curiae is essential. In principle, when the public petitioner's request is approved, he is a formal party to all intents and purposes. To a large extent, he "controls" the procedure regarding timing, the nature of the requested remedies, the pleadings, and more. In contrast, the amici are always limited to submitting a written position on a particular issue, often of principle, raised by the formal litigants.

2.5 Summary

In recent years, the use of the legal practice known in Latin as "Amicus Curiae" (in short—amicus), which means "friend of the court" (amicus—friend; curiae—of the court), has flourished. This is a practice by which a third party who is not formally involved in a legal proceeding but has an interest in it presents his position to the court by submitting a written brief. Amicus briefs are typically used to add arguments that the formal litigants did not present to the court or to provide the court with additional information (e.g., social, economic, historical, or environmental) from a broader perspective. For example, in a case from 2012, which dealt with equal rights in marriage for LGBT couples, 156 briefs were submitted to the Supreme Court of the United States on behalf of hundreds of different amici.

Today, Amicus Curiae is used in several legal systems that differ from each other in the way the legal process is conducted and in the rules of discussion that are used: the common law method (in countries such as the United States, Canada, England, and Australia), the continental method (used for example in France, Germany, and Spain) and international law (for example in the European Court for human rights). In addition, amicus has become popular among rights organizations, ordinary citizens, professional guilds, and even politicians in recent years.

In recent decades, following legal, social, and economic developments, the courts have developed a series of practices designed to give particular representation to various third parties (see Table 2.1). There are significant differences between these

[99] See for example High Court of Justice 90/49 Nochimovski v. Minister of Justice, 4 (1949); High Court of Justice 40/70 Becker v. Minister of Defense, (1970).

[100] In a long series of rulings, the High Court of Justice recognized the status of the "public petitioner." High Court of Justice 428/86 Barzilai v. the Government of Israel, (1986). High Court of Justice 869/92 Zoili v. Chairman of the Central Election Committee for the Thirteenth Knesset, 692 (1992); HC 744/97 Gozlan v. Judge Aminoff, (1997). In general, see: Kay (2006).

Table 2.1 Types of Amici Curiae and Court Influencers—roles, characteristics and rights

Intervenor	Modern /Political / Lobbying Amicus	Litigating Amicus	Supporting Amicus	Bystander Amicus	Classic Amicus Curiae	Type
• Direct, tangible interest in the case • Applies to join the proceedings	• Clear agenda/interest aligned with one party's position • Often, non-profit or advocacy groups	• Hybrid between amicus and formal party • Clear interest aligned with one party	• Has an interest aligning with one formal party • Subdivided into categories: 1) Representing unrepresented litigant 2) Direct interest in the outcome 3) presenting public interest	• Offers assistance/perspective on their own initiative, not invited • No formal support for any party	• A neutral third party, usually an expert • Invited by the court • No personal interest	Characteristics
• Directly advocate for their own interests affected by the case outcome	• Influence the court's decision by emphasizing arguments, presenting public lobby behind a party, conveying broader policy messages	• Directly advocate for the supported party's interests	• Support the position of a formal party • Ensure interests are represented	• Present a viewpoint or information not raised by formal parties	• Assist the court by providing advice, expertise, or information not presented by formal parties • Help the court avoid errors and reach a complete decision	Purpose
• Permitted to fully participate (file briefs, oral arguments, evidence etc.) • Subject to cost obligations	• Often permitted to file written briefs, sometimes oral arguments • No financial obligations	• Sometimes permitted full rights of the formal party at the court's discretion (submissions, evidence, cross-examination, etc.) • Potential cost obligations	• Usually limited to written briefs, sometimes oral arguments • No financial obligations	• Limited to submit a written brief • No financial obligations	• Limited to submit written briefs. • No financial obligations	Rights/ obligations

representation mechanisms. However, the general common denominator of these representation mechanisms, and the “friend” in them, is the possibility of third parties to express their interests in the courts. As described later, the Amicus Curiae integrates with third-party representation mechanisms and vastly changes the nature of litigation in the courts.

References

Aiyar R (1997) The Law Lexicon 102 (2d ed) (referring to 1 Edward Coke, Institutes of the Lawes of England 178 (London: J. Flesher, 1622))

Alarie BRD, Green AJ (2010) Interventions at the supreme court of Canada: accuracy, affiliation and acceptance. Osgoode Hall Law Journal 48(3/4):381–410

Banner S (2003) The myth of the neutral amicus: American courts and their friends, 1790–1890. Const Comment 20:111

Bernstein DE (2008) Expert witnesses, adversarial bias, and the (partial) failure of the Daubert revolution. IA Law Rev 93:451

Beyer GW, Redden KR (2001) Modern dictionary for the legal profession, 3rd edn. W.S. Hein, Buffalo, N.Y, p 41

Box-Steffensmeier JM, Christenson DP, Hitt MP (2013) Quality over Quantity: Amici influence and judicial decision making. Am Polit Sci Rev 107(3):1–15

Brodie I (2000) Lobbying the supreme court. In: Westmacott M, Mellon H (eds) Political dispute and judicial review, p 195

Brooke H (2007) Interventions in the court of appeal. Pub Law 401

Caldeira GA, Wright JR (1990) Amici curiae before the supreme court: who participates, when, and how much? J Polit 52(3):782–806

Callaghan GD (2020) Intervenors at the supreme court of Canada. Dal Law J 43(1):33

Campbell E (1998) Intervention in constitutional cases. Pub Law Rev 9:225, 256

Champagne A, Shuman D, Whitaker E (1992) Expert witnesses in the courts: an empirical examination. Judicature 76(1992):5

Chan JMM (2009) What the court of final appeal has not clarified in its clarification: jurisdiction and amicus intervention. In: Chan JMM, Fu HL, Ghai Y (eds) Hong Kong’s constitutional debate, p 171

Clark E (2005) The needs of the many and the needs of the few: a new system of public interest intervention for New Zealand. Victoria Univ Wellington Law Rev 36:71

China Strategic Ltd. [1997] H.K.L.R.D. 131 (C.F.I)

Collins PM Jr (2007) Lobbyists before the United States Supreme Court: Investigating the influence of Amicus Curie briefs. Polit Res Q 60(1):55–70

Collins PM Jr (2008) Friends of the Supreme Court: Interest groups and judicial decision making

Collins PM Jr (2004) Friends of the court: examining the influence of amicus curiae participation in United States supreme court litigation. Law Soc Rev 38(4):807–832

Collins PM Jr (2018) The use of amicus briefs. Annu Rev Law Soc Sci 14:219–237

Collins PM Jr, McCarthy LA (2017) Friends and interveners: interest group litigation in a comparative context. J Law Courts 5(1):55–80

Collins PM Jr, Corley PC, Hamner J (2015) Influence of amicus curiae briefs on U.S. Supreme Court opinion content. Law Soc Rev 49:917

Eliantionio M, Backes C, Rhee van CH, Spronken TNBM, Berlee A (2012) Standing up for your right(s) in Europe - a comparative study on legal standing (locus Standi) before the EU and member states’ courts. Policy Department for Citizen’s Rights and Constitutional Affairs, European Parliament. https://doi.org/10.2861/10624

Fiss OM (1996) The political theory of the class action. Wash Lee Law Rev 53:21

Fletcher WA (1988) The structure of standing. Yale Law J 98(2):229–291
Franze AJ, Anderson RR (2015) Record breaking term for amicus curiae in Supreme Court reflects new norm. Nat Law J. http://www.nationallawjournal.com/supremecourtbrief/id=1202735095655
Franze AJ, Anderson RR (2020) Amicus Curiae at the Supreme Court: Last Term and the Decade in Review, NAT'L l.j., November 18.2020, https://www.arnoldporter.com/-/media/files/perspectives/publications/2020/11/amicuscuriae-at-the-supreme-court.pdf
Larsen AO, Devins N (2016) The amicus machine. Va Law Rev 102:1901
Gleason SA, Ivy DK (2021) As she was saying: The role of gender and narratives in oral argument amicus success. Just Syst J 42(3–4):416–433
Goldman P (2011) Note, should the supreme court stop inviting amici curiae to defend abandoned lower court decisions? Stan Law Rev 63:907, 909–907, 911
Hansford TG (2004) Lobbying strategies, venue selection, and organized interest involvement at the United States supreme court. Am Politics Res 32(2):170–197
Harris MJ (2000) Note, amicus curiae: friend or foe? The limits of friendship in American jurisprudence. Suffolk J Trial App Advoc 5(2000):1
Hensler DR (2009) The globalization of class actions: an overview. Annals Am Acad Pol Soc Sci 622:7
Kay RS (2006) Standing to raise constitutional issues: a comparative analysis. Bruylant, Bruxelles
Krislov S (1963) The amicus curiae brief: from friendship to advocacy. Yale Law J 72:694–721
Klement A (2002) Who should guard the guardians—a new approach for monitoring class action lawyers. Rev Litig 21:25
Larsen AO (2014) The trouble with amicus facts. Va Law Rev 100:1757–1818
Lester A (1988) Amici curiae: third-party interventions before the European court of human rights. In: Matscher F, Petzold H (eds) Protecting human rights: the European dimension, p 341
Loveland I (2009) Constitutional law, administrative law, and human rights: a critical Introduction, 5th edn, pp 543–544
Lowman MK (1992) Comment, the litigating amicus curiae: when does the party begin after the friends leave? Am Univ Law Rev 41:1243, 1245
Marcus D (2012) The history of the modern class action, part I: Sturm und Drang, 1953-1980. Wash Univ Law Rev 90:587–595
Mcdorman RE (2010) Liberty and scientific evidence in the courtroom: Daubert v. Merrell Dow Pharmaceuticals, Inc. and the New Role of Sciencftific Evidence in the Criminal Courts
Mclauchlan JS (2005) Congressional participation as amicus curiae before the U.S. Supreme Court. In: Wrbka S, van Uytsel S, Siems M (eds) American legal institutions collective actions: enhancing access to justice and reconciling multilayer interests?. 2012
Mellinkoff D (1992) Dictionary of American Legal Usage 27
Metcalfe E (2009) To Assist the Court: Third Party Interventions in the UK 1
Mohan SC (2010) The amicus curiae: friends no more? Sing J Legal Stud 2:352–374
Murray C (1994) Litigating in the public interest: intervention and the amicus curiae. S Afr J Human Rights 10:240, 242
O'Connor K, Epstein L (1981) Amicus curiae participation in U.S. Supreme Court litigation: an appraisal of Hakman's "Folklore,". Law Soc Rev 16:311
Saks MJ (1990) Expert witnesses, nonexpert witnesses, and nonwitness experts. Law Hum Behav 14(4):291
Saks MJ (2003) Expert witnesses in Europe and the United States. In: Adversarial versus inquisitorial justice: psychological perspectives on criminal justice systems, pp 235–244
Solomon SM, Hackett EJ (1996) Setting boundaries between science and law: lessons from Daubert v. Merrell Dow pharmaceuticals, Inc. Sci Tech Human Values 21:131
Shaw K (2015) Friends of the court: evaluating the supreme Court's amicus invitations. Cornell Law Rev 101:1533
Solimine ME (2013) The solicitor general unbound: amicus curiae activism and deference in the supreme court. Ariz St Law J 45:1183

The Massachusetts Digest (1823) Being a Digest of the Decisions of the Supreme Judicial Court of Massachusetts, Volume 2

Thompson DC, Wachtell MF (2009) An empirical analysis of supreme court certiorari petition procedures: the call for response and the call for the views of the solicitor general. Geo Mason Law Rev 16:237, 242

Welch J (1985) No room at the top: interest group interveners and charter litigation in the supreme court of Canada. Toronto Fac Law Rev 43(2):204

West's Encyclopedia of American Law (2d ed. 2008)

Zweigert K, Kötz H (1998) An introduction to comparative law (Tony Weir trans., 3rd ed)

Chapter 3
The Advantages and Disadvantages of the Amicus

3.1 The Advantages of the Amicus

3.1.1 Potential for the Most Complete and Correct Judicial Decision

The first, and perhaps the most important advantage of using Amicus Curiae is that the information presented through amicus briefs may reduce errors in the decision-making processes of the courts, potentially leading to the best and most complete decisions possible. Using amicus briefs allows these decisions to be based on the broadest information available under the circumstances and institutional limitations under which the courts operate. An English court ruled in 1656 concerning an amicus, "It is for the honor of a court of justice to avoid error in their judgments," and it seems that these words have not expired.[1]

The potential of additional information—factual, legal, or social—presented by the amici to reduce errors in the decision-making process of the courts lies in the possibility that interests of third parties having bearing on the proceedings may not be heard in court without the presence of these amici.[2] Furthermore, the practice of the Amicus Curiae makes it possible to introduce into judicial systems extensive knowledge from a broad spectrum of third parties with some interest in the procedure, possessing various fields of opinion, different from those presented by the formal parties.[3] The amici may make principled claims that have future, broad implications and not focus only on the concrete claims of the case. In this way, the

[1] Protector v. Geering (1656), 145 Eng. Rep. 394, 394; Hardres 85, 85, 86.

[2] Spriggs and Wahlbeck (1997), pp. 365–386. [The article challenges the conventional wisdom that amicus briefs provide the Supreme Court with information that is not otherwise supplied by litigants and that the Court finds this information useful. The authors found that amicus briefs often contribute unique arguments, but they also commonly reiterate their party's brief].

[3] See Johnson and Tuerk (2005), p. 24.

S. Farber, *The Amicus Curiae Phenomenon*, Ius Gentium: Comparative Perspectives on Law and Justice 119, https://doi.org/10.1007/978-3-031-67225-5_3

amicus may prevent reliance on exclusive (and sometimes incorrect) sources of knowledge presented to the court by the formal litigants without consideration of additional interests,[4] including the interests of third parties.[5] It can be assumed that the broader and more complete the information presented to the court, the less the chance of error.[6]

Using an amicus does not guarantee that errors will not be made in judicial decisions[7] but may undoubtedly improve the situation.[8] The assumption is that judges are interested in receiving all the essential, legal, or factual information to properly and efficiently decide the case before them. The role of the amici may not necessarily be expressed in the presentation of all the information but rather in directing the court to the most suitable and accurate materials.[9] If judges believe that the addition of third parties as amici (or as intervenors) may increase the chance of a better and more complete decision (of course, relatively) through the presentation of significant and innovative information that was not presented by the formal parties (or that the formal parties do not wish to present such information; or they are unable to do so), then they will tend to approve the request from these third parties to join the procedure.

3.1.2 The Amicus As a Generator of Influence on Court Rulings

The information presented by the amici can influence the ruling results. This may depend on the position or perspective that the amicus wishes to promote. The question of how the Amicus Curiae affects the decision-making processes is complex and ambiguous. Empirical studies claim that mentions or explicit quotations of the information presented by amici in judgments do show that amici influence the decisions.[10]

---

[4]Umbricht (2001), p. 783 [The article analyzes the nature of the institution of Amicus Curiae and outlines different options for tackling the amicus question by the WTO dispute settlement bodies. The author highlights the complexities entailed in this process and draws a distinction between policy arguments and legal arguments].

[5]Levine (2011), pp. 200–224. Regarding amicus involvement in international investment arbitration, Levine wrote on p. 217 that: For instance, in *AES* it is possible that neither Hungary nor the investor would have an interest in emphasizing the fact that the contracts between them may violate the European Commission's restrictions on State aid.

[6]Schachter (2004), p. 111.

[7]See for example Hami Ben Nun (2009), p. 177.

[8]Doron et al. (2015), pp. 145–164.

[9]Viñuales J (2012) Foreign investment and the environment in international law, Cambridge, p. 115; Alarie and Green (2010).

[10]Lynch (2004), pp. 33, 46–56; Abramowicz and Colby (2009). ("There has been no shortage of praise in the legal literature for the ability of amicus briefs to 'inform the court of implications of a decision'...[and] provide relevant factual information not offered by the parties").

For example, in about a third of the judgments given from the middle of the twentieth century to the first decade of the twenty-first century in the American Supreme Court, the information presented in amicus briefs submitted to the Court are mentioned or referred to in some way in the judgement. This phenomenon has been increasing in recent years as well. Between 2015 and 2016, in approximately 54% of the judgments given in the American Supreme Court, there was an explicit reference in the judgment to information presented by amici.[11] Between 2010 and 2016, in about 50 percent of the cases in which a verdict was given, the court mentioned, cited, or referred to the information presented by amici.[12] Data showing the widespread use of information presented by "amici" in court rulings can also be found in international judicial bodies such as the Latin American Court[13] of Human Rights or the European Court of Human Rights.[14]

This data supports the hypothesis that the courts were influenced in some way by the amicus briefs submitted to them, although it is not possible to determine precisely to what extent, in what way, and exactly how this was done. These studies admit that it is possible to disagree on the degree of influence of an amicus brief on the court, but its citation or mention shows that the court considered the brief in some way and took it into account.

However, this criterion should be used very carefully for several reasons. First, research shows that judges sometimes cite briefs from amici on both sides to present an equally objective picture of the situation. Also, judges may quote amici in their judgment to show that the positions of the amici and that of the formal litigants are the same. Furthermore, judges may allow the amici to argue orally and therefore not find it necessary to refer to their words in the judgment; in other cases, judges are not interested in citing specific briefs due to the public image of these organizations and the fear of expressing public support for their actions.[15] In general, we, therefore, should mindful that quotes from amici can have additional explanations other than influencing the verdict. In any case, it is possible to disagree about the degree of influence of an amicus brief on the court, but its citation or mention shows, with due caution, that the court considered the brief in some way and took it into account among its other considerations.[16] The citations of the information presented by the amici show that it has been helpful in the court's decision-making process.

[11] Franze and Anderson (2015).

[12] Collins et al. (2015). Between 2010 and 2016, Judge Ginsberg, in 45 percent of the rulings she wrote, referred to information presented to her by "amici." Judge Kennedy made use of information given to him by amici in 42% of his rulings. (Sotomayor—40%; Roberts—40%; Breyer—39%; Kagan—35%; Alito—27%; Scalia—24%; Thomas—22%) Franze and Anderson (2015).

[13] Juaristi (2014) see footnote 640.

[14] Van Den Eynde (2019). See also Lester (1988).

[15] Franze and Anderson (2016) and Larsen and Devins (2016). See also Mauro (2016), Feldman (2016) and Lynch (2004).

[16] For a representative example, see the reference of the President of the United States Supreme Court, John Roberts, to an "amicus" brief of a former White House adviser regarding the alleged corruption of the governor of Virginia. Coyle (2016) http://www.law.com/supremecourtbrief/almID/1202756102813.

Other studies rely on in-depth interviews with judges to prove the influence of the amici on the work of the courts. For example, from Simard's research that examined amici joining cases in the United States federal courts, it appears that the majority of federal judges (about 77% of the judges in the Circuit Courts and about 82% of the judges in the District Courts) believe that the briefs from an amicus which are served to them help them reach a fuller understanding of the expected general consequences of the court's rulings on the interests of third parties.[17]

Another way to examine the influence of the amicus on the work of the courts is related to the "social information" that the judges draw about the undercurrent of public opinion through the amici. For some judges, briefs from amici are a "social barometer" for the public's position.[18] The role of the amici is not limited to "only" presenting information, but the presence of the amici, in some cases, as incorporated interest groups, creates pressure on the judges to accept the position that the interest group promotes.[19]

This approach of interest groups "broadcasting" to the court their desired result is based on the assumption that judges tend not to stray too far from the public consensus, that they are attentive to the public's positions, and that they give considerable importance to the positions of interest groups, in particular to influential interest groups. In other words, the courts accept the arguments in a brief from an amicus not only because of the formal content of the brief, which should help them in their work, but also because of the interest groups behind the submission. Since judges tend to consider public opinion in certain matters more than in everyday disputes, especially if these matters are "explosive" issues or have a public dimension, they look at the "amicus" memos as a kind of social indicator that helps them understand the expected consequences of their decision.[20]

3.1.3 Low Economic Costs

The costs of using an "amicus" are low in comparison to alternatives such as submitting an independent petition or involving an additional formal party in the proceedings. Amici are not required to pay various fees (such as the fee for opening a procedure). In addition, amici are not charged additional fees since the formal parties

[17] Simard (2008), p. 696.

[18] Collins Jr (2004), pp. 814–815. Many studies emphasize that the most dominant component of these processes originates from "responsiveness to social demand" which has increased in part due to the efforts of interest groups to achieve through the courts what cannot be achieved by the Authority the legislature and the executive. Zannoti (1995), https://doi.org/10.18574/nyu/9780814770078.003.0014.

[19] Kearney and Merrill (2000), pp. 743–855.

[20] Collins Jr (2004), pp. 807–832.

pay the fees, and the "amicus" only joins the proceedings. Other costs associated with the proceedings are also not imposed on them.[21]

For example, the amici are not required to guarantee other parties' expenses in the proceedings. In addition, if the proceedings to which the "amicus" joined ends in a ruling on court costs, the formal party is the one who bears the burden, and the "amicus" is not exposed to these costs.

In addition, writing a brief by amici is relatively simple and cheap compared to an independent petition's alternatives. The brief writing procedure is usually shorter than the other litigation alternatives, which require considerable time. This is because it is not necessary to refer to all of the parties' arguments, to refute them, or to contradict them. An "amicus" may discuss one issue while the formal parties must argue all the issues that arise in the case. In many cases, "amici" briefs are free (or relatively inexpensive)[22] because students in legal clinics at universities and colleges write them.[23] In addition, there is a common practice in which various interest groups come together to write a joint brief as they share the same values and the desire to save financial expenses.

Even in the discussion aspects of the proceedings, as mentioned above, the results of the amicus procedure do not establish a judicial act towards the "amici," neither in predicate nor non predicate offenses. Furthermore, a person who is not a party to the proceedings ("the amicus") cannot claim to remain silent in his own favor, and it is impossible to claim to stay silent against him. Other silences, such as the judicial silence or reasons due to the lack of good faith, do not apply to the "amicus" either.

---

[21] Although in some places there is a principled authority to impose legal costs on third parties (mostly, it is about imposing costs on "intervenors," but costs can also be imposed on "amici"). However, the use of this authority is rare. For cases in which court costs were imposed on amici, see for example: in the case of "In re Amoco Cadiz" (1981), the United States Court of Appeals for the Fifth Circuit imposed sanctions on an Amicus Curiae for filing a brief that was deemed to be "frivolous" and "misleading." The court ordered the amicus to pay the opposing party's legal costs. In the case of "Trexel v. Granville" (2000), the United States Supreme Court imposed sanctions on an Amicus Curiae for filing a brief that contained improper arguments and misrepresentations. The court ordered the amicus to pay a $500 fine. In the case of "West Virginia Highlands Conservancy v. Island Creek Coal Co." (fourth Cir. 1983), the United States Court of Appeals for the Fourth Circuit imposed sanctions on an Amicus Curiae for filing a brief that contained false and misleading statements. The court ordered the amicus to pay the opposing party's legal costs.

[22] See, for example, *The Center's Civil Rights & Criminal Justice Advocacy*, Seattle Univ. Sch. of Law (2016), www.law.seattleu.edu/centers-and-institutes/korematsu-center/litigation/the-civil-rights-amicus-brief-project (last visited Oct. 16, 2019). *Civil Rights Amicus Brief Project*, Seattle Univ. Sch. of Law (2016), www.law.seattleu.edu/centers-and-institutes/korematsu-center/litigation/the-civil-rights-amicus-brief-project. For example, in Fisher v. University of Texas at Austin (2016) (Affirmative action in college admissions), several university legal clinics filed amicus briefs. For instance, the Supreme Court Litigation Clinic at Stanford Law School submitted a brief on behalf of a group of leading social scientists, supporting the University of Texas at Austin's admissions policy. See *supra* notes 22 and 38.

[23] In light of this, it is no wonder that important social struggles are organized today by legal clinics in universities and colleges, and not by private individuals. For example, in Fisher v. University of Texas at Austin (2016).

3.1.4 Cooperation and Strengthening of Ties Between Social Organizations

Joining the proceeding as amici may be a fertile ground for creating collaborations and strengthening working relationships between different social organizations. These collaborations enhance civil society and should not be seen as a mere means but also as a worthy end. There are various means of forming collaborations between social organizations around joining legal proceedings as amici and creating "coalitions" of amici with these, including: writing a joint brief on behalf of several social organizations, sharing brainstorming sessions, work meetings, and regular consultations between the representatives of the organizations about the arguments that should be included. Sometimes, working relationships between organizations are expressed as "amici" in the creation of existing legal materials, scientific or social studies, or in the appointment of experts (for example: experts in environmental sciences or the field of labor law) for the partner organization in the coalition.[24]

Sometimes, collaborations between social organizations in connection with using the Amicus Curiae practice include building a joint action strategy to manage the procedure.[25] The "invitation" for cooperation in connection with the submission of a supporting amicus brief does not only exist between public and non-governmental organizations. It crosses sectors and also occurs between state institutions and social organizations.[26]

In addition, when several organizations join together and voice a united front in court as a coalition of amici, this may create a more significant impression on the court and the public. At the same time, as mentioned, it isn't easy to establish a broad consensus on the content of the position that will be presented on the united front's tactics and methods of operation.[27] Furthermore, not only is the writing of a joint

[24]In Israel, for example, in two cases related to the protection of privacy (intrusion into an employee's e-mail box; and a biometric attendance clock at the workplace), the "Civil Rights Association" and the "Worker's Line" collaborated in writing an "amicus" brief to the court. On the one hand, the association Experts in the field of information privacy and on the other hand—the "Worker's Line" which made available to the association expertise in labor law. See Labor Appeal (national) 90/08 Inbar–v. State of Israel—Commissioner for the Women's Labor Law (8.2.2011).; In the case of United States v. Windsor, the ACLU, the Human Rights Campaign, and the National Center for Lesbian Rights filed a joint amicus brief in support of Edith Windsor, who was challenging the Defense of Marriage Act (DOMA). See United States v. Windsor, 133 S.Ct. 2675 (2013).

[25]For example, in the process of appointing interpreters for the Arabic language in the committees of the National Insurance in East Jerusalem, the "The Center for the Protection of the Individual" which submitted the petition to the organization "BiZchut" for the latter to present to the court its point of view regarding the rights of people with disabilities, ignoring the political orientations that arose during the hearing of the petition. The matter of the Center for the Protection of the Individual from the foundation of Dr. Lotte Salzberger.

[26]See Carter et al. (2016), pp. 264–332 [discusses the role of NGOs in court proceedings and their use of Amicus Curiae briefs]. See also Van Den Eynde (2019), pp. 96–119.

[27]Behuniak-Long (1991), pp. 261–262.

brief by several entities likely to strengthen the power of the brief and may save on the overall expenses of the "amici," but it may also facilitate the court's work, which will read and study fewer memos, thus saving judicial time.

3.1.5 Protection of the Public Interest

Briefs from amici may help protect the "public interest," especially in developing countries or in proceedings where there are significant power differences on various issues: human rights, environmental quality, workers' rights, protection of local heritage, and the fight against corruption. The argument is that there are conflicts in which there is no expression of essential interests, even though they are discussed (either directly or indirectly) in the proceedings. In some cases, the amici are the only ones interested (or able) to present proper interests, other than the commercial (and legitimate) interests of the formal parties. In light of this, the information presented by the amici, which was not presented by the parties, must be brought to the arbitrators' attention.

Moreover, sometimes, the formal parties do not have the tools, the ability, or the unique and professional knowledge possessed by amici. On the other hand, amici, especially if they are international organizations with experience and expertise, can offer a different point of view or assist the arbitrators from a legal, factual, or technical point of view.[28] In doing so, they may focus the court on substantial public claims.

3.1.6 Public Transparency

There are some claims that investment tribunals, especially the WTO dispute settlement institutions, suffer from a lack of transparency in their proceedings and decision-making.[29] One of the benefits of having Amicus Curiae briefs in court is the transparency they produce. By allowing third-party individuals or organizations to provide information to the court, the court gains a broader perspective on the legal issues presented in the case. This, in turn, can help promote transparency in the legal system by ensuring that all relevant arguments and perspectives are considered before a decision is made.[30] As explained above, the Amicus Curiae can help ensure

---

[28] For example, in the case of Biwater Gauff, Award (2008), the author stated in paragraph 359 that the "amici" approach[ed] the issues in this case with interests, expertise and perspectives that have been demonstrated to materially differ from those of the two contending parties, and as such have provided a useful contribution to these proceedings.

[29] McRae (2004), p. 12. see Lacarte (2004), pp. 685–686.

[30] Kearney and Merrill (2000), pp. 743–855.

that the court's decision is not based on incomplete or biased information but instead reflects a well-rounded understanding of the legal issues.[31] For example, in several investment arbitration cases, Amicus Curiae applicants opined that their participation would "allay public disquiet as to the closed nature of arbitration proceedings."[32]

A further example is found in the intervention of amici in international arbitration procedures, which affect the institutional regime of international institutions and result in a more transparent and democratic activity.[33] Sometimes, the media coverage that the amici receive leads to a public discussion of issues that the formal parties try to influence, thus increasing public criticism of procedures that otherwise may sometimes be carried out behind closed doors.[34]

3.2 The Amicus's Shortcomings

3.2.1 Encouraging Politicization of the Legal Process

The "modern amicus" has shortcomings not associated with the traditional "true amicus," with the claim made that the "modern amicus" is not a "true amicus" of the court but actually the opposite.[35] Instead of maintaining neutrality and presenting additional information, it is feared that the "modern amicus" may result in the politicization of the court and turn the court into an arena for the promotion of the political interests of various groups. The "modern amicus" copies, so to speak, political debates from the legislative and executive authority to the judicial authority, thereby causing the judicial system to be perceived as an avowedly political arena.[36] One gets the impression that there is an attempt to influence the courts by recruiting

---

[31] Martin (2014), pp. 527–562; Johnson (2016), pp. 47, 116–129. [His article suggests that amicus briefs can play an important role in ensuring that the Court's decisions are based on the best available information. Corbin (2017), pp. 593–624 [Corbin argues that the Court should take steps to increase transparency in the amicus brief process. He argues that the Court should require amicus briefs to be filed under the same rules as briefs filed by the parties to the case. He also argues that the Court should make amicus briefs more accessible to the public].

[32] Methanex v. USA, decision of the tribunal on petitions from third persons to intervene as 'amici curiae,' 15 January 2001, para. 5. See Vick p. 64.

[33] Kawharu (2007), pp. 2–3.

[34] Graham (2012), pp. 6–10. Naturally, while the arguments in favor of the involvement of third parties are mainly voiced by non-governmental public organizations, the main arguments against the adoption of the amici are mostly voiced by developing countries, investors and capitalists.

[35] Also see in general—Beckwith and Sobernheim (1948), p. 38. [article also argues that the Amicus Curiae should not be used as a tool for advocacy, but rather as a means of providing the court with impartial information].

[36] Franze and Anderson (2015). Some call the judges in the United States "politicians in black robes" GLICK 1983). On the other hand, other researchers pointed to the emphasis on the court's autonomy and its immunity to political pressures. Davis (1994).

amici. In general, in certain cases, it now appears that the party with more amici (especially if they are influential and powerful) has the higher chance of winning the case. Throughout history, there have been several notable incidents of using an amicus to influence the judges overtly and directly in a declared manner. For example, in the 1960s, the newspaper "The Daily Worker" called on United States citizens to submit amicus briefs directly to the judges who heard the *Lawson* case, which dealt with refusing to answer questions from a Senate committee about membership in the Communist Party.[37] In the eyes of the interest groups that formed the basis of this call, the use of amici was seen as a formal expression of a political struggle, and therefore, sending letters to sitting judges by citizens, which is tantamount to crossing red lines in the eyes of the legal community, was seen in their eyes as a proper and reasonable activity.

Criticism of the use of an Amicus Curiae for political needs was reinforced by former Supreme Court Judge Antonin Scalia, who, in the Jaffee ruling, criticized the growing pressure of non-governmental organizations ("pushy NGOs") on the judges, which may create a bias in the results of the trial.[38] This ruling was another expression of the critical position of some of the judges of the Supreme Court, which called for a return to the objective interpretation of the amicus ("the classic amicus" who assists in the work of the court through advice, usually at the request of the court). That is, an amicus brief should only be submitted if the "amicus" has new factual or legal information that helps in the work of arbitration, which the formal parties did not present.

3.2.2 *Use of an Amicus by Powerful Groups*

It is claimed that the use of "amicus briefs" favors highly organized, powerful interest groups that have the resources to use amici to promote their own interests. These powerful forces in society (such as energy companies, banks, and financial companies) or large organizations (such as employers' organizations) have an advantage in general when making use of the law, and the use of the Amicus Curiae practice further extends their ability to promote their interests.[39] From a study based on a 50-year database, commercial corporations and various professional groups, including powerful interest groups, filed over 58% of the amicus briefs filed with the United States Supreme Court. In contrast, human rights organizations, consumer

[37] Lawson v. United States, 176 F.2d 49 (D.C. Cir. 1949).

[38] Jaffee v. Redmond, 518 U.S. 1, 35–36 (1996). Emily Bazelon, "Antonin Scalia Didn't Trust Science," NY TIMES MAG. (12/21/16) (quoting Professor John Donahue) ("Scalia was willing to cite work that was thoroughly refuted by an accepted scholarly institution," while rejecting the most rigorous research on the subject).

[39] Johnson (2016), pp. 116–129. Johnson finds that amicus brief participation is highly concentrated among a small number of organizations. The top ten organizations filed over 50% of all amicus briefs in the Supreme Court between 2000 and 2015.

organizations, environmental organizations, and labor organizations filed less than 42% of the "amicus" briefs submitted.[40]

Furthermore, the amici are often sent by powerful interest groups to strengthen their arguments in sophisticated ways, allowing the perception that they are "neutral amici" and not partners of the formal parties in the proceedings. Sometimes, attorneys of interest groups hire different "amici" (often without the knowledge of the authorized officials in these organizations) to complete their arguments from various points of view to create an impression of strong public support for the interests of those sending them.

As will be expanded on in the second part of the book, this criticism is one of the reasons for the creation of "due disclosure" rules in many judicial systems in connection with the participation of amici in proceedings (as in most states within the United States and in most international institutions such as the European Court of Human Rights).[41] This also takes into account that an independent "amicus brief" written by an individual is not comparable to one written by an organization, supported by funding, with the assistance of, or "commissioned" by, one of the official litigants.[42] There is a concern, therefore, that parties may manipulate and influence the courts' decision-making by inviting many influential "amici" (or, on the contrary, refrain from doing so to make the impression of being the "underdog").

The court may get the mistaken impression that when many bodies support a particular litigant that, public opinion supports him, while these "amici" were actually "invited." Furthermore, their briefs may well have been written or financed by the "commissioning" party. In these cases, the "amici" were only instructed to submit the brief to generate public support for one party's position. For example, in a specific response to this criticism, the advisory committee for writing the rules of procedure of the state of Minnesota stated in connection with Amicus Curiae that: "This rule is intended to encourage the participation of independent amici, and to prevent the courts from being misled about the independence of amici or being exposed to a mirage of amicus support that emanates from the petitioner's word processor."[43]

As mentioned above, various studies, mainly conducted in the United States, have shown that in a significant part of the cases in which briefs are filed, the "amici" who join the proceedings are lobbyists or interest groups that support "powerful" forces

---

[40] Bradley and Gardner (1985), pp. 78, 91; Regarding the disproportionate influence of interest groups on legislative procedures, see Farber and Frickey (1991). In any case, these data shows that "strong" entities have a greater ability (mainly from the resource aspect) to make use of "amicus" to influence the legal process. Kelleher and Yackee (2006), pp. 629–643.

[41] Compare with Thornton (2003) With Friends Like These... the Weight of 90-plus Amicus Briefs in the Michigan Cases Ought to Influence the Court. Legal Times, March 31 at 70.

[42] For more, see Rustad and Koenig (1993), pp. 91, 157–158 [The article argues that the use of junk social science in amicus briefs can lead to selective distortion of the facts and can have a significant impact on the court's decision-making process].

[43] Minn. R. App. P. 129.01 Advisory Committee cmt.

within society (for example, banks and giant corporations).[44] Sometimes these are "amici" sent by the formal parties in sophisticated ways while complying with the legal rules to strengthen their arguments by presenting a public atmosphere sympathetic to the activity of the formal disputants. In other words, there is a concern that instead of promoting proper public values, the "amici" who participate in the proceedings (or those who are "hired" to present a false representation) support the positions of commercial interest groups such as energy, cigarette, finance, alcohol and weapons corporations.[45]

Other scholars have suggested that the participation of corporations in Amicus Curiae briefs can undermine the legitimacy of the legal system and lead to a perception that justice is for sale to the highest bidder. In addition, some scholars have also suggested that corporations' use of Amicus Curiae briefs can contribute to the "capture" of regulatory agencies, where these agencies become more responsive to the interests of the industries, they are meant to regulate rather than the interest of the general public. This can lead to a situation where corporations have undue influence over regulatory policy, which can be detrimental to the environment, public health, and consumer protection.[46]

On the other hand, the opposite criticism was voiced towards the use of "amici," mainly in international courts (but not only) when it was argued against them that in international proceedings, the "amici" tend to be one sided, with that side, almost "automatically" being in favor of the "weak" parties or countries. This claim found the Amicus Curiae process favored the "poor" against powerful countries or groups of investors and capitalists, regardless of the examination of the facts.[47]

In other words, opening the doors to third parties to express their interests as "amici" in ongoing proceedings may serve those powerful economic forces who can make best use of "amici," although this may not always be the case. Furthermore, powerful interest groups will be able relatively quickly to "buy" or organize different "amici," who may influence the courts in accordance with the interests of their senders. The ability of powerful economic actors to file amicus briefs can lead to a perception that the legal system is biased in favor of corporate interests rather than being impartial and fair to all parties involved. This can contribute to disillusionment

---

[44] There is a concern that these companies may have a specific agenda or interest that they are advocating for, which can lead to a perception of bias or lack of objectivity. For example, in the case of Citizens United v. Federal Election Commission, several oil and gas companies filed Amicus Curiae briefs arguing that campaign finance laws violated their free speech rights. Similarly, in the case of American Bankers Association v. National Credit Union Administration, the banking industry filed Amicus Curiae briefs arguing that a credit union regulatory rule was unlawful. Sachs and Revesz (2010), pp. 787–823.

[45] Wohl (1996) and Ward (2007).

[46] Kagan (1991), pp. 1–18; Sachs and Revesz (2010), pp. 787–823.

[47] Mourre (2006), p. 266; Gruner (2003), p. 955; Hobér (2008), p. 155.

and mistrust in the legal system, particularly among those who feel their voices are not being heard.[48]

A prominent voice raising concerns about the modern amicus process is Senator Sheldon Whitehouse. In his 2021 Yale Law Journal Forum essay "A Flood of Judicial Lobbying: Amicus Influence and Funding Transparency," Whitehouse argues that wealthy and influential groups, particularly those aligned with conservative or Republican interests, have exploited amicus briefs as a tool for coordinated judicial lobbying. He contends that donor networks have funded extensive "amicus armadas" in high-profile cases like Americans for Prosperity Foundation v. Bonta, while also influencing judicial nominations. Whitehouse asserts that this onslaught of amicus influence, combined with a lack of transparency around funding sources, undermines judicial independence and public faith in the courts.

While Whitehouse raises valid concerns about the potential for abuse, his claims regarding ideological capture could be viewed as overstating the issue. Liberal and progressive groups also routinely participate as amici and have their own donor bases. Additionally, amicus briefs can provide courts with valuable perspectives, especially from underrepresented or marginalized groups not formally party to a case. The long tradition of amicus participation underscores its important role in the judicial process.

Nonetheless, Whitehouse's central criticism highlights the need for robust disclosure requirements surrounding amicus funding sources. Anonymous or obscured amicus spending raises potential conflicts of interest. By mandating disclosure of significant funders, as proposed through Whitehouse's AMICUS Act, courts and the public could better evaluate the motivations behind each brief while still benefiting from amicus participation's informational value. Reasonable disclosure rules could address legitimate concerns while preserving this important tradition.

3.2.3 Little Control Over the Legal Process

As mentioned previously, the amicus procedure has some distinct advantages which have been discussed, such as low costs and relatively low legal expenses. It also allows the involvement of third parties who are not interested in submitting their own independent petition, including those who may be afraid of the costs associated with the entering into the status of being a full party to the proceedings. This being said, there are also distinct disadvantages, including disadvantages to the "amici" themselves, who do not have full control over the legal proceedings. Those who choose to participate in a particular legal process as an Amicus Curiae consciously decide to be

[48] In addition, "flooding of information" by "amici" may result in the courts rejecting the information that will reach them from the "amici" and leaving only the information that is based and supported by expert opinions. This will give an advantage to strong groups and sectors that have the power to finance scientific opinions over weaker groups. Goldman (2011), pp. 907, 909–911; Larsen (2014).

a passive partner in the proceedings (other than the "disputing amicus," sometimes referred to as "Amicus Plus," but as mentioned, this mechanism is not common). Apart from presenting their position in writing, the amici cannot control the judicial process in any way. The involvement of the amici in the proceedings is usually limited to submitting a written brief and, on rare occasions, to an oral argument. The formal litigators are the ones who manage the procedure under the auspices of the court and are able, at their discretion, to decide to delete, reject, withdraw a petition, or compromise the procedure without consulting the amici who wrote the briefs.

When a person or organization submits an amicus brief, they also have no direct control over the legal strategy or decision-making process of the formal parties involved. This lack of control can limit their ability to shape the arguments or outcomes in a manner that aligns perfectly with their interests.[49]

3.2.4 Low Contribution to the Legal Process and Fear of Harming the Formal Parties

One general argument against joining third parties as amici is that some of them make no real contribution to the work of the courts. The claim is that the briefs submitted by the "amici" may not update essential information for the court (these briefs are sometimes called "Me too briefs"). They often replicate arguments made by the formal litigators in different ways.

Beyond that, the amici may burden the courts with much information that is not only not essential to their work but causes a waste of judicial time, harming the parties' rights to an efficient and speedy procedure.[50] The possibility of submitting an "amicus brief" without clear procedural limitations (such as the test that will be proposed below, according to which only if the information offered by the amicus is new information can the memo be accepted) may impose a considerable burden on the courts in the form of too many briefs. As mentioned, this may result in substantial damage to the effectiveness of the judicial procedure and damage to the deliberative rights of the formal parties to an effective procedure.

Submitting multiple "amicus briefs" can inundate the court with extensive documents, including diverse perspectives and arguments. This influx of information may overload the court's capacity to thoroughly analyze and evaluate each brief,

---

[49] Hansen and Watson (2009), pp. 86–106. [The authors conclude by calling for greater transparency and accountability in the filing of amicus briefs. They recommend that courts require amici to identify their interests and to disclose any financial or other ties to the parties in the case. They also recommend that courts provide more guidance to amici on the types of arguments that are appropriate for amicus briefs].

[50] Ramseyer and Rasmusen (2008), pp. 224–232 [Courts often have limited resources, including staff, time, and budget. The additional work associated with reviewing and considering amicus briefs can strain these limited resources, potentially affecting the court's ability to efficiently handle its overall caseload and delaying the resolution of cases].

potentially compromising the quality and efficiency of the decision-making process.[51]

Furthermore, when it comes to the use of an amicus in arbitration proceedings (or other procedures whose common denominator is the agreement of the parties to the outline of the procedure), then it must be remembered that an arbitration procedure is by its nature a procedure of agreement and free will between two parties, therefore when a particular party does not wish to add amici to the arbitration procedure, such a move cannot be forced on him because such coercion goes against the rationale of the arbitration procedure (see Sect. 3.2.8).[52] Opponents to amicus participation argue that the amicus can interfere with the parties' autonomy because it introduces external voices into a process designed to be consensual and confidential. They argue that allowing amicus submissions can disrupt the balance between the parties and may unduly influence the decision-making process of the arbitral tribunal.[53]

Another criticism in connection with this is directed, among other things, to the methods of operation of certain lawyers or organizations who submit briefs in cases with a broad media profile. Their main purpose in doing this may be to present to the public their experience and expertise on the subject in the hope that this will bring them publicity, money, or new clients. Recently, the presence of lawyers in the media has increased, and they are often interviewed as spokesmen for their clients and celebrities in their own right.[54] In some cases, lawyers or non-governmental organizations use the media to present their legal arguments and receive articles that outline their worldview.[55]

Some even claim that non-governmental organizations submit "amicus briefs" to show their work to the general public to motivate others by creating a kind of "jealousy" between competing organizations. That is, a specific non-governmental organization submits an "amicus brief" and thus motivates a public organization from the same "side" who supports the same position "not to be left behind." This second organization may, therefore, also submit an amicus brief simply to remain in the public view, especially when there is a struggle between organizations for

[51] Nelson (2011), pp. 121–186.

[52] First Mexican 1128 Submission ¶ 5, United Parcel Serv. of Am., Inc. v. Canada (NAFTA Arb. June 11, 2001).

[53] Born and Forrest (2020), pp. 626–665; see also Levine (2011). The article explores the growing phenomenon of third-party participation in international arbitration, including the role of Amicus Curiae. It discusses the benefits, challenges, and potential impact of amicus participation on the parties' autonomy and the decision-making process. See also: Savarese (2007), pp. 99–121. The article examines the participation of Amicus Curiae in investor-state arbitration. It analyzes the potential effects on the autonomy of the parties and the arbitral process, and discusses the various approaches and rules adopted by different arbitral institutions and tribunals: See also Kaufmann (2016).

[54] Sherwin (2003), pp. 147.

[55] Wohl (1996) and Ward (2007). See also Bell and Odysseos (2002), pp. 653–669.

resources, donations, and public sympathy.[56] Another possible criticism claims that organizations submit "amicus briefs" to the courts not necessarily out of genuine interest in the case itself but out of fear that other organizations will precede them (this phenomenon is known in political science theory as the "Arms Race").

3.2.5 Increasing the Costs of the Legal Process

A similar criticism to that made above is also made concerning the modern amici. It is claimed that the briefs submitted by these "amici" do not necessarily update the courts with essential information to decide the procedure, but rather, the "amici" are replicating arguments made by the formal litigants. Sometimes, these briefs only use different wordings or different emphases, but the essence is the same as the points made by the formal parties. As suggested above, in these cases, the "amici" may burden the courts with extensive information that is not only not essential to the court's work also burdens the judicial time, which is considered one of the most critical resources of the judiciary.[57]

Furthermore, according to this criticism, as more "amicus briefs" are submitted and as the participation of interest groups as amici becomes more comprehensive, the costs associated with managing the procedures imposed on the parties multiply. The process itself also become cumbersome and excessively long.[58] According to this claim, amici burden the proceedings, prolonging them unnecessarily and thus generate increased costs on the formal litigants. Those who hold this criticism cite the rulings of Judge Richard Posner of the federal appeals court in Chicago on this matter. In the Ryan ruling, Judge Posner stated that the Amicus Curiae institution failed to assist the courts. In his view, the amici make the courts' work more difficult and waste the most critical judicial resource—precious working time. He claimed that most of the briefs submitted by the amici are submitted by "allies" of the formal litigants. He also claimed that these briefs duplicate the parties' arguments and so do not assist the work of the courts.[59]

True to this approach, in the ruling *Nat'l Org. for Women, Inc. v. Scheidler*, Judge Posner ruled that whether to grant third-party permission to submit a brief as an amicus is a matter of grace and not a right. He reiterated that he would not approve

---

[56] As is known, the influence of an interest group depends, among other things, on the number of its members. This is a matter of "membership density," meaning who joins the interest group as a percentage of all those eligible to join. Total membership gives the group more authority and a strong bargaining position at decision-making nodes.

[57] Posner (1993), pp. 1, 23–30.

[58] Flechtner (2013), pp. 1211–1263. [examining the economic implications of amicus participation in international commercial arbitration within the United States].

[59] Ryan v. Commodity Futures Trading Comm'n, 125 F.3d 1062, 1063 (seventh Cir. 1997) "The tendency of many judges of this court, including myself, has been to grant motions for leave to file Amicus Curiae briefs without careful consideration."

brief submissions that repeat the original parties' positions. He emphasized that the proper legal policy is to grant permission to amici to submit a brief only in a limited number of situations: when a formal party will not be adequately represented or will not be represented at all; when the amicus can indicate a direct interest that may be harmed if he does not present this interest to the court; when the amicus has essential information that is not in the hands of the formal parties; or when the information offered is required for justice.[60]

Similar to this approach, in a survey conducted among Florida court judges, many complained that "too many briefs are useless" and that "many amici are just an 'echo' of the party brief."[61] This criticism has permeated through different courts in recent years with various results. Some courts are trying to be more aware of the content of the briefs submitted to them. For example, the Tennessee Court of Appeals determined that the role of the "amicus" should be limited and that "As a general matter, appointing an amicus is reserved for rare and unusual cases that involve questions of general or public interest."[62] The positions of Judge Posner, who led (before his retirement) a conservative line against the addition of amici, were widely quoted around the world when opinions were divided between those who believed that his position expressed a positive trend that should be adhered to[63] and those who thought that his position expressed a conservative trend which may lead to problems.[64]

[60] 223 F.3d 615 (seventh Cir. 2000). See also United States v. Michigan, 940 F.2d 143, 164 (sixth Cir. 1991. pp. 164–165. In Voices for Choices v. Ill. Bell Tel. Co., 339 F.3d 542, 5[45] (seventh Cir. 2003), the President of the Illinois Senate and the Speaker of the House They asked to submit an "amicus" brief on behalf of the House of Representatives and the litigants agreed to the request. Nevertheless, Judge Posner refused the request and stated that the Illinois State Select men's brief repeats the arguments of the parties and does not assist the court. He added and stated that an appeal in court does not constitute a congressional hearing. See also Scourfield McLauchlan and Gay (2015), p. 79.

[61] Walbolt and Lang Jr. (2003) him other courts in the United States, adopted Posner's approach.

[62] State ex rel. 'Comm'r of Transp. v. Med. Bird Black Bear White Eagle, 63 S.W.3d 734, 758 (Tenn. Ct. App. 2001). Similar to this approach, the Mississippi Court of Appeals and the Louisiana Supreme Court also take a (relatively) conservative approach to the criteria for the inclusion of "amici." Miss. R. APP. P. 29(A); LA. SUP. CT. R. 7–12.

[63] For example, Harris (2000). Harris advocates imposing significant substantive and deliberative restrictions on non-governmental "amici." A well-known ruling in this area is Eldred v. Ashcroft, 255 F.3d 849, 851 (D.C. Cir. 2001). In this regard, The Court of Appeals for the District of Columbia denied an "amicus'" motion to file a brief on the grounds that these arguments open up a new front in the case. Other federal judges have held to Judge Posner's approach. See, e.g., Sciotto v. Marple Newtown Sch. Dist., 70 F. Supp. 2d 553, 555 (E.D. Pa. 1999).

[64] Munford (1999). Munford criticized Posner's position and claimed that adopting this position could weaken the "amicus" institution. Judge Posner's approach is not acceptable to all judges of the appeals courts. For example, in the case of Neonatology Assoc., P.A. v. Comm'r, 293 F.3d 128, 133 (3d Cir. 2002), Judge Alito (later appointed to the Supreme Court) rejected Posner's approach. He argued that a narrow approach towards the "Amicus' institution conveys an unfortunate message about the openness of the court."

Another claim is that briefs from "amici," which do not assist in the work of the courts, lead to an increase in the overall costs of the legal process.[65] As more "amicus briefs" are submitted and the participation of interest groups becomes more comprehensive, the overall costs of managing the procedures multiply, with the procedures becoming cumbersome and excessively long.[66]

In some of the proceedings, there is a concern that the "amici" will flood the courts with non-essential information and materials, which ultimately harm the ability of the courts to act quickly and efficiently.[67] Judge Richard Posner (formerly) of the Federal Court of Appeals in Chicago was one of the representatives of this criticism. He has ruled on several occasions that the "amicus" representation mechanism (as interpreted by most United States courts) has failed in its duty to assist the courts. In his view, the amici make the work of the courts more difficult, waste valuable judicial time, and increase the legal process's costs.[68]

In addition, in arbitration proceedings in which amici are attached, it is further argued that the amici cause unnecessary delays in the arbitration procedure, which is intended to be short and efficient, rather than going to other courts, thereby increasing the costs imposed on the parties who tried to avoid it in advance by going to arbitration.[69] In other cases, also mainly related to arbitration proceedings, amici ask the arbitrators to order the parties to transfer commercial documents and various materials that the parties to the conflict do not necessarily wish to share. In doing so, they harm the autonomy of the parties to conduct the arbitration as they want and cause the costs of the procedure to increase.[70]

3.2.6 Uselessness of "Amici" Due to Courts' Ability to Obtain Information Independently

In today's era of accessible information, both due to the information available on the Internet and due to the ability to obtain many types of information through various technologies (such as artificial intelligence or similar elite technologies), judges can

---

[65] Posner (1993), pp. 23–30.

[66] Flechtner (2013), pp. 1211–1263. [examining the economic implications of amicus participation in international commercial arbitration within the United States]. See also Williamson (2010), pp. 491–518. It focuses on the relationship between costs and the involvement of Amicus Curiae in the Canadian legal system. The author conducts an empirical study to explore the impact of amicus participation on the overall costs of legal proceedings. The study examines the costs associated with Amicus Curiae participation in different types of cases, such as appellate litigation or constitutional matters, within the Canadian context.

[67] Goldman (2011), pp. 907, 909–911; Larsen (2014).

[68] Ryan v. Commodity Futures Trading Comm'n, 125 F.3d 1062, 1063 (seventh Cir. 1997) at p. 1063; 223 F.3d 615 (seventh Cir. 2000).

[69] Sabater (2010), p. 51.

[70] Ishikawa (2010), p. 393.

now simply and efficiently obtain for themselves the information offered to them in the past by amici. This makes many "amicus briefs" superfluous.[71] Beyond that, modern "amici" flood the courts with information and materials, which ultimately harm the ability of the courts to act quickly, flexibly, and efficiently, considering "you cannot see the forest for the trees." Moreover, in some cases, the "flooding of information" (both quantitatively and qualitatively) from various amici may result in the courts rejecting the information that reaches them from amici, leaving only the information that they deem to be correct.[72]

3.2.7 Using Unfounded Research Methods

It is claimed that some amici use research methods that are not scientifically based, meaning that the court cannot draw clear conclusions from their briefs. According to this claim, judges must be aware that not all the information presented by amici is reliable and well-founded. Rustad and Koenig argued that in light of the possibilities for amici to present information in an exaggerated or unreliable manner, the courts must appoint a professional expert who will provide independent advice concerning briefs that contain different types of information, in particular, from the field of social sciences and humanities.[73] Larsen warned against judgments that cite information from "amici" and rely on them as unequivocal facts that cannot be disputed, even if these are scientifically questionable. She wrote, "It is a mistake to conclude that the Justices can easily tell which of these amici are real factual experts and which are not."[74] She suggested that, in appropriate cases, "amici" should present to the courts a detailed scientific explanation about the methods (and the criticisms of the information presented, if any) they relied on in the brief.[75]

---

[71] Castells (2014), pp. 127–148.

[72] Goldman (2011), pp. 907, 909–911; Larsen (2014) The article challenges the process of citing amicus briefs as authority and addresses the failure of the parties to act as an adequate check.

[73] Rustad and Koenig (1993), pp. 91, 157–158.

[74] Cf. Larsen (2014), p. 1762. In this context, see also the concerns raised in Dwyer (2023). Dwyer argues that there is a growing problem with Amicus Curiae briefs that are filed by individuals or organizations who do not have a legitimate interest in the case and who are not truly advocating for the interests of the parties involved. Dwyer calls these briefs "faux advocacy" briefs. He claimed that courts should be skeptical of amicus briefs that are filed by organizations with a clear agenda. These organizations may be more interested in advancing their own agenda than in providing the court with accurate and unbiased information.

[75] Larsen (2014). Larsen relies to some extent on the series of steps proposed by HUBER, footnote 1256, to prevent the misuse of legal proceedings through idle science.

3.2.8 The Criticism of the Use of Amicus Curiae in International Arbitrations

Using amici has also become common in international commercial arbitrations (primarily the World Trade Organization). This is because international commercial arbitrations involve not only the commercial interests of the parties to the arbitration but also broader interests such as human rights or environmental quality.[76] When dealing with the practice of "Amicus Curiae" in arbitration proceedings in general and in international arbitration proceedings in particular, additional criticisms about the use of "amici" are added, which are listed below.

First (as noted in Sect. 3.2.4), an arbitration proceeding, by its nature, is a process of agreement conducted between two parties of their own free will. When a particular party does not wish to add "amici" to the arbitration procedure (and this was the case quite often), such a move cannot be forced upon him because such coercion goes against the primary rationale of the arbitration procedure. For example, in the NAFTA arbitration regarding UPS, Mexico claimed it was "very disturbed" by adding amici to the arbitration process. It claimed that this development in procedural law that allows third parties to present their position is a move that is contrary to the organization's tradition and Mexico's consent to the arbitration process.[77]

Second, amici may not be necessary for arbitration proceedings since the arbitrators are free and authorized to obtain any information they need on their own independently.[78]

Third, to achieve what they want, amici sometimes request access to commercial documents and various materials that the parties to the arbitration do not wish to hand over. In doing so, the amici violate the autonomy of the parties to conduct the arbitration in a manner that is in line with their interests.[79]

Fourth, according to the experience gained so far concerning the participation of amici in international arbitrations, it seems that, for the most part, the "amici" side

[76] Charwat (2016); Howse (2003), pp. 496–510; Keller (2005), pp. 449–470.

[77] First Mexican 1128 Submission 5, United Parcel Serv. of Am., Inc. v. Canada (NAFTA Arb. June 11, 2001). In the NAFTA arbitration regarding UPS, Mexico claimed that it was "very troubled" by the addition of "amici" to the arbitration process and claimed that this development in procedural law is a dangerous move that is contrary to the tradition of the organization. Rogers (2006), p. 1301; see also Born and Forrest (2020), pp. 626–665.

[78] For example, in the case of UPS, it was claimed by the investor group that "amicus briefs should only be submitted in the event that the Tribunal determines the disputing parties are unable to provide the necessary assistance and materials needed to decide the dispute." Investor's Response to the Petition of the Can. Union of Postal Workers & the Council of Canadians 17, United Parcel Serv. of Am., Inc. v. Canada (NAFTA Arb. May 28, 2001).

[79] Ishikawa (2010), pp. 393 [the author argues that third-party participation can enhance the legitimacy and transparency of investment treaty arbitration, but it also raises concerns about the confidentiality of the proceedings and the potential for abuse. The article concludes that third-party participation should be allowed in investment treaty arbitration, but with appropriate safeguards to protect the interests of the parties involved].

with the "weak" and "poor" countries against strong countries or a group of investors and capitalists.[80]

Fifth, even in international arbitration proceedings, the "amici" increase the legal expenses imposed on the parties and cause significant delays in the arbitration procedure, which is intended to be short and efficient compared to going to other courts.[81]

3.3 Summary

In summary of this chapter, it has been seen that in recent years, countless issues in society reach the courts accompanied by the submission of Amicus briefs. The amici writing the briefs may be representatives of social organizations, students writing in amicus clinics, private individuals, politicians, various interest groups, or professionals employed by commercial companies. It has been seen that upon comprehensive examination of the issue, there are various advantages and disadvantages to making use of amici. Beginning with the advantages, using the Amicus Curiae may, first and foremost, lead to a complete and better legal decision that also considers the interests of third parties who may be affected by court rulings. Second, the amicus is a tool that can influence court rulings in areas of public interest and concern of ecological, economic, and social importance. Third, using an Amicus Curiae has relatively low costs and low financial risks. Fourth, submitting a shared amicus brief increases cooperation between interest organizations, different social groups, and the third and public sectors. These collaborations strengthen civil society and have great intrinsic value. Fifth, the Amicus Curiae supports the institutional legitimacy of the courts because the very willingness of the courts to listen to the arguments of various amici shows appreciation on the part of the courts for the amici and creates a more significant commitment to them to respect the judgments.

Using the Amicus Curiae practice also has several disadvantages: first, there is a fear of turning the court into a political arena through the involvement of Amicus Curiae. Second, there is widespread concern about extensive use of Amicus Curiae by "powerful" interest and professional groups. Third, the amici themselves have little control over managing the way in which their brief may be used within the legal process. Fourth, courts may be overloaded with irrelevant and useless information presented by amici in order to serve their own purposes rather than being solely motivated to help the court proceedings. Fifth, the multiple amicus briefs may lead to a continuation of proceedings and a potential violation of the rights of the formal

[80] Mackenzie (2005), pp. 295, 296 (Tullio Treves et al. eds., 2005).

[81] Sabater (2010), pp. 47, 51 [The author discusses the potential risks and challenges associated with increased transparency, such as the protection of sensitive business information, the potential for undue influence from public opinion, and the erosion of party autonomy].

litigants. Sixth, Amicus Curiae briefs using unfounded research methods need more scientific credibility.

References

Abramowicz M, Colby TB (2009) Notice and comment judicial decision making. Univ Chicago Law Rev 76:965:987

Alarie BRD, Green AJ (2010) Interventions at the Supreme Court of Canada: accuracy, affiliation and acceptance. Osgoode Hall Law J 48(3/4):381–410

Bazelon E, "Antonin Scalia Didn't Trust Science," NY Times Mag

Beckwith E, Sobernheim R (1948) Amicus Curiae --Minister of Justice. Fordham Law Rev 17:38

Behuniak-Long S (1991) Friendly fire: amici curiae and Webster v. reproductive health services. Judicature 74:261–262

Bell RB, Odysseos P (2002) Sex, drugs, and court TV? How America's increasing interest in trial publicity impacts our lawyers and the legal system. Georgetown J Legal Ethics 15:653–669

Born G, Forrest S (2020) Amicus curiae participation in international commercial arbitration. ICSID Rev Foreign Invest Law J 34(3):626–665

Bradley and Gardner (1985) Underdogs, Upperdogs and the use of the amicus brief: trends and explanations. Justice Sys J 10:78, 91

Carter LE, Ellis MS, Jalloh CC (2016) NGO intervention in court proceedings through amicus curiae briefs. In: The international criminal court in an effective global justice system. Edward Elgar Publishing, Cheltenham, pp 264–332

Castells M (2014) The impact of the internet on society: a global perspective. Change 19:127–148

Charwat N (2016) Who participates as amicus curiae in World Trade Organization dispute settlement and why? New Zealand Univ Law Rev 27

Collins PM Jr (2004) Friends of the court: examining the influence of amicus curiae participation in United States supreme court litigation. Law Soc Rev 38(4):807–832

Collins PM Jr, Corley PC, Hamner J (2015) Influence of amicus curiae briefs on U.S. Supreme Court opinion content. Law Soc Rev 49:917

Corbin CR (2017) Amicus curiae and transparency in the supreme court. Ohio State Law J 78(3): 593–624

Coyle M (2016) Roberts singles out former White House Counsel for 'Extraordinary' brief. LAW. COM. http://www.law.com/supremecourtbrief/almID/1202756102813

Davis R (1994) Decisions and images: the supreme court and the press

Doron II, Totry-Jubran M, Enosh G, Regev T (2015) An American friend in an Israeli court: an empirical perspective. Israel Law Rev 48(2):145–164

Dwyer JG (2023) Faux Advocacy in Amicus Practice. Pepperdine L Rev 50:633–718

Farber DA, Frickey PP (1991) Law and public choice: A critical introduction

Feldman A (2016) The most effective friends of the court, empirical SCOTUS. https://empiricalscotus.com/2016/05/11/the-most-effective-friends-of-the-court

Flechtner HM (2013) The economic impact of amicus participation in U.S. international commercial arbitration. UC Davis Law Rev 47(4):1211–1263

Franze AJ, Anderson RR (2015) *Record Breaking Term for Amicus Curiae in Supreme Court Reflects New Norm*, Natl Law J. http://www.nationallawjournal.com/supremecourtbrief/id=1202735095655

Franze AJ, Anderson RR (2016) In unusual term, big year for amicus curiae at the Supreme Court. Nat Law J. https://www.apks.com/~/media/files/perspectives/publications/2016/09/in-unusual-term-big-year-for-amicus-curiae-at-thesupreme-court.pdf

Graham C (2012) Advocates for Int'l Dev., a "How To" guide to amicus curiae & international investment arbitrations, pp 6–7 (Feb. 29)

Goldman P (2011) Note, *should the supreme court stop inviting amici curiae to defend abandoned lower court decisions?* Stan Law Rev 63:907, 909–907, 911
Gruner M (2003) Accounting for the public interest in international arbitration. Columb J Transnational Law 41:955
Hami Ben Nun (2009) Cognitive biases and judicial decisions. Gates of Law 177
Hansen W, Watson AH (2009) The role of amicus curiae briefs in the Federal Appellate Courts. Just Syst J 30(1):86–106
Harris MJ (2000) Note, amicus curiae: friend or foe? The Limits of Friendship in American Jurisprudence. Suffolk J Trial App Advoc 5, 1(2000)
Hobér K (2008) Arbitration involving states. In: Newman L, Hill R (eds) The leading arbitrators' guide to international arbitration, New York, chapter 8, p 155
Howse R (2003) Membership and its privileges: the WTO, civil society, and the amicus brief controversy. Eur Law J 9(4):496–510
Ishikawa T (2010) Third party participation in investment treaty arbitration. Int Comp Law Q 59: 373, 393
Johnson TJ (2016) Amicus curiae participation in United States supreme court cases: a network analysis. Soc Networks 47:116–129
Johnson L, Tuerk E (2005) CIEL's experience in WTO dispute settlement: challenges and complexities from a practical point of view. In: Treves T et al (eds) Civil society, international courts and compliance bodies, p 24
Juaristi FJR (2014) The amicus curiae in the Inter-American Court of human rights (1982–2013). Available at SSRN https://ssrn.com/abstract=2488073
Kagan A (1991) Adversarial legalism and American government. J Policy Anal Manage 10(1):1–18
Kaufmann G (2016) Center for International Dispute Settlement
Kawharu A (2007) Public participation and transparency in investment arbitration: recent developments and future challenges. IHLRes 2:2–3
Kearney JD, Merrill TW (2000) The influence of amicus curiae briefs on the supreme court. Univ Pa Law Rev 148:743–855
Kelleher CA, Yackee SW (2006) Who's whispering in your ear? The influence of third parties over state agency decisions. Polit Res Q 59(4):629–643
Keller J (2005) The future of amicus participation at the WTO: implications of the sardines decision and suggestions for further developments. Int J Leg Inf 33(3):449–470
Lacarte J (2004) Transparency, public debate and participation by NGOs in the WTO: a WTO perspective. J Int Econ Law 7:685–686
Larsen AO (2014) The trouble with amicus facts. Va Law Rev 100:1757–1818
Larsen AO, Devins N (2016) The Amicus machine. Va Law Rev 102:1901
Lester A (1988) Amici curiae: third party interventions before the European court of human rights. In: Matcher F, Petzold H (eds) Protecting human rights: the European dimension. Studies in honor of Gérard J. Wiarda, Cologne, p 342
Levine E (2011) Amicus curiae in international investment arbitration: the implications of an increase in third-party participation. Berkeley J Int Law 29(1):200–224
Lynch KJ (2004) Best friends? Supreme Court law clerks on effective amicus curiae briefs. J Law Pol 20(33):46–56
Mackenzie R (2005) *The* amicus curiae *in international courts*: *toward common procedural approaches*. In: Treves T et al (eds) Civil society, international courts and compliance bodies, vol 295, p 296
Martin AD (2014) Strategic amici curiae and supreme court decision-making. Law Soc Rev 48(3): 527–562
Mauro T (2016) Bolstered by briefs, liberal justices lash out during contraceptive debate. Nat Law J. Mar. 23. https://www.law.com/supremecourtbrief/almID/1202752957056
McRae D (2004) What is the future of WTO dispute settlement? J Int Econ Law 7:12
Mourre A (2006) Are amici curiae the proper response to the public's concerns on transparency in investment arbitration? Law Practice Int Courts Tribunals 5:266

Munford LT (1999) When does the curiae need an amicus? J App Prac Process 1:279
Nelson WE (2011) Taking interests into account: amicus curiae participation in supreme court litigation. Stanford Law Rev 63(5):121–186
Posner RA (1993) What do judges and justices maximize? (The same thing everybody Else does). Supreme Courts Econ Rev 3(1):23–30
Ramseyer JM, Rasmusen EB (2008) When are amicus curiae briefs unhelpful? Int Rev Law Econ 28(3):224–232
Rogers C (2006) Transparency in international commercial arbitration. Univ Kanas Law Rev 54: 1301
Rustad M, Koenig T (1993) The supreme court and junk social science: selective distortion in amicus briefs. North Carolina Law Rev 72:91, 157–91, 158
Sabater A (2010) Towards transparency in arbitration (a cautious approach). Berkeley J Int Law Publicist 5:47, 51
Sachs B, Revesz RL (2010) Corporate amicus briefs. Mich Law Rev 108(5):787–823
Savarese E (2007) Amicus curiae participation in investor-state arbitration. Italian Yearb Int Law Online 17(1):99–121
Schachter M (2004) The utility of pro bono representation of U.S.-based amicus curiae in non-U.-S. and multi-national courts as a means of advancing the public interest. Fordham Int Law J 28: 111
Scourfield McLauchlan J, Gay T (2015) When congress speaks, does the Suprem amicus curiae before the U.S. Supreme Court during the Rehnquist court. Texas Rev Law Politics 20:79
Sherwin RK (2003) Celebrity lawyers and the cult of personality. NYLS J Human Rights 19:147
Simard LS (2008) An empirical study of amici curiae in Federal Court: a fine balance of access, efficiency, and Adversarialism. Rev Litig 27:669. (referring to Grutter v. Bollinger, 539 U.S. 306 (2003)
Spriggs JF, Wahlbeck PJ (1997) Amicus curiae and the role of information at the supreme court. Polit Res Q 50(2):365–386
Thornton LT (2003) With friends like these... the weight of 90-plus Amicus briefs in the Michigan cases ought to influence the court. legal times, March 31 at 70
Umbricht G (2001) An "amicus curiae brief" on amicus curiae briefs at the WTO. J Int Econ Law 4: 783
Van Den Eynde L (2019) The consensus argument in NGO's' Amicus Curiae briefs: Defending minorities through a creatively used majoritarian argument. Building Consensus on European Consensus: Judicial Interpretation of Human Rights in Europe and Beyond. pp. 96–119
Walbolt SH, Lang JH Jr (2003) Amicus briefs: friend or foe of Florida courts? Stetson Law Rev 32: 269
Ward SF (2007) Friends of the court are friends of mine. ABA J 24(93):11
Whitehouse S (2021) A flood of judicial lobbying: amicus influence and funding transparency. Yale LJF 131:141
Williamson (2010) Costs and the participation of amicus curiae in Canada: an empirical study. Dalhousie Law J 33(2):491–518
Wohl A (1996) Friends with agendas. J ABA 82:11
Zannoti Francesca (1995) "The judicialization of judicial salary policy in Italy and the United States". The Global Expansion of Judicial Power

Chapter 4
The Historical Development of "Amicus Curiae" and the Reasons for Its Emergence

As mentioned in the previous chapter, nowadays, Amicus Curiae is used in several legal systems that differ from one another in their rules of conduct and their overall legal process. These systems include: the common law system (in countries such as the United States, Canada, England, and Australia), the continental system (practiced, for example, in France, Germany, and Spain), and international law (for example, in the European Court of Human Rights). In addition, the amicus practice has become popular among rights organizations, ordinary citizens, professional guilds, and even politicians in recent years. But what are the historical roots of this practice? Where did it first appear, and how did it begin to evolve? What historical factors led to its resurgence and spread in recent years?

This chapter provides a general overview and outlines Amicus Curiae's historical and intellectual evolution, examining its vital historical milestones. It begins with the Roman era (from around 27 BCE), then moves on to England and its colonies (particularly between the thirteenth and eighteenth centuries) and concludes with the modern-day United States (from the early eighteenth century to the mid-twentieth century). This chapter focuses particularly on the development of Amicus within the common law framework, which is the legal system practiced in English-speaking countries.

From a methodological perspective, not all contextual details are known regarding a small portion of the mentioned legal precedents in this chapter. The reason is that until the first half of the nineteenth century, legal proceedings were conducted mainly orally in many courts, and there was no official body responsible for the organized publication of legal precedents as is customary today. Therefore, the aim of this chapter is exceedingly modest: to describe the contribution of historical circumstances to the existence and development of a legal practice that has been utilized for centuries and has experienced a revival and gained momentum in recent years.

S. Farber, *The Amicus Curiae Phenomenon*, Ius Gentium: Comparative Perspectives on Law and Justice 119, https://doi.org/10.1007/978-3-031-67225-5_4

4.1 The Amicus in Roman Law

According to one version of the history of the Amicus Curiae practice, its historical origin can be traced back to Roman law. According to this approach, Amicus Curiae corresponds to well-known practices in Roman law, whereby a consultative council (consilium) was established, mainly consisting of jurists, who advised the ruling authority in the empire.[1] The establishment of the council was likely a result of reforms initiated by Emperor Augustus (Gaius Julius Caesar Octavianus) in 27 BCE, where the right of appeal to the people was abolished, and appellants were directed to the emperor's court instead. The emperor held the ultimate appellate jurisdiction and presided over it alone but sought assistance from the council he established and consulted with. The council mainly consisted of learned individuals with legal expertise and a few members from the emperor's inner circle. The jurists, who were educated and held high social status in Roman society, were referred to as "masters of the law" or "legal experts" (iuris prudentes) or as "advisors or expounders of the law" (iuris consulti). They provided legal opinions to parties interested in seeking advice and provided non-binding consultations to the courts and the rulers who controlled the judicial system. The jurists who were members of the consultative council also advised on the role of the Roman praetor, a political position that dealt with distinct legal matters and assisted in formulating edicts and regulations.[2]

The role of "iuris prudentes" (legal experts) also involved drafting legal texts and provisions that governed the legal proceedings in the courts. John Crook argued that this practice was based on an earlier tradition in which individuals in public office did not make decisions regarding public matters on their own. According to the legal tradition prevalent in Rome, any decision concerning public affairs had to be made after consulting professional experts. In other words, important decisions regarding public matters were only reached after the advisory council members, who were independent and impartial advisers, provided their input. Furthermore, Crook contends that the role of "iuris prudentes" extended beyond legal consultation to rulers or the courts themselves, as they played a broader role in shaping legal procedures. Crook believes that the "iuris prudentes" actually assisted in most areas concerning senior public office, particularly political and administrative matters. In addition to providing legal counsel to the courts, they assisted ordinary citizens throughout the empire in various civil and public legal matters, including drafting contracts, wills, inheritances, property transfers, and more. The exclusive and elitist "iuris prudentes"

[1] Those who hold this opinion are Fowler V. Harper & Edwin D. Etherington, Lobbyists Before the Court, 101 U. Pa. L. Rev. 1172 (1953) and Angell (1967).

[2] See Covey Jr. (1959). Beckwith and Sobernheim (1948). [the article discusses the role of the Amicus Curiae as a "minister of justice" and how the Amicus Curiae can assist the court in reaching a just decision. The article also argues that the Amicus Curiae should not be used as a tool for advocacy, but rather as a means of providing the court with impartial information].

significantly influenced the development of lifestyles within the Roman Empire.[3] Among the well-known advisors were Cassius Dio (155–235 AD)[4] and Herodian (170–240 AD),[5] who served as amici in the advisory council during their respective periods.

Several characteristics connect the "amicus" of the Roman era to the "amicus" of today. Like its Roman counterpart, the assistance provided by contemporary amici is purely advisory, and the recipients are not obliged to act upon it. Amici also possess, for the most part, a high level of education and specific professional expertise. They, too, serve as advisors to the court only after receiving approval or a specific request from the court or the commissioning party. They are considered external and independent consultants who are not part of the judicial system. Lastly, similar to the Roman amicus, the modern amicus is regarded as having professional prestige and symbolizes a position of honor.

The advisors who were members of the Roman consilium bear a strong resemblance to the counselors who were members of His Majesty's Most Honorable Privy Council in England, which likely began to take shape during the Norman rule in England from 1066.[6] The Privy Council was a prominent body of advisors to the ruling monarch of the United Kingdom. Today, its members include lords, politicians, lawyers, and judges. Its original purpose was to advise the king on matters of governance and legislation of great importance. Over the years, democratic institutions such as Parliament, responsible for legislation, and the court system have emerged. According to custom, the decisions of the Privy Council and its subordinate committees are purely advisory, and, over time, the king or queen would receive their advice and recommendations and approve them.

However, the difficulty in the approach connecting the amicus and the Roman consilium is that the term "Amicus Curiae" is not mentioned in any text, legislation, or Latin dictionary from this period. This fact is unusual and raises real reservations because the information about the litigation procedures in Roman law is quite well established. Latin dictionaries mention, for example, the terms "Amici Augusti" (friends of the emperor), "Amicitia" (friendship), and "Amicus Populi Romani" (friend of the Roman people), but "Amicus Curiae" as a term describing a third party who provides external assistance to the court, is not explicitly mentioned in any known source.

In addition to this difficulty, it is impossible to infer with certainty and definitively conclude that the term "amicus," being of Latin origin, stems from Roman practice.

---

[3]Crook (1955), p. 26 [Crook's book is a valuable contribution to the study of the Roman imperial council. The book provides a comprehensive overview of the council's history and role in the government of the empire.].

[4]For more on his character, see Aalders (1986), pp. 282–304.

[5]For more on his character, see Chrysanthou (2020), pp. 621–651.

[6]Macpherson (1873), Macpherson provides a comprehensive overview of the functioning of the Judicial Committee, including its jurisdiction, composition, and the types of cases it heard. The book delves into the procedural aspects of appeals brought before the Committee, covering topics such as the filing of petitions, preparation of cases, oral arguments, and the rendering of judgments.

The reason is that in medieval Europe and the early modern period, Latin was the language of intellectuals in various fields of knowledge, such as literature, theology, science, and law. Furthermore, even when Latin ceased to be a spoken and living language, it continued to be used for scientific and religious writing as well as legal literature. Latin terminology abounds in these disciplines without them being derived from Roman times. In modern law, hundreds of terms are used today that, although derived from Latin, have no direct connection with Roman law. Therefore, it is impossible to draw definitive conclusions from the fact that "amicus" is a term of Latin origin.[7]

The Hebrew legal system, part of which developed in a period parallel to the development of Roman law, also recognized the procedure of external consultation to the court. There are several references to the consultation of judges with parties outside the court's jurisdiction, such as with the judge's rabbi or with another scholar whose knowledge of Jewish Law surpasses that of the judge. According to Jewish Law, the appropriate authorities must be consulted before making important decisions in public affairs, for if the Almighty God consults with angels, then *a fortiori* humans can consult with experts.[8]

4.2 The Amicus Curiae in Common Law

Despite the similarities between the amicus and Roman law and administration, it appears that the practice of Amicus Curiae developed or, at the very least, took shape and solidified noticeably during a later period, around the fourteenth century or slightly earlier, within the Common Law system of England. As is well known, the Common Law system follows the adversarial method, in which the judge passively adjudicates between two opposing parties, and it is the parties' responsibility to present evidence before the judge.[9] This approach contrasts with the inquisitorial method, which is widely used in continental European countries (such as Germany, Spain, and France) and most Latin American countries, where the judge has a more active role in managing the proceedings. In the inquisitorial system, for example, the judge personally investigates the witnesses and does not leave the task to the parties' attorneys, as is customary in the Common Law system.[10] One of the distinct

[7]Collins (2008); For more also see: Izarova and Szloc-Nartows (2019) https://doi.org/10.1556/2052.2019.60103.

[8]Epstein (1884–1908). For a more detailed examination of the Amicus practice in Jewish Law, see Farber and Cohen (2023), pp. 16–21.

[9]For a history of the common law system see Holmes (1991) and Hale (1792). The book is a comprehensive history of the development of the common law in England, from its origins in the Anglo-Saxon period to the seventeenth century. The book is divided into two volumes and covers a wide range of topics, including the origins of the common law, the development of the jury system, and the role of judges in the legal system.

[10]Jolowicz (2003), pp. 281–295. Parisi (2002), pp. 193–216.

characteristics of Common Law is that the judge must make decisions based on custom, tradition, or precedent. This is known as casuistic reasoning, which is based on principles established in a prior case and the comparison between the case under consideration and previous cases, relying on shared facts among them.[11]

The development of the amicus within the Common Law system was influenced by several social and historical factors that shaped its role within the realm of the judiciary. Firstly, there was a relatively common public involvement in the management of judicial proceedings, which was prevalent during the medieval period and even to some extent in later times. Secondly, amici became involved in representing defendants who were not entitled to legal representation. Thirdly, informal collegial relationships between judges and attorneys played a role, as attorneys informally advised judges on cases in which they did not participate. Other areas where amici intervened include collecting third-party legal information, submitting it to the court, and preventing errors to uphold the court's dignity. Lastly, it is worth mentioning the attempts by third parties to present their interests in cases in which they lacked formal standing, but there was a concern that the court's decision could affect them. All of these aspects will be examined further below.

4.3 Public Involvement in Judicial Proceedings

The emergence of the practice of Amicus Curiae within the common law system was rooted in the prevalent custom of public participation, particularly among the middle to upper-class population, in judicial proceedings in England. Legal precedents recorded in the yearbooks of the late fourteenth century and even slightly earlier demonstrate that in English law during the later medieval period, anyone in the courtroom could actively participate in the trial, request to be an Amicus Curiae, and present critical information.[12] Within this practice, individuals—sometimes possessing legal expertise but often uneducated—would provide the judge with information on a specific matter in which the judge was either uninformed or uncertain about how to proceed. During that time, many trials took place in the town or village square, and any person with relevant information, whether legal or factual, could intervene in the process, even if they lacked formal education.[13]

For example, in the year 1293, in a case concerning the interpretation of a deed, a particular individual whom the court referred to as Amicus Curiae—and whose exact level of education is unknown (he presumably possessed some form of education)—provided the court with knowledge of a legal precedent that could assist in the ruling

[11] Pound (1907), p. 383.

[12] Cohen (1929), pp. 4, 12.

[13] The people who hold this opinion are Lowman and Covey. See Lowman (1992), pp. 1243, 1245 and Covey Jr. (1959).

of the case.[14] Additional examples can be found in the Year Book of 1573, which describes three cases where amici present in the courtroom drew the judge's attention to irregularities in judicial orders. This assistance was given to prevent the court from making errors.[15] In a Scottish judgment from 1757 dealing with the emancipation of a Jamaican slave, a private individual requested to join the proceedings as an Amicus Curiae to assist in the enslaved person's emancipation. The court rejected the request but noted that the amicus presented "varied and learned arguments."[16]

An English court ruling from 1736 illustrates an additional intriguing aspect of public participation in legal proceedings. The case revolved around financial fraud committed by Mrs. Phillips against an unidentified plaintiff. During the trial, it was revealed that at the time of her marriage to Mr. Millman, Mrs. Phillips was already married to another man. Consequently, the ecclesiastical court declared her marriage to Millman invalid. The plaintiff argued that the promissory note signed by Mrs. Phillips was weak since, according to the court's decision, her marriage to Millman was deemed invalid. In defense, Mrs. Phillips contended that her previous husband was also married, thereby asserting the validity of her marriage to Millman and the authenticity of the promissory note, and according to the procedural practice that followed then, an application for contempt of court needed to be submitted out of concern for potential court deception to clarify the matter.

In this case, Lord Hardwicke was required to consider who among the parties was entitled to file the application for contempt of court. He noted that when there is a risk of collusion between two formal parties in a legal proceeding, there is no impediment for a third external party—in this case, Mr. Millman—to submit the application as an Amicus Curiae. Indeed, Mr. Millman approached the court as an Amicus Curiae, presented the fraud committed by Mrs. Phillips, and succeeded in securing her conviction for contempt of court. If her scheme had succeeded, the Amicus Curiae (Millman) himself could have been adversely affected. Therefore, this case can be seen as a precedent for the intervention of a third party as an Amicus Curiae when their interest is at stake.[17]

4.4 Representation of Defendants Who Are Not Entitled to Legal Representation

Another factor that may have contributed to the Amicus Curiae's development was the prevailing legal practice until the early eighteenth century, whereby the defendant in criminal proceedings was not entitled to legal representation on his

[14] YB 21 Edw. 1, p. 149, Easter (1293).

[15] Brooke (1573), p. 33.

[16] Sheddan v. A Negro, (1757) Mor 14545.

[17] Coxe v. Phillips, (1736) 95 Eng. Rep. 152; 1 Cas. t. Hard. 237. See in general Smith (2013), pp. 42, 44.

behalf.[18] The defendant was required to respond to the charges brought against him, and no person was allowed to represent him. In general, it can be said that defendants in English law were deprived of most of the rights necessary to protect themselves—they did not receive a detailed account of the charges against them, nor did they always know what those charges were. They were not allowed to testify under oath. They were not allowed to call witnesses on their behalf, even if such witnesses were present in court and willing to testify. And indeed, they were not permitted any legal counsel. This approach's rationale was that "there is one truth," meaning that if the prosecution proved its case to the required standard of proof, there couldn't be any other truth in favor of the accused. Moreover, according to the prevailing rule at that time, all of the property of anyone who confessed to a crime, together with their family's property, was forfeited to the king, in addition to the punishments imposed on them in the trial. Therefore, accused individuals who believed they would be convicted preferred to remain silent during their interrogation, even if it hastened their death. Numerous cases are known where accused individuals chose to die under the severe torture inflicted by English investigators rather than confess to guilt and jeopardize their family's property.

However, according to the prevailing legal principles practiced at that time, observers who were present in court and were considered to have a certain level of education, even if they were not necessarily legally trained, may have assisted in officially defending the accused to some extent when they appeared as amici curiae. The jurist Edward Coke wrote that "[if] the accused did not have a lawyer with whom he could consult [...] any educated person present at that time was entitled to present arguments to the court on his behalf."[19] The presentation of arguments by amici curiae not only aided the accused but also indirectly benefited the courts, particularly in ensuring proper conduct of the proceedings. Nevertheless, by the end of the nineteenth century, with the professionalization of legal advocacy in England and the establishment of rules allowing accused individuals to have formal representation by lawyers, this practice of amicus intervention for unrepresented defendants dwindled.[20]

Another contribution to the development of Amicus Curiae in English criminal law arose from the fact that amici curiae were often, in practice, de-facto advocates for the accused. According to legal historian Stuart Banner, when defendants were granted legal representation, lawyers would present arguments on behalf of the accused as amici rather than as advocates. The reason behind this was the concern that if they argued formally and their argument was rejected, it would be difficult to

---

[18] Pittman (1935), pp. 763–789; Langbein (1993), pp. 1047.

[19] Coke (1644), p. I29 (Brooke ed. 1779).

[20] Langbein (1993). The article examines the historical origins of the privilege against self-incrimination in the common law of England and its evolution in the United States. The author argues that the privilege against self-incrimination has its roots in the medieval ecclesiastical courts, where the accused was protected from being forced to confess to a crime.

rectify the situation. Although this may seem like a peculiar maneuver, it was likely deemed legitimate and persisted until the end of the eighteenth century.[21] A case in Connecticut, United States, in 1823 illustrates this point: an attorney representing a defendant named Judson argued before the court as an Amicus Curiae that the accused had no connection to the charges against him. After the court rejected this argument, the attorney presented himself as Judson's formal advocate and continued representing him in the case as if nothing had transpired.[22]

The case of Sir Roger Casement in 1916, regarding his prosecution for treason, provides another interesting example that illustrates this aspect. Casement was an Irish nationalist, poet, human rights activist, and revolutionary who played a role in forming the Irish Volunteers, a nationalist military organization fighting for Irish independence.[23] In 1914, Casement traveled to the United States to gather political support and funds for the organization's activities. He met with German diplomats in New York and even attempted to raise an Irish brigade composed of Irishmen serving in the British Army.[24] Shortly after his return to Ireland, Casement was arrested and imprisoned in the Tower of London on charges of treason, sabotage, and espionage against the Crown. Given the gravity of the case, a battery of top-notch legal practitioners was assembled to prosecute him, including Sir George Cave, the Home Secretary, Lord Chancellor-to-be and judge-to-be Lord Birkenhead, and Attorney General and close friend of Churchill, Sir Humphreys.

The English law of treason stipulated that in cases of treason, the accused was entitled to a maximum of two legal representatives. However, the defense team sought to expand the framework of the defense and, to circumvent the legal limitations imposed by the law, appointed "Lord Chief Justice" Lord Reading and Professor John Morgan from the University of London as amici curiae.[25] Professor Morgan was an informal part of the defense team and presented to the court the legislative history of the treason law and constitutional arguments in favor of the accused. Despite these efforts, they did not ultimately assist the accused, who was ultimately convicted and hanged.

---

[21] Banner (2003), pp. 1790–1890. Banner challenges the common perception that Amicus Curiae briefs are neutral and impartial presentations of legal arguments. Instead, he argues that amici have historically been driven by their own interests and biases, and their briefs have often served as tools for advancing specific agendas or influencing court decisions.

[22] Judson v. Blanchard, (1823) 4 Conn. 557.

[23] Laffan (2009).

[24] Barmann (1977), pp. 215–216.

[25] Keeton (2004).

4.5 Collegial Working Relationships Between Judges and Lawyers

Another factor that seemingly contributed to the development of amicus practice was the casual and informal working relationships between judges and barristers in the legal community. Judges who felt they needed some form of assistance, typically in the form of legal opinions or advice on proceedings, would often turn to barristers who had appeared before them in other matters or barristers with whom they had a personal acquaintance, relying on the natural trust that judges placed in members of the same elite legal profession. Friendly and collegial relationships between judges and barristers in the legal community, often stemming from shared personal backgrounds or involvement in professional activities, were quite common and widely accepted, and to a large extent, they still exist today in various levels of the legal profession.[26]

An amusing example illustrating such relationships comes from a case that occurred in 1830. A lawyer found himself in a bankruptcy proceeding in which one party, consistently represented by the lawyer, was sued by another party, who was also usually represented by the same lawyer. He did not know to which of his clients the duty of representation applied and how he should proceed, so he sought a decision from the court. Lord Chancellor, claiming that he himself lacked legal authority to recommend to the barrister which client to choose, appointed himself as an Amicus Curiae solely for the discussion and, in that capacity, provided recommendations to the barrister on how to proceed.[27]

4.6 Collection of Legal Material and Its Transfer to the Court

Another critical area in which the Amici operated was their role as a source of information. Among them were those who served as a repository of the process of legal rules and precedents. In Common Law, as explained above, judges are required to decide based on custom, tradition, or precedent, and courts are required to draw casuistic conclusions in cases before them by comparing them to previous cases and according to the principles established in previous cases. However, judges needed to have organized, systematic databases where they could search for legal rules and precedents. In England, for example, official case summaries began to appear only in the seventeenth century, edited by Edward Coke, a well-known English jurist. However, only after many years did collecting, editing, and publishing court judgments become established in the accepted legal system.

---

[26] Krislov (1963), p. 694. See also Dunn (2018).

[27] Ex parte Elysee, Monte 69, 70 na (Ch. 1830).

Until then, judges did not have organized, systematic information about their own or other judges' precedents, and no official body was entrusted with publishing court judgments (or their summaries). Lawyers who participated in legal debates or observed them for study purposes would write concise legal reviews of orally given judgments. Often, these summaries served as the primary documentation source for court judgments. As such, judges frequently turned to the lawyers and sought their assistance in locating such information, which could be oral and not necessarily recorded in writing.

Such an institution, a third-party entity that assists the court in documenting and organizing precedents, existed in Hebrew law even during the Talmudic period (70–640 CE). In Jewish Talmudic literature, the term "Tanna" (plural: Tannaim) often appears, meaning a person (usually highly educated in Torah) who reviews legal rules and previous judgments before senior judges; in other words, a kind of amicus. Yaacov Epstein emphasized that "this institution is central and elementary in the world of Jewish scholars, and without it, one cannot fathom the study in the *Amorah yeshivas* [study halls of later sages], just as one cannot fathom study in our world without books and libraries, as the Tannaim were the living libraries of the *yeshivas*."[28] These anonymous sages preserved thousands of living legal rules and customs in their memory and were the exclusive substitute for written books.[29]

Another example of this type of amicus can be seen in a case that occurred in the United States in 1800. The chief prosecutor of the state of Pennsylvania requested the state's Supreme Court to prioritize a particular case, in which the state was a party, over other cases pending in the court clerk's office. Another lawyer, Alexander Dallas, who was also involved in publishing judgments of both the Supreme Court of Pennsylvania and the Supreme Court of the United States, was present during the hearing of this request. Dallas requested the court to present his position as an amicus and informed the court that he was aware of an unpublished judgment from the Supreme Court of the United States. This judgment established that cases in which the state is a party receive priority in the court's proceedings regarding hearing cases involving citizens.[30]

4.7 Assistance to Courts to Prevent Judicial Errors

The role of the amicus also developed in relation to safeguarding the court's dignity against judicial errors. Third parties, whether attorneys or citizens present in the courtroom during a hearing, observed that the court may render judgments contrary to the law or based on incorrect facts. They then assisted the court by providing vital

---

[28] Epstein (1982), p. 48.

[29] Farber and Cohen (2023), pp. 16–21.

[30] Respublica v. Cobbett, 3 Yeates 93 (Pa. 1800). the case is also notable for being one of the earliest cases in American legal history to address the issue of libel.

factual or legal information. Such a case occurred, for example, in England regarding Geering in 1656, where an amicus sought to draw the judges' attention to several factual errors that happened during the proceedings. The court permitted the assistance of the amicus and held that "avoidance of errors in judgment is an honor to the court" and that "barbarianism may enter between the walls of the court if it is prohibited to inform the court of gross and evident errors within its walls."[31]

In such cases, the assistance of the amicus was not formal, and any formalities or procedures did not bind their position. Furthermore, a formal request by the amicus to present vital information to the court was not required. The court accepted third-party information as needed on a case-by-case basis to avoid judicial errors.

The *Falmouth* affair of 1706 illustrates this development. A civil case between two parties was decided in favor of the defendant. The judgment was given in the absence of the parties, and it later emerged that the defendant had passed away the day before. This raised the legal question of whether the judgment was valid or should be annulled. The court ruled that it was a factual question, instructed the plaintiff to submit a request to amend the judgment, and added that if the defendant passed away during the period in which the judgment was rendered, then the judgment would be valid. It noted that in such a case, one should act as an amicus and update the court on important factual matters, such as the death of one of the parties, to assist the court in avoiding problematic judgments.[32]

Another example occurred in 1811 in Massachusetts. The state's Supreme Court discovered that one of the jurors in a criminal proceeding was the complainant against the defendant. Attorney Joseph Story, who was present in the courtroom, requested, on his initiative, to be appointed as an amicus. He argued that based on existing precedents, the court should disqualify the juror and replace him with another.[33] He pointed out to the court that there was a precedent from the Supreme Court of Virginia, where the court disqualified a juror for the same reason. However, the court rejected Story's argument. Judge Marshall, who himself served as a judge in the U.S. Supreme Court, stated that the fact that the juror was acquainted with the defendant could actually contribute to a better understanding of the truth. Such familiarity, the court emphasized, would assist the jurors in understanding the true character of the defendant.[34]

---

[31] Protector v. Geering (1656), 145 Eng. Rep. 394, 394; Hardres 85, 85, 86.

[32] Falmouth v. Strode, (1706) 88 Eng. Rep. 949; 11 Mod. 136.

[33] See Newmyer (1970), pp. 112–135.

[34] For extension, see Newmyer (1985). The book examines Story's life and career, including his role as a statesman during the early years of the American Republic.

4.8 Overcoming the Principle of Duality of the Adversarial System

Finally, as Samuel Krislov noted, the practice of using amici assisted in overcoming inherent difficulties in the adversarial justice system in England, as well as in the United States and other countries. These difficulties stemmed from the lack of representation of interests other than those of the formal parties involved in the proceedings. In the prevailing adversarial conception of justice, in its pure form, two opposing parties confront each other, and the judge does not actively search for the facts of the case. Instead, information is presented to the judge by the parties themselves.[35] The philosophical theory underlying the conventional legal system viewed the court as a kind of arena where a battle between two champions took place, and at times, it was even referred to as "trial by combat."[36]

According to this tradition, the principle of dignity dictates not intervening in the conflict of a third party. Although, in some instances, a dispute between two parties may affect a non-formal party in the process, this judicial tradition saw the battle between the two parties as the primary focus. As such, there existed numerous difficulties in presenting the interests of additional parties. The involvement of third parties whose interests could be adversely affected by the court's decision was excluded.

To overcome this difficulty, the use of Amicus Curiae was employed. The amicus was a flexible tool for the third party to present its position in court, even if it was not an official party to the proceedings. Using amici, courts were exposed to additional interests related to the proceedings. Even in the late medieval period, there were cases in the conventional legal system where the court allowed the hearing of a third party in a proceeding in which that party was not formally involved. Most of these cases occurred in courts of equity, which operated according to more flexible legal principles.[37]

Indeed, such cases were relatively rare because they went against the chivalry principle of the Common Law system, which dictated that a third party should not interfere in a dispute between two gentlemen. However, in cases where the involvement of a third party was permitted, that third party was referred to as an "amicus." Even in such proceedings, courts emphasized the principle that the amicus should

[35] Sward (1988), p. 301; Strier (1992), p. 109. [The article argues that the American system, which is based on the adversarial model, is often criticized for being too focused on winning and losing, rather than seeking the truth. The inquisitional system, on the other hand, is more focused on finding the truth and is less adversarial in nature. The article suggests that the American system could benefit from adopting some of the features of the inquisitional system, such as allowing judges to take a more active role in questioning witnesses and gathering evidence.

[36] Neilson (1891).

[37] For a description of the history and characteristics of these courts, see: Oleck (1951), pp. 23. [The article argues that equity jurisprudence has its roots in the ancient concept of natural justice, which predates the development of formal legal systems]. Holdsworth (1914), p. 293.

maintain neutrality. As the Indiana Supreme Court stated in 1859, "The Amicus Curiae does not work for any party. He works only for the court."[38]

Due to its federal structure, the lack of representation of third-party interests has been reinforced in the United States' legal system. In cases involving disputes between states or between an individual and the government, third parties' issues and interests often arose beyond the original conflict between the formal parties in the proceedings. Over time, United States courts began to recognize the potential implications of a dispute between two formal parties on third parties, who, due to the dualistic nature of the process, were not represented, and their voices were not heard. Therefore, specific categories were gradually and cautiously established to allow official government representatives to be described as "Amicus Curiae" when a conflict between two parties affects the government.

This occurred, for example, in 1812 when the Supreme Court of the United States allowed the Attorney General of the United States, William Pinkney, to intervene in a legal proceeding involving the American Navy, even though the Navy was not a direct party to the case.[39] The courts concluded that they had the authority to grant third-party intervention if the non-expression of their position could harm them.

The first official mention of Amicus Curiae in American jurisprudence can be found in the case of *Green v. Biddle* in 1823.[40] The case involved a question of land ownership in the state of Kentucky, and the court issued a ruling without hearing the state's position. However, the state argued that the judgment was erroneous and did not consider its interests, so it turned to the prominent lawyer Henry Clay (who later served as Secretary of State under John Quincy Adams' administration) and requested that he represent the state as an Amicus Curiae in court.[41] The court granted Clay's request for further deliberation, stating that "Mr. Clay, as Amicus Curiae, requested further argument, alleging that the interest involved affected the rights and property of many settlers on the land."[42] However, the court emphasized that the state of Kentucky, as an Amicus Curiae, does not assist any party in the proceeding but merely presents its interests.

About 30 years later, in the landmark case of *Florida v. Georgia,* in 1854, the United States Supreme Court was required for the first time to consider the possibility of involving a third party in the proceedings despite the formal parties' objections. The state sought to present its position, but both parties were concerned about potential harm to their interests. However, the Chief Judge of the Supreme Court at the time, Judge Roger Taney, determined that if the United States government wished to present its position, "it is the familiar practice of the Court to hear the

[38] Campbell v. Swasey, 12 Ind. 57, 58 (1859).

[39] Schooner Exchange v. McFaddon, 11 U.S. (7 Cranch) 116 (1812).

[40] Green v. Biddle, 21 U.S. (8 Wheat.) 1, 17–18 (1823).

[41] For further reading on Clay's character, see Klotter (2018) and Clay (2023).

[42] Green v. Biddle, 21 U.S. (8 Wheat.) 1, 17–18 (1823).

Attorney General in suits between individuals when he suggests that the public interests are involved in the decision."[43]

There have been other cases in which states in the United States have sought to join ongoing proceedings as amici curiae when the outcome could potentially affect them, and their requests were granted. For example, in 1865, the U.S. Supreme Court presided over a conflict between a law of the state of California and the United States Constitution. The Attorney General of California filed an Amicus Curiae brief, stating that, in his view, the law was consistent with the Constitution.[44] Another interesting example is "*The Gray Jacket*" case of 1867. In this case, the Attorney General of the United States, Henry Stanbery, formally presented the position of the Department of Justice, but the Department of the Treasury sought to present a different position. In a relatively exceptional move, the Supreme Court allowed representatives of the Treasury Department to present their position, not as formal parties, but rather as amici curiae. This was justified on the grounds that they wanted to receive all relevant information on the matter to reach the best decision.[45]

Over time, courts gradually began to allow the participation of third parties as amici curiae even in private litigation, particularly vis-à-vis commercial companies seeking to protect their business interests. Examples of such companies included insurance, construction, transportation, energy companies, as well as stockholders in the alcoholic beverages industry. These companies, familiar with the legal system and aware of its imperfect regulation, employed various practices, with Amicus Curiae being one of them, to advance their interests in court. However, despite the increasing use of this practice, courts were somewhat hesitant in granting Amicus Curiae status, fearing that the inclusion of amici in the proceedings might harm the formal parties and compromise the dignity observed in the courts. An American court decision from 1911 established that the authority to participate as Amicus Curiae is a matter of grace, bestowed solely by the court's benevolence and for its purposes. It vividly stated: "These graces do not come through the consent of the other party. Similar to the mercy, they fall like the gentle and refreshing dew from the sky."[46]

The American body that has made use of the Amicus to the greatest extent has been the Department of Justice. During the tenure of Charles Bonaparte (the nephew of the French Emperor Napoleon I) as the Attorney General of the United States from 1906 to 1909, the Department of Justice extensively utilized the practice of Amicus Curiae to influence the courts.[47] This period marked a fertile time for the Amicus Curiae practice and its establishment in public litigation. These years witnessed

[43] Florida v. Georgia, 58 U.S. (17 How.) 478, 491 (1855).

[44] Steamship Co. v. Jolliffe, 69 U.S (2 Wall.) 450, 454 (1864).

[45] The Gray Jacket, 72 U.S. (5 Wall.) 370 (1867). This is a case in which the Supreme Court of the United States held that a ship that had been seized by the United States Navy during the American Civil War could not be forfeited to the United States government.

[46] *Ex parte* Brockman, 134 S.W. 977, 982 (Mo. 1911).

[47] For a detailed examination of Bona'arte's life, see Bishop (1922).

significant liberal developments that touched upon the rights of various interest groups, including African-Americans, women, minorities, and immigrants. To represent the government's positions on social issues in cases where the government was not a formal party, Bonaparte instructed state attorneys to participate in the proceedings as amici curiae and present relatively liberal positions. Krislov argues that the Department of Justice, during Bonaparte's tenure, granted the government's position as Amicus Curiae in numerous social cases, and this influenced the character of the United States.

The person who may have had the most significant influence on the establishment of Amicus Curiae in the American legal system was lawyer and judge Louis Brandeis.[48] In the landmark case of *Muller v. Oregon* in 1908,[49] Brandeis, who was then an attorney and participated in the case as an Amicus Curiae, utilized medical and social science research to prove that the long working hours for women harmed their health. He submitted a document to the court comprising over a hundred pages.[50] Only two pages were dedicated to legal arguments. The rest of the document presented sociological information that supported his contention that labor laws should be tailored to accommodate women workers. This case served as an early precedent for a practice that would later become highly popular in numerous courts worldwide: the presentation of social and cultural data using the Amicus Curiae practice.[51]

However, the use of this practice by non-governmental public organizations, particularly human rights organizations, has led to the most remarkable development and popularization of Amicus Curiae. The first documented case in which a human rights organization utilized the Amicus Curiae practice was a case involving the expulsion of the Asian population from New York in the early 1920s.[52] In this case, the Supreme Court was requested to approve the expulsion of a person of Chinese descent, and the New York Chinese Charitable and Benevolent Association sought to join the proceedings as an Amicus Curiae, arguing that the expulsion of Chinese-American citizens was discriminatory, and in contradiction to the American Constitution.

Throughout the twentieth century, the use of Amicus Curiae among rights organizations, such as women's organizations, immigrant organizations, environmental organizations, labor organizations, and religious organizations, increased persistently. Based on amicus briefs, it was determined, for example, that non-white citizens were entitled to vote in local elections,[53] and the United States

[48] For a general biography of Brandies, see Lief (1936) Brandeis. See also: Urofsky (1981).

[49] Muller v. Oregon, 208 U.S. 412 (1908).

[50] https://louisville.edu/law/library/special-collections/the-louis-d.-brandeis-collection/the-brandeis-brief-in-its-entirety.

[51] Johnson (1992). See also Yovel and Mertz (2004), p. 414. For a modern examination of using Amicus briefs in social sciences, see Horn et al. (2020), pp. 449–476.

[52] Ah How v. United States, 193 U.S. 65 (1904).

[53] Smith v. Allwright, 321 U.S. 649 (1944).

Supreme Court abolished racial segregation in schools based partially on the information presented by various amici curiae.[54] Similarly, in the famous *Miranda* case, which established that law enforcement authorities must inform suspects of their right to consult with an attorney and remain silent, numerous amicus briefs were submitted by non-governmental organizations.[55]

Throughout the twentieth century in the United States, rights organizations submitted thousands of amicus briefs to the courts in pivotal cases dealing with the right to abortion,[56] the right to death,[57] affirmative action,[58] freedom of expression,[59] and LGBT rights.[60] This extensive use by non-governmental rights organizations led to a shift in the traditional role of Amicus Curiae. As the flow of requests from non-governmental organizations to participate as amici curiae increased, Amicus Curiae ceased to be a neutral institution assisting the court in avoiding errors, recalling prior precedents, and clarifying the law (as it likely was in its early versions). It became an active participant and sometimes a sharp and vociferous advocate among the participants in the legal process. It became a third party that clearly supports the formal side that it advocates for, trying with all its might to secure victory for the side it supports. The amicus, in its classical sense (i.e., neutrality), has faded away. Krislov coined the term "from friendship to advocacy" and describes a continuous process in which the use of Amicus Curiae, previously in the hands of a neutral party, has passed into the hands of an interested party whose "friendship" lies with one of the formal sides. Either way, it is no longer a "true friend" of the court.[61]

To complete the picture, the historian Banner provides a contrasting perspective on the transformation of Amicus Curiae practice in the United States. He contends that Amicus Curiae was never a purely neutral entity that solely assisted the court. Even in the early nineteenth century, amici curiae with distinct interests sought to participate in legal proceedings to further their own agendas.[62] Additionally, Banner argues against the notion of a shift from friendship to advocacy, as both elements coexisted even during earlier periods. Instead, by the mid-nineteenth century, amici curiae with vested interests *outnumbered* the neutral ones. Banner attributes this increase in interest-driven amici curiae during the late nineteenth century to a change in the style of courtroom debate, transitioning from oral arguments to written submissions. As attorneys began presenting their arguments in writing, their physical

[54] Sweatt v. Painter, 339 U.S. 629 (1950).

[55] Miranda v. Arizona, 384 U.S. 436 (1966).

[56] Webster v. Reproductive Health Services, 74 Judicature 261, 262.

[57] Cruzan v. Dir., Mo. Dep't of Health, 497 U.S. 261 (1990).

[58] *Regents of the University of California v. Bakke*, 438 U.S. 265 (1978).

[59] Pac. Gas & Elec. Co. v. Pub. Utils. Comm'n of Cal., 475 U.S. 1 (1986).

[60] Romer v. Evans, 517 U.S. 620 (1996).

[61] Krislov (1963), pp. 694–721.

[62] Banner (2003), pp. 1790–1890.

presence in the courtroom diminished, along with the level of assistance they had previously offered to the court.

4.9 Summary

The Amicus Curiae practice is a significant phenomenon in public litigation in numerous courts worldwide. In recent years, the use of this practice for the promotion of interests has become increasingly popular among private individuals, professional guilds, commercial companies, rights organizations, and politicians. As mentioned above, its origins may be traced back to the Roman period, but a more plausible explanation links it to historical and intellectual developments within the common-law system of England that subsequently spread to other countries.

Examining historical landmarks in the evolution of the Amicus Curiae practice reveals an adaptable legal institution that takes on various forms according to societal and historical needs. The Amicus Curiae has fluctuated over time between substantive elements (legal principles determining what society is entitled to) and procedural aspects (general judicial management rules determining how society's entitlements can be enforced). The uses of Amicus Curiae, ranging from providing neutral advice and assistance to the court to safeguarding the dignity of the judiciary, blur the distinction between substance and procedure. While formally categorized as a procedural practice, Amicus Curiae transcends that designation, evolving into a popular social tool allowing societal groups to navigate the judicial system and influence their worlds.

The multifaceted societal use of this practice over the centuries and the adaptability of its mechanism are evidence of the inherent interconnectedness between substantive and procedural law and its mutual influence. The legal practice of Amicus Curiae, ostensibly belonging to the realm of procedure, has substantially shaped the historical trajectory of social rights in many societies. This brief historical overview demonstrates that it is not merely a technocratic tool in the administration of courts and legal practitioners but a substantive procedure that has contributed and continues to contribute to the advancement of people's rights. Superficially, Amicus Curiae appears to be a legal practice serving interest groups. However, a deeper historical examination reveals that it embodies profound processes rooted in the societal role of the law.

The renewed appearance of Amicus Curiae on the historical stage in its modern form reflects the revival of the perception of the legal process as a broad social phenomenon involving not only formal litigants but also other parties, including experts and professional advisors, as was customary in medieval justice and perhaps even earlier, in the Roman consilium.

4.10 First Part Summary

The Amicus Curiae is a legal institution by which a third party who is not formally involved in the ongoing legal process but has some interest in it may present his point of view to the court by submitting a brief. Sometimes, the amici will be allowed to present their arguments orally or actively participate in the proceedings, similar to the formal disputants. Generally, there is a difference, and sometimes a difference of substance, in the characteristics of the amicus between the countries and the international institutions that use it. Sometimes, there is a difference in the use of amici between different courts in the same region. De facto, the amicus has many faces, and on one side of the spectrum stands the "classic amicus," who helps the court without any personal interest. On the other side of the spectrum is the "modern amicus" (the lobbyist) who participates in the proceedings to advance his agenda in court.

The roles played by the amicus during history changed significantly according to the historical, legal, and social circumstances that prevailed in the judicial systems that adopted it. Therefore, one can find contradictions—in law and fact—between different amici. Another reason for the conceptual confusion is related to the fact that there are other legal institutions that are used to fulfill purposes similar to an amicus, headed by the "intervenor," who in many ways participates in the same category of third parties joining a legal proceeding, with the main difference being that the intervenor has a tangible interest in the case.

Despite the significant influence of amici on the court's decision-making processes, the practice of Amicus Curiae is not without criticism. It is argued that using an amicus causes the politicization of the court and turns it into an arena of clashes between political actors. Also, the participation of amici in ongoing proceedings sometimes "increases the volume" of the debate. It was also claimed that amici often promote anti-social and anti-liberal values. Indeed, various studies have shown that financial organizations, arms industries, and energy companies use amicus briefs most effectively to promote their (legitimate) goals in the courts.

In addition, it is argued against the amici that they often do not contribute to the court's work. In other words, "in general," they mostly repeat the things presented by the formal parties. This repetition of the parties' claims, even if it is from a different or broader point of view, wastes judicial time, which is considered the most valuable resource in the judicial system, and increases the costs of the procedure imposed on the formal litigants and the public as a whole.

There are several possible hypotheses about the reasons for the appearance of the amicus: a desire to consult with external expert consultants; community involvement in the judicial proceedings; dynamics of assistance and work relations between judges and lawyers; maintaining the dignity of the court against judicial errors; and finally, overcoming the lack of representation of additional interests other than the interests of the formal litigants which was the dominant approach in the common law.

Following the attempts of non-governmental organizations to influence the courts through the amicus, the amicus ceased to be a neutral institution that helps the court avoid mistakes or clarify the law objectively. The tone changed, and the amici became active participants and sometimes the most acrimonious participants in the legal process. The "friendship" in the classical sense—died out.

The uses made of amicus, beginning with providing neutral advice and assistance to the work of the courts and ending with preserving the court's honor, show that the amicus's practice obscures the binary distinction between substance and procedure. In principle, the amicus brief is merely a procedural legal practice. In practice, however, it is much more than that. Over the years, the Amicus Curiae has become a social tool that allows groups in society to influence their world and society.

References

Aalders HGJD (1986) Cassius Dio and the Greek world. Mnemosyne 39(3–4):282–304

Angell E (1967) The amicus curiae: American development of English institutions. Int Comp Law Quart 16:1017

Banner S (2003) The myth of the neutral amicus: American courts and their friends, 1790–1890. Const Comment 20:111

Barmann LF (1977) The lives of Roger casement. Thought: Fordham Univ Q 52(2):215–216

Beckwith ER, Sobernheim R (1948) Amicus Curiae--Minister of Justice. Fordham Law Rev 17:38

Bishop JB (1922) Charles Joseph Bonaparte: his life and public services. C. Scr'bner's Son, New York

Brooke R (1573) Le Graunde Abridgement

Chrysanthou CS (2020) Herodian and Cassius Dio: a study of Herodian's compositional devices. Greek Roman Byzantine Stud 60(4):621–651

Clay H (2023) The life and speeches of Henry Clay, vol I. BoD–Books on Demand

Cohen H (1929) A history of the English bar and attornatus to 1450, at 4, 12

Coke E (1644) Institutes of the Laws of England 29 (Brooke ed. 1779)

Collins PM Jr (2008) Friends of the Supreme Court: interest groups and judicial decision making

Covey FM Jr (1959) Amicus curiae: friend of the court. Depaul Law Rev 9:30

Crook J (1955) *Consilium Principis: Imperial Councils and Counsellors from Augustus to Diocletian* (Cambridge), p. 26

Dunn ME (2018) Bridging the great divide:(inn) formal communication between judges and lawyers. Judges J 57:16

Epstein Y (1982) Introduction to the commentary of the geniuses on purity (Jerusalem and Tel Aviv, [1984]), 48

Epstein's *"Choshen Mishpat"* on the *"Aruch Hashulchan"* (Warsaw 1884–1908) chapter 13, section 11

Farber S, Cohen Y (2023) Third parties intervention in Jewish law: new friends (amicus) in the rabbinical courts litigation. Jewish Law Annual 22:21–16

Hale M (1792) The history of the common law. James Moore, College-Green

Holdsworth W (1914) Early history of equity. Mich Law Rev. 13:293

Holmes OW (1991) The common law. Courier Corporation

Horn CL et al (2020) Shaping educational policy through the courts: the use of social science research in amicus briefs in fisher I. Educ Policy 34(3):449–476

Izarova I, Szloc-Nartows B (2019) Amicus curiae: origin, worldwide experience and suggestions for east European countries. Hungarian J Legal Stud 60:1. https://doi.org/10.1556/2052.2019.60103

Johnson JW (1992) Brandeis Brief. In: Hall K (ed) The Oxford companion to the supreme court of the United States. Oxford University Press, New York, pp 100–101
Jolowicz JA (2003) Adversarial and inquisitorial models of civil procedure. Int Comp Law Q 52(2): 281–295
Keeton GW (2004) Morgan, John Hartman (1876–1955). Oxford dictionary of national biography (online ed.). Oxford University Press, Oxford
Klotter JC (2018) Henry Clay: the man who would be president. Oxford University Press, Oxford
Krislov S (1963) The amicus curiae brief: from friendship to advocacy. Yale Law J 72:694–721
Laffan M (2009) Casement, Sir Roger David. dictionary of Irish biography
Langbein JH (1993) The historical origins of the privilege against self-incrimination at common law. Mich Law Rev 92:1047
Lief A (1936) Brandeis: the personal history of an American ideal. Stackpole Sons, Mechanicsburg
Lowman MK (1992) Comment, The litigating amicus curiae: when does the party begin after the friends leave? Am Univ Law Rev 41:1243, 1245
Macpherson W (1873) The practice of the judicial committee of her Majesty's most honorable privy council
Neilson G (1891) Trial by combat, vol 1. Macmillan
Newmyer RK (1970) Justice Joseph story on circuit and a neglected phase of American legal history. Am J Legal History 14(2):112–135
Newmyer RK (1985) Supreme Court Justice Joseph Story: Statesman of the Old Republic. The book examines Story's life and career, including his role as a statesman during the early years of the American Republic
Oleck HL (1951) Historical nature of equity jurisprudence. Fordham Law Rev 20:23
Parisi F (2002) Rent-seeking through litigation: adversarial and inquisitorial systems compared. Int Rev Law Econ 22(2):193–216
Pittman RC (1935) The colonial and constitutional history of the privilege against self-incrimination in America. Va Law Rev 21(7):763–789
Pound R (1907) Common law and legislation. Harv Law Rev 21:383
Smith AM (Sept. 2013) The history and evolution of Amicus Curiae in West Virginia, W. Va. Law., at 42, 44
Strier F (1992) What can the American adversary system learn from an inquisitional system of justice. Judicature 76:109
Sward EE (1988) Values, ideology, and the evolution of the adversary system. Ind Law J 64:301
Urofsky MI (1981) Louis D Brandeis and the progressive tradition
Yovel J, Mertz E (2004) The role of social science in legal decisions. In: Sarat A (ed) The Blackwell companion to law and society. Blackwell Publishing, Malden, p 414

Part II
The Phenomenon of the Amicus Curiae and the Rise of Third Parties in the Trial

Introduction

The first part of this book introduced the Amicus Curiae, describing its various possible origins and its evolution to the present day. The diverse uses of this practice in different judicial systems were presented, together with an analysis of the historical, social, and cultural influences that continue to shape the nature and quantity of amicus briefs submitted to courts at all levels. Based on the criteria mentioned above, this part will draw, map, and analyze one of the essential developments of the modern judicial procedure in recent decades, which the author calls the "amicus phenomenon." In so doing, this section aims to present the scope and contribution of the Amicus Curiae to modern law and the work of the courts today.

Discussions in this part will demonstrate how the amicus practice has become so common and significant in judicial systems worldwide, including in European countries, South American countries, African countries, and Asian countries. The far-reaching effects of the phenomenon will be exemplified by examining its influence on politicians, non-governmental organizations, lawyers, and other legal agents. The comparative information regarding the amicus phenomenon will allow an analysis and discussion of the causes of the formation of the phenomenon and its effect on the design of modern law and the work of modern judicial systems (This discussion will be held in the third part).

In general, the dynamics in most countries that have adopted the Amicus Curiae practice are similar. In the first stage, there is a principled objection that is usually based on broader rules, according to which there is no room to allow the addition of third parties in proceedings where they are not formal parties. In the second stage, this approach undergoes a change, often appearing to be some kind of "softening" tendency. This usually arises in the face of a series of issues in which the courts understand that the presence of third parties is appropriate and justified—mainly because the procedure may affect wider groups. In the third stage, the amicus practice is adopted. Sometimes formally and sometimes semi-formally, without a formal announcement of this. In the fourth stage, the amicus practice is established in the state or supra-state law in which it was absorbed. Initially, only a small number of amicus briefs are submitted, in a few select cases, in what can be described as a relatively small trickle.

In the fifth stage, there is an intensification in the use of Amicus Curiae, which is expressed in a variety of ways: an increase in issues in which amicus briefs are submitted to courts, an increase in the types of judicial courts to which the brief are submitted; an increase in the number of briefs submitted in "mega cases;" and an increase in types of entities that use amicus as a way to influence court rulings. Other developments, such as the opening of many clinics around the world that train students to submit brief as amici on diverse topics, also reflect the expansion of the amicus phenomenon. This has also been accompanied by an increasing media coverage of briefs submitted by amici, leading to greater public awareness of these activities. Finally, the growth of the phenomenon is also reflected in the planning and building courtrooms with unique seating for amici, even though they are not formal parties to the proceedings.

The structure of this part of the book will be as follows: First, the author will outline and analyze the arrangements in place in some leading countries in the (Anglo-American) common law system in which Amicus Curiae is used, primarily the United States, Canada, Australia, England, South Africa, Hong Kong, and Singapore. In the second chapter within this section, the author will examine the reception of Amicus Curiae in international law, particularly in international judicial systems and international dispute settlement institutions. The chapter will review the European Court of Human Rights, the International Court of Justice in The Hague, the World Trade Organization, and more.

In the third chapter of this section, the author will describe the development of the amicus phenomenon in civil law within the continental legal system that includes countries in Latin America (such as Brazil, Argentina, and Peru), Africa (Rwanda, Ethiopia, and Namibia), Asia (such as South Korea, Thailand) and Europe (such as Spain, Austria, and the Czech Republic). The reason for prioritizing the description of developments in international law over that of continental law, as will be explained in detail later, is that the development of the amicus phenomenon in the continental legal system is based on, and is primarily influenced by, the development of the amicus in international law. As mentioned, certain countries have a long and well-established judicial tradition regarding including third parties in ongoing proceedings. In these countries, the information is more accessible, broader, and more comprehensive, so all the criteria (or the absolute majority) can be examined for them. On the other hand, the database is more limited concerning other countries, especially those in the civil law system.

Chapter 5
The Common Law

5.1 United States

The significant and dramatic transformation of the Amicus Curiae in terms of the extent of its implementation and the nature of the amici curiae operating within the legal arena began in the United States, starting in the 1960s and is known as: "From Friendship to Advocacy." This process, which later spread to many other countries—both those belonging to common law and those operating continental style civil law, expresses the idea that the amici ceased to be neutral and became parties that openly and unilaterally support a formal litigant involved in the legal proceedings.[1]

In the mid-twentieth century, Amicus Curiae in the United States was a common legal procedure within judicial systems including both state and federal courts.[2] The American amicus is a form of lobbyist concerned with persuading the court to rule according to the worldview of the amicus ("the lobbying amicus").[3]

The amici curiae that appear in the various United States courts influence the judge's decision-making process. Although the amici are "secondary" players to the original litigants, some of the most critical judgments in the United States have been decided on the basis of information presented exclusively by amici curiae. For

[1] Krislov (1963), p. 697.

[2] As known, a court at the lowest federal level is called: "The District Court of the United States." In total, there are 94 district courts. District courts are divided on a regional basis and each state has one or more federal judicial districts. A court in the Second Federal Circuit, which is the buffer between the district courts and the Supreme Court, is the "United States Court of Appeals." There are a total of 12 appeals courts. In addition, there are seven federal courts that are limited to a certain subject, ruling over the entire United States. For example, "United States Tax Court" or "United States Court of International Trade." https://web.archive.org/web/20071201145552/http://www.uscourts.gov/index.html.

[3] Reagan and Vasaly (2004), pp. 23–30.

S. Farber, *The Amicus Curiae Phenomenon*, Ius Gentium: Comparative Perspectives on Law and Justice 119, https://doi.org/10.1007/978-3-031-67225-5_5

example, in a case dealing with the rules of "habeas corpus," the Supreme Court found its decision almost exclusively on the amici's arguments.[4]

In other significant cases in the history of the United States, amicus briefs submitted by various organizations and interest groups were an essential factor in shaping the ruling. These rulings have profoundly influenced the image of the United States, and they include:[5] the right to abortion,[6] the right to die,[7] affirmative action,[8] freedom of speech,[9] climate change,[10] electioneering,[11] the right to bear arms,[12] protection against discrimination because of sexual or gender identity,[13] or the right to artificial abortion.[14] These critical cases, and thousands of others, express the ability of amicus as a judicial practice to influence the courts' decision-making processes.

Following the developments in the Amicus Curiae phenomenon in the United States and other countries that use the common law, there are three main categories of amici. The first group is the representative group of the state branches (the public sector): the legal counsel for the government and the attorney general, the legal counsel for the states, the legal counsel for the cities and Municipal authorities throughout the United States, and statutory government authorities (such as the Tax Authority, the Immigration Authority, and the Anti-Drug Authority). Generally, this group enjoys an "open door" from the courts when its representatives wish to voice their position as amici.[15]

The second group includes private organizations that belong mainly to the business sector, as well as professional organizations, such as the Bar Association or the Accountants' Association, as well as financial organizations and commercial associations, among others. The third group ("the third sector") includes diverse interest groups. This third sector mainly contains public benefit associations, endowments organizations, charities, cooperative societies, and international

---

[4]Teague v. Lane, 489 U.S. 288 (1989); In the Mapp v. Ohio, 367 U.S. 643, 646 n.3 (1961), the Court interpreted the Constitution based on a brief submitted to it by the American Human Rights Association.

[5]See for example: Huang and Roemheld (2016) https://arxiv.org/pdf/1606.04672.

[6]Webster v. Reproductive Health Services, 74 Judicature 261, 262. Thomas E. Dobbs, State Health Officer of the Mississippi Department of Health, et al. v. Jackson Women's Health Organization, et al 2022.

[7]Cruzan v. Dir., Mo. Dep't of Health, 497 U.S. 261 (1990).

[8]*Regents of the University of California v. Bakke*, 438 U.S. 265 (1978).

[9]Pac. Gas & Elec. Co. v. Pub. Utils. Comm'n of Cal., 475 U.S. 1 (1986).

[10]**Massachusetts v. Environmental Protection Agency,** 549 U.S. 497 (2007).

[11]**Citizens United v. Federal Election Commission**, 558 U.S. 310 (2010).

[12]R.G. & G.R. Harris Funeral Homes, Inc., Petitioner, v. Equal Employment Opportunity Commission and Aimee Stephens, Sup. Ct. R. 18-107 (2019); Adams v. Sch. Bd. of St. John's County, 318 F. Supp. 3d 1293 (M.D. Fla. 2018).

[13]Bostock v. Clayton Cty., 140 S. Ct. 1731 (2020).

[14]Romer v. Evans, 517 U.S. 620 (1996).

[15]O'Connor (1982), p. 256.

organizations.[16] These groups often defend a religious, racial, gender, or ethnic minority, such as the American Association for Human Rights, organizations promoting African-American rights, LGBT organizations, and women's organizations. As will be described, groups that belong to the third category are the ones who brought about the significant change in the judicial climate regarding Amicus Curiae in the United States and around the world, with the contribution of these groups to shaping modern law through amicus being highly significant.[17]

The arrangements regarding Amicus Curiae were first formally anchored in the rules of the Supreme Court in 1937. This legislation was a formal anchoring of rules and procedures regarding the amicus that had been used in the Supreme Court since the appearance of the amicus for the first time officially in 1823. Since then, many amendments were made to these rules at the court's initiative, but the core of the settlement remained as it was: an amicus brief that brings to the court's attention information that the original parties did not present will be welcomed. On the other hand, a brief that does not serve this purpose is undesirable as it burdens the court.[18] The rules from 1937 stated that it is necessary to receive the consent of the formal parties and the court's approval to submit an amicus brief. In 1949, the rules were amended so that amici were allowed to file a brief with the court's approval even without the consent of the formal parties.[19] However, a requirement was added that the request to submit the brief be submitted within a reasonable period before the decision is issued.

In addition, it was determined that the request to submit the brief would be separate from the brief itself.[20] The addition of this rule indicates the dissatisfaction of the courts with the practice that prevailed before, in which the request to join as an amicus and the brief itself were bound together. This could have influenced the decision to add the applicant as an amicus. In 1954, a limit was added to the number of pages of the brief. In the United States Supreme Court, amicus briefs are limited to approximately 9000 words, while formal parties are limited to 15,000 words.[21]

It is interesting to note that the limitation regarding the length of the brief has been "adopted" by various courts worldwide. For example, it is customary in the Supreme Court of Canada and in international arbitrations, such as ICSID, that the brief length should be at most twenty pages.[22] In other states within the United States (such as

[16] DiMaggio and Anheier (1990), pp. 137–159.

[17] See Wasby (1995), pp. 219–235; George and Epstein (1991), p. 314; Howard (1988), p. 241; Pfeffer (1981), p. 83; See also Collins (2008).

[18] Sup. Ct. R. 37.1.

[19] Amendment of Rules, 338 U.S. 959, 959–60 (1949).

[20] Ibid.

[21] Sup. Ct. R. 33.1(g).

[22] Rules of Procedure for Arbitration Proceedings (Arbitration Rules), Rule 37. Although according to the rules, the length of the brief cannot exceed twenty pages, the courts allow, if they find reason for it, an exception to this. Murray (1994), p. 256.

Kentucky or Missouri), the length allowed for amici is fifteen pages.[23] In contrast, other states allow more extraordinary lengths. For example, in Maine, an amicus brief's maximum length is fifty pages.[24] In Wyoming, the entire length is limited to thirty-five pages.[25] The federal courts of appeals have held as a matter of principle that the length of the brief shall not exceed half the length permitted to the formal parties.[26] Elsewhere, the limit is by the number of words. For example, the Court of Appeals in the State of New York determined that the limit is 7,000 words (about half of the scope allowed for formal litigants).[27] Another established rule is that the time for the oral argument of an amicus, if such leave is granted, shall be detracted from the time allotted for the argument of the formal party supported by the amicus.[28]

In 1967, the Rules of the Court were reorganized and worded more clearly.[29] In 1990, after over 80 briefs were filed by dozens of amici in a case dealing with the right to have an abortion (the *Webster* case),[30] a further revision of the rules arose. The *Webster* case is one of the high points of the participation of non-governmental public organizations in the decision-making process of the Supreme Court. It raised questions among various public organizations related to litigation tactics, where one of the main questions in this context is "What is the correct strategy - to submit as many individual briefs as possible or to organize coalitions of large organizations?"[31] The court amended rule 37 while emphasizing that only briefs that contain

[23] Ky. R. Civ. P. 76.12; Miss. R. App. P. 29(b).

[24] Me. R. App.I 9(e)(1).

[25] WYO. R. APP. P. 7.12(d). In the case of City of Fairmont v. Pitrolo Pontiac-Cadillac Co., 308 S. E.2d 527, 539–40 (W. Va. 1983), the judge criticized the length of the amici briefs and noted that one of the briefs was "certified by the Clerk of Court as weighing one and three-eighth pounds" See. Smith (2013), p. 42, 44x.

[26] FED. R. APP. P. 29(d). Some countries have also adopted this formula (the length of the amicus brief is about half the length allowed for the formal parties). This is the case, for example, in Nebraska and Iowa. IOWA R. APP. P. 6.906(3); NEV. R. APP.P. 29(e).

[27] N.Y. Ct. App. R. 500.11. See also, Joel (2016), http://www.newyorklawjournal.com/id=1202760161078.

[28] For an interesting analysis of the oral argument aspect see: Gleason and Ivy (2021), pp. 416–433. [They argue that gender stereotypes can influence how amicus briefs are perceived by the Supreme Court, and that narratives can be used to overcome these stereotypes].

[29] Sup. Ct. R. 42, 388 U.S. 931, 973–75 (1967).

[30] Behuniak-Long (1991), pp. 261–262.

The dozens of memoranda that were submitted represented over 420 different organizations from across the spectrum of political opinion in the United States, which represented a total of 5469 interest groups and individuals: liberal interest groups, African-American interest groups, the Civil Rights Association, organizations that specialize in medical ethics, the umbrella organization of churches in the United States, women's organizations, the American Medical Association, the American Association of Deans of Medical Schools and educational organizations.

[31] Behuniak-Long (1991), pp. 261–262. Behuniak-Long argues that the amicus briefs filed in Webster were largely ineffective in influencing the Court's decision. Behuniak-Long concludes by arguing that the amicus briefs filed in Webster are a reminder of the limitations of Amicus Curiae briefs.

new and relevant information concerning the information presented by the original parties will be accepted. In contrast, a brief that does not comply with this rule "simply burdens the staff and is not favored."[32]

In 1997, the rules of the courts on the Amicus Curiae issue were amended once more, and an obligation was imposed on amici to disclose the relationship between them and the formal parties as well as to disclose the identity of those entities that participated in financing the preparation of the brief. In addition, the amici were required to indicate whether they were financially supported by a formal party to the proceedings and if a formal party assisted in writing the brief.[33] The Supreme Court did not specify why it tightened its rules and demanded increased disclosure obligations from potential amici. The author estimates these requirements originate from the judges' desire to read and evaluate the brief correctly. An independent brief written by an anonymous person is nothing like a brief written with funding, assistance, or "commissioned" by one of the official litigants.[34] Another possible explanation for the due disclosure rules imposed by the court is the fear that formal litigants will continue their arguments through their amici curiae.

In cases where there is a formal or ethical impediment, a formal party can contact an Amicus Curiae and request him to submit a brief including those arguments from which the arguments he is either prevented from arguing or does not wish to be present himself to the court. Another example of continuing arguments through an amicus is when the court limits the pleadings of formal parties to several pages. In such cases, these parties may turn to amici to continue their line of argument within the court's guidelines. Sometimes, these are "unpleasant" arguments that the formal party prefers that another party present to the court so that if the matter does not go well, any consequences will not fall on his shoulders but on those of the amicus.

Another explanation for tightening the rules is that the parties may manipulate and influence the courts' decision-making by inviting amici. The court may get the wrong impression that if many public organizations support a particular litigant, it also means that public opinion supports that side. However, in the meantime, these amici were "invited" to submit a brief to the proceedings, or the inviting party actually wrote the amicus brief, and the amici were only instructed to submit the brief to generate public support for this position. That is, if it were not for the "due disclosure" rules, it could be thought that there was widespread political or public support for a particular litigant, while this was not necessarily the case.[35]

---

[32] Sup. Ct. R. 37.1, 493 U.S. 1099, 1145–47 (1989).

[33] Sup. Ct. R. 37.6, 519 U.S. 1159 (1997).

[34] For more, see Rustad and Koenig (1993), pp. 157–158.

[35] For due diligence rules in various states, see for example ARIZ. R. CIV. APP. P. 16, cmt.; CAL. R. CT. 8.520(f)(4); CONN. R. APP. P. 67-7; ID. APP. R. 8; MD. R. 8-511(b); MINN. R. CIV. APP. P. 129.01; N.D. R. APP. P. 29(c); TEX. R. APP. P. 11; W. VA. R. IP. P. 30(e).

Rule 37 of the Supreme Court Rules entitled "Brief for an Amicus Curiae" determines the arrangements for receiving amicus briefs.[36] This arrangement is fundamental because it has been copied by many countries worldwide (for example, Canada, India, South Africa, and several international institutions led by the World Trade Organization). Section 5.1 of the rule establishes the guiding principle that only briefs that present new and relevant information that the original parties did not present will be considered briefs that contribute to the court. Section 5.2 establishes the following individual arrangements: the applicant to be Amicus Curiae must obtain the consent of the formal parties or the consent of the court;[37] if the amicus wishes to assist the appellant or the petitioner, he must submit his brief within thirty days from the date of submission of the petition to the House the trial; the amicus must make sure that the attorneys of all the parties involved in the proceedings are aware that he intends to submit a brief at least ten days before the date on which he must submit the brief to the court; the amicus must furthermore indicate in his request whether the formal parties have agreed to his request; and finally the amicus must indicate which formal side of the procedure he supports.

In brief, the third section states that a request for oral arguments by Amicus Curiae will be submitted with the consent of the parties or if the court grants this right, but in any case, the request will be submitted, at the latest, within seven days of the submission of the brief. The fourth section sets out a list of entities that do not need the consent of the parties or the consent of the court to file a brief: the Attorney General of the United States; a representative of a government authority; an Attorney General of a state, territory, county, city, or similar legal entity. Section 5.5 states that the application must be submitted per strict procedural instructions, such as the length of the application must not exceed 1500 words; The application shall include a detailed explanation of the applicant's interests and the relevance of the brief to the hearing in court. Section 5.6 states that the amicus must indicate whether one of the parties to the formal procedure was a participant in drafting the brief or whether the brief was drawn up with his assistance. Also, the amicus must indicate whether one of the formal parties funded the research cited in the brief or contributed to the establishment of research on which the brief is based.

Despite the rules that put limitations on amici joining proceedings and require that the amicus briefs must be "recent and relevant," over the past three decades, the United States Supreme Court has taken a liberal approach to the submission requests from amici, allowing amici to join hearings almost automatically. For example, the Supreme Court under former President Rehnquist denied only a few amici requests

[36] SUP. CT. R. 37.1. The guiding principle states: "An Amicus Curiae brief that brings to the attention of the court relevant matter not already brought to its attention by the parties may be of considerable help to the Court. An Amicus Curiae brief that does not serve this purpose burdens the court, and its filing is not favored."

[37] That is, in the United States a party can be Amicus Curiae if both formal parties have agreed to it. In this case, a judicial decision of the court is not required. On the other hand, in other courts such as the Supreme Court of Canada, the court's consent is required in any case, even if both formal parties agreed to the request to join.

to file a brief in his entire tenure. In 1990, for instance, he denied only one request out of 115 requests to join proceedings in that year.[38] Although, in principle, an organization that is not a governmental authority must receive the consent of both parties to participate as an amicus,[39] in almost all cases, amici do join the proceedings. Even if the parties' consent for the involvement of an Amicus Curiae was not given, the potential amicus might apply to the court, which usually approves the request.[40] Court rulings cite amici briefs, often from interest groups or activists, who applied to the court to submit their briefs, even when the formal parties refused their requests to be involved.[41]

As a result of the Supreme Court's liberal approach towards the desire of third parties to express their position in ongoing proceedings, a kind of practice has arisen whereby the formal litigants tend not to refuse amici requests, even if the information presented by them is against their interests. Among litigators in the Supreme Court, it is a well-known fact that opposing an amicus request, even if his interest is against the party's interest, means that the amicus will himself apply to the court, and the court will probably approve. These appeals by amici to the court cause a burden to the courts and take up valuable judicial time, so the formal litigants fear that if they resist the requests of third parties to submit a brief as amici, they may be perceived as not protecting the court's time. Thus, there is a kind of informal understanding according to which the formal parties do not oppose, except in exceptional cases, amici who support the opposing side out of consideration of the overall benefit of the procedure ("he will not oppose my amici and I will not oppose his amici") and so all amici curiae who wish to present their position can do so.

In 2023, the U.S. Supreme Court instituted several notable revisions to its rules governing amicus curiae participation. Firstly, as stated in the first paragraph of the letter from the Supreme Court Clerk, the Court eliminated the requirement for amici curiae to obtain consent from the parties before filing a brief.[42] This change streamlined the amicus process and fostered a more diverse range of perspectives before the Court. Secondly, while still mandating hard copies, the Court now also requires electronic submission of amicus briefs through its e-filing system,

---

[38] Epstein (1993), p. 650. Epstein found that interest groups were more likely to file amicus briefs in cases that were ideologically salient, that involved complex legal issues, or that had the potential to affect a large number of people.

[39] Sup. Ct. R. 37.3(a).

[40] George and Epstein (1991), pp. 314. Between 1969–1981, the Supreme Court refused to accept amicus briefs in less than 11 percent of the cases it heard.

[41] See also Caldeira and Wright (1990), p. 782; Songer and Sheeham (1993), p. 339. The article explores various factors that may contribute to interest group success in the Court, such as the credibility and expertise of the amici, the alignment of their interests with those of the Court, and the stage at which the amicus briefs are filed.

[42] Rules 37.2, 37.3.

facilitating efficient management and public access to case documents.[43] Thirdly, word limits were imposed, with amicus briefs at the petition stage restricted to 6000 words,[44] and at the merits stage, 9000 words for governmental entities and 8000 words for other amici.[45] Fourthly, as per the Clerk's fourth paragraph, deadlines for filing were clarified as 30–60 days after the supported party's filing at the petition stage and 7 days after the merits stage.[46] Collectively, these revisions aimed to enhance efficiency, accessibility, and the value of amicus participation in Supreme Court proceedings.[47]

5.1.1 Regulation of the Amicus in the Federal Courts

The arrangement in the federal courts regarding joining amici curiae is similar to the Supreme Court protocol, with a difference.[48] Rule 29 of the Federal Rules of Appellate Procedure provides, in essence, the following arrangement: First, the Attorney General of the United States, a representative of one of the authorities of the United States, or the Attorney General of a state may submit a brief as amicus as well without the consent of the parties or the consent of the court. On the other hand, any other amicus must receive the court's permission.[49] Third, the amicus must perform due diligence: he must submit his identity, his interest in the case, and the legal basis for his request. Fourth, there are restrictions on the brief length, date, and manner of submission. Fifth, the amicus may argue orally if he has received the court's permission.[50]

---

[43] Rules 33.1(f), 29.7; Supreme Court of the United States Clerk. (2023, June 15). Letter regarding changes to Supreme Court amicus curiae rules effective 2023 [Letter]. Supreme Court of the United States [from now: "Clerk's letter"], para. 2.

[44] Rule 33.1(g)(x); Clerk's letter, para. 3.

[45] Rules 33.1(g)(xi)-(xiv); Clerk's letter, para. 3.

[46] Rules 37.2, 37.3.

[47] Clerk's letter, para. 4.

[48] FED. R. APP. P. 29. Smallman (1999). For more, see Garcia (2008).

[49] See: https://cafc.uscourts.gov/wp-content/uploads/RulesProceduresAndForms/FederalCircuitRules/FederalCircuitRulesofPractice.pdf; for a discussion regarding possible changes in federal courts following the changes in the supreme courts see also: https://www.ohioappeals.com/2023/02/articles/trending/consent-requirements-for-amicus-briefs/.

[50] Once the brief is filed, the amicus' formal role is over, and the brief cannot be amended or filed again. Stern et al. (2002). For more on the subject of the amicus in the federal courts, see Harrington (2005). Case W. Rsrv. L. Rev. 667. FED. R. CIV. P. 11(b)(1) states: "[the paper presented to the court] is not being presented for any improper purpose, such as to harass, cause unnecessary delay, or needlessly increase the cost of litigation."

5.1.2 Regulation of Amicus Curiae in the States Within the United States

In all states in the United States, there is the possibility of joining third parties as amici curiae. The rules in most states are similar to the guiding rules of the Supreme Court or the rules of the federal courts of appeals.[51] At the same time, there is a significant difference between the various states related to the judicial conduct of the State Supreme Court, how the state judges perceive the role of the amicus, and the concerns arising from its excessive use.[52] This is the case, for example, in Alaska, Arizona, Iowa, Maine, Missouri, and Nebraska.[53]

On the other hand, some states allow the submission of an amicus brief only after the court's approval, even if the parties' consent has been obtained (such as California, Colorado, Delaware, Massachusetts, and Tennessee).[54] In some states (Texas, Georgia, and Pennsylvania), an amicus brief can be submitted even without the party's consent or the court's approval. However, the courts can reject amici briefs according to their discretion.[55] Regardless of these or other rules, all state courts have the authority to appoint themselves amici according to their discretion and the circumstances of the case.[56]

In general, one of the most notable changes in the judicial procedure in the United States in the twentieth century is related to the presence of the amici.[57] In the first half of the twentieth century, almost no amici briefs were submitted to the Supreme Court, even though it was possible under the court's ruling as early as 1823 and certainly under the Supreme Court's rules from 1939.[58] Between 1920 and 1966, amicus briefs were submitted in less than ten percent of the cases heard in the

[51] See, for example, ALA. R. APP. p. 29; ALASKA R. APP. P. 212(9); COLO. APP. R. 29; Me.I APP. P. 9 (e)(1); MASS. R. APP. P. 17; OHIO APP. R. 17; R.I. SUP. CT. R. 16(h); S.C. APP. CT. R. 213.

[52] For example, in Mississippi and Louisiana there are additional criteria that applicants to be amici must meet. Such as: a statement about the type of interest they intend to present (private or public); and that if they had not joined as amici, their legitimate interests might be harmed. See MISS. R. APP. p. 29; LA. SUP. CT. R. 7.

[53] See ALASKA R. APP. P. 212(A)(9); ARIZ. R. CIV. APP. P. 16(A); IOWA R. APP. P. 6.906(1); I. R. APP. P. 9(e)(1); Mo. SUP. CT. R. 84.05(f); NEV. R. APP. P. 29(a).

[54] See CAL. R. CT. 8.520(f); COLO. APP. R. 29; DEL. SUP. CT. R. 28(a); MASS. R. APP. P. 17; TENN. R. APP. P. 31(a).

[55] Ga. Sup. Ct. R. 23; Pa. R. App. P. 531(a); Tex. R. App. P. 11.

[56] Franze and Anderson (2015), p. 397.

[57] One of the main empirical studies on the subject is Kearney and Merrill (2000). Alongside this, there are many empirical studies in the field that have investigated various issues in connection with Amicus Curiae. See for example Bradley and Gardner (1985); Songer and Sheeham (1993); Deen et al. (2003); Epstein et al. (1994); Laroche (2009).

[58] Sup. Ct. R. 28, 37.

Supreme Court.[59] This trend reversed beginning in the 1970s and 1980s, and the rate of presence of amici in the House of The Supreme Court has grown significantly every decade. Between 1975–1966, 54 percent of the cases heard in the Supreme Court had amicus briefs filed. Between 1975–1985, 73 percent of the cases heard in the Supreme Court had amicus briefs filed. Between 1985 and 1995, about 85 percent of the cases discussed in the court were accompanied by amicus briefs. Between 2011–2014, amici joined in 96 percent of all cases discussed in the Supreme Court.[60]

Between 2014 and 2015, in approximately 98 percent of all cases discussed in court, amici curiae joined (in fact, only one case discussed in the Supreme Court was not joined by amici).[61] Between 2015 and 2016, amici joined approximately 92 percent of all the cases discussed in court. In total, between the years 2015–2016, about 863 amicus briefs were submitted to the court, which is an average of about 13 amici briefs in each case.[62] This is an increase of over 800 percent since the 1950s and about 95 percent since 1995. Between 2019–2020, about 97% percent of all cases discussed in court were joined by amici.[63]

The number of briefs submitted in "mega cases" has also increased significantly in recent decades. While between 1946 and 1955, only three cases discussed in the United States Supreme Court had ten amici curiae briefs submitted, between 1986 and 1995, over 120 cases discussed in the court contained at least ten amici briefs in each case. In addition, between 1985 and 1995, more than twenty briefs were submitted in more than twenty cases. For example, in a case that dealt with equal rights in connection with marriage in 2013, 156 briefs from different amici were submitted.[64] In the ruling that discussed health care reform in the United States, hundreds of various interest groups united and submitted 136 amici briefs to the Supreme Court.[65]

---

[59] One of the pioneering studies conducted in the United States was by Nathan Hakman. Hakman noted that, beginning in the middle of the twentieth century, the participation of amici curiae in the Supreme Court increased significantly. However, Hakman noted that, despite the increase in the rate of participation of non-governmental organizations in the judicial system. Their influence on the Supreme Court was negligible and was probably created due to the "folklore of various theories in political science." He concluded his words and claimed that organized interest groups "appear to play a relatively minor role in Supreme Court decision-making." Hakman (1966), p. 50.

[60] Kearney and Merrill (2000), p. 754. From the middle of the twentieth century to the end of the century, about half of the cases heard in the Supreme Court included amicus briefs.

[61] Franze and Anderson (2015).

[62] Franze and Anderson (2016). 2010–2011 (717 amicus briefs; 9 amici in each proceeding), 2011–2012 (715 amici briefs, 10 amici in each proceeding), 2012–2013 (1003 amici briefs, 14 in each proceeding), 2013–2014 (818 amici briefs, 12 amici in each proceeding), 2014–2015 (790 amici briefs, 12 amici in each proceeding). 2015–2016 (863 amici briefs, 13 amici in each proceeding). The distribution of the files is as follows: 783 memoranda of non-governmental organizations, 32 memoranda of the US government, 48 memoranda of the states.

[63] Franze and Anderson (2020).

[64] United States v. Windsor, 133 S.Ct. 2675 (2013).

[65] Nat'l Fed'n of Indep. Bus. v. Sebelius, 132 S. Ct. 2566 (2012). In this case, the Supreme Court cited numerous memos including memos that described the history of health care reforms.

Similarly, in a case dealing with same-sex marriage in 2015, 147 briefs were submitted representing thousands of non-governmental organizations and various interest groups (women's organizations, religious organizations, etc.).[66] In a case dealing with affirmative action in university admissions in 2016, 85 requests were submitted by amici curiae to express their position.[67] Furthermore, in the matter that dealt with tightening conditions for abortion in 2016, 82 groups of amici submitted briefs to the Supreme Court.[68] In a case dealing with the counting of votes in the United States elections in 2000, the court in the state of Florida ordered a recount of the votes. The Bush campaign appealed the recount order to the Supreme Court, arguing that it violated the Equal Protection Clause of the Fourteenth Amendment. In this case, 100 Amicus Curiae briefs were submitted, representing various interests.[69]

In recent years, the average number of briefs submitted to the Supreme Court has been about five hundred each year, containing thousands of pages.[70] From the middle of the twentieth century until today, over 25,000 amicus briefs have been submitted in over 5000 cases heard by the Supreme Court.[71] A cross-sectional examination of the last fifty years shows an increase of over 800 percent in the number of amici in the Supreme Court. The percentage of participation of amici in Supreme Court cases is increasing every year, and in the eyes of attorneys specializing in public litigation in the Supreme Court—"the peak is still ahead of us." It is likely that in the coming years, every case in the United States Supreme Court, without exception, will be joined by dozens of amici curiae.[72]

In terms of the use of Amici Curiae brief by the courts, it appears that in about a third of the cases discussed from the mid-twentieth century to the 2000s, the court referred, mentioned, or referred in some way to the information presented to it through one of the brief submitted.[73] This phenomenon increased significantly,

[66] Obergefell v. Hodges, 576 U.S. 644. (2015).

[67] The Fisher case, *supra* notes 22 and 38. For more, see Larsen & Devins, *supra* note 35.

[68] Whole Woman's Health v. Hellerstedt, 136 S. Ct. 2292 (2016). See also Adam Liptak, Justices Overturn Texas Abortion Limits, N.Y. Times, June 28, 2016, at A1.

[69] Bush v. Gore, 531 U.S. 98 (2000).

[70] Kearney and Merrill (2000), p. 754.

[71] Collins (2008), p. 48.

[72] An interview conducted with attorney Franze of the Arnold & Porter law firm. Mark (2013), p. 16.

[73] In a study conducted in relation to the years 2012–2013, it was found that Supreme Court judges mention or quote memos of interest groups with a fairly high frequency. For example, out of 16 rulings written by Judge Sotomayor, she cited information from an amicus brief 11 times explicitly (69 percent of her rulings). Judge Ginsburg cited amicus briefs in 8 out of 16 rulings she wrote (50 percent of her rulings). The president of the court, Judge Roberts, cited memos in 4 out of 15 judgments he wrote (about 35 percent of his judgments). Even judges who are perceived as conservative such as Alito and Scalia cited memos in at least 3 out of about 23 judgments they wrote (about 13 percent). Name. In general, between the years 2010-2016, Judge Ginzoberg, in 45 percent of the rulings she wrote, referred to the information presented to her by amici. Judge Kennedy used information presented to him by amici in 42 percent of hi– rulings (Sutmayor – 0 percent; Roberts – 40 percent; Breyer – 39 percent; Kagan – 35 percent; Alito – 27 percent; Scalia – 24 percent; Thomas – 22 percentage).

and in recent years, the court cited or mentioned an amicus brief in more than half of the cases.[74] For example, in the years 2015–2016, in about 54 percent of the judgments given in the American Supreme Court, there was a reference to the information presented by amici.[75] This trend of increasing reliance on amicus briefs is consistent with Hazelton and Hinkle's analysis, which found that as the number of amicus briefs has proliferated over recent decades, their impact on shaping the Court's opinions has intensified. Specifically, they demonstrate that both individually and in the aggregate, the side whose amicus briefs contain more shared citations and language exerts greater influence over the content of majority opinions.[76] There was then a slight rise with a reference to the information presented by amici made in about 57 percent of the judgments given in the American Supreme Court in the years 2017–2018.[77] This rose to 59 percent of the judgments given in the American Supreme Court in the following year.[78] Then, in the years 2020–2021, there was a more significant rise to about 65 percent of the judgments given in the American Supreme Court, including a reference to the information presented by amici.[79]

Going back to the start of the last decade, between 2010 and 2016, in about fifty percent of the cases in which a verdict was given, the court mentioned, cited, or referred to the information presented by amici.[80] In general, between 2010 and 2016, Judge Ginzberg referred to the information presented to her by amici curiae in 45 percent of her rulings. Judge Kennedy used the information presented to him by amici in 42 percent of his rulings. (The rest of the justices: Sotomayor—40 percent; Roberts—40 percent; Breyer—39 percent; Kagan—35 percent; Alito—27 percent; Scalia—24 percent; Thomas—22 percent).[81]

Data collected about the Supreme Court Judges' use of amicus briefs show that they are more likely to quote from a brief submitted by state bodies led by the United States Attorney General than from those submitted by public, non-governmental organizations.[82]

These data support the hypothesis that the briefs submitted to them influenced the courts in some way, although it is impossible to determine precisely to what extent.

---

[74] Franze and Anderson (2015). In addition to the increasing reliance o' the state attorney's memoranda, court judges tend to cite memoranda that deal with the legal background of the legislation before them, often by state prosecutors who present to them the legislative history of the statute that is being attacked in the House the trial.

[75] Franze and Anderson, Unusual Term (2016).

[76] Hazelton and Hinkle (2022).

[77] Franze and Anderson (2018), pp. 547–563.

[78] https://www.scotusblog.com/statistics/.

[79] Franze and Anderson (2020).

[80] Collins et al. (2015), p. 936.

[81] Franze and Anderson (2016).

[82] Sometimes referred to as "green memos" in light of the fact that they are submitted in a green cover, as opposed to memos submitted by state bodies. https://www.supremecourt.gov/casehand/AmicusGuide2019.pdf.

However, its citation or mention shows that the court took the brief into account in some way among its other considerations.

Other studies bring up additional conclusions: First, the Amicus Curiae most cited by Supreme Court Judges is the United States State Attorney. In forty percent of the cases in which he submitted a brief, he was cited by the Supreme Court. Sometimes, his brief is called the "king of the citation-frequency hill." For example, between 2010-2015, in eighty percent of the cases in which the United States government appeared as Amicus Curiae in the Supreme Court proceedings, the Attorney General's brief was cited in the judgment. It also seems that when the court's decision is close, for example, five judges against four judges, there is a greater tendency to cite amici, especially the Attorney General's brief, than in decisions with a large majority.[83]

There are several hypotheses behind the fact that the courts "consider" the state attorney's position in a unique way. First, the state attorney usually represents the broad public interest in the best way by virtue of the powers granted to him and by the reputation he has gained. Therefore, the judges of the Supreme Court give more weight to his position than to the positions of other amici curiae. Since judges tend not to stray too far from the public consensus, and the state attorney embodies this consensus, the judges often tend to accept or at least consider his position. Secondly, another explanation for the success of the state attorney in his role as Amicus Curiae in the American Supreme Court stems from his unique relationship with the judges due to his multiple appearances before the court and his high and respected position in American politics as someone who represents the majority of the American people.[84]

Second, amicus briefs filed by respected firms, recognized public organizations, and experienced attorneys were cited more than those filed by those not experienced or recognized in the field. As Hazelton and Hinkle note, 'attorney experience carries weight not just in crafting persuasive briefs but also in establishing credibility and trust with the justices. Seasoned Supreme Court advocates, who cannot afford to mislead the Court, enjoy an advantage in having their arguments taken seriously, an intangible benefit beyond the substantive merits of their briefs.[85] Third, briefs filed by repeat participants in the Supreme Court have had better success than casual participants.[86]

The enormous and increasing number of briefs submitted to the courts deal with all areas of life. It is true that the judgments that are subject to strong public

[83] Franze and Anderson (2015).

[84] See O'Connor (1983), p. 256; Segal (1988), pp. 135–136. See also Collins (2004), p. 827 (a list of organizations that the Supreme Court tends to refer to due to the prestige and status it confers on the writers of the brief). For example, in *Regents of the University of California v. Bakke*, 438 U.S. 265 (1978), Judge Powell cited from a joint brief written by the deans of Harvard, Columbia, Stanford and Pennsylvania universities. See also McGuire (1995), pp. 187, 194.

[85] Hazelton and Hinkle (2022).

[86] See also Collins (2004), pp. 807–832.

controversy "attract" an immense number of briefs.[87] However, in practice, amici join all the cases and all the legal issues discussed in court: tort law, criminal law, environmental quality, labor law, family law, privacy law, tax law, and commercial law. Finally, the rise in the amicus phenomenon in the United States has not only taken place in the Supreme Court but also exists in the various state courts and the federal courts on their two levels (Circuit Courts and District Courts).[88]

In the lower federal courts (district courts), the Amicus Curiae's participation is at a level of about five percent of the proceedings discussed. This rate increases when discussing amici's intervention in the federal courts above them.[89] An explanation for this is that in the first instance, the main questions discussed are factual, and therefore, the frequency of amici is lower. However, the main discussion in the appeals courts revolves around legal or social questions.[90]

As for the use and prevalence of amici curiae in state courts, studies show significant variation between the different states.[91] Amici have a relatively high prevalence in Alabama, California, Florida, Massachusetts, Michigan, New Jersey, New York, North Carolina, Ohio, and Washington.[92] It has been found that the states with the strictest policies towards amici did so due to increasing use of the Amicus Curiae practice.[93] For example, a study on the California Supreme Court showed that 1868 amicus briefs were filed in 422 civil proceedings (out of 707 in total) between 2000 and 2009.[94] Other studies have shown the following trends: In 2010, the Washington Supreme Court accepted amici curiae briefs in 49 cases out of 141 judgments it issued (35 percent). The California Supreme Court accepted amici briefs in 54 of 102 rulings (53 percent). The Arizona Supreme Court received nine amici briefs out of 41 judgments (22 percent).[95]

---

[87] For example, in the ruling regarding affirmative action in universities in the United States, Grutter v. Bollinger, 539 U.S. 306 (2003).

More than sixty amicus briefs were attached which supported the universities' affirmative action policy. The memoranda presenters include United States universities, law student organizations, the Society of Sociologists, the Bar Association, the National Association for the Advancement of Colored People, former United States President Gerald Ford, several senators, retired United States Army generals, companies Commerciality.

[88] Box-Steffensmeier and Christenson (2012). http://Amicinetworks.com. Box-Steffensmeier and Christenson (2014), pp. 82–96.

[89] Simard (2008), pp. 686–687.

[90] Songer and Sheeham (1993), pp. 339–354 (an empirical study of the influence of amici on state supreme courts); Simard (2008); Laroche (2009), p. 701.

[91] Corbally et al. (2004) Filing of Amicus Curiae. Briefs in State Courts of Last Resort: 1960–2000, 25 Just. Sys. J. 39, 44–46. The authors also find that the number of amicus briefs filed in state supreme courts increased significantly during this period, from an average of 1.5 briefs per case in 1960 to an average of 10.5 briefs per case in 2000.

[92] Ibid, p. 46.

[93] Ibid, p. 53.

[94] Sungaila (2010), p. 6.

[95] Anderson (2015).

Simard's research that examined the joining of amici curiae in the United States federal courts shows that most federal judges (about 77 percent of the judges in the Circuit Courts and about 82 percent of the judges in the District Courts) believe that the amicus briefs that are served to them help them to better understand the expected general consequences of the court's ruling.[96] Among the judges who participated in the study, there was broad support for amici briefs, which drew attention to the social, environmental, or other consequences associated with the rulings. In contrast, there was weak support among judges who participated in the research to the amici who elaborated at length on their ideological doctrine and informed the court of their support for a particular side.[97]

Most judges believed that briefs of this type were unnecessary and did not provide assistance. The research also revealed that over fifty percent of the federal court judges believed briefs submitted by academic professors, in general, and law professors, in particular, are successful briefs. These findings are because they manage to get right into the court's opinion and present their ideas with a legal or social analysis that the original parties still need to present.[98] In the eyes of the judges who participated in the research, the Amicus Curiae briefs are the most appropriate procedural tool through which the legal academy should actively participate in shaping the development of the law through the presentation of theoretical and practical information.[99]

The study also revealed a broad consensus among federal court judges that amicus briefs submitted by representatives of state authorities: the attorney general, federal agencies, and regulators are the most preferred briefs over those from other interest groups. Fifty percent of the Circuit Court judges indicated that the assistance provided by the amici was beneficial.[100] They found the briefs submitted by the State Authorities to be objective by nature, relating to the wider implications of the issue before them. Another explanation is that the state is a "recurring actor" in the courts, and as such, its attorneys are skilled and experienced in writing effective briefs.[101]

To summarize this section, we have seen that the Amicus Curiae in the United States is a common legal procedure in almost all courts. Thus, it is possible for third parties—government representatives, business companies, or non-governmental

---

[96] Simard (2008), pp. 669.

[97] Ibid., at p. 692. See Fallon (2012), pp. 223, 225–226 (citing survey of Justices and their clerks), 228 (referring to "distinctively scholarly expertise and perspective" and "an implied warranty of scholarly integrity").

[98] Ibid., pp. 699–700.

[99] For the role of the legal academy in the decision-making process of the various courts, see for example Edwards (1992).

[100] Simard (2008), p. 697. In relation to District Court judges, about 30 percent indicated that the amicus briefs of the state authorities helped significantly, while about 55 percent of them indicated that the memos helped more moderately. 12 percent of judges These stated that the amicus memoranda of the governing authorities did not help at all; Ibid., p. 697, 127.

[101] For the status of the governmental authorities as Amicus Curiae, see Lowman (1992), pp. 1261–126.

organizations—not officially disputing the procedure to present their views in the courts. The Amicus Curiae has existed in American law Ever since 1823 (and even earlier but in a semi-formal manner). Since the seventies and eighties of the twentieth century, a constant increase in its use has been recorded.

In the first half of the twentieth century, almost no amicus briefs were submitted to the Supreme Court, although it was possible to do so. This trend was reversed in the 1970s and 1980s, and the rate of amici submitting briefs to the Supreme Court increased significantly every decade. For example, in 2015 and 2016, in approximately 92 percent of all cases discussed in court, dozens of amici joined in and asked to present their opinion. This is an increase of over 800 percent since the 1950s and about 95 percent since the mid-1990s. The average number of briefs submitted to the Supreme Court in recent years has been over five hundred each year, containing thousands of pages. From the middle of the twentieth century until today, about 25,000 amicus briefs have been submitted in about 5000 cases heard in the Supreme Court. The number of briefs submitted in "mega cases" has also risen consistently over recent decades.

In the United States, there is extensive and comprehensive regulation, both in the state and federal courts, on the subject of Amicus Curiae. From 1937 until today, many amendments to the rules have been made, at the court's initiative, to adapt to the changing reality. One of the significant amendments was made in 2023 when it was determined that it is no longer necessary to obtain the parties' consent before submitting the brief to the court. In general, amici have a somewhat "open door" in the courts, particularly in the Supreme Court. Despite the rules of the court that require that the brief be "recent and relevant," in practice, a liberal approach is taken that allows amici to join proceedings quite conveniently.

Regarding the use of amici briefs by courts, it appears that in about a third of the cases discussed from the mid-20th century to the 2000s, the court referred, mentioned, or cited in some way to the information presented to it through one of the briefs submitted. This phenomenon has increased significantly. This finding is limited because sometimes, judges cite briefs from amici on both sides to present an equally objective picture of the situation (or to show that the position of the amici and the position of the formal litigants is the same). With that, it has some weight in the decision-making process.

Finally, the enormous and increasing numbers of amicus briefs submitted to the courts deal with all possible branches of law. There is almost no legal field or issue, even if it is relatively insignificant, where you cannot find amici who want to present their perspectives in the discussion. Accordingly, the increase in the use of Amicus Curiae exists not only in the Supreme Court but also in the various state courts on all levels, particularly in the federal courts.

5.2 Canada

The phenomenon of the Canadian Amicus Curiae is slightly different to that described above in the United States. Like elsewhere, in Canada, the Amicus Curiae is a person or group that is not a party to a legal proceeding but may submit a brief to the court to provide information or arguments that may be useful to the court in its decision. The practice of filing Amicus Curiae briefs in Canada is also derived from the same tradition as described for the United States, which began in the Roman Empire and was first adopted in English courts in the sixteenth century. This practice was officially recognized in Canadian courts in the nineteenth century.[102]

In Canada, there are two main mechanisms for third-party participation in legal proceedings: amicus curiae and interveners. The formal role of an amicus curiae is to assist the court in the development of legal principles, often at the invitation of the court itself, without having a direct interest in the outcome of the proceedings.[103] Unlike the American amicus curiae, which may promote the agenda of a particular group, the Canadian amicus curiae is expected to provide a more objective perspective to aid the court's understanding. An amicus curiae is not a formal party to the proceedings and cannot perform actions reserved for litigants, such as presenting new evidence.

Alongside amici curiae, diverse interest groups (human rights organizations, environmental groups, or corporations) may present their positions in court through "interveners." Unlike amici curiae, who have no direct stake in the results, an intervener is a third party with a genuine interest in the outcome of the proceedings. Once granted intervener status by the court, interveners effectively become formal parties to the case, similar to an amicus curiae in the American sense. They are permitted to present arguments, evidence, and participate actively to advance their specific interests.[104]

From the point of view of third parties who wish to influence ongoing proceedings, the Amicus Curiae and the "intervenor" are on the same continuum, where the amicus (except the American Amicus Curiae) is usually a more objective third party who comes to help develop the principles of the law or to fulfill additional functions in the procedure. The amicus often joins the proceedings according to the court's invitation. On the other hand, the intervenor has a direct interest in the procedure, and after the request of the intervenor is accepted, he becomes a formal party.

The Canadian Amicus Curiae briefs are most often filed by interest groups but can also be filed by individuals, businesses, and government agencies. In a study of Amicus Curiae briefs filed in the Supreme Court of Canada between 2000 and 2015,

---

[102] Mirsane (2021), p. 669.

[103] Peter (2007).

[104] Clark v. Canada (Att'y Gen.) (1978), 17 O.R. (2d) 593 (Sup. Ct.); Borowski v. Canada (Minister of Justice) (1983), 23 Sask. R. 259 (Q.B.); Canada (Att'y Gen.) v. Aluminum Co. of Can. (1987), 10 B.C.L.R. (2d) 371 (C.A.).

it was found that the most common types of organizations filing Amicus Curiae briefs were interest groups (44%), government agencies (22%), individuals (17%), business (11%).[105]

One of the precedent rulings on the distinction between the amicus and intervenor from the point of view of third parties is the case *Reference re Secession of Quebec*, in which the Supreme Court of Canada ruled that the Province of Quebec may not unilaterally withdraw from the Canadian Federation.[106] In this case, the court was assisted by legal and social information presented to it by both intervenors and amici. Another example is the case "*Reference Re Certain Titles to Land*" in Ontario, which dealt with the constitutionality of real estate transactions in Ontario. In this case, several third parties also appeared before the court, some as amici and some as intervenors, all in connection with the applicants' interests.[107]

It is important to note that the federal government of Canada, the cabinet, may refer questions of law or fact to the Supreme Court for it to discuss and express its opinion regarding them, including regarding the interpretation of the Constitution, the constitutionality or interpretation of a law, and the powers of the Canadian Parliament. The court may notify any interested person of the holding of the hearing, and they are entitled to be heard at the hearing. By its very nature, it strengthens the amicus phenomenon in Canada.[108]

The arrangements regarding the intervention of third parties in legal proceedings were anchored in the rules of the Canadian Supreme Court.[109] In summary, the rules state that the request to join as a third party shall include a description of the applicant, usually the organization or person behind the request to join, and a detailed description of the applicant's interest in the procedure. Also, the application shall include an explanation of the effect that may be caused to the applicant's interest if his application is rejected.[110] Similar to the United States, the rules state that the Attorney General of Canada or the Attorney General of one of the provinces may join the proceedings without the need to obtain the court's permission.[111] In addition, the request must include details about the position proposed to the court and an explanation of how the arguments are relevant, valuable, and different from the parties' original arguments.[112]

---

[105] Ibid.

[106] Reference re Secession of Quebec, [1998] 2 S.C.R. 217.

[107] Ibid.

[108] Rules of the Supreme Court of Canada, SOR/2002-156 r 53–55. Also see: Hogg (2002).

[109] Ibid. Rule 18.

[110] Ibid. Rule 57(1).

[111] Ibid. Rule 61(4). Procedurally, rule 37 titled "Service and Filing of Intervener's Documents" sets the rules on the subject. The rule that deals with Amicus Curiae's rule 92 entitled "Appointment of Amicus Curiae" which states that the court in full composition or in a single hearing may appoint an amicus in an appeal process. The rest of the procedures were determined by the rulings of the courts.

[112] Ibid. Rule 57(2)(b).

The two primary considerations of whether to allow a third party (both amici and intervenors) to present their position are whether their arguments will help the court decide the case and whether their arguments differ from the arguments of the formal parties. And according to Canadian Supreme Court Judge John Sopinka: "Third-party intervention will be welcomed if the applicant provides the court with new information or a new perspective on a constitutional matter or an important public issue."[113] Moreover, there are other legal considerations, such as the time of submission of the brief, its length, and financial guarantees to be paid to the original disputants if they are harmed due to the intervention. In addition, unlike the Amicus Curiae, the court may determine whether the "intervenor" will be allowed to present new evidence and argue orally.[114]

Beginning in the 1980s, the federal courts and courts in the various provinces also started to receive briefs from third parties.[115] As part of the new rules, it was determined that the request to submit the brief must include a description of how the applicant wishes to influence the legal proceedings and how his participation will assist the court in a factual or legal matter related to the proceedings.[116] Most Canadian provinces regulate the rules regarding joining third parties, amici, and intervenors in their procedural regulations. For example, in the Province of Ontario, Rule 13 of the Rules of Procedure is divided into two categories—a request to join an intervenor as an additional litigant and a request to intervene as an Amicus Curiae.[117] The same applies in the provinces of Manitoba[118] and Nova Scotia.[119]

In general, it can be said that the Canadian Supreme Court has, in the last three decades, had a liberal approach regarding the participation of third parties in legal proceedings conducted before it.[120] The courts even tend, especially since the late 1980s, to invite various amici on their initiative to assist them in issues of public

[113] Reference re Workers' Comp.

[114] Rules of the Supreme Court of Canada, SOR/2002-156, r 56(a), 59(1)(b), 59(2) 59(3).

[115] If permission to intervene was granted, the court will determine the concrete procedural rules in relation to the intervention such as: hearing rights and the joining dates. Federal Courts Rules, SOR/98-106, r 109.

[116] Federal Courts Rules, SOR/98-106, r 109.

[117] Rules of Civil Procedure, R.R.O. 1990, Reg. 194 in relation to the Amicus Curiae, it was determined in the civil procedure as follows: "Any person, after receiving the permission of the court, or if the court has invited him, and without being a formal party to the proceedings, may be a 'friend of the court' to assist the court by way of presenting an argument."

[118] In the province of Manitoba, the provision governing the summoning and character of amici curiae is the Court of Queen's Bench Rules, Man. Reg. 553/88, r 13, and the rules regarding the joining of amici and interveners are very similar to the rules in Ontario.

[119] The Nova Scotia Civil Procedure Rules (N.S. Gaz., Nov. 19, 2008, r 35.10, 90.19) also make a distinction between joining as an intervener versus joining as an Amicus Curiae, when an intervener will be allowed to join the proceedings if there is an interest His personal and directness is on the agenda.

[120] Bryden (1987), p. 490.

consequence and allow third parties to present their position.[121] This approach has not always been dominant in the Canadian judicial system.

The attitude of the Canadian Supreme Court towards the desire of third parties to present their position in the courts can be divided into two main periods. In the first period, from adopting the Canadian Bill of Rights in 1982 until 1987, the Supreme Court did not sympathize with the interventions of third parties in the proceedings discussed before it.[122] This judicial approach has been criticized, arguing that the court was failing in its social role entrusted with protecting human rights and preserving Canada's democratic values. Another criticism was concerned with the fact that the court did not explain the reasons for accepting or rejecting a request from a third party to join the procedure in its decisions, which led to the laws in the field not being adequately defined. Creating legal certainty regarding the distinction between the amici curiae and the intervenors was impossible. It was also argued that the courts' decisions regarding approving or rejecting requests to join as third parties were not uniform and coherent.[123]

On the other hand, in the second period, from about 1987 onwards, a change took place in the courts' approach, and they began to take a relatively liberal approach towards the desire of third parties to present their position in the courts. Indeed, until 1987, only some third-party accession applications were approved. By contrast, from 1987 until today, most of the requests submitted by third parties—both amici and intervenors—have been accepted.[124]

Studies show a consistent increase in third-party intervention in Canadian Supreme Court proceedings. For example, in 1983, the percentage of participation of third parties in ongoing proceedings was about 18 percent; in 1987, it was about 20 percent, and by 1990 it had reached 35 percent. This trend remained relatively constant until 1997. In 1999—in 40 percent of the procedures discussed in the Canadian Supreme Court, the court allowed third parties (for example, rights organizations or financial organizations) to express their position. In 2001, there was a drop to 35.1 percent. In 2003, there was a sharp rise to 56 percent, with a slight drop in 2005 to 54.1 percent, and a further rise in 2007, when in 61.8 percent of the procedures, third parties were involved. In ninety percent of the proceedings in the Supreme Court of Canada in the years described above that dealt with constitutional matters, third parties joined.

The average number of third parties intervening in each case discussed in the Supreme Court in the nineties was 5.6 third parties in each proceedings. In the 2000s,

---

[121] See for example Cooper v. Canada (Human Rights Comm'n), [1996] 3 S.C.R. 854; R.v. O'Connor (1995), p. 411. See generally Bruce (1998) p. 9.

[122] Canadian Charter of Rights and Freedoms: Charte canadienne des droits et libertés). The Charter was proclaimed in force by Queen Elizabeth II of Canada on April 17, 1982, as part of the Constitution Act, 1982.

[123] Koch (1990), p. 500.

[124] The non-governmental public bodies that have been most successful are the Canadian Civil Liberties Association and the rights organization LEAF (Legal Education and Action Fund). Brodie (1992).

on the other hand, there was an increase to 7.6 third parties in every proceeding discussed in the Supreme Court.[125] More evidence of a turn concerning third parties in the Supreme Court can also be found in a series of rules installed in the Canadian Supreme Court in the late 1980s and early 2000s, which more liberally allowed interventions by third parties.[126]

Additional empirical studies show that between 2000 and 2009, in about half of the cases discussed in the Supreme Court of Canada, third parties (amici and intervenors) participated. In appeal proceedings discussed in court, the participation percentages were higher—about 60.6 percent.[127] During the presidency of the Chief Judge of the Supreme Court of Canada, Beverley McLachlin, the court allowed an average of about 176 third-party interventions each year—a total of 1,583 third-party interventions in those years. About 94 percent of the third parties' requests to participate in a case were accepted during these years.[128] In the division between intervention requests of state bodies versus non-state organizations, it was found that the tendency of the courts to approve was higher when it comes to requests of state bodies. For example, 98 percent of the Attorney General's requests were honored. In contrast, requests from entities or private individuals were only approved in 76 percent of the cases.[129]

The growth of the amicus phenomenon in Canada over the past two decades has manifested in several ways. First, there has been a significant increase and diversification of the number and type of interest groups that try to influence the decision-making process through the submission of a brief.[130] For example, in 2012 alone, over sixty percent of Supreme Court proceedings were accompanied by briefs from third parties (amici and "intervenors"). In the seventy-five cases heard in court, over

[125] Alarie and Green (2010), p. 398. In criminal proceedings, the average is about 2.6 third parties in proceedings. This is a fairly significant increase from the beginning of the century, from 1900 to 1982, there were no cases at all in the Supreme Court of Canada in which joinder was allowed of a third party (as Amicus Curiae or as an intervener). In 1982, ten cases were discussed in which 14 interveners were added. Starting in 1989, there was a moderate increase when in 12 discussed cases 30 interveners were added, in 1991, in 18 cases 36 interveners were added. In 1993, 49 intervenors were added to 22 cases discussed in court. In 1999, 45 interveners were added to 15 cases discussed in court.

[126] Rules of the Supreme Court of Canada S.O.R.2002-156, as amended by S.O.R./2006-203.

[127] Alarie and Green (2010). In 2000, 45 percent of the appellate proceedings heard in the Supreme Court were accompanied by interventions by third parties. In 2001, 35.1 percent. 2002 (45.3 percent). 2003 (56 percent) 2004 (52.4 percent), 2005 (54.1 percent), 2006 (47.5 percent), 2007 (61.8 percent), 2008 (49.3 percent).

[128] Numerically, in 1983, third parties intervened in fifty proceedings, in 1990, third party interventions were recorded in 200 different proceedings. In 1993, there was a drop to fifty procedures per year. In 1997, third parties intervened in 125 proceedings. In 2002, in 160 procedures. In 2005, in 225 procedures. In 2007, in 120 procedures. Alarie and Green (2010), p. 397.

[129] Ibid. p. 398.

[130] Box-Steffensmeier et al. (2013), pp. 1–15. Collins et al. (2015), pp. 917–994. See *supra* note 33; Collins (2008).

221 third-party briefs were submitted.[131] Today, the interventions of third parties come from throughout the spectrum—representatives of the government's legal advisory position, various government authorities, financial entities, huge companies, private associations dealing with multiple issues, and more.

Second, there was an increase in the number of cases and legal issues in which third parties were allowed to express their position. Today, in almost every possible legal area, third parties appear in Canadian courts—tort, family, high-tech and technology, labor, corporate, environmental, antitrust, insurance, constitutional, criminal, tax, and intellectual property. Third, there has been an increase in the number of briefs in files of public significance ("mega cases").[132] Fourth, there has also been an increase in the number of citations or references of amici curiae in court rulings.[133]

In general, it can be said that the deep involvement of Canadian courts in society has resulted in issues related to sex, race, multiculturalism,[134] religion, nationality, indigenous rights, and environmental rights have become relatively common issues in Canadian courts. Accordingly, diverse interest groups began to present their position increasingly as third parties, as "intervenors" or as amici, to advance their position in court. Public litigation is crucial for these groups to increase their court positions.[135]

In summary, the Canadian Amicus Curiae's role is to assist the court in its work, usually at the court's invitation and without having a direct interest in the proceedings, unlike the American Amicus Curiae. In addition to the amicus, another common representation mechanism of third parties with some interest is the "intervenor." From the point of view of third parties who wish to influence an ongoing procedure, the amicus and intervenor are on a continuum, with the amicus usually being a more objective third party. On the other hand, the intervenor has a direct interest in the proceedings, and after his request is accepted, he becomes a formal party.

There are several aspects to the use of these representation mechanisms in Canada: First, the joining of third parties to ongoing proceedings (as amici or intervenors) has become common since the 1990s in almost all the various courts in Canada and, in particular, in the Supreme Court. Secondly, following the courts'

---

[131] Lorne Neudorf (2013), pp. 16, 19.

[132] Brodie (2002). As I will discuss in detail in the third chapter, the rise of the amicus phenomenon in Canada is related to a broad climatic change in which the court perceived its function in society in a different way than it was in the past and accordingly softened its previous position and adopted a liberal approach towards the wishes of third parties to influence ongoing proceedings.

[133] Ibid.

[134] See for example the Canadian Multiculturalism Act, 1988 as well as other laws enacted in the provinces which all strengthened the participation of third parties in the legal process. See for example: The Manitoba Multiculturalism Act, 1992. Human Rights, Citizenship and Multiculturalism Act, 2000 of the State of Alberta. Multiculturalism act 1996 of the province of British Columbia. Multiculturalism act 1989.

[135] Smith (1994), pp. 60, 75.

demands, the arrangements regarding the intervention of third parties in legal proceedings were anchored in the rules of the Canadian Supreme Court and other federal and provincial courts. The rules have been updated, at the courts' initiative, several times. Thirdly, there has been a consistent increase in third-party interventions in the Supreme Court of Canada proceedings. Fourthly, there is an increase in the number of interventions by third parties in each procedure. Fifthly, there is a significant increase and diversification of the interest groups that try to influence the decision-making process (rights organizations, commercial companies, and politicians). Finally, there is an increase in the number of citations and references of amici in court rulings.

5.3 England

The English Amicus Curiae has a long history as its first use was made in the sixteenth century, and since then, it has become a regular and accepted practice in English law. Initially, the practice of Amicus Curiae was mainly used by the government. However, over the years, it has become more common among various organizations, including interest groups, charities, and even individuals. It is unique in several ways. First, it is not limited to the parties to the case, meaning that any person or organization, regardless of their interest in the case, can file an amicus brief. Second, the English Amicus Curiae is not limited to providing legal arguments. It can also provide information or an expert opinion.[136]

The English Amicus Curiae is subject to the rules of civil procedure, introduced in 1998.[137] The rules governing the English Amicus Curiae are relatively liberal, so this means that it is relatively easy to submit an amicus brief. The rules governing English Amicus Curiae also allow the court to refuse to consider an amicus brief, which is rarely done in practice.[138]

The English Amicus Curiae is used for various purposes, such as providing the court with additional information, presenting arguments, presenting the possible future consequences of a particular decision, or persuading the court to reach a specific result.

The English Amicus Curiae is a third party invited to the court to assist in the court's work and is supposed to represent an objective and neutral position. In some cases, although this is not very common, the courts in England ask amicus to take a more adversarial role in the proceedings. In the *Allen* judgment, Judge Salmon noted:

---

[136] Pannick (1992).

[137] Civil Procedure Rules 1998 (SI 1998/3132).

[138] Ian Loveland, Constitutional Law, Administrative Law, and Human Rights: A Critical Introduction (5th edn 2009) pp. 543–544; Eliantonio et al. (2012).

> I had always understood that the role of an Amicus Curiae was to help the court by expounding the law impartially, or if one of the parties needed to be more represented, by advancing the legal arguments on his behalf.[139]

Courts in England accept amici briefs mainly in four situations: First, when a particular dispute involves an important public issue that may affect large groups other than the formal litigants.[140] Second, to help the court avoid a judicial error when the amicus presents aspects that the court does not know. Thirdly, when an unrepresented party cannot help the court rule on the case or manage the procedure correctly. Even when a lawyer acts on behalf of an unrepresented party as an amicus, he is not considered a lawyer "on behalf of," and from the court's point of view, his definition as an amicus remains the same.[141] Fourth, when a legal issue that has arisen does not directly concern the parties or the parties have no interest or ability to assist the court. However, the court wishes to develop a legal rule on the subject and needs additional information. Usually, social information presents the broad general implications of court policy.

Due to the lack of clarity about the role of the "amicus" in the English judicial system, the Supreme Court of England decided in 2011 to change its rules so that the title of the proceedings on Amicus Curiae was changed from "Amicus Curiae" to "Advocate to the Court." This is not a semantic change but a fundamental issue. In this way, the English judicial system sought to emphasize and clarify to potential amici that the English Amicus Curiae is not a friend of a party to the procedure, as exists in the United States and other countries, but only of the court.[142] That is, the formal role of the English amicus is to assist the court only and not to support or assist one of the parties.

Even in England, the distinction between the amicus and the intervenor is accepted. The practice of intervening in proceedings as third parties, the amicus, and the intervenor, exists in most judicial courts in England: The Administrative Court, the Court of Appeal, the Privy Council of the United Kingdom,[143] the House of Lords, and in the Supreme Court which replaced the House of Lords.

Concerning intervention in the Supreme Court, Rule 26(1) of 2009 states that:

---

[139] Allen v. Sir Alfred McAlpine & Sons Ltd. [1968] 2 QB 229 (CA) 266.

[140] Morelle Ld. v. Wakeling [1955] 2 QB 379 (CA) ;[1967] 1 QB 443 (CA); In re Scandinavian Bank Plc. [1988] Ch 87, 99.

[141] *In re* Harris and Sheldon Grp. Ltd. [1971], (Ch) 900.

[142] Lord (2002), pp. 35.

[143] The Queen's Council also has judicial functions, which are usually delegated to the Judicial Committee. The committee consists of senior judges: judges of the Supreme Court of the United Kingdom and senior courts in England and Wales, Scotland and Northern Ireland. In the past, before most of the Commission's powers were transferred to the Supreme Court, the Council served as a court of appeals for the British Empire as a whole, and it still hears appeals from British Overseas Territories, sovereign base territories and the British Commonwealth of Nations. In light of the fact that most of the powers of the Queen's Council have been delegated to the Supreme Court, the participation of third parties in recent years has been low. See Judicial Committee (Appellate Jurisdiction) Rules Order 2009, SI 2009/224, r 27(1).

(a) any official body or non-governmental organization seeking to make submissions in the public interest,
(b) any person with an interest in proceedings by way of judicial review,
(c) any person who was an intervener in the Court below or whose submissions were taken into account under rule 15, may apply to the Court for permission to intervene in the appeal.[144]

Although the practice of joining third parties in ongoing proceedings has been institutionalized and common since the 1990s, there is a significant difference between the various courts regarding the entitlement of a third party to present its position in the courts, the ways of submitting applications, and the content of the brief.

For example, the court's rules for administrative matters state that any person can apply a request to present his position to the court. The request must contain an explanation about who the applicant is, a description of the argument that will be presented, and an explanation of how this is intended to participate in the discussion. On the other hand, the Court of Appeals does not have explicit rules. However, there is a practice that determines how to examine each request according to the circumstances of the matter. The essential considerations are submitting the request as early as possible, the agreement of the formal litigants, and considering the contribution of the matter to the court. The rules of the United Kingdom Supreme Court and the Privy Council of the United Kingdom are similar to those of the House of Lords. In essence, a public body or public, non-governmental organization may submit a brief in the name of the public interest; also, any person who has an interest in a proceeding involving judicial review and any person who was involved as a third party in a lower court may submit a request to present his position.

The House of Lords had no rules justifying its considerations in applications for the accession of third parties. However, in the Northern Ireland Rights Commission, Lord Slynn ruled that: "The courts will only allow or invite assistance when they feel it necessary or helpful."[145] Lord Woolf added that the court should balance the benefit of adding a third party to the process and hearing his position and the inconvenience that may be caused to the formal parties.[146]

The 1990s and early 2000s marked a turning point in the approach of the English judicial system regarding the involvement of third parties (amici and intervenors) in ongoing proceedings.[147] The courts in England began to constantly and increasingly allow a series of third parties to present their position in proceedings in which there

---

[144] Supreme Court Rules 2009, SI 2009/1603, r 26(1). See R (Prudential plc.) v. Special Comm'r of Income Tax [2013] UKSC 1, [2013] 2 AC 185 (appeal taken from Eng.), which discusses the application of these rules.

[145] *In re* N.I. Human Rights Comm'n [2002] UKHL 25, [25] (appeal taken from N.I.).

[146] Ibid.

[147] Similar to the process that took place in other countries in the world, initially the first third parties allowed to participate in legal proceedings in England were governmental bodies, while gradually the courts allowed non-governmental public organizations to present their position.

were no formal parties. These parties included public bodies, private individuals, commercial companies, and non-governmental public organizations; The 1996 judgment of the House of Lords in the *Khan* case, in which the submission of a brief by a human rights organization was allowed for the first time, is a turning point in the approach of the English courts to non-governmental third parties.[148] The then Lord Chancellor described it well in the following words:

> So, as at present advised... that our courts will be ready to permit amicus written briefs from non-governmental organisations; that is to say briefs, but not to treat them as full parties.[149]

This ruling institutionalized the practice of third-party intervention in the English judicial system. Since then, the cases in which the courts have allowed, and sometimes requested, third parties to come and present additional aspects or different perspectives regarding the procedure have multiplied.[150] By the time the Appeals Committee of the House of Lords issued its final judgment in July 2009 and was superseded by the Supreme Court, the practice of submitting briefs by third parties had become institutionalized and regular, with third parties requesting to voice their position in almost every case heard before the court.[151]

For example, in 2005, out of 73 proceedings discussed in the House of Lords, the accession of third parties was approved in six proceedings. In 2006, out of 59 proceedings discussed in the House of Lords, third parties joined in 13 proceedings (22 bodies of different third parties). In 2007, out of 58 proceedings discussed in the House of Lords, in 19 proceedings, third parties joined (40 various third parties in total). In 2008, out of 75 proceedings discussed, in 21 proceedings, third parties joined (about 36 third parties in total) about). In 2009, out of 45 proceedings discussed, third parties joined in 9 proceedings (about 14 third parties in total). Nearly half of the intervenors during this period were state bodies, about 40 percent were various non-governmental organizations, and about 10 percent were private or individual bodies.[152]

Another example that illustrates the increase in the role of third parties in England: between the years 2005–2009 (the last year of the work of the House of Lords), third parties were added by about 25 percent, while between the years 2009–2012 there is an increase of about 35 percent in the Supreme Court. For example, in 2015 alone, out of 79 judgments of the Supreme Court, in 38 proceedings, third parties (one or more) were involved—public non-governmental

[148] R v. Khan [1997] AC 558 (HL) (appeal taken from Eng.). See also Harlow (2002).

[149] 24 Nov. 1997, Parl. Deb. HL (2007) col. 833 (Lord Irvine).

[150] For example, in 1998 the House of Lords allowed the Amnesty organization and Human Rights Watch to submit a brief regarding the extradition of the dictator Pinochet. R v. Bow St. Metro. Stipendiary Magistrate, ex parte Pinochet Ugarte (No. 1) [2000] 1 AC 61 (HL) (appeal taken from Eng.).

[151] Even in their latest decision, R (Purdy) v. DPP [2009] UKHL 45, [2010] 1 AC 345 (appeal taken from Eng.), a large number of third parties participated in the judicial proceedings. See Lorne Neudorf (2013).

[152] Metcalfe (2009), pp. 18–26.

organizations, human rights organizations, or private individuals (almost fifty percent of the proceedings). Between 2009 and 2016, out of 423 proceedings discussed in the Supreme Court, 228 different interveners were joined in 141 proceedings according to the following division: 91 public bodies, 101 public, non-governmental organizations, and 41 private bodies.[153] Beginning in the late 1990s, the practice of involving third parties in ongoing proceedings in England has increased yearly. Third parties were added in about a third of the cases heard in the 2000s by the Appellate Committee of the House of Lords.[154]

The growth of the Amicus Curiae phenomenon in the English judicial system is reflected not only in the number of cases in which third parties (intervenors and amici) were approved to submit their position but also in the number of accessions in each case.[155] For example, in the case of *JFS*, which dealt with the question of "who is a Jew" (to admit students to high schools according to their affiliation with the orthodox stream), Lord Phillips received extensive social information from a long list of organizations and groups: the umbrella organization of British Jews, the Commission Equality and Human Rights United Kingdom, Secretary of State for Children, some private schools and families, the umbrella organization for Churches in the United Kingdom.[156] Most of the principled cases from a public point of view discussed in the House of Lords were followed by many requests from interest groups to present their position.[157]

In addition, in about a third of the cases in which third-party intervention was approved in the 2000s, a coalition of interest groups formed, which presented the courts with different points of view that the official litigants did not present. In the famous ruling that dealt with evidence obtained using a form of torture known as pressure bordering, the coalition of intervenors and amici (most of them non-governmental organizations) joined together in submitting a joint brief.[158] In 2009 (the first year of the work of the Supreme Court in its modern form), third parties were added in 35 percent of the cases. The numbers remained fairly steady, with 30 percent of cases including briefs submitted by third parties in 2010–2030 percent; about 40 percent in 2011, and about 37 percent in 2012.[159] The increase in the phenomenon of the intervention of third parties starting in the 1990s is not

[153] Justice and Freshfields Bruckhaus Deringer (2016).

[154] Brooke (2007), p. 403.

[155] Metcalfe (2009), p. 13.

[156] R (E.) v. Governing Body of JFS [2009] UKSC 15, [2010] 2 AC 728 (appeal taken from Eng.).

[157] For example, the ruling YL v. Birmingham City Council [2007] UKHL 27, [2008] 1 AC 95 (appeal taken from Eng.), which dealt with the definition of "public authority" under the English Human Rights Act, was followed by submissions from various interest groups: human rights organisations, Elderly organizations and women's organizations. Similarly, in the ruling Van Colle v. Chief Constable of Hertfordshire [2008] UKHL 50, [2009] 1 AC 225 (appeal taken from Eng.), which dealt with police tort liability for witness protection was joined by various interest groups.

[158] A. v. Sec'y of State for the Home Dep't (No 2) [2005] see footnote 640.

[159] Lorne Neudorf (2013), p. 25.

unique only to the House of Lords and then to the Supreme Court that replaced it. However, there is also an impressive increase in other courts in the English judicial system.[160]

Another aspect of the amicus phenomenon in England is giving third parties the right to argue orally. By the end of the 1990s, it was clear that third parties could present their position orally. This was the case, for example, in the matter of removing the immunity of the dictator Pinochet, which was discussed in the House of Lords.[161] Lord Hoffmann succinctly described the change of attitude in the following words:

> In recent years, the House has frequently been assisted by the submissions of statutory bodies and non-governmental organisations on questions of general public importance. Leave is given to such bodies to intervene and make submissions, usually in writing but sometimes orally from the bar, in the expectation that their fund of knowledge or particular point of view will enable them to provide the House with a more rounded picture than it would otherwise obtain. The House is grateful to such bodies for their help.[162]

Alongside those mentioned above, following the growing increase in the presence of third parties and their influence on formal litigants, the Criminal Justice and Courts Act 2015 was enacted.[163] The Act establishes rules for awarding costs to interveners in the Administrative Courts and the Court of Appeal of England and Wales proceedings. The new regime of ruling costs for interveners is designed to prevent abuse of the procedure by interveners and to direct their behavior so that they assist the court in the public matter they sought to join. Lord Faulks, the minister in charge of the House of Lords, explained it this way:

> [W]ith this clause we hope to deter inappropriate interventions and also to make interveners think about the scale of their intervention so as to reduce the costs for all parties, whether applicants or respondents, and to ensure that those interventions are relevant and genuinely assist the court.[164]

The new law established a series of cases in which the court has the discretion to award costs against third parties who intervene in the proceedings: (a) an intervener has behaved unreasonably, or (b) has in effect taken on a role as one of the main parties to the dispute; or (c) an intervention is not of significant assistance to the court, or (d) relates in significant part to matters which are not necessary for the court to consider. Non-governmental social organizations criticized this legislation,

[160]Brooke (2007), p. 403.

[161]In practice, the average length of time for an oral argument ranges from about half an hour to an hour. If there are several third parties, they share this time together and the time of each body wishing to argue orally is shortened.

[162]E.v. Chief Constable of the Royal Ulster Constabulary [2008] UKHL 66, [2], [2009] 1 AC 536, 542 (appeal taken from Eng.). The decision of the House of Lords to extradite Pinochet was overturned due to the discovery that Lord Hoffmann was connected to Amnesty, an organization active in the fight for human rights that submitted an affidavit to the court in favor of removing Pinochet's immunity.

[163]c. 2, § 87.

[164]756 Parl Deb HL (5th ser.) (2014) col. 998–99.

claiming, among other things, that it would cause excessive deterrence of non-governmental organizations that wish to assist the courts by joining the process as a third party.[165]

In summary, The 1980s and 1990s show a change in trend regarding the intervention of third parties in England. The courts in England began to allow a series of third parties constantly and increasingly: public bodies, private individuals, commercial companies, and non-governmental public organizations, to present their position in proceedings in which they were not formal parties. Compared to isolated cases of third-party interventions until 1996, submitting briefs by third parties has become institutionalized and regular. Today, the mechanisms of representation of third parties (the amicus and the intervenor) exist in almost all judicial courts in England. Moreover, almost all the judicial courts in England have established rules of accession concerning the intervention of third parties.

The increase in the involvement of third parties in the English judicial system is reflected not only in the cases in which third parties (intervenors and amici) were approved to submit their position but also in the number of accessions in each case. For example, in about a third of the cases in which the intervention of third parties was approved in the 2000s, a coalition of interest groups was formed that presented the courts with different points of view that the official litigants did not present.

5.4 Australia

Compared to other common law jurisdictions, such as Canada, the United States, and South Africa, Australia has a much more conservative approach regarding the interventions of amici and other third parties.[166] Academics have suggested that this may be a result of the reluctance of the Australian Judiciary (and specifically the Australian High Court) to adopt an approach of legal realism (which gained significant traction in the mid-1900s) in favor of a more traditional, formalistic jurisprudence.[167] Notwithstanding this, the concepts of intervention and Amicus Curiae have significantly risen in recent decades.[168] This has occurred both practically, in terms of the number of amici that have appeared in front of courts, and in the world of jurisprudence, as expressed in academia, court rules, and (often dissenting) legal judgments.

[165] Justice and Freshfields Bruckhaus Deringer (2016).

[166] For a comparative analysis of the way in which the Australian High Court has differed from many other common law countries, see Williams (2000), p. 365.

[167] See Hopper (2017), p. 82.

[168] In Australia, there are two mechanisms by which a third party may enter the proceedings: as either an 'intervener' or an amicus. An overview of the differences between these mechanisms is presented later in this section. For a more detailed explanation of the similarities and differenced between amici and interveners, see Williams (2000), p. 365.

An acute expression of both the overall reluctance of the Australian judiciary to accept third-party interventions, as well as an advocation for a shift towards an approach of acceptance, can be found in the publications of the Honourable Judge Michael Kirby.[169] Judge Kirby has described the High Court's approach to third-party intervention as "hostile"[170] and provides four primary notions that underscore this hostility. First, the general belief that non-part intervention is a corrupting influence on the sanctity of the courtroom should have dispute resolution between parties as its primary responsibility. Second, the development of societal goals and human rights issues should fall to the responsibility of the litigator and not the unelected justices. Third, the self-interest-focused ideology of adversarial judicial tradition means that the formal parties will already present their arguments most effectively, and allowing outside intervention will not usually help matters. Fourth, the extent of intervention in the courtroom should be decided by legislation, not precedent.[171]

As a result, as mentioned above, the Australian judiciary has seen a much lower number of amicus interventions than many other Western countries. For example, in 2013, there was intervention by amici in under 9% of cases that were argued before the High Court. Compare this to the data from the United States Supreme Court from the same year, whereby over 95% of cases accepted some form of amicus intervention.[172]

Formally, the Australian amicus is defined as a disinterested third party that assists the court in a legal or factual issue. Indeed, in *Corp Affairs Comm'n v Bradley*, the Supreme Court adopted the lexical definition as defined in *Jowet*, and determined that an "Australian amicus" shall be defined as follows:

> [a] friend of the Court, that is to say a person, whether a member of the Bar not engaged in the case or any other bystander, who calls the attention of the Court to some decision, whether reported or unreported, or some point of law which would appear to have been overlooked.[173]

In Australia, alongside the institution of the amicus, there is also the option of intervention by a third party in a proceeding through the use of the "intervener" practice. Both express the involvement of third parties in ongoing proceedings, but the difference lies in the fact that interveners usually have a direct interest in the

[169] Kirby (2011), pp. 537–564; See also Hon Kirby (1997), pp. 650–652; Attorney General (Cth) v. Breckler (1999) 197 CLR 83, pp. 134–137.

[170] Kirby, ibid.

[171] Ibid. See also Hopper (2017), p. 91.

[172] See Hopper (2017), pp. 84–85, who combines data from numerous sources. 2013 was not picked because it is an outlier (either for the United States or America), rather, this trend of an astonishing difference in the number of interventions can be seen in any year from recent decades.

[173] See *Corp Affairs Comm'n v Bradley* [1974] 1 NSWLR 391.

outcome of the process, whereas the amicus' purpose is to assist the court.[174] In the words of the Australian Law Reform Commission:

> The role of Amicus Curiae can be distinguished from the role of an intervener. While the role of an Amicus Curiae is to assist the court, the role of an intervener is to represent the intervener's own legal interests in proceedings.[175]

At face value, it seems that the Australian judiciary thus sees the Amicus Curiae as an entirely disinterested third-party (what has been referred to previously in this book as the "traditional amicus"), whereas the intervener is a party with partisan interests (the "lobbying amicus"). However, it is not so clear whether this distinction holds up against academic scrutiny, especially when juxtaposed with the development of the Amicus Curiae phenomenon that has gained traction around the world. In situations where the intervening party has no legal standing rights but has a personal interest in the outcome of the case, there may be a significant overlap between the amicus and the intervener.[176]

The court's considerations regarding whether to allow the inclusion of amici or interveners are based on three main tests: (1) some deficiency in the arguments of the parties; (2) some interest (initially, some concrete, usually financial interest) of the third party in the case; (3) the ability of the amicus to add something substantial to the proceedings.[177]

Already from 1930, the first two of these tests had been established in case law. Judge Dixon stated:

> Normally parties, and parties alone, appear in litigation. [...] The discretion to admit appearances by counsel is a very wide one; but I think we would be wise to exercise it by allowing only those to be heard who wish to maintain some particular right, power or immunity in which they are concerned.

As such, the High Court has since had a keen focus on the rights of the parties in litigation, as well as a contention that these rights are exclusive and should not be violated without the existence of a concrete interest of a potential intervener. In 1997, the question of the participation of third parties in proceedings was addressed in a significant ruling by the High Court of Australia (the *Lange* case) dealing with the issue of freedom of expression.[178] Due to the issue's importance, numerous interest groups, particularly media companies and human rights organizations,

---

[174] One of the central distinctions between an intervener and an amicus is that if the intervener's request is granted, they may become an official party and be granted substantive rights and obligations in the proceedings, whereas the amicus is authorized to make submissions only. See, for example, *Lange v Austl Broad Corp* (1997) 189 CLR 520.

[175] https://www.alrc.gov.au/publication/serious-invasions-of-privacy-in-the-digital-era-dp-80/15-new-regulatory-mechanisms/amicus-curiae-and-intervener-roles-for-the-australian-information-commissioner/, Accessed on 12/07/2023.

[176] Williams (2000), p. 365.

[177] Willheim (2010).

[178] *Lange v Austl Broad Corp* (1997) 189 CLR 520. This ruling was given in tandem with *Levy v. Victoria* (1997) 189 CLR 579.

sought to express their positions. The High Court allowed them to participate in the proceedings, some as interveners and others as amici. The court stated that its authority to hear additional viewpoints and positions from the public derives from general principles of natural justice. It was also noted that the hearing of an Amicus Curiae is entirely in the court's discretion. That discretion is exercised on a different basis from that which governs the allowance of intervention. The footing on which Amicus Curiae is heard is that that person is willing to offer the Court a submission on law or relevant fact which will assist the court in a way in which the Court would not otherwise have been assisted.[179]

In explaining his change of approach concerning requests from third parties to join the proceedings, Judge McHugh specifies that:

> Although this is litigation between parties, part of this Court's function is to declare the law for the nation and that means the Court has got to look at issues that go beyond [...] the particular parties.[180]

Here, the High Court recognized the third test: a significant addition that will be made to the court by the amicus or intervener. Henceforth, the Australian Judiciary has recognized that litigation has implications beyond those that exist solely for the formal parties involved. In an admission of such implications, the High Court has stated:

> It is recognised by the courts that the resolution of disputes serves the public as a whole, not merely the parties of the proceedings.[181]

In 2004, the High Court of Australia established new rules regarding the participation of third parties.[182] These rules provide a set of criteria for submitting an application to join proceedings, specify time limits for filing, and determine the level of detail required in the submissions. These rules indeed improved the procedure regarding the inclusion of third parties, but they are not without difficulties. For example, the rules do not address critical procedural issues related to the amicus, such as the disclosure process that the amicus must undertake, the relationships they have with the parties, and the distinction (or lack thereof) between an amicus and an intervener.[183]

In Australia, government representatives are entitled to present their position as third parties in ongoing proceedings without the need for the consent of the parties involved. Representatives of Attorneys General do indeed exercise this right and participate in proceedings whenever a significant issue arises before the court.[184] Similar to the United States and Canada, courts in Australia generally prioritize

---

[179] *Levy v. Victoria* (1997) 189 CLR 579 p. 601.

[180] *Superclinics Austl Pty Ltd v. CES* [1996] HCATrans 357, at 15 (appears in the protocol of the hearing from Judge McHugh).

[181] Aon Risk Services Australia Ltd v. Australian National University [2009] HCA 27 para 113.

[182] *High Court Rules* 2004 (Cth) pt. 44.

[183] Owens (1998).

[184] Campbell (1998), pp. 225, 265.

submissions made by government representatives over those of non-governmental interest groups. The former submissions are perceived as representing the public interest in the best possible way.[185] Indeed, in a lengthy series of previous court decisions in Australia, the government's position as a third party has been mentioned or cited in the court's rulings.[186]

The Amicus Curiae phenomenon in Australia has manifested itself, among other ways, in a change in the courts' approach toward the willingness to allow third parties to join proceedings and express their positions. Until the 1990s, influenced by the adversarial philosophy of common law, the Supreme Court refused to grant third parties the authority to express their positions in proceedings where they did not have formal standing.[187] The court argued that third parties must demonstrate a concrete and tangible interest that may be affected to be allowed to express their positions.[188] This approach changed in 1998 when it was established in the *United States Tobacco* case:

> The general principle is that the parties are entitled to carry on their litigation free from the interference of persons who are strangers to the litigation. But there is an overriding right of the court to see that justice is done. An *amicus* may be heard if good cause is shown for doing so and if the court thinks it proper.

The court added:

> In particular, in the present state of the Anglo-Australian authorities . . . no clear line appears to differentiate that which can never be included as part of the role of an *Amicus Curiae* from what in a given case and as a permissible exercise of discretion, the court may permit or require of an *amicus.*[189]

---

[185] Generally, courts tend to favor statutory organizations and demonstrate a greater degree of liberalism towards them. This is the case, for example, in relation to the Human Rights and Equal Opportunity Commission, which advises the courts on issues of race, gender, and discrimination. Although this commission is not neutral, its role is to present professional considerations. Some argue that this commission, to some extent, legitimizes the involvement of various interest groups in human rights issues, as it is considered by the courts the "best amicus." See *Minister of State for Immigration & Ethnic Affairs v. Teoh* (1995) 183 CLR 273; *Qantas Airways Ltd v Christie* (1998) 193 CLR 280.

[186] See, for example, *Wik Peoples v. Queensland* (1996) 187 CLR 1 (property rights of indigenous peoples).

[187] The first case in the High Court of Australia that dealt with a request for amici to join the proceedings was *Austl Rys U'ion v. Vic Rys Comm'rs* (1930) 44 CLR 319. The judgment was based on the English decision that prohibits the participation of third parties without a direct interest being affected, without their consent.

[188] Despite statements by the court regarding strict criteria for the inclusion of third parties in proceedings, in practice, the right has been granted on several occasions for non-governmental organizations to present their positions. This was the case, for example, in the judgment dealing with the preservation of wilderness in Tasmania, *Commonwealth v. Tasmania* (1983) 158 CLR 1, pp. 50–51. In this case, the Tasmanian government supported the establishment of a hydroelectric dam in their state, while the federal Australian government opposed it on grounds of land conservation. The court was aware of the far-reaching implications and allowed various groups to present before the court the ecological, public, and societal consequences of the matter.

[189] *Nat'l Austl. Bank v Hokit* (1996) 39 NSWLR 377, 381; *US Tobacco Co v. Minister for Consumer Affairs* (1988) 20 FCR. p. 533–534, 536.

The Amicus Curiae phenomenon is accentuated not only in a more lenient and liberal approach towards the requests of amici to present their positions but also in the fact that the courts have started to grant them much greater freedom to argue orally, and even to participate in the proceedings actively.[190]

The use of the amicus in Australia is also associated with increased judicial activism in recent years and the growing involvement of the High Court in public issues, human rights, and civil rights matters.[191]

The amicus phenomenon is also related to a series of laws concerning human rights and multiculturalism that have been enacted in Australia in the twenty-first century, which have led to the significant involvement of amici, who seek to influence the decision-making processes of the courts. For example, two states in Australia, Victoria and New South Wales, established legislation following a federal declaration of their commitment to multiculturalism.[192] These laws are considered exceptional in the sense that they are not legally enforceable. Their essence lies in an attempt to focus on a discourse of identities and foster dialogue among different groups. Engaging with these issues in legislation naturally invites greater involvement of third parties seeking to influence the emerging discourse.

In summary, it can be observed that the growth of the amicus phenomenon in Australia has been relatively moderate in comparison to the increase in activities of amici and interveners in other countries.[193] However, there is a growing call from academia to increase the willingness to accept amicus interventions, particularly in proceedings of broad public interest.[194] Notwithstanding this, the amicus phenomenon in Australia has manifested itself in several aspects. Firstly, there is a nuanced approach by the courts towards the desires of interveners and amici to present their positions, which began to develop primarily in 1997 (in the *Lange* case). Secondly, new legal procedures have been established regarding the participation of third parties in some courts, particularly the High Court. These rules define a list of criteria for filing an application to intervene, the deadlines for submission, and the level of detail required in the submission. Thirdly, there is a relatively lenient approach towards the requests of amici to present their position through oral

[190] Campbell (1998); Owens. This was the case, for example, in the judgments of *Garcia v. Nat'l Austl Bank Ltd* (1998) 194 CLR 395 (validity of loan enforcement against vulnerable groups); *Project Blue Sky v. Austl Broad Auth* (1998) 194 CLR 355 (regulation of communication). For further details, see Campbell (1998).

[191] Blake (2006); Williams (2000). See, for example, *Multicultural Victoria Act 2004* (Vic); *Multicultural NSW Act 2000* (NSW) *below*.

[192] See *Multicultural Victoria Act*, No. 100 (2004) (Australia). Additionally, the *Community Relation Commission and Principles of Multiculturalism Act 2000* provide relevant provisions. For example, Section 3 of the latter law establishes recognition by the parliament of the existing linguistic, religious, racial, and ethnic diversity, and the right of individuals, either individually or with their communities, to maintain and preserve their linguistic, religious, racial, and ethnic heritage. It further stipulates that all citizens should be provided with the best possible opportunity to participate in relevant areas of life.

[193] Williams (2000), p. 365.

[194] Kristen (2010)' pp. 111, 125.

arguments and even actively participate in the proceedings. However, in general, and especially when compared to the activities of amici and interveners in other countries, notably the United States and Canada, it appears that the amicus phenomenon has had a significantly more moderate effect on the Australian Judiciary.

5.5 New Zealand

The use of Amicus Curiae in New Zealand was already in practice from the 19th century. The first known case in which an Amicus Curiae was appointed was in 1862, in the case of *R v. Jones*.[195] In that case, the Supreme Court appointed the Attorney General as amicus to provide the court with information on conspiracy law.[196] Today, the use of the amicus in New Zealand is still limited, although there has been significant growth in recent years.[197]

Formally, in New Zealand, the Amicus Curiae has several potential roles: to present legal arguments on behalf of a party who is not present or otherwise unable to appear before the court;[198] to represent a group of individuals who may be adversely affected by a court's decision;[199] and to weigh in when the issue at hand raises significant questions, usually regarding human rights.[200] The New Zealand Court of Appeal has even taken a step further than the courts in England and Canada, establishing that there is no objection to the amicus assisting the court in a supportive role for one of the parties and even taking on an adversarial function.[201] The assumption is that when an amicus is appointed by the court to represent the interests of an unrepresented party, they unavoidably take a side in the dispute; there can never be a truly natural amicus.[202]

In a similar fashion to other common law countries, the guiding principle underlying the involvement of amici in New Zealand is the extent of their potential contributions to the process. In the case of *Auckland Area Health Board*, the Supreme Court deliberated on whether the withdrawal of life support from a patient with Guillain-Barre syndrome would be considered murder. The government's legal advisor sought to intervene in the proceedings as an amicus, but the court rejected

[195] ***R. v. Jones*** [1866] NZLR 131.

[196] Ibid.

[197] A 2018 study found that only about 1% of New Zealand Supreme Court cases involved Amicus Curiae briefs. However, the use of Amicus Curiae has been increasing in recent years. In 2022, 12 amicus briefs were submitted to the High Court, which is more than double the number of memoranda submitted in 2018. Prof Mark Henaghan Otago University.

[198] *Wanganui District Council v. Tangaroa* [1995] 2 NZLR 706 (HC); *R. v. Kim* [2009] NZCA 294 (the amicus is appointed to represent the position of a defendant who has fled the country).

[199] *N.Z. Dairy Workers Union Inc. v. N.Z. Milk Prods. Ltd.* [2004] 3 NZLR 652 (CA).

[200] *Siemer v. Solicitor-General* [2009] 2 NZLR 556 (CA).

[201] *Solicitor-General v. Miss Alice* [2007] 1 NZLR 655 (CA).

[202] *Beneficial Owners of Whangaruru Whakaturia No. 4 v. Warin* [2009].

the request, determining that the government's legal advisor would be recognized as an "intervener" in the process rather than an amicus. The court further stated that when a party seeking to intervene intends to present legal arguments when they have a direct interest in the proceedings, it is appropriate to classify said party as an intervener rather than an amicus.[203] In contrast, considering the similarity between the amicus and the intervener, the New Zealand Law Commission has recommended that they should be treated in the same manner.[204] Nonetheless, both the amicus and the intervener represent different forms of third-party involvement in ongoing proceedings.

The Amicus Phenomenon has impacted New Zealand's judiciary in a similar way to that of other common-law countries. Until the 1990s, New Zealand's courts held a conservative, non-intervention approach in the interests of formal parties. However, since the early 2000s, the involvement of amici and interveners has become increasingly accepted, albeit still relatively restrained.[205] Since 2004, dozens of third-party interventions have been recorded in ongoing proceedings. The most prominent interveners include the government's legal advisor,[206] human rights organizations,[207] commercial entities,[208] and the New Zealand Bar Association.[209]

The Amicus Curiae phenomenon is manifested not only in the change of approach and gradual growth in the number of amici and interveners but also in the fact that courts have started to provide numerous opportunities for third parties to present their *oral* positions (as opposed to written submissions, which was essentially the case in the past). The amicus phenomenon in New Zealand is also rooted in constitutional developments, including the adoption of the Bill of Rights in 1990, the establishment of the Supreme Court in 2004 (after the Queen's Privy Council ceased to serve as the highest appellate authority in the country), and the recognition of the courts' creative power and influence on society. In a long line of judgments, particularly those related to the New Zealand Bill of Rights, the Supreme Court of New Zealand has sought to obtain broad social information and additional perspectives from the public. This is because cases dealing with this issue inherently involve interests and broad public considerations beyond those of the formal parties involved.[210]

---

[203] *Auckland Area Health Bd. v. Attorney-General* [1993] 1 NZLR 235 (HC) at 240; Clark (2005).

[204] The New Zealand Law Commission is a statutory government committee established to create reform and consolidation in the judiciary. See *Report 126, Review of the Judicature Act 1908 (2012).*

[205] See Clark (2005).

[206] *Ngai Tahu Props. Ltd. v. Central Plains Water* [2009] NZSC 24.

[207] *Zaoui v. Superintendent, Auckland Central Remand Prison* [2004] NZSC 22.

[208] *Austin Nichols & Co. v. Stiching Lodestar* [2007] NZSC 103; *Bryson v. Three Foot Six Ltd.* [2005] NZSC 54, [2005].

[209] *Chamberlains v. Lai* [2006] NZSC 70, [2007] 2 NZLR 7.

[210] Clark (2005).

To summarize, no specific data was found regarding all the criteria presented in the methodology section regarding New Zealand. With caution, it can be said that the main innovation concerning the use of the Amicus Curiae representation mechanism in New Zealand lies in the softening of the reluctance that existed in the courts until the early 2000s regarding third-party requests to present their positions (amici and interveners) in ongoing proceedings.

5.6 South Africa

Until the mid-1990s, the Amicus Curiae in South Africa was a "friend of the court" who did not assist or support the formal parties but exclusively assisted the court. The Supreme Court noted that the amicus is:

> a person who, if he observes the judge in doubt about something, or likely to fall into error through failure to recollect a fact of which he ought to take cognizance, such as a legal decision or a statute, asks leave to come to his assistance and to mention it, and thus help the judge by pointing out what appears to be in danger of being overlooked.[211]

However, starting in the 1990s and especially after adopting the South African Constitution, the South African Amicus Curiae slowly morphed, becoming similar to the American Amicus Curiae (the lobbyist) rather than the classical "friend of the court."[212] In recent years, the amicus in South Africa has adopted a broad range of characteristics, some of which are of a lobbying nature, which has allowed the amicus to play a significant role in shaping the society and the legal system in the country. However, similar to other countries with a common law system, the amicus also serves to present legal arguments on behalf of an unrepresented party,[213] or to represent the interests of individuals who may be affected by the court's decision, significantly when the issue raises weighty questions of public consequence.[214]

In the mid-90s, the South African Constitutional Court's rules were formulated in a way that reflects the shift from the Amicus Curiae's focus on court interests

---

[211] *Connock's (SA) Motor Co. v. Pretorius* 1939 TPD 355, 356–57.

[212] Murray (1994), p. 244. It noted that despite the relatively high frequency of amicus and third-party interventions in South African courts, particularly in the Supreme Court and Constitutional Court, courts are hesitant to delve into the reasoning behind their permission or denial of amicus requests, resulting in unclear guidelines on the matter. For a description of the impact of the amicus on human rights-related proceedings. See also Viljoen and Abebe (2014), pp. 22, 24.

[213] For example, in the case of *Ex Parte de Villiers, In Re Carbon Devs. (Pty) Ltd. (in liq.) 1993 (1) SA 493 (A)* the court appointed a number of amici as there was an important issue that the court wanted to address but was not adequately argued by the parties.

[214] See, for example, *Govender v. Manikum* 1981 (1) SA 1178 (N) at 1182; Amanda Spies, Amicus Curiae Participation, Gender Equality and the South African Constitutional Court (June 9, 2014) (unpublished Ph.D. dissertation, University of the Witwatersrand).

towards inclusion in the amicus' own interests.[215] These rules stipulate that a request from an organization or individual to be recognized as an Amicus Curiae should include a description of the interest they have in the proceedings, a description of the position they seek to present, and an explanation of why the submitted brief may prove helpful to the court and why it is distinct from the arguments presented by the formal litigants.[216] In addition, the rules dictate that the amicus must acquire the consent of all the formal parties involved in a proceedings before being granted the right to stand. If permission is not obtained, the amicus is allowed to appeal to the court's president. Should the court grant the amicus' request to make submissions, the court must, as part of its decision, determine the specific rights of the amicus in the proceedings.[217] For example, the court may establish that the amicus' rights are similar to those of a formal litigant, allowing them to present official, scientific, technical, or statistical information to the court. However, an amicus will be allowed to intervene by means of written submissions only, they may not make oral arguments before the court.[218] An Amicus Curiae brief will be accepted provided that it does not reiterate the parties' arguments and that it presents arguments that assist the court in its judicial work.

Naturally, lower courts have adopted similar regulations with necessary modifications. As such, amici curiae can participate in most judicial settings in South Africa, including the Constitutional Court,[219] the Supreme Court of Appeal,[220] the High Court,[221] the Labor Appeal Court,[222] the Land Claims Court,[223] and the Labor Court.[224]

The South African Constitution grants a wide range of bodies the right to approach the courts with an allegation of a violation of constitutional rights. Therefore, the prevalence of the Amicus Curiae practice is not surprising, as South African courts rely on and encourage the submission of third-party briefs. According to the South African constitution,[225] should one-third of the members of Parliament feel the need to do so, they have the right to approach the Constitutional Court to decide

[215] The Constitutional Court's Rules were drafted in 1995. With the amendment of the rules in 2003, amicus participation is now presented in rule 10.

[216] Rules of the Constitutional Court rule 10(6), GN R165 of GG 25726.

[217] Ibid, rule 10(4).

[218] Ibid, rule 10(8). However, some South African jurists have argued that the amicus may be granted special permission to argue orally in specific situations. See Budlender (2006), p. 1 at 8–10.

[219] Ibid rule 10. See also Jason and du Plessis (2011), p. 152.

[220] Rules Regulating the Conduct of the Proceedings of the Supreme Court of Appeal of South Africa, r. 16, GN R.1523 (1998).

[221] Rules Regulating the Conduct of the Proceedings of the Several Provincial and Local Divisions of the High Court of South Africa, r. 16A, GN R.48 (1965), as amended.

[222] Labour Appeal Court Rules, r. 7, GN 1666 of GG 17495 (1996).

[223] Land Claims Court Rules, r. 14, GN R.300 of GG 17804 (1997).

[224] Labour Court Rules, r. 19, GN 1665 of GG 17495 (1996).

[225] Sections 79 and 80 of the Constitution of South Africa.

on the constitutionality of a law. Similarly, the President of the country[226] and the province's premier[227] are authorized to approach the Court regarding the constitutionality of a proposed law. The Court's decision is binding. When disagreements arise in Parliament (or in a provincial legislative proceeding) regarding the constitutionality of a law, as mentioned, one-third of the members of Parliament (or 20% of the provincial legislature) have the right to approach the Constitutional Court to rule on the matter. The Court may announce the existence of the hearing to any potentially interested party who will be entitled to be heard during the hearing. This inherently strengthens the amicus phenomenon in South Africa.

Indeed, according to Professor Klaaren, the formulation of the rules of the courts since 1995 regarding the involvement of the Amicus Curiae in judicial proceedings demonstrates a departure from the previous South African governance structure. These rules were designed to enable various interest groups, particularly non-governmental organizations, to actively participate in shaping the country's legal discourse to focus on human rights and to allow for deep public involvement in the decision-making process.[228] Researchers Mubangizi and Mbazira argued that, generally speaking, the legal frameworks of the different courts regarding the intervention of third-party actors as amici curiae (presented above) reflect this perspective.[229]

A 2012 court ruling regarding the *Children's Institute* underscores the significance of the Amicus Curiae in South Africa.[230] In this context, one of the amici sought to present statistical evidence on the anticipated impact of the court's decision on children. The lower court determined that the court's rules only allow the Amicus Curiae to present *legal arguments* and therefore rejected the submission of the statistical evidence.[231] However, the Constitutional Court reversed the decision, stating, "Rule 16A does not prohibit the introduction of evidence by an amicus in a High Court."[232] Furthermore, it added that the court has the discretion to allow the

[226]Ibid, section 80.

[227]Ibid, section 121.

[228]Klaaren (1995), p. 499. For example, in the case of S. v. Lawrence 1997 (4) SA 1176 (CC), which dealt with the prosecution of a person selling alcoholic beverages on a public holiday, alcohol companies joined as amici on the side of the accused. In the case of *S. v. Mamabolo* 2001 (3) SA 409 (CC), which addressed the constitutionality of prosecuting a person for contempt of court, interest groups, including media organizations and human rights organizations, joined as interveners arguing for the right to freedom of expression. In the case of *S. v. Jordan* 2002 (6) SA 642 (CC), which dealt with the prohibition of prostitution, various interest groups, including women's groups, joined as amici. For further reading, see Jason (2006), p. 391.

[229]Mubangizi and Mbazira (2012), pp. 199–200.

[230]*Children's Inst. v. Presiding Officer of the Children's Court* [2012] ZACC 25, (2013) 2 SA 620.

[231]The contention is seemingly based on the fact that the Constitutional Court Rules 10(8) forbids an amicus from raising new facts in a case. However, rule 31(1) allows an amicus to canvas factual materials not appearing in the records. For a detailed explanation of this issue, see *supra* note 553, Budlender in Woolman et al. (2006), p. 8.

[232]Ibid para 26.

amicus to present evidence based on considerations of justice and that the rules of the court are:

> [S]pecifically intended to facilitate the role of amici in promoting and protecting the public interest. In these cases, amici play an essential role first, by ensuring that courts consider a wide range of options and are well informed. and second, by increasing access to the courts by creating space for interested non-parties to provide input on important public interest matters, particularly those relating to constitutional issues.[233]

Similarly, in a case concerning the constitutionality of the death penalty, Chief Judge Chaskalson of the Constitutional Court, who was aware of the societal and political implications of this issue following the end of apartheid rule, reached out to various interest groups. These groups included human rights organizations, conservative organizations, university professors, and spiritual and religious leaders. He invited them to present their positions to the court.[234] This judgment illustrates the importance that the South African judicial system attributes to the role of Amicus Curiae in shaping the country's jurisprudence.[235] A vivid depiction of the Amicus Curiae phenomenon in South Africa can be found in the *Children's Institute* case, where the Constitutional Court affirmed that the amicus plays a significant role in shaping South African society:

> amici curiae have made and continue to make an invaluable contribution to its jurisprudence and . . . their participation in litigation is to be welcomed and encouraged.[236]

The relatively liberal adoption of the Amicus Curiae practice in South Africa and the significant involvement of amici in decision-making processes within the courts has inspired other countries on the African continent, such as Uganda,[237] Kenya, Ethiopia,[238] and Namibia,[239] which have gradually embraced the practice of Amicus Curiae in their judicial proceedings. Furthermore, there is a growing call from academia for other African countries to follow suit and adopt aspects of the South African practices regarding Amicus Curiae. There is a belief that doing so may have a transformative effect on the jurisprudential landscape of the continent, encouraging the furthered protection of human rights in private law.[240]

[233] Ibid para 26.

[234] *S. v. Makwanyane* 1995 (3) SA 391 (CC). For a description of the impact of the amicus on human rights-related proceedings. See also Viljoen and Abebe (2014), p. 24.

[235] Klaaren (1995), p. 508. For a description of the trends, see Klaaren et al. (2011). For a description of the contribution of amici to the development of human rights law in South Africa, see: Spies (2015), pp. 136, 156–167.

[236] *Children's Inst. v. Presiding Officer of the Children's Court* [2012] ZACC 25, (2013) 2 SA 62 para15.

[237] Kasirye (2012); Mbazira (2009); Mubangizi and Mbazira (2012), pp. 199–200.

[238] Badwaza (2011). Viljoen and Abebe (2014).

[239] Hinson and Hubbard (2012). Viljoen and Abebe (2014).

[240] Jonas (2019); Jonas (2015), pp. 329–354; Nekura et al. (2022) Comparative Perspectives on Amicus Curiae Practice in Africa. Accessed at: https://home.creaw.org/wp-content/uploads/2022/05/ISLA_Insights_Issue_3_Comparative_Perspectives_on_Amicus_Curiae_Practice_in_Africa_Ebook.pdf; Viljoen and Abebe (2014).

In sum, the Amicus Curiae phenomenon has manifested in South Africa in several vital aspects: Firstly, since the early 2000s, there has been widespread use of the amicus procedure, particularly in proceedings related to human rights (but not limited to them). The Amicus Curiae as a protector of human rights in South Africa has been a fascinating case study, not least due to the country's apartheid background, which has triggered a significantly larger NGO-per-capita ratio than most other countries and a vigorous passion for public involvement in legal proceedings.[241] As such, the amicus has been a critical character in the South African judiciary, as exemplified in the *Children's Institute* case, where the Constitutional Court extolled the significant role of the amicus in shaping South African society.[242] Secondly, there has been significant development and diversity vis-a-vis the types of judicial interventions involving amici, which were initially limited to the Constitutional Court but have branched out to the Supreme Court of Appeals and extended to the Land Court, encompassing almost everything in between. Thirdly, a wide range of interest groups now utilize the Amicus Curiae as a tool to represent their interests. Fourthly, there has been the formulation and consolidation of rules regarding the involvement of amici in court proceedings.

5.7 Ireland

The Amicus Curiae practice in Ireland is an extraordinarily new phenomenon. Remarkably, an amicus was only explicitly recognized by the Irish judiciary for the first time in 2003, following a ruling by the Supreme Court in the case of *Iwuala*.[243] In this matter, which dealt with recognizing Iwuala as a refugee, the United Nations High Commissioner for Refugees (UNHCR) requested to submit a brief as an Amicus Curiae. The UNHCR argued that the brief would assist the court in adopting a proper interpretation of the issue and that the amicus status in European courts had become customary.[244] Despite the absence of regulations regarding the acceptance of third-party positions as Amici in the Irish judicial system, the Supreme Court granted the request of the UNHCR to participate as amicus in the ongoing proceedings.

---

[241] Jonas (2019) ibid.

[242] *Children's Inst. v. Presiding Officer of the Children's Court* [2012] ZACC 25, (2013) 2 SA 62.

[243] I. v. Minister for Justice, Equality & Law Reform [2003] 3 IR 197. From a legislative perspective, the only mention of Amicus Curiae was in section 8(h) of the Human Rights Commission Act 2000, which recognised, in an extremely limited way, the right of the Human Right Commission to appear to the high court as an amicus. In terms of precedent, the judgment of the aforementioned case recognised that a previous decision, Brady v. Cavan Co. Council [1999] 4 IR 99., had recognized the right to intervene, which sowed the seeds for the outright recognition of the amicus practice.

[244] See examples from England: R v. Immigration Appeal Tribunal; *ex parte* Shah [1999] 2 AC 629 (HL) (appeal taken from England); Sepet v. Secretary of State for the Home Department [2001] EWCA Civ 681.

Ironically, while the practice has very little history in Irish jurisprudence, Ireland provides us with a uniquely acute lens with which to understand the overall development of the Amicus Curiae phenomenon. In Iwuala, precisely because of the lack of local legislative and common law, Judge Keane was forced to consider a broad perspective of the Amicus Curiae, as it has appeared and developed in other countries.[245] The Supreme Court judgment recognised that the "traditional amicus," disinterested by nature and intended solely for the court's benefit, has developed a more partisan role:

> The role of the Amicus Curiae, however, in those jurisdictions where its nature has been the subject of reasonably extensive judicial discussion, notably the United States, has changed considerably with time. While it is still the case that an Amicus Curiae is allowed to appear because the court would be thereby assisted in coming to a correct resolution of an issue in dispute by being informed of all the relevant cases, statutes and other materials relevant to its determination, the amicus is no longer expected to be wholly disinterested in the outcome of the litigation.[246]

In what may be considered, in my opinion, to be an extraordinary example of judicial activism (at least insofar as the court was not restrained by lack of legislation or precedent), the Supreme Court ruled that it was within their "inherent jurisdiction"[247] to allow the intervention of an amicus. They cited an inherent flaw in the adversarial judicial system as a primary reason for such:

> It is an unavoidable disadvantage of the adversarial system of litigation in common law jurisdictions that the courts are, almost invariably, confined in their consideration of the case to the submissions and other materials, such as relevant authorities, which the parties elect to place before the court. Since the resources of the court itself in this context are necessarily limited, there may be cases in which it would be advantageous to have the written and oral submissions of a party with a bona fide interest in the issue before the court which cannot be characterised as a meddlesome busy body.[248]

I believe that this case provides a prime accentuation of a broad and universal movement whereby the jurisprudence of the world at large (or at least, of the Western world) has begun to recognize the social and humanistic role of the courtroom. Eschewing a rigid and unflinching commitment to formal legislation or precedent, *Iwuala* reflects the judiciary's understanding of how legal systems can impact society.

In Ireland, the decision of whether to accept an Amicus Curiae in judicial proceedings is left to the exclusive discretion of the court.[249] Unlike in other common law countries, even representatives of the state authorities are required to

---

[245] The court considered examples primarily from Australia, the United States, and England. See Hippolitus Iwuala v. The Minister for Justice, Equality and Law Reform 2003 IESC 42.

[246] Ibid p. 6.

[247] Ibid p. 12.

[248] Ibid pp. 12–13.

[249] Ibid. Even though no party formally objected to the amicus brief, the court still insisted on deciding on the issue. See also Kingston (2014). The article discusses the role of amici curiae in public interest litigation in Ireland and examines the requirements and limitations of the practice.

submit a request to present their position as amici. One of the criteria for including amici is a balance between the potential contribution of the amici and the burden that including the amici may impose on the litigants.[250] In Ireland, alongside the option to intervene as an amicus, third parties are also allowed to express their position as "third party interveners," but such interventions are generally limited to specific situations such as matrimonial disputes and admiralty actions.[251]

The Iwuala judgment, given in the early 2000s, represents a significant milestone in the approach of Irish courts regarding the Amicus Curiae phenomenon.[252] Since the decision was issued, Irish courts have shown readiness to expand the use of the Amicus Curiae concerning various non-governmental public organizations and various issues.[253] One of the bodies that frequently appears before the Irish High Court is the Irish Human Rights Commission. Since 2005, the Commission has been allowed to intervene in various cases before the Irish judicial system, including providing legal assistance to defendants, protecting information, psychiatric detention, psychiatric treatment in institutions, and refugee rights.[254]

One of the famous cases is the case of *P.P. v Health Service Executive* (HSC) in 2014.[255] In this case, the Irish High Court allowed several organizations to make written submissions as amici curiae on the issue of whether the Eighth Amendment of the Irish Constitution prohibited termination of pregnancy in cases of fatal fetal abnormality.[256]

The new assumption of Irish courts is that the modern judicial role requires a broader understanding of their judgments' societal implications, including information often available from various sources and interest groups beyond the formal litigants. However, as a matter of practical reality, the courts are still wary of using the amicus in many judicial proceedings.[257]

In summary, the fact that Ireland has a very limited history with the Amicus Curiae practice has proved a bittersweet datum. On the one hand, it has allowed us to capture the way in which the Supreme Court was able to analyse the issue unbiasedly

---

[250] In contrast, the Supreme Court of India has held that the opposition of the parties to the appointment of an amicus is of no significance when the court deems it necessary to appoint an amicus to the court. See S.K. Sundaram vs Unknown on 15 December, 2000; See also Supreme Court Rules, 2013, Order IV para. 1(a).

[251] HI p. 5.

[252] O'Brien (2004).

[253] Kingston (2014).

[254] *Amicus Curiae or Friend of the Court*, Irish Human Rights & Equality Comm'n, http://www.ihrec.ie/legal/amicuscuriae.html.

[255] P.P. v Health Service Executive [2014] IEHC 622.

[256] Kingston (2014).

[257] Amicus Curiae briefs have been used in cases involving constitutional rights and public interest issues but are not frequently used in Ireland compared to other jurisdictions. See de Londras and Enright (2008). The article notes that Amicus Curiae briefs have been used in cases involving constitutional rights and public interest issues but are not frequently used in Ireland compared to other jurisdictions.

and succinctly from a relatively external perspective while considering an acute fault with the adversarial system. On the other hand, complete data regarding all the criteria presented in the methodological chapter was not available for Ireland. However, cautiously speaking, it can be said that the main innovation concerning the use of the Amicus Curiae in Ireland is the actual acceptance of this institution in 2003 and the establishment of common law rules regarding its utilization.

5.8 Hong Kong and Singapore

Due to the significant similarities between the legal systems of Singapore and Hong Kong (former British territories) regarding their respective adoption of Amicus Curiae, they will be referred to collectively.[258] Formally, in Hong Kong and Singapore, the Amicus Curiae is used in four main situations: Firstly, during a hearing when a legal issue of public importance arises, and the court wishes to hear additional opinions from third parties other than the formal litigants. In such cases, the court itself will appoint an individual or organization to assist in the proceedings. For example, in the case of *Leung Chi Yuen*, which dealt with the duty of defense counsel to assist the court when instructed by the accused to act differently, the court appointed an Amicus Curiae to provide their opinion on the matter.[259] Similarly, in the *AG v. Choi Yan Kwong* case, the court appointed an amicus after the question arose whether the court was authorized to decide against the accused in conflict with the wishes of the general prosecution, which had already withdrawn its arguments.[260] Secondly, when the accused is unrepresented, and there is no legal obligation to appoint counsel, the court faces difficulties in managing the proceedings.[261] Thirdly, in applications made by one party where the court seeks to understand the public interest, the state's representatives are not legally required to be present in the proceedings.[262] And fourthly, in cases where the appointment of an Amicus Curiae is necessary to safeguard the interests of a third party who may be

[258] See Mohan (2010), pp. 352–374.

[259] R v. Leung Chi Yuen, [1989] 2 H.K.C. 24 (C.A.). Similarly, in Chan Lee Kuen v. Chan Sui Fai, [1966] H.K.L.R. 796, an amicus was invited when the question arose as to whether the court has the authority to enforce divorces for Chinese citizens for the purpose of preventing polygamy.

[260] AG v. Choi Yan Kwong, [1989] 1 H.K.C. 131 (C.A.).

[261] Chan (1997), p. 396. See Lei Sau Fong v. Tai Wai Ying, [1991] 1 H.K.C. 61 (C.A.), which dealt with the question of whether a poorly drafted contract could constitute a ground for rescission. Similarly, in the case of Tam Hing Yee v. Wu Tai Wai, [1991] HKCA 201, the application of Hong Kong's Bill of Rights in private disputes was discussed.

[262] For example, in the case of *S.* China Strategic Ltd., [1997] H.K.L.R.D. 131 (C.F.I), where the question of sanction against a company for breach of its obligations was deliberated. The court appointed an amicus to assist in rendering a decision on the appeal. For additional examples from Hong Kong, see the case of Carrian Holdings Ltd. (In Liq.), [1990] 1 H.K.C. 320 (C.F.I.); the case of *Grandeur Constr.*, *supra* note 119; Re Sing. Ins. Co., [1985] 2 H.K.C. 244 (C.F.I.).

affected by the outcome of the proceedings and is not formally part of the process or does not understand their rights as a matter of law.[263]

In Singapore and Hong Kong, it is customary that if the court invites an amicus to assist in the proceedings, the state treasury pays his expenses. However, the court has the authority to impose the expenses of the amicus on one of the formal parties. In fact, the courts may even award costs against the amicus in cases where they abuse their power or their argument is contentious or harassing.[264]

The frequency of third-party interventions in Hong Kong and Singapore is relatively low. Each year, there are only a few isolated instances of amici appointed by the courts (and even fewer cases of intervenors who have a more direct interest in the litigation).[265] However, research indicates that in cases where amici are indeed involved (notwithstanding the rarity of the occurrence), the courts heavily rely on them to obtain information, particularly on international legal doctrines, which assist in developing domestic law.[266]

One of the central judicial decisions regarding the Amicus Curiae phenomenon in Hong Kong is *Hong Kong v. Ma Wai-Kwan*.[267] The court case dealt with the question of whether the common law continues to be the dominant law in Hong Kong following its transfer to China. The Court of Appeal dismissed the request of the Law Society of Hong Kong to submit a position as an Amicus Curiae. It noted that the submission's content contradicted the amicus's neutral and traditional role in Hong Kong.

This judicial decision has been subject to considerable criticism, as it is argued that it is unclear why the court refused to allow the Law Society's participation as an Amicus Curiae, given that it is a well-established practice in Hong Kong to include it as an amicus in various matters. Furthermore, it is contended that the court erred in its determination that the request did not meet the criteria for court participation since the Amicus Curiae, by its very definition, does not need to complete the conventional standing requirements, as it is not a formal party. Thirdly, the court's approach of rejecting attempts by third parties to join proceedings reflects a stance that opposes the constitutional development of the legal system in Hong Kong. In other words, the court's treatment of the Amicus Curiae institution, as demonstrated in the *Ma Wai-Kwan* case, does not reflect the prevailing approach of the judiciary in Hong

[263] See, for example, the case of C v. D, [1992] 2 H.K.C. 248 (C.F.I.). In this case, the question of removing the custody of the children from a person was deliberated, and the state prosecutor was appointed as an amicus to ensure the well-being of the children.

[264] See, for example, the case of S. China Strategic Ltd., [1997] H.K.L.R.D. 131 (C.F.I). In practice, interest groups or individuals are not allowed to be amici without the permission of the court, and such permission is granted based on the anticipated contribution of the amicus to the proceedings, their expertise, and professional experience.

[265] Lee Zhe Xu et al. (2015).

[266] There, p. 52. See, for example, the case of Tang Kin Hwa v. Traditional Chinese Med. Practitioners Bd., [2005] 4 S.L.R. 604 (H.C.).

[267] Hong Kong v. Ma Wai-Kwan, [1997] 12 H.K.C. 315, 359 (C.A.).

Kong. Since this judgment, the courts have shown a much more liberal attitude towards the wishes of third parties to present their positions.[268]

In addition, political and constitutional developments that took place in the 1990s and early 2000s, as well as various court decisions, have led to a certain increase in the involvement of courts in public issues and individual rights.[269] These developments have prompted diverse interest groups, often including international organizations (such as human rights organizations), to attempt to influence the court's decision-making processes as third parties to ongoing proceedings.[270] These developments have included, for example, the enactment of the Hong Kong Bill of Rights, the dispute over the right to abode in Hong Kong, the enactment of China's National Security Law in Hong Kong, political interference in opposition districts, the extrajudicial targeting of human rights organizations in Hong Kong, and the protests against the Extradition Law Amendment Bill in 2019.[271]

5.9 Israel

Similar to other common-law countries, the rise of the Amicus Curiae phenomenon in Israel is part of the widespread legal and social processes that have taken place throughout the Western world in recent decades. These include significant processes that have occurred simultaneously vis-à-vis society, politics, and the role of judicial systems. Israel is part of the global "Amicus Curiae phenomenon," but it is characterized by unique aspects. The amicus phenomenon in Israel has reciprocal relationships with social and legal phenomena that have occurred in the global environment, as well as with developments within Israeli society, politics, and the Israeli legal system. It appears that it is not coincidental that during a period in which reliance on the judiciary and various legal procedures to organize and address issues about core matters of social, economic, and political policy has been increasing in Israel, the Amicus Curiae practice has been increasingly adopted into the Israeli legal system.

The judicial precedent that first brought about the adoption of the Amicus Curiae practice into the Israel judiciary was the *Kozali* case. In this case, involving five defendants accused of child murder, the defense focused on the alleged failure in the initial legal representation provided to the defendants, the quality of their legal protection, and the flawed manner in which their confessions were obtained.

In light of these circumstances, the Public Defender's Office approached the Supreme Court and, for the first time in the Israeli judiciary, submitted a request to join the proceedings as an Amicus Curiae. In principle, the Public Defender's Office argued that due to its expertise in studying criminal cases and the substantial legal

[268] Kwan (2022), pp. 71–91.

[269] Ibid.

[270] For further discussion, see Johannes and Ghai (1993).

[271] Chan (1997), p. 396.

questions that arose regarding the quality of legal representation, it was appropriate for the court to adopt the institution of Amicus Curiae and allow the involvement of the Public Defender's Office in this case. The office contended that there is considerable value in promoting the independent appearance of an Amicus Curiae rather than pursuing separate petitions, as there is no need for the public petitioner to invest all the resources associated with filing a distinct appeal. Utilizing an Amicus Curiae would save the court's time while allowing the amicus to focus resources on presenting the legal position. Furthermore, it argued that recognizing an Amicus Curiae could encourage public entities unwilling or unable to file separate appeals and reluctant to bear the expenses associated with direct party status to participate in legal discussions.

The defendants in the *Kozali* case agreed to the request for the participation of the Public Defender's Office as an Amicus Curiae. In contrast, the Attorney General's Legal Advisor opposed the request based on three grounds. Firstly, recognizing the Public Defender's Office as an Amicus Curiae would undermine its position as the exclusive representative of the interests of the public as a whole.[272] The inclusion of the Public Defender's Office as an amicus would imply its role solely as a general claimant and not as someone presenting the comprehensive public interest before the court.[273] Secondly, it was argued that the possibility of including the Public Defender's Office as an amicus does not align with the prevailing legal system in Israel, whereby on one side of the scale stands the state represented by the prosecution, and on the other side, the defendant, represented by the defense, without any other entities having the authority to intervene in the proceedings. Thirdly, in the Attorney General's view, the correct definition of an "Amicus Curiae" should be just that—a "friend of the court"—a neutral and objective representative who draws the court's attention to a legal point that the court may have overlooked.

After reviewing the parties' arguments, the President of the Supreme Court of Israel at the time, Aharon Barak, agreed to the public defender's request to join the proceedings as an Amicus Curiae. He wrote:

> The Amicus Curiae institution has been recognized in various legal systems for hundreds of years. Its essence is assistance to the court in some issue, by someone who is not a direct party to the conflict in question. Initially, this institution was a tool for presenting only a neutral position in the proceedings, while providing objective assistance to the court. But later, the Amicus Curiae institution developed as a party to the proceedings, which is not necessarily neutral and objective, but rather represents - by virtue of its role or occupation - an interest or expertise that deserves to be heard before the court in a specific conflict. Thus, in those cases where there is a third party - which is not involved in the dispute itself - it will

[272] See sections 62 and 231 of the Criminal Procedure Code (Consolidated Version) 5724–1982.

[273] This position is valid when it comes to a request for a retrial in which special status is given to the Attorney General as he is not a party to the proceedings in the traditional sense but rather assists the President of the Supreme Court in deciding on the existence of grounds for a retrial. The basis of this decision was the determination that the public defender's office in itself has no status within the related procedures on the question of holding a retrial. The status is given either to the convicted defendant's representative or to the attorney general. See section 31 (B) Criminal Procedure Code (Consolidated version) 5726–1984.

> be possible to add [said party] as an Amicus Curiae, if their presence in the proceedings is in order to contribute to the formation of the common law on a particular matter, on the basis of presenting all the relevant positions on the matter in question, and while providing representation, a chance to intervene, and knowledge, of representative and professional bodies.[274]

This ruling presents an "open" list of factors that the judge must consider when deciding whether to allow the inclusion of a party as an Amicus Curiae before the court, including the potential contribution of the proposed position; the nature of the requesting party seeking to join the process; their expertise, experience, and the representation they provide to the interest they seek to represent in the proceedings; the type of process and procedure being followed; the parties involved in the process; the stage at which the application for inclusion is submitted; and the nature of the issue at hand.[275]

The criticism of the court's ruling suggests that the intention of the Supreme Court in adopting the Amicus Curiae in Israel is unclear.[276] It is unclear which particular model of Amicus the Israeli judiciary has adopted. Is it the "classical amicus" (similar to the English concept), perhaps it is the "modern amicus" (the American concept), or maybe it is another model that falls within the spectrum of these categories?

5.9.1 Specific Reasons for Adopting the Israeli "Amicus"

Regarding the adoption of the Amicus Curiae in Israel, there are also unique explanations that led to the adoption of the amicus in Israel regarding *Kozali*.[277] The first explanation is that the Supreme Court wanted to establish and strengthen the power and public status of the Public Defender's Office as a parallel body to the State Attorney's Office, and its addition as an amicus was an appropriate means for

---

[274]The Supreme Court President, Aharon Barak, agreed that the public defender should join the proceedings as an "Amicus Curiae" but should limit her contributions to two topics: firstly, the effect of the alleged failure in the initial legal representation provided to the defendants in their trial; and secondly the precise meaning of the concept "a significant concern that the conviction caused a miscarriage of justice" For the Kozali case. See: The State of Israel vs. Kozali 19.10.1985, 349/84; Kozali vs The State of Israel 9.5.1991 906/85; Kozali vs The State of Israel 3081/91 1991, President Shemgar; Kozali vs The State of Israel 7929/96 1999.

[275]The court emphasized that all these factors are not conclusive criteria and are not sufficient to determine in advance when it would be appropriate to join a party to the proceedings as an Amicus Curiae.

[276]It is my contention that Barak was influenced, albeit selectively, by the principles of Amicus Curiae participation in the United States Supreme Court. For discussion, see Farber (2018), pp. 547–563.

[277]The State of Israel vs. Kozali 19.10.1985, 349/84. The court emphasized that all of these are not exhaustive criteria and there is no point in deciding in advance when it will be appropriate to add a party to the proceedings as an "Amicus Curiae."

this purpose. It seems that it was easier for the court to "digest" or accept recognition of a new amicus in the form of an organization from within the state rather than a foreign and unknown organization. It seems that the fact that it was a state body that presented considerations that supported one side but were of a professional nature facilitated the adoption of the amicus for the first time. If another body had asked to join as an amicus before any other precedents had been established, the Supreme Court would probably have rejected its request. The intensification of the discourse about the rights of defendants in criminal law, and in particular, after the enactment of the fundamental laws in 1992,[278] also contributed to the recognition of the public defender as an amicus that sheds light on criminal issues from the point of view of those involved in crimes.[279]

Moreover, in the Israeli criminal procedure, there is no alternative in which a third party can present his point of view (except for crime victims in certain circumstances) before the courts. In the adversarial method, the criminal procedure is a "closed" procedure, where the prosecution reflects the public interest, while the accused, through his attorney, presents his defense, and third parties cannot intervene in the procedure.[280] Thus, the amicus was the court's way of adopting the positions of third parties in criminal proceedings, which later allowed the addition of amici in other branches of law.

Second, the request of the defense was the first request submitted to the Supreme Court to join as an Amicus Curiae, and the Supreme Court was led by Judge Barak, who was interested in the development of the law on the issue of public litigation. He saw this as an opportunity to fulfill his judicial view. Also, in Barak's early writings, it can be seen that he believed that the law on the subject of "the public interest litigant" should be developed by adopting the amicus practice. As an example of the development of the public interest litigator who assists the courts, Barak pointed to the amicus in the United States.[281] It seems, therefore, that the court had "looked for" the first opportunity that came its way to develop the practice of the amicus in Israel. Furthermore, about a decade and a half after Barak published his position regarding the development of the amicus in Israel, the appropriate judicial opportunity finally came his way, and he did take advantage of it.

---

[278] Basic Law: Human Dignity and Liberty, 1992.

[279] Barak (1994, 1996).

[280] As a rule, the accused is at a disadvantage compared to the accuser. I will mention only a few examples that illustrate this: the defense attorney arrives late at the scene of the investigation—a scene that is managed exclusively by the investigating authority; the normative determination regarding the incriminating meaning of the right to remain silent; and conviction based on statements given outside the walls of a court. Also, the ethos of the prosecution as a protection of the public and the presumption of propriety applied to the activity of the government is, to a certain extent, opposed to the protection of defendants.

[281] Barak (1983).

5.9.2 The "Amicus Curiae Phenomenon" in Israel

According to the data I collected, starting with the adoption of Amicus Curiae in Israel in 1999, there has, since then, been a significant increase in the scope of the use of this practice.[282] In the first years after the amicus's adoption, amici were hardly used, and only a few applications were submitted to the courts. However, since that time, this trend has changed, and from the middle of the first decade of the 2000s, a significant increase in the use of amicus can be observed. For example, compared to an average of a few requests per year in the early 2000s, the scope of use has increased to hundreds yearly. About half of the requests for amici to join proceedings are submitted to the Supreme Court, both when it sits as the High Court and when it sits as a court of appeals, with over ninety percent of the amici requests submitted to three courts: the Supreme Court, the courts for administrative matters and the National Labor Court.[283] Most applications are submitted by non-governmental organizations seeking to support the position of private litigants conducting legal proceedings against the state or corporations wishing to influence court policy.

In addition, starting with the adoption of amici in Israel in 1999, a significant increase in the number of public organizations that use amici to express their position is evident. As mentioned above, the first body that used an amicus brief was a government body—the Public Defense Office.[284] However, several non-governmental public organizations working for various issues of public interest began to use this institution and applied it to the courts to present their positions as third parties. These include: (1) human rights organizations;[285] (2) women's rights organizations;[286] (3) 'green' sustainability organizations;[287] (4) religious

[282] According to my last examination made in three databases in the Hebrew language - Nevo, Takdin and Pador (last checked in September 2023).

[283] Ibid.

[284] Following this, the Public Defender's Office was joined in a large number of founding and precedent cases. For a list of the various positions expressed by the defense as a "Amicus Curiae" on key issues of criminal law, see "Amicus Curiae position" The Public Defense Office (2021) https://www.gov.il/he/departments/publications/reports/amicus_curiae. The Public Defense Office has the highest number of accessions as an Amicus Curiae.

[285] Association for Civil Rights in Israel; *Amuta Lema'an Ichut HaShilton* (The Movement for Quality Government in Israel) HCJ 155/97 E.G.E. Alonim Services Company Ltd. V. Minister of the Interior (February 12, 2001); Request for Administrative Appeal Permission 7696/16 Arie v. Ministry of the Interior – Population and Immigration Authority (January 4, 2017).

[286] NA'AMAT – Movement of women workers and volunteers – Clal Insurance Company Ltd. (September 11, 2001); Dantz 18/15 Anonymous v. The Special Courts for Conversion (decision of 4/30/2015); OJ (national– 13359-12-13 Manit – Anonymous (7/31/2014).

[287] *Adam Teva VeDin* – Israel Union for Environmental Defense; *Zalul; Chayim VeSviva.* TA (Shalom Beer Sheva) 4814–03 State of Israel – Ministry of Environmental Quality v. Bromine Compounds Ltd. (17.5.2004); AJM 7014/14 Mustafa v. Jerusalem Municipality (12.4.2016).

organizations;[288] (5) organizations for patients' rights.[289] In addition to these various non-governmental groups, organizations with economic, social, or political power also began to use "amici" as a means to promote their goals: the Bar Association,[290] the "Industrial Association,"[291] or the Bank Association.[292] Political parties,[293] local authorities,[294] politicians, and parliament members also make use of the "amicus" institution.[295]

From the adoption of the amicus in 1999 until 2022, not only has the number of briefs and requests to join as amici increased, but the topics the briefs deal with and the types of legal courts to which the brief are submitted have also increased and diversified. If in the past, amici only joined proceedings before the Supreme Court, the courts for administrative matters, and the National Labor Court, now amici join all possible tribunals, including family courts, disciplinary courts,[296] statutory commissions,[297] and military courts.[298] In Israel, requests to join amici are submitted to almost all legal courts in the country, including the magistrates'[299] and small claims courts.[300]

---

[288] *Ne'emanei Tora veAvoda- a religious Zionist movement.* HCJ 5224/13 in Tito v. Minister of Religious Services (July 30, 2013).

[289] Access Israel. Criminal Appeals Authority 5273/12 Guy v. State of Israel (May 9, 2013).

[290] In recent years, the number of cases in which the Chamber requested to join as a "Amicus Curiae" has increased. If in the past, the Bar Association requested to join as an "amicus" in matters closely related to its powers such as: collection of fees, protection of the profession or attorney-client privilege, then in recent years the Bar Association also requests to join in general matters. See, for example, HCJ–43/16 OMC Movement - Citizens for Proper Administration and Social and Legal Justice v. the Government of Israel.

[291] Additional civil hearing 4998/15 Tempo Beer Industries Ltd. v. Director of the Customs and VAT Division - Purchase tax (8/31/2015); HCJ 4374/15, *supra* note 620.

[292] Civil appeal 4303/15 Leumi Bank of Israel Ltd. v. Kogan trustee and Baumgarten trustee (September 21, 2015).

[293] Additional hearing High Court of Justice 10007/09 Gluten v. The National Labor Court, P.D. Su (1) 518 (2013).

[294] Additional Civil Hearing 6298/15 The local committee for planning and building Petah Tikva against Divon (15.6.2016).

[295] See the request of MK Elazar Stern in the 5026/16 Gigi v. Chief Rabbinate of Israel (February 16, 2017).

[296] Local authority Tiberias Municipality vs Elyahu, 46/06 (17.12.2008).

[297] The Decision of the Committee on Compensation and Royalties in accordance with Section 109 of the Patent Law, 1967-577 (23.5.2013).

[298] Appeal to a disciplinary court 84/14 L. 20 v. the Chief Military Prosecutor (unpublished, April 18, 2016).

[299] See, for example, TA 5090/06 Nirgad Car Company Ltd. vs. Khayke (published in Nevo 17.6.2012); TA 18445-08-12 World organization of Libyan Jews vs Duani (published in Nevo 11.12.2014) among many others.

[300] See Small Claims (Small Claims Court) No. 8518-03-09 Narozini v. Kovner (11/24/2009). In this case, the "Association of Art Lovers in Israel" requested to join the lawsuit that was conducted in the small claims court as an "Amicus Curiae."

In addition, the increase in the number of amicus briefs submitted to the courts is not limited to constitutional cases, with amicus briefs also being submitted in other areas, such as labor law, tort law, privacy protection law, planning and construction law, environmental law,[301] family law, criminal law, administrative law, bankruptcy law, and property law.[302]

The amicus practice in Israel has grown rapidly in recent years, especially in cases of extensive public significance. Examining what is happening in the content of social organizations in connection with their activity in the legal arena shows that joining a procedure conducted as amici is fertile ground for creating collaborations and strengthening working relationships. Collaborations between organizations regarding joining legal proceedings as amici and "coalitions" of amici can be brought about in various ways: writing a joint brief on behalf of several organizations, mutual brainstorming between the organizations' activists about the position that should be submitted as an amicus brief, work meetings and regular consultations between the representatives of the organizations about the arguments that should be included in the briefs.

In some cases, working relationships between organizations are manifested in connection with joining as amici in the submission of existing legal materials, scientific or social studies, or in the appointment of experts (for example, experts in environmental sciences or experts in the field of labor law) for the partner organization in the coalition. In a certain sense, the court serves as a sort of forum in the original meaning, as the "town square" where individuals and organizations meet for social and legal activity. For example, in two cases of principle related to the protection of privacy with far-reaching implications (intrusion into an employee's email box;[303] and a biometric attendance clock at the workplace[304]), the "Civil Rights Association" and "Kav LaOved" (Workers Help-line) collaborated in writing an amicus brief to the court.

In addition, when several organizations join together and voice a united front in court as a coalition of amici, this may create a more significant impression on the court and the public. As mentioned, amicus collaborations and coalitions are also common in other countries. Over the past twenty years, collaborations, and coalitions between many different organizations regarding joining the proceedings as amici.[305]

---

[301] See class action (districts of BS) 49319-12-14 Levi Pirsak v. Eilat Ashkelon Pipeline Company Ltd. (9.8.2016).

[302] In general, less than a third of the requests concern constitutional matters, while the legal branch with the highest percentage of requests is administrative (nearly forty percent of the requests).

[303] Labor Appeal (national) 90/08 Inbar–v. State of Israel - Commissioner for the Women's Labor Law (8.2.2011). Known as Tali Isakov-Inbar case.

[304] Appeal of a national collective dispute 7541-04-14 New General Workers' Union South Triangle Region - Kalansawa Municipality (March 15, 2017).

[305] For example, in the famous ruling that dealt with evidence obtained by means of pressure bordering on torture, coalitions of "intervenors" and "amici" (most of them non-governmental organizations) joined together in a joint memo. A. v. Sec'y of State for the Home Dep't (No 2)

5.9.3 *Criteria for Adding Amici in Israeli Courts*

In Israeli jurisprudence, several guiding tests (criteria) have been established regarding the addition of amici to ongoing proceedings:

(1) "The potential contribution of the proposed position"—Similar to most common law countries, this criterion was placed at the top of the court's scale when examining a request to join as an amicus. For example, in the *Ben Haim* case, the request of the Association for Civil Rights to join the process was rejected because "its claims do not make any real contribution to the judicial investigation required in the applications before us for the appellate authority more than the claims made by the applicants of the memos themselves."[306]
(2) "The essence of the body requesting to join the proceedings"—is similar to that accepted in other common law countries; as long as it is a professional body that represents interests of public importance, the courts will tend to accept the request to join as an amicus. On the other hand, when the amicus represents an independent and narrow position or interests of no public importance—the court will tend to reject the request.[307]
(3) "His expertise, experience and the representation that the amicus gives to the party in whose name he wishes to join"—the degree to which the amicus has expertise in his field, extensive knowledge, proficiency, and experience, matches the degree to which room will be made for him to present his position.[308]

[2005] UKHL 71, [2006] 2 AC 221 (appeal taken from Eng) For the Human Rights Tribunal of Latin America see: Juaristi FJR (2014).Available at: SSRN: https://ssrn.com/abstract=2488073. See also: Moyer (1985).

[306]Criminal Appeals Authority 10141/09 Ben Haim v. The State of Israel, Judgment Sa (3) 305, 326–327 (2012 Various Civil Applications (Tel Aviv Districts) 22414/07 Gil v. Lev, Pass 6 (15.1.2008). The rejection of a lawyer's request to express a position contrary to the "Amicus Curiae" in the case—The Bar Association - because "in the case before us, the applicant did not point to the contribution of his attachment to the present proceeding, but on the contrary, it seems that his words indicate that his attachment to the proceeding may even result in harm to the effectiveness the discussion." The considerations for the inclusion of an "amicus" are dealt with in Doron and Totari-Jobran (2006).

[307]For example, Yissacharov vs The Chief Military Prosecutor case 5121./98 (2006) the court allowed the addition of the Bar Association and the Public Defender's Office as "amici." It noted that: given the role of the bodies mentioned above, their expertise, and experience in representing defendants, their addition to the proceedings may contribute to deepening the discussion and clarifying it.

[308]For example, in the matter of property management property tax, the late Judge Azar came to the general conclusion that the bar association should be seen as an Amicus Curiae and noted that: one of the essential goals of the bar association is to take the following actions to ensure the level, reliability, and purity of the legal profession. This goal is so important that in a matter that raises the question of transgressing the boundaries of the profession, it is essential to hear the position of the Israel Bar Association (Tel Aviv District) 22050/03 Israel Bar Association - Tel Aviv District Board Property Management (1965) Ltd. (4.2.2004). In general, the reasons underlying most of the decisions in Israel to accept request for joining as "amici" were that this was a body representing an important public interest and that it was a fundamental or complex issue. See Doron et al. (2011).

(4) "The type of proceedings and the procedures used in them"—the type of proceedings primarily reflects the public interests at stake as well as the interests of the parties directly involved. Therefore, and following the current situation in most countries of the world, to the extent that the issue includes public interest elements or questions of legal or social weight, the tendency to approve the joining of a party to the proceedings as an amicus will increase. On the contrary—when the proceedings are supposed to be quick and efficient, there is a greater inclination not to add amici.[309]
(5) "The parties to the procedure itself"—where a formal party to the procedure in its nature and essence represents the public interests or a broad point of view, which also covers the same information or the position of the applicant to be an amicus, then the tendency will be not to accept the request of the amici.[310] In addition, to the extent that the formal parties themselves are ready and willing to allow the submission of the amicus's position, the positive weight will be added to the court's discretion to grant the request, and vice versa.[311] In most countries where the amicus is recognized, the consent of the parties to the proceedings, and at the very least their position, must be obtained.[312] The assumption is that when the formal parties agree to allow the addition of an amicus, they declare that their rights in the discussions will not be harmed due to the addition of the amicus, therefore, their consent makes it easier for the court to add amici.[313]
(6) "The stage at which the request to join was submitted"—the earlier the stage at which the request to join was submitted is within the procedure, the greater the tendency of the courts to approve the joining.[314]

---

[309] See Simon Wiesenthal Museum of Tolerance, Jerusalem High Court, 2008. Due to the many public interests related to harming the religious feelings of the Muslim population in Jerusalem, several social organizations were allowed to join the process as amici.

[310] See Koffman case, 3471/07 Tel Aviv (published in Nevo 12.3.2007).

[311] See for example AB (Jerusalem areas– 2669/04 Foxbromer - Civil Service Commission (September 13, 2009) (The plaintiff and the Civil Service Commission agreed to the merger of the Bar Association, thus paving the way for submitting a brief to the court.

[312] See Bryden (1987). For example, the Supreme Court of Canada, the consent of the court is required, even if both formal parties have agreed to the request for joinder.

[313] I believe that an additional subtest should be adopted that examines not only the position of the original parties but also their ability to present their position in court. That is to say, in cases where the court gets the impression that due to its economic, social, or public inferiority or for—some other reason—a formal party could not bring to light the arguments supporting its position. The court will tend to approve the joining of an amicus. This test should be subjective and not objective when the focus should be on the practical ability of the parties to present their arguments so that fairness is created in the process.

[314] For example, Dr Maria Mahamid case, Tel Aviv District Court, 23.01.17 which dealt with employment discrimination against a dentist based on nationality, the Equality (*Shivyon*) Commission asked for opportunities to join as an "amicus." The Labor Court approved the request and noted, among other things, that the receipt of the opinion at the stage when the parties' affidavits have not yet been submitted and the first hearing of the case has not yet taken place "will not hinder the procedure or delay it and the parties will be able to refer to the opinion late in the proceedings."

(7) "The nature of the issue to be decided"—the more the issue being examined in the court folds into an obligation Broad public considerations, political considerations, or innovative legal issues that have not yet been clarified in court, the courts will likely allow "amici" to present their position.[315]

5.9.4 The Israeli Amicus: An Intermediate Model between the American Amicus and the Classic Amicus

Israeli law has never given its opinion explicitly on the question of what the characteristics are of the desired amicus figure. Instead, the Supreme Court decided to take the path towards defining the acceptable characteristics of amici through negation: it is not interested in the modern, political, and self-interested "amici" similar to the "American amicus" of today. The Israeli law in practice today establishes the following conditions: First, only third parties who are not directly involved in the dispute will be allowed to join as amici. This means the Israeli amicus is not similar to the intervenor model accepted worldwide. Second, amici will only be accepted to join proceedings only if they are capable of making a real contribution to the judicial ruling on a particular matter. In other words, the addition of a third party as an amicus is intended to provide significant assistance to the court in the formulation of a judgement or the formulation of legal doctrine and not for any other reasons. This is substantially different to the addition of a third party who intends to support one side (similar to a certain extent to the "modern amicus"). Third, it will be possible to add an amicus who will present a balanced, accurate, and complete picture, unlike "modern amici," whose sole purpose is to support a particular side.[316] Fourth, only professional and representative bodies will be allowed to join the procedure. This again differs from the practice in some parts of the world where private individuals also submit amicus briefs on topics close to their hearts.[317] On the other hand, the courts in Israel reject, as a matter of principle,

[315] For example, Migdal case, AA 11152/04 Anonymous v. Migdal Insurance Company Ltd. (4.4.2005) requests were received from the Center for Assistance to Foreign Workers and Victims of Human Trafficking and the Clinic for Combating Trafficking in Women to join the procedure in which compensation was awarded to fund an escort institute. The court determined that the issue of recognizing the damage of "escort services" is innovative and precedential, and it has not yet been discussed and decided by the Supreme Court in the case of Migdal, AA 11152/04 Anonymous v. Migdal Insurance Company Ltd. (4.4.2005).

[316] In addition, this observation teaches us about another difference from the modern "amici" whose minority provide information without factual basis when the court cannot examine the facts to confirm them. Rustad and Koenig (1993), pp. 91, 157–158.

[317] In the United States, for example, it is common for private individuals to write memoranda to the courts and seek to present their worldview on a particular issue. See, for example, a memo submitted by a retired military officer who noted the negative impact on the military of affirmative action in universities, in the Grutter case, Grutter v. Bollinger, 539 U.S. 306 (2003).

requests from individuals or entities lacking professional experience to submit an amicus brief.[318]

Furthermore, the Israeli model is not similar to the objective model of the amicus but is a distinct entity that may be regarded as a sort of intermediate model: First, the "classic amicus" as it exists in most countries of common law and continental law is represented by amici who are usually invited to join proceedings in order to help the court by using their expert knowledge or professional expertise, while in Israel—it is the third parties who apply to the court to join as amici as they wish to express their position. Second, a "classic amicus" is allowed to raise any argument that will help the work of the court, while, in contrast, in Israel, the amici are only allowed to present certain arguments: specifically, they are not allowed to present claims against a defendant in a criminal proceeding.[319] Third, the "classic amicus" is a disinterested amicus whose purpose is to assist the court with particular proceedings. The situation in Israel is different since the Israeli amicus does not usually have a direct interest in the case, but he certainly has some interest in the subject matter under discussion. To this, it should be added that many of the amici who have joined so far in Israel same arguments that have already been presented to the court (briefs known as "me too briefs"), but in practice, the briefs that are submitted do often strengthen a specific side. In my humble opinion, the "Israeli amicus" is not similar to the "modern amicus." However, on the other hand, it is not entirely identical to the "classic amicus." It has many of the characteristics of the "intervenor" (except for the fact that the "Israeli amicus" does not become a formal party). It is a unique model.

5.10 Summary

The "amicus phenomenon" in Anglo-American countries significantly impacts court litigation procedures. There is a significant increase in the use of the amicus practice in all the countries that belong to this legal method—the United States, Canada, England, and South Africa. Concerning other common law countries (such as Australia, New Zealand, Hong Kong, and Singapore), there is a more moderate increase in the use of amici. In general, since the 1990s, the courts of common law have taken a liberal approach regarding the participation of third parties ("amici" and

---

Brief from a San Francisco citizen to the California Supreme Court on same-sex marriage, Divine Queen Mariette Do-Nguyen Lockyer v. City & County of San Francisco, 95 P.3d 459 (Cal. 2004) (No. S122923).

[318] See, for example, the request of attorney Yoram Shaftel regarding the prosecution of former president Moshe Katsav. The court noted that it is not necessary to say that the fact, in itself, that a certain person has an opinion or view, one way or another, in relation to the procedure that is being revealed in the court, cannot make that party a party to the proceedings, certainly not on the status of an "Amicus Curiae." Criminal proceedings (peace of Jerusalem) 5735/08 State of Israel v. Katsav (24.3.2008).

[319] Criminal case reference Tel Aviv 40230/07 State of Israel vs Gabriel Zizubi 15.11.2007 Takdin.

"intervenors") in legal proceedings before them, and the courts tend to invite "amici" on their own initiative to assist them in issues with broad implications. The number of subjects the briefs deal with and the number of judicial courts to which the briefs are submitted are also increasing significantly. Studies show an increase in the number of briefs submitted to various courts in the last two decades. In addition, the subjects in which individuals and public organizations seek to be amici deal with all areas of life.

In the eyes of many, the Amicus Curiae is the primary tool available to public organizations, enabling them to participate in the legal process to promote their position on a topic of interest to them. There are proceedings in which hundreds of amici join, representing thousands of interest groups. In common law, amici join proceedings conducted in all possible tribunals: courts for administrative matters, family courts, lower courts, labor courts, military courts, arbitration proceedings, and even statutory committees. In addition to all of these, the variety, type, and nature of the public bodies and organizations that began using the amicus to influence court rulings increased considerably. These include human rights organizations, "green" organizations working for sustainability and the quality of the environment, organizations working to strengthen democracy, religious organizations, LGBTQIA organizations, welfare organizations, "concerned" citizens, corporations, and groups with economic, social, or political power.

In the United States, the amicus serves as a lobbyist who supports the position expressed by one of the formal litigants and tries to convince the court to adopt his view. In contrast, in other countries, the "amicus" is usually a more objective third party who comes to assist in developing legal principles or to fulfill additional functions. Alongside the amicus, another institution allows participation in proceedings as a third party—the intervenor. From the point of view of third parties who wish to influence an ongoing case, the "amicus" and the "intervenor" are positioned on a continuum where the amicus is usually the more objective third party. In comparison to the amicus, the intervenor has a more direct interest in the procedure, and after the request of the intervenor is accepted, he becomes a formal party.

From a comparative perspective, it can be said that in most common law countries, a similar pattern is seen in adopting or increasing the use of an amicus. Initially, there is resistance on the part of the courts to the inclusion of third parties when the assumption underlying this approach is the common law philosophy, which is "hostile" to interference in the proceedings by third parties. After that, there is a "softening" trend in this approach in the face of dealing with issues with broader societal consequences. In the subsequent phase, the courts are "ready" to adopt intervention practices, sometimes formally and clearly and sometimes semi-formally. After the establishment of the practice, which takes a few years, there is an "explosion" in the way this practice is used, which is reflected in the diversity in the range of topics in which amicus briefs are submitted; an increase in the types of judicial courts to which the briefs are submitted; an increase in the number of briefs submitted in "mega cases," and more.

The Amicus Curiae phenomenon is not uniform in all common law countries. In some countries (such as the United States), the phenomenon's intensity is particularly noticeable, and its social consequences are broad. On the other hand, in other countries (such as Australia or New Zealand), the amicus phenomenon is not very noticeable. The courts' response to the desire of amici to express their position in the proceedings is based on the perception of their role. Indeed, in general, there is a correlation between the perception of the judicial role and the amicus phenomenon. This is expressed as a tendency towards active amici who participate in many proceedings, trying to influence the policy of the courts in places where the courts have broad powers and are deeply involved in society (such as the United States or South Africa). On the other hand, amici are less active in countries where courts are less actively involved in shaping society. Courts that sympathize with amicus interventions and welcome them tend to see their role as broader than dispute resolution.

References

Alarie BRD, Green AJ (2010) Interventions at the Supreme Court of Canada: accuracy, affiliation and acceptance. Osgoode Hall Law J 48(3/4):381–410

Anderson HA (2015) Frenemies of the court: the many faces of amicus curiae. Univ Rich Law Rev 49:361

Badwaza YM (2011) Public interest litigation as practiced by south african human rights NGOs: any lessons for Ethiopia?

Barak A (1983) Judicial legislation. Mishmatim 13:25

Barak A (1994) Human dignity as a constitutional right. The Advocate 41:271

Barak A (1996) The constitutionalization of the legal system following the basic laws and its consequences for the criminal law (substantive and deliberative). Legal Stud 13:5

Behuniak-Long S (1991) Friendly fire: amici curiae and Webster v. reproductive health services. Judicature 74(261):262

Blake DW (2006) Human rights law Res. Cwebstertr., role of Amicus Curiae and intervenors in the promotion and protection of human rights (Apr. 13, 2006)

Box-Steffensmeier JM, Christenson DP (2012) Database on Supreme Court Amicus Curiae briefs. Version 1.0. http://Amicinetworks.com

Box-Steffensmeier JM, Christenson DP (2014) The evolution and formation of amicus curiae networks. Soc Netw 36:82–96

Box-Steffensmeier JM, Christenson DP, Hitt MP (2013) Quality over quantity: amici influence and judicial decision making. Am Polit Sci Rev 107(3):1–15

Bradley RC, Gardner P (1985) Underdogs, upperdogs and the use of the amicus brief: trends and explanations. Just Syst J 10:78, 91

Brief from a San Francisco citizen to the California Supreme Court on same-sex marriage, Divine Queen Mariette Do-Nguyen Lockyer v. City & County of San Francisco, 95 P.3d 459 (Cal. 2004) (No. S122923)

Brodie I (1992) Interest groups and the charter of rights and freedoms: interveners at the Supreme Court of Canada. (unpublished M.A. thesis). University of Calgary

Brooke H (2007) Interventions in the court of appeal. Public Law 401

Bruce R (1998) A court in need and a friend indeed: an analysis of the arguments of the Amicus Curiae in the Quebec secession reference. Const Forum 10:9

Bryden PL (1987) Public interest intervention in the courts. Can Bar Rev 66:490

Budlender G. (2006) Amicus Curiae. In: Woolman et al (eds) Constitutional law of South Africa, 2nd edn. Juta and Co, pp 1 at 8–10
Caldeira GA, Wright JR (1990) Amici curiae before the Supreme Court: who participates, when, and how much? J Polit 52:782
Campbell E (1998) Intervention in constitutional cases. Public Law Rev 9:225, 256
Chan J (1997) Amicus curiae and non-party intervention. Hong Kong Law J 27(3):391–404
China Strategic Ltd., [1997] H.K.L.R.D. 131 (C.F.I)
Clark E (2005) The needs of the many and the needs of the few: a new system of public interest intervention for new Zealand. Victoria Univ Wellington Law Rev 36:71
Collins PM Jr (2004) Friends of the court: examining the influence of amicus curiae participation in United States Supreme Court litigation. Law Soc Rev 38(4):807–832
Collins PM Jr, Corley PC, Hamner J (2015) Influence of amicus curiae briefs on U.S. Supreme Court opinion content. Law Soc Rev 49:917
Collins PM Jr (2008) Friends of the Supreme Court: interest groups and judicial decision making
Corbally SF, Bross DC, Flango VE (2004) Filing of Amicus Curiae. Briefs in state courts of last resort: 1960–2000. Just Syst J 25:39, 44–46
de Londras F, Enright M (2008) Public interest litigation and the European Convention on Human Rights in Ireland. Irish Jurist
Deen RE, Ignagni J, Meernik J (2003) The solicitor general as amicus, 1953–2000: how influential? Judicature 87:60
DiMaggio PJ, Anheier HK (1990) The sociology of nonprofit organizations and sectors. Ann Rev Sociol 16:137–159
Doron Y, Totari-Jobran M (2006) The birth and development of the Israeli "Amicus Curiae". Alei Mishpat 65
Doron, Y, Totari-Jobran M, Anush G, Regev T (2011) A decade of the Israeli Amicus. Iyunei Mishpat
Edwards HT (1992) The growing disjunction between legal education and the legal profession. Mich Law Rev 91:34
Eliantonio M, Backes CW, van Rhee CH, Spronken TNBM, Berlee A (2012) Standing up for your right(s). In: Europe - a comparative study on legal standing (Locus Standi) before the EU and Member States' courts. European Parliament
Epstein L (1993) Interest group litigation during the rehnquist court era. J Law Polit 9.4:639–717
Epstein L, Segal JA, Spaeth HJ, Walker TG (1994) The Supreme Court compendium: data, decisions, and developments
Fallon RH Jr., (2012) Scholars' briefs and the vocation of a law professor. J Legal Anal 4:223, 225–226, 228
Farber S (2018) Amicus Curiae Phenomenon. Legal Stud 32:733
Franze AJ, Anderson RR (2015) Record breaking term for amicus curiae in Supreme Court reflects new norm. Natl Law J. http://www.nationallawjournal.com/supremecourtbrief/id=1202735095655
Franze AJ, Anderson RR (2016) In unusual term, big year for amicus curiae at the Supreme Court. Natl Law J. https://www.apks.com/~/media/files/perspectives/publications/2016/09/in-unusual-term-big-year-for-amicus-curiae-at-the-supreme-court.pdf
Franze AJ, Anderson RR (2020) Amicus curiae at the Supreme Court: last term and the decade in review. Natl Law J.. https://www.arnoldporter.com/-/media/files/perspectives/publications/2020/11/amicuscuriae-at-the-supreme-court.pdf
Franze AJ, Anderson RR, Unusual Term; Larsen AO, Devins N (2016) The amicus machine. Va Law Rev 102:1901
Franze JR, Anderson DA (2018) Record-breaking reliance on amicus briefs by the U.S. Supreme Court. J Polit 80(2):547–563
Garcia RJ (2008) A democratic theory of amicus advocacy. Fla St Univ Law Rev 35
George TE, Epstein L (1991) Women's rights litigation in the 1980s: more of the same? Judicature 74:314

Gleason SA, Ivy DK (2021) As she was saying: the role of gender and narratives in oral argument amicus success. Just Syst J 42(3–4):416–433
Hakman N (1966) Lobbying the Supreme Court – an appraisal of political science folklore. Fordham Law Rev 35(15):50
Harlow C (2002) Public law and popular justice. Mod. Law Rev 65:1
Harrington J (2005) Amici curiae in the federal courts of appeals: how friendly are they. Case Western Res Law Rev 55:667
Hazelton MLW, Hinkle RK (2022) Persuading the Supreme Court : the significance of briefs in judicial decision-making. University Press of Kansas
Hinson Z, Hubbard D (2012) Access to justice in Namibia: proposals for improving public access to courts: amicus curiae participation. Legal Assistance Centre
Hogg PW (2002) Constitutional law of Canada. York University, Toronto
Hon. Kirby's dissenting judgments in *Levy v. Victoria* (1997) 189 CLR 579 pp 650–652; Attorney General (Cth) v. Breckler (1999) 197 CLR 83, pp 134–137
Hopper BR (2017) Amici Curiae in the United States Supreme Court and the Australian High Court: a lesson in balancing amicability. J Marshall Law Rev 51:81, 82
Howard J (1988) Retaliation, reinstatement, and friends of the court: amicus participation in brock v. roadway express, Inc. How Law J 31:241
Huang A, Roemheld L (2016) Constitutional Precedent of Amicus Briefs. https://arxiv.org/pdf/1606.04672
Jason B (2006) Note, the intervention of amici curiae in criminal matters. South Afr Law J 123:391
Jason B, du Plessis M (2011) Current development/case note, two's company, three's a crowd: public interest intervention in investor-state arbitration (Piero Foresti v South Africa). S Afr J Human Rights 27:152
Joel S (2016) Court of Appeals Limits Length of Briefs. New York Law J June 16, 2016, http://www.newyorklawjournal.com/id=1202760161078
Johannes C, Ghai YP (1993) The Hong Kong bill of rights: a comparative approach, p 220 et seq
Jonas O (2015) The participation of the "Amicus Curiae" institution in human rights litigation in Botswana and South Africa: a tale of two jurisdictions. J Afr Law 59(2):329–354
Jonas O (2019) The participation of amicus curiae in the African human rights system, PhD thesis. University of Bristol Law School
Juaristi FJR (2014) The amicus curiae in the inter-American Court of human rights (1982–2013). Available at SSRN: https://ssrn.com/abstract=2488073
Justice & Freshfields Bruckhaus Deringer 2016 To Assist the Court: Third Party Interventions in the Public Interest 9
Kasirye A (2012) Uganda Law Society Report of Ad Hoc Committee on the Reform of the Civil Procedure Rules
Kearney JD, Merrill TW (2000) The influence of amicus curiae briefs on the Supreme Court. Univ Pa Law Rev 148:743–855
Kingston S (2014) The Amicus Curiae and public interest litigation in Ireland. Irish Law Times
Kirby M (2011) Deconstructing the law's hostility to public interest litigation. Law Quart Rev 127: 537–564
Klaaren J (1995) Comment, becoming friendly with the constitutional court: an interpretation of the Court's amicus curiae rules. South Afr J Human Rights 11:499
Klaaren J. Dugard J, Handmaker J (2011) Public interest litigation in South Africa: special issue introduction. South Afr J Human Rights 27:1
Koch J (1990) Making room: new directions in third party intervention. Univ Toronto Faculty Law Rev 48:151
Krislov S (1963) The Amicus Curiae brief: from friendship to advocacy. Yale Law J 72:694–721
Kristen W (2010) Amici curiae and access to constitutional justice: a practical perspective. Bond Law Rev 22:111, 125
Kwan M (2022) Is the Hong Kong Courts' ability to refer to foreign authorities unrestrained? Amicus Curiae 4:71–91

Laroche M (2009) Is the New York state court of appeal still "Friendless?" an empirical study of amicus curiae participation. Albany Law Rev 72:701
Lee Zhe X et al (2015) The use of academic scholarship in Singapore Supreme Court Judgement: 2005–2014. Sing Law Rev 33:25
Lord G (2002) Advocate to the court. Law Society Gazette, p 35
Lorne Neudorf L (2013) Intervention at the UK Supreme Court. Cambridge J Int Comput Law 2(16):19
Lowman MK (1992) Comment, the litigating amicus curiae: when does the party begin after the friends leave? Am Univ Law Rev 41:1243, 1245
Mark W (2013) It was another big term for amicus curiae briefs at the High Court. ABA J p 16
Mbazira C (2009) Public interest litigation and judicial activism in Uganda: improving the enforcement of economic, social and cultural rights. Human Rights & Peace Ctr., Working Paper No. 24
McGuire KT (1995) Repeat players in the Supreme Court: the role of experienced lawyers in litigation success. J Polit 57:187, 194
Metcalfe E (2009) To assist the court: third party interventions in the UK 1
Mirsane M (2021) The roles of Amicus Curiae (friend of the court) in judicial systems with emphasis on Canada and Alberta. Alberta Law Rev 59:669
Mohan SC (2010) The amicus curiae: friends no more? Singapore J Legal Stud 2:352–374
Moyer C (1985) The Role of Amicus Curiae in the Inter-American Court of Human Rights, in Inter-American Human Rights Institute, La Corte Interamericana de Derechos Humanos, Estudios y Documentos
Mubangizi JC, Mbazira C (2012) Constructing the amicus curiae procedure in human rights litigation: what can Uganda learn from South Africa. Law Democr Dev 16(199):200
Murray C (1994) Litigating in the public interest: intervention and the amicus curiae. South Afr J Human Rights 10:240, 242
Nekura R, Ndashe S, Jonas O (2022) Comparative perspectives on amicus curiae practice in Africa. Accessed at: https://home.creaw.org/wp-content/uploads/2022/05/ISLA_Insights_Issue_3_Comparative_Perspectives_on_Amicus_Curiae_Practice_in_Africa_Ebook.pdf
O'Brien Z (2004) The courts make a new friend? Amicus Curiae Jurisdiction in Ireland. Trinity College Law Rev 7:5
O'Connor K (1982) The Amicus Curiae role of the US solicitor general in Supreme Court litigation. Judicature 66:256
O'Connor K (1983) The amicus curiae role of the U.S. solicitor general in Supreme Court litigation. Judicature 66:256
Owens RJ (1998) Interveners and amicus curiae: the role of the courts in a modern democracy. Adelaide Law Rev 20:193
Pannick D (1992) The law of amicus curiae in England. Oxford University Press
Peter H (2007) Constitutional Law of Canada 20–56 5th ed
Pfeffer, L (1981) Amici in church-state litigation. Law Contemp Probs (Spring), p 83
Reagan WS, Vasaly MR (2004) The amicus brief: how to be a good friend of the court 23–30, 2nd edn. Amer Society of Civil Engineers
Rustad M, Koenig T (1993) The Supreme Court and junk social science: selective distortion in amicus briefs. North Carolina Law Rev 72:91, 157–91, 158
Segal JA (1988) Amicus curiae briefs by the solicitor general during the warren and burger courts: a research note. Western Polit Quart 41(135):136
Simard LS (2008) An empirical study of amici curiae in federal court: a fine balance of access, efficiency, and adversarialism. Rev Litig 27:669. (referring to Grutter v. Bollinger, 539 U.S. 306 (2003)
Smallman DB (1999) Amicus practice: new rules for old friends, litigation. Winter, p 25
Smith AM (2013), The history and evolution of amicus curiae in West Virginia. West Va Law, pp 42, 44

Smith L (1994) Have the equality rights made any difference? In: Bryden P, Davis S, Russell J (eds) Protecting rights and freedoms: essays on the charter's place in Canada's political, legal and intellectual life. University of Toronto Press, Toronto, pp 60, 75
Songer DR, Sheehan RS (1993) Interest group success in the courts: amicus participation in the Supreme Court. Polit Res Q 46:339
Spies A (2015) Considering the impact of amicus curiae participation on feminist litigation strategy. South Afr J Human Rights 31(1):136
Stern RL, Gressman E, Shapiro SM, Geller KS (2002) Supreme Court practice: for practice in the Supreme Court of the united states, 8th edn. p 684
Sungaila MC (2010) Effective advocacy through amicus briefs. S.F. Daily J, June 28, p 6
Viljoen F, Abebe AK (2014) Amicus curiae participation before regional human rights bodies in Africa. J Afr Law 58:22, 24
Wasby SL (1995) Race relations litigation in an age of complexity. University Press of Virginia, pp 219–235
Willheim E (2010) Amici Curiae and access to constitutional justice in the High Court of Australia. Bond Law Rev 22
Williams G (2000) The amicus curiae and intervener in the High Court of Australia: a comparative analysis. Fed Law Rev 28:365

Chapter 6
International Law

There are two main developments that have recently taken place forming part of the "Amicus Curiae phenomenon" in international law, which relate to public law (as seen, for example, in the European Court of Human Rights) and to international commercial matters. This book deals with the description of the "amicus phenomenon" from the point of view of international law rather than the development of the phenomenon in continental law for two reasons. First, the "amicus phenomenon" in international law was influenced by Anglo-Saxon law, especially by American law (for example, you can see copying or selective copying of the rules of the American Supreme Court in international institutions). Second, the "amicus phenomenon" in the continental legal system is highly based on the development of the "amicus" in international law.

6.1 The European Court of Human Rights

The European Court of Human Rights approach towards the wishes of third parties to express their position in ongoing proceedings was not sympathetic until the end of the early 1990s. Over the years, there have been only a few cases in which the European Court of Human Rights allowed the submission of briefs by an amicus or by other third parties with different interests who were not a formal part of the proceedings. On the other hand, as happened in common law countries starting in the late 1990s, international tribunals led by the European Court of Human Rights gradually changed their attitude and began to receive requests from diverse interest groups, mainly international non-governmental organizations, to give their position to the courts.[1]

[1] Van den Eynde (2013), p. 271; Lester (1988).

S. Farber, *The Amicus Curiae Phenomenon*, Ius Gentium: Comparative Perspectives on Law and Justice 119, https://doi.org/10.1007/978-3-031-67225-5_6

The first request for admission as Amicus Curiae in the ECtHR occurred in the *Winterwerp v. the Netherlands* case. The government sought to file a brief on the interpretation of Article 5(4) ECHR, which was relevant in several pending ECtHR cases against it. The government argued that the court could allow it to participate based on its investigative powers.[2] The President of the Court refused the request for oral participation but allowed the government to make a written submission.[3]

This was the case in many topics and issues that were brought before the European Court of Human Rights: the issue of freedom of association;[4] illegal wiretapping;[5] freedom of expression;[6] the rights of prisoners;[7] or extradition laws.[8] The change in the trend of the European Court of Human Rights towards third parties was characterized, among other things, by softer and more liberal court orders towards amici; a diversification of entities that were allowed to participate in the proceedings (for instance, various non-governmental organizations) as well as an increase in their numbers; and the opportunity given to them to argue orally in the courts. Oral participation was granted where the Amici Curiae possessed special knowledge due to their involvement in the case or longstanding involvement in the matters under discussion.[9] While written Amicus Curiae participation has always been the norm in the ECtHR, the number of oral submissions has noticeably decreased over time, possibly due to the overall increase in the court's caseload and efforts to conduct proceedings most efficiently.[10]

---

[2]Petitioners sought to rely on former Rule 38(1) ECtHR Rules which concerned the ECtHR's investigative powers. The provision determined that a chamber could hear 'any person whose evidence or statements seem likely to assist in the carrying out of its task.' The ECtHR did not use the provision to accept amicus briefs. Instead, it arranged for a written submission to be made through the representatives of the EComHR. See Winterwerp v. the Netherlands, Judgment, 24 October 1979, ECtHR Series A No. 33. The oral proceedings were interrupted for two weeks to allow the EComHR to present the statement. See also Matscher (1980), p. 539.

[3]Matscher (1980), p. 539. For a detailed analysis of the first cases of Amicus Curiae participation before the ECtHR and the role of British legal practitioners therein, see Dolidze (2015), p. 851; Wiik (2018).

[4]Young v. United Kingdom, 44 Eur. Ct. H.R. (ser. A) (1981).

[5]Malone v. United Kingdom, 82 Eur. Ct. H.R. (ser. A) (1984).

[6]Lingens v. Austria, 103 Eur. Ct. H.R. (ser. A) (1986).

[7]Monell v. United Kingdom, 115 Eur. Ct. H.R. (ser. A) (1987).

[8]Soering v. United Kingdom, 161 Eur. Ct. H.R. (ser. A) (1989).

[9]Mahoney assumed that this would only occur regarding factual aspects. Practice shows that this is not the case. See Mahoney (1983), p. 146; Wiik (2018).

[10]The first admission of Amicus Curiae allowed oral submissions. See Young, James and Webster v. the United Kingdom, Judgment of 13 August 1981, Series A No. 44. Between 2003 and 2010, seven amici curiae were granted leave to present oral sub- missions. See Karner v. Austria, No. 40016/98, 24 July 2003, ECHR 2003-IX; Pini and others v. Romania, Nos. 78028/01 and 78030/01, 22 June 2004, ECHR 2004-V; Bosphorus Hava Yollari Turizm Ve Ticaret Anonim Sirketi v. Ireland [GC], No. 45036/98, 30 June 2005, ECHR 2005-VI; Saadi v. Italy [GC], No. 37201/06, 28. February 2008, ECHR 2008; Opuz v. Turkey, No. 33401/02, 9 June 2009, ECHR 2009; Perna v. Italy [GC], No. 48898/99, 6 May 2003, ECHR 2003-V; Muňoz Díaz v Spain Archives 2009, No. 49151/07, 8 December 2009, ECHR 2009; Wiik, A (2018) *supra* note 657.

In an interview with him, the former secretary of the European Court also said that the court has begun to develop a tolerant approach that considers the requests of third parties to present their positions in the courts.[11] One of the main rulings that expressed this change in the court's approach is the Chahal ruling from 1996, which dealt with the deportation of a separatist Sikh to India in which the European Court of Human Rights granted several amici the right to express their positions.[12]

It seems that the adoption of Protocol 11 to the European Convention in 1994 marks the turning point in the court's attitude towards the desire of third parties to present their position and the "amicus phenomenon" in general. Before the protocol's adoption, there were no formal rules regarding the intervention of third parties in ongoing proceedings. On the other hand, the adopted protocol stated that:

> The President of the Court may, in the interest of the proper administration of justice, invite any High Contracting Party which is not a party to the proceedings or any person concerned who is not the applicant to submit written comments or take part in hearings.[13]

Shelton's research has shown that the inclusion of amici in the proceedings at the European Court of Human Rights increases the chance of an essential ruling by the court regarding the violation of human rights (in 75 percent of the cases in which amici joined) compared to cases in which amici did not join (about fifty percent).[14] Following dozens of briefs submitted over the years, it became necessary to update the court rules, and the new rules further expanded the possibility of adding third parties (amici and intervenors) to the proceedings, and they were even given the formal opportunity to argue orally.[15]

The presence of non-governmental organizations as third parties in the European Court of Human Rights has increased significantly in the last decade, when their briefs often include comparative arguments that present, for example, comparisons between national law with international law.[16]

The number of interventions by interested third parties in pending proceedings has increased considerably during the last two decades. In 1985, there were 3 interventions in pending proceedings. In 1993 the same number. Starting in 1998, an

---

[11] Hodson (2011), p. 52.

[12] Chahal v. United Kingdom, 1996-V Eur. Ct. H.R. 1831, for example, Amnesty International, Aire Centre, Liberty Justice.

[13] European Convention on Human Rights, art. 36, ¶ 2, Nov. 4, 1950, E.T.S. 5 (following Protocol No. 11 to the Convention for the Protection of Human Rights and Fundamental Freedoms, Restructuring the Control Machinery Established Thereby, May 11, 1994, E.T.S. 155). For more on the subject, see Frigessi di Rattalma (2005), p. 131.

[14] Shelton (1994), pp. 611, 637. See there also the limitations of her research and among them the low numbers of "amici" as of the time of the research.

[15] European Court of Human Rights, Rules of Court, r. 44 (2016). For example, INTERIGHTS was allowed to argue orally in Opuz v. Turkey, App. no. 33401/02, 50 Eur. H.R. Rep. 28 (2009). Unlike common law, it is not necessary to obtain the consent of the official parties to submit a position and the only requirement is that the request be reasoned and written in one of the official languages of the court (English or French).

[16] Van den Eynde (2013), pp. 271–313; Interights (1997).

increase was recorded (6 interventions). In 2005–2025 interventions; in 2008–2021 interventions; in 2009–2023 interventions; in 2010–2030 interventions; in 2011–2042 interventions; In 2012–2035 interventions and in 2013–2025 interventions.[17] In 2018, there was a conference in Copenhagen on the reform of the European Convention system, in which the importance of third-party intervention by member States was highlighted. The final declaration calls on member States to engage in a dialogue with the Court through this instrument and to do so in a coordinated manner. It also invites the Court to support third-party interventions.[18]

For example, more amicus briefs were submitted in 2012–2013 than in the whole of the previous decade. In recent years, about a quarter of the cases heard at the Human Rights Court have been submitted by amicus brief, and the percentage of participation in cases of high interest (mega cases) is increasing significantly every year.[19] Numerically, in the 1990s, only a few amicus briefs were submitted yearly. On the other hand, since 2005, between 20 and 45 brief have been submitted every year.[20]

In addition, in controversial proceedings of great public significance (mega cases), many coalitions of third parties have often joined together to write a consolidated brief. By 2015, out of the 294 cases in which the court allowed the submission of an amicus brief, 92 of them involved cases in which third parties joined together to present a unified front.[21] For example, in the *Al-Skeini* case that dealt with the extraterritorial application of the Convention on human rights, dozens of non-governmental organizations united and submitted a joint amicus brief.[22]

In 2023, The European Court of Human Rights published an updated version of the Rules of the Court, which incorporates amendments in respect of Rule 44 §§ 2 and 3 (b) on third-party intervention. These amendments were adopted on 3 March 2023 and entered into force on the same date. These amendments concern the third-party intervention of the Council of Europe's Commissioner for Human Rights and set out the conditions and deadlines for requests to intervene as a third party both by written procedure and in a hearing before a Chamber. These clarifications are the culmination of a process initiated after the 2018 high-level conference in Copenhagen on the reform of the Convention system, which encouraged the Court to support third-party intervention.[23] Only 3 days before the amendment of the rules, the Court had announced that 26 member States would intervene in the combined case

[17] Van den Eynde (2013), p. 280.

[18] Batura (2023).

[19] Van den Eyne (2013), p. 280.

[20] Ibid, at p. 280. In total, until 2013, there were interventions by third parties in approximately 237 cases.

[21] Metcalfe (2009), p. 90.

[22] Al-Skeini v. United Kingdom, 2011-IV Eur. Ct. H.R. 99.

[23] The Registrar of the Court (2023).

concerning the full-scale invasion of Ukraine in 2022 and the conflict in eastern Ukraine that began in 2014.[24]

Relative to other courts in common law countries (and particularly in the United States Supreme Court), the numbers of amicus interventions in the European Court of Human Rights seem relatively "low." However, this can be explained in several ways: First, the database about the number of times in which The European Court of Human Rights refused requests from third parties to express their position is relatively limited.[25] Second, some argue that, relatively speaking, the influence of the third parties' briefs on the court is not high, which reduces the incentive for potential third parties to join the process.[26] There are differences between the working styles of the European Court of Human Rights and the United States Supreme Court related to the legal culture to the judicial tradition that grants increased powers to the representatives of the state to intervene in the law in the name of the public interest, to civil society, and lots of other fundamental differences that make the comparison almost impossible.[27]

6.2 The International Court of Justice in The Hague

The International Court of Justice in The Hague (ICJ) also refused until the mid-nineties to accept briefs from third parties in ongoing proceedings. In particular, it did not favor receiving any interventions, including amicus briefs from non-governmental organizations.[28] However, from the beginning of the mid-nineties, the tribunal began to allow requests for the accession of third parties. Initially, it allowed state bodies to submit briefs both when disputes between states are being discussed and also when the ICJ gives opinions on issues referred to it by the General Assembly or by the Security Council of the United Nations.[29] Despite the relative flexibility of the procedure, the ICJ initially did not allow a non-governmental public organization to submit an "amicus" brief in an ongoing proceedings.[30]

The rules of the ICJ state, for example, that in disputes between countries, only international public organizations are allowed to submit an amicus brief on their

[24] Batura (2023).

[25] Mahoney (2005), p. 151, 155 (Hélène Ruiz Fabri & Jean-Marc Sorel eds.,).

[26] Bartholomeusz (2005), p. 209, 236.

[27] For writing about the court see for example Leach (2011). Mowbray (2005), pp. 57–79.

[28] Mackenzie (2005), p. 296; Shelton (1994), pp. 620–623.

[29] Land, Island & Maritime Frontier Dispute (El Sal. v. Hond.), Application to Intervene, Judgment, 1990 I.C.J. 92 (Sept. 13); Statute of the International Court of Justice, art. 34, par. 2, art. 66, par. 2, June 26, 1945, 33 U.N.T.S. 993 (hereinafter: the Constitution of the International Court of Justice).

[30] Bartholomeusz (2005), pp. 209, 236.

initiative or at the invitation of the court.[31] On the other hand, in the consultation procedures that the tribunal provides on legal issues referred to it by the UN institutions, other organizations, and bodies are also allowed to submit written and oral arguments, and in exceptional cases and with the approval of the court, even respond to the arguments of the formal parties. In addition, countries that have any interest in an ongoing proceedings that turns out to be between two other countries are also allowed to join the procedure as third parties.[32] In 2004, the rules of the court were amended, and it was determined that briefs submitted by international organizations would not be a formal part of the process but would be placed in the Peace Palace, where formal parties will be allowed to consult and use this information if necessary.[33]

Third-Party intervention in the ICJ has become increasingly significant in contemporary international law. In September 2020, Canada and the Netherlands issued a joint statement suggesting their intention to intervene in an ongoing contentious case at the ICJ.[34] This was a case on the Application of the Convention on the Prevention and Punishment of the Crime of Genocide (*The Gambia v. Myanmar*). On July 22, 2022, the ICJ decided, by fifteen votes to one, that it has authority under the Genocide Convention to hear the application filed by The Gambia against Myanmar in November 2019.[35] The Gambia's application alleges that Myanmar's military and other security forces perpetrated genocide by systemically destroying—through mass murder, rape, and different kinds of sexual violence—villages of the Rohingya in the Rakhine province of Myanmar. While in the past, states have brought cases before the ICJ under the Genocide Convention, this is the first time that a state has invoked its authority to seek redress for alleged genocidal acts committed against the citizens of another state. As reflected in their joint statement, the intervention was to support efforts that concerned all of humanity. The right of a third party to intervene accrues if interest is of a legal nature that may be affected by the decision in the case arises (Article 62) or construction of a Convention to which States other than those concerned parties is in question (Article 63). The ICJ has strictly interpreted applications by third states. To put it into perspective, it has

[31] S. 34(2) of the Constitution of the International Court of Justice.

[32] "States and organizations having presented written or oral statements, or both shall be permitted to comment on the statements made by other states or organization'."

[33] Ibid, S. 34; Int'l Court of Justice, Practice Directions, practice direction XII; Mackenzie (2005), p. 296;Van den Eynde (2013), p. 280.; Palchetti (2002), p. 139. Palchetti argues that the current rules on third-party intervention are too restrictive because they make it difficult for third states to participate in ICJ proceedings.

[34] Alexander (2022). https://papers.ssrn.com/sol3/papers.cfm?abstract_id=4107651.

[35] Application of the Convention on the Prevention and Punishment of the Crime of Genocide (Gam. v. Myan.), Judgment on Preliminary Objections (July 22, 2022), https://www.icj-cij.org/public/files/case-related/178/178-20220722-JUD-01-00-EN.pdf [hereinafter Judgment]. While Judge *ad hoc* Kress voted with the majority of the Court, he appended a separate declaration. Judge Kress raised his concern as to the Court not adequately dealing with the issue of change in Myanmar's representatives in the proceedings before the Court happening as a consequence of the military coup in February 2021; See Wiik (2018).

merely entertained 20 and 29 percent of applications and declarations under Article 62 and Article 63, respectively.[36]

6.3 The Latin American Court of Human Rights in Costa Rica (InterAmerican Court of Human Rights: IACtHR)

The Latin American Court of Human Rights in Costa Rica (InterAmerican Court of Human Rights—IACtHR) also started in the early 2000s to liberally allow the addition of third parties to ongoing legal proceedings.[37] The rules for adding an Amicus Curiae are like the rules of the European Court of Human Rights, and they result from an accumulation of rulings on the matter and a desire to update the rules.[38] The legal procedural rules from 1980 did not explicitly refer to the practice of the amicus. However, a backlog of various rulings accumulated over the years resulted in the fact that in 2009, the court instituted new rules on the subject. Paragraph 2(3) of the Rules of Procedure states that the "amicus" is:

> the person who is unrelated to the case and the proceeding and who submits to the Court reasoning [sic] about the facts contained in the application or the legal considerations over the subject matter of the proceeding, using a document or an argument presented in the hearing.

Rule 41 of the procedural rules states under the title "Arguments of Amicus Curiae" that:

> The brief of one who wishes to act as Amicus Curiae may be submitted to the Tribunal, together with its annexes, at any point during the contentious proceedings, but within the term 15 days following the public hearing. If the Court does not hold a public hearing, amicus briefs must be submitted within the term 15 days following the Resolution setting deadlines for the submission of final arguments and documentary evidence. Following consultation with the President, the Amicus Curiae brief, and its annexes shall be immediately transmitted to the parties for their information.[39]

The frequency of requests by amici to submit their positions to the IACtHR tribunal has increased in recent years: in the 1980s, about 40 amicus briefs were submitted. In the nineties, about 23 amicus briefs were submitted, and in the 2000s, 172 briefs were submitted. Between the years 2010–2013 alone, 177 briefs were submitted from many dozens of amici (which make up about 43 percent of all the "amicus" briefs submitted up to that time). In total, 412 amicus briefs were submitted in

[36] Alexander and Shouvik (2022), https://ssrn.com/abstract=4107651.

[37] Formally, the first case in which an "amicus" joined was in 1982. "Other Treaties" Subject to the Consultative Jurisdiction of the Court (Art. 64 American Convention on Human Rights), Advisory Opinion OC-1/82, Inter-Am. Ct. H.R. (ser. A) No. 1 (Sept. 24, 1982).

[38] Rules of Procedure of the Inter-American Court of Human Rights, art. 44 (2009).

[39] Ibid. The rules establish another series of procedural rules: how the brief must be submitted, deadlines for submission, who is authorized to submit; The proposed argument, and more.

98 proceedings heard by the court (1987–2013). That is, in 35 percent of the proceedings discussed at the court, amici were allowed to express their positions. In 2012 alone, 107 amicus briefs were submitted to the court.

During these years, about 58 percent of the amici were non-governmental human rights organizations (29 percent of which were international organizations and the rest local organizations), 24.5 percent—academic institutions, and 14 percent—private individuals. Three percent of various state officials (politicians, representatives of local authorities, legislators, or the states themselves through the attorney general). Only 0.5 percent—were various commercial companies. Here, too, various groups began to make increasing use of amicus briefs in court as a tool to advance their interests ("green" organizations and human rights organizations, academic research institutions, UN institutions, etc.).[40]

In addition, the judges of the IACtHR refer to and rely on the information presented to them by various amici in their rulings, in particular to information from international non-governmental organizations acting as amici.[41] Starting in the 1980s, the IACtHR received over 500 amicus briefs. This is particularly surprising because the tribunal issued a total of 275 rulings (between 1982–2013) and another twenty advisory decisions. That is to say, the court received more interlocutory documents from third parties than from formal parties to the proceedings.[42] Two cases discussed at the Court that dealt with the adoption of children by same-sex couples (the *Artavia Murillo* case and the *Atala Riffo and Daughters* case) attracted about 98 briefs from dozens of amici, mainly non-governmental organizations and academic institutions. In total, amici submitted briefs in approximately 35 percent of all proceedings conducted at the AICtHR.

The IACtHR accounts for the largest number of Amicus Curiae participation in relative terms. Out of 317 concluded contentious cases, Amicus Curiae briefs were submitted in 122, with a notable increase in submissions over the last decade, particularly in cases engaging fundamental ethical questions. The IACtHR has received Amicus Curiae submissions in twenty of its twenty-two advisory opinions.[43]

The court's openness to public interest-based Amicus Curiae is illustrated also by its public call for Amicus Curiae submissions from different entities and the public society in general through its website.[44] The IACtHR's reluctance to assign a private interest-based function to Amicus Curiae has led it to hear on an ad hoc basis people

[40] Ibid, on page 5.

[41] Mónica (2005), pp. 47, 55–56.

[42] Juaristi (2014); Mayer (2011), p. 911. Between the years 1987–2013, a total of 412 memoranda of "amicus" in 98 proceedings were conducted.

[43] Woolaver (2016).

[44] Articulo 55 de la Convención Americana Sobre Derechos Humanos, Advisory Opinion No. OC-20/09, 29 September 2009, IACtHR Series A No. 20, pp. 28–32.

directly affected by its judgment, but not as Amicus Curiae.[45] Still, it receives in contentious and advisory proceedings submissions from institutions which are active advocates on the issues in dispute. On occasion, these groups may be affected by the court's judgment, but this is not the reason for their admission.[46]

Based on statements by former court officials, obiter dicta in some judgments, and a comparison of Amicus Curiae submissions with judgments, the court regularly relies on Amicus Curiae submissions both in contentious and advisory proceedings. Padilla, a former employee of the court, conveys: "Judges of the Inter-American Court have told me that the Amicus Curiae have provided invaluable contributions to the court's deliberations and judgments."[47]

In conclusion, the amicus in the IACtHR is very important. First, starting from the beginning of the 2000s, and even before the establishment of clear rules of procedure on the subject, the court began to permit in a rather lenient manner the addition of third parties as amici to ongoing legal proceedings. Secondly, an accumulation of different rulings and the increase in the use of amici resulted in the fact that in 2009, the court established clear rules on the subject, which clarified the importance and role of the amicus in the court. Third, the frequency of requests by amici to submit their positions to the tribunal has consistently increased. In these years, the IACtHR received more interlocutory documents from third parties than from formal parties to the proceedings. Fourth, there has been a diversification and expansion of the range of entities that use amicus—human rights organizations, academic institutions, private individuals (often the victims of the crime), and politicians.

6.4 International Criminal Courts

International criminal tribunals and international criminal courts established ad hoc, also began to allow for the first time in the early 2000s the receipt of briefs from "amici." This was the case at the ad hoc Special International Criminal Tribunal for the Investigation of Crimes Committed in Yugoslavia (ICTY),[48] the International

[45] Atalo Riffo y niñas v. Chile, Judgment of 4 February 2012, IACtHR Series C. No. 239. The court decided to hear the testimony of three minors in a case concerning their mother's loss of custody and their removal from the family home due to her sexual orientation. The children's father's request for his and his daughters' direct participation as interveners was denied and he was not allowed to present substantive arguments or evidence as Amicus Curiae.

[46] See Compulsory Membership in an Association Prescribed by Law for the Practice of Journalism (Articles 13 and 29 American Convention on Human Rights), Advisory Opinion No. OC-5/85 of 13 November 1985, IACtHR Series A No. 5, pp. 6–9.

[47] Padilla (1993), pp. 95, 111. See also Umbricht (2001), p. 791.

[48] Int'l Crim. Trib. for the Former Yugoslavia, Rules of Procedure and Evidence, r. 74, IT/32/Rev.50 (July 8, 2015).

Criminal Tribunal for the Investigation of Crimes in Rwanda (ICTR),[49] and the International Criminal Court for the Investigation of Crimes in Sierra Leone (SCSL).[50] In all these cases, for the first time, third parties who were not directly part of the conflict were allowed to express their position by submitting a brief to the court. In addition, the International Criminal Court in The Hague (ICC) instituted in 2002 explicit rules on the subject stating that it may invite or give permission to a state, organization, or private person to submit as a third party a written or oral position in any matter that the court deems appropriate, and at every stage of the ongoing legal process.

The term “Amicus Curiae” is explicitly mentioned in the governing laws of the ICTY, the ICTR, in the ICC and the SCSL Rules of Procedure and Evidence, the IACtHR Rules of Procedure, and in numerous cases before the ECtHR, the IACtHR, the ICC, the ICTY, the ICTR, the SCSL, the STL, WTO panels, the WTO Appellate Body and investor-state arbitration tribunals. Some international courts and tribunals choose not to use the term to avoid connotations associated with any national legal concept.[51]

The position of the ICC is that the acceptance of briefs from third parties is subject to the sole discretion of the court and is not subject to the consent of the formal parties. Likewise, in other judicial courts, the main criterion for accepting a third-party brief in international criminal courts is the question of whether the brief assists the court in its work.

The Rules of Procedure and Evidence of the ICC also provide for the admission of amicus briefs. Rule 103 allows the Chambers to “invite or grant leave for a State, organization or person to submit” oral or written amicus submissions whenever “it considers it desirable for the proper determination of the case.” As with the ad hoc and hybrid tribunals, therefore, the ICC Chambers have a broad discretion to admit amicus.

According to the figures that we have compiled for applications made up to early 2016, approximately 85 applications for amicus status have been received by the ICC Chambers. These applications have been made by a variety of actors, including States, intergovernmental organizations, defense representatives from other cases, academics and other individuals, and civil society organizations. The civil society groups are primarily non-governmental organizations, both large international NGOs and small “local” NGOs, but also include professional groups such as defense associations. The proposed submissions deal with a wide range of subject matter, including submissions on both legal and factual issues, such as victims’ issues,

[49] Int’l Crim. Trib. for Rwanda, Rules of Procedure and Evidence, r. 74. As is known, the wars in Yugoslavia and Rwanda and the atrocities committed within the framework of these conflicts put on the agenda the necessity of the existence of a forum to judge war criminals and were a catalyst for the establishment of the International Criminal Court.

[50] Special Court for Sierra Leone, Rules of Procedure and Evidence, r. 74. For more, see Gómez (2012), p. 510.

[51] Report of the UNCITRAL Working Group II (Arbitration and Conciliation on the Work of its fift^y fifth session), 55th Session, UN Doc. A/CN.9/736 (2011), para. 71 [Emphasis added].

defense rights, historical background, evidentiary or procedural issues, and contempt proceedings. Thus far, victims' issues are the most popular topic of proposed amicus submissions. These proposals, therefore, align most often with the submissions of the victims' representatives (29% of applications). Surprisingly, the second-most common alignment is with defense interests (26% of applications), and only a small number of applications received so far align with prosecution interests (4% of applications).[52]

Alongside the low rate of accepting amici at the ICC, the judicial practice that we have examined indicates that criteria for the admission of amici may not be consistently applied. As mentioned above, Rule 103 requires only that the Chamber in question "considers it desirable for the proper determination of the case" to grant amicus status, leaving the discretion broadly defined. Without further directions or guidelines, the Chambers have used divergent criteria when assessing amicus applications. Some Chambers have applied a demanding threshold that amicus submissions will be allowed "only on an exceptional basis" or where they would provide "an indispensable aid." In other cases, amici have been admitted simply because they "may assist" the Court. This suggests that some amicus applications are subject to more stringent tests for admission than others, making it difficult to predict which applications will be successful.

To complete the picture, I will point out that there is a criticism that claims that the international criminal courts have not internalized the rationale for the use of amici and their roles in these proceedings. In three different international criminal tribunals, the "amicus" served in several different roles: once as a "classical amicus" who impartially provided information. Another time, as a kind of "intervenor" who tried to influence the proceedings from a certain point of view, and a third time, when the amicus was used as a defense attorney for the accused, and finally, the amicus was also used to express the voice of crime victims. The second criticism is that amici have often been given a lot of weight in the courts, similar to the weight of the official parties. The powers granted to them were broad, and in one case, contrary to the purpose of the amicus, the amicus was authorized to file an appeal and formally represent the interests of one of the formal parties.[53]

6.5 International Trade and Investment Dispute Settlement

The amicus curiae phenomenon has been particularly evident in international economic institutions and dispute settlement mechanisms related to trade and investment matters in the last two decades. These institutions operate under specialized international legal frameworks, such as the World Trade Organization's Dispute Settlement Understanding, the North American Free Trade Agreement (NAFTA),

---

[52] See Williams and Palmer (2016), pp. 40–46.

[53] Gómez (2012).

and the Convention on the Settlement of Investment Disputes between States and Nationals of Other States (ICSID Convention). Rather than handling purely private commercial disputes, they resolve disputes between sovereign states, or between states and investors, concerning issues such as trade agreements, investment treaties, and state-investor relationships. The prominent institutions in which the "amicus phenomenon" is especially prominent are (1) the World Trade Organization (WTO); (2) The North American Free Trade Agreement (NAFTA); (3) The International Center for Settlement of Investment Disputes (ICSID). The main reason behind the "amicus phenomenon" in these institutions and the desire of third parties to participate is that the disputes they handle not only involve commercial interests but also encompass issues of human rights, environmental quality, political rights, and other public issues. Various third parties began to recognize that these institutions and their dispute settlement procedures, with their substantial broad implications, represent a significant arena in which they can influence decision-making.[54]

There are other significant reasons for the intervention of amici in various international arbitration procedures. First and foremost, briefs from amici help protect the public interest, especially in developing countries, on multiple issues: human rights, environmental quality, workers' rights, protection of local heritage and culture and struggles against corruption. From the amicus' point of view, the formal parties to the arbitration do not present the arbitrators with the complete picture of the arbitration. For example, they do not present broad environmental or cultural consequences for the population in whose territory the transaction is conducted. From the point of view of the amici, it is vital that the information presented by the amici, which is not necessarily presented by the formal parties (or hidden from the arbitrators), is brought to the attention of the arbitrators.[55] Secondly, the parties to the arbitration procedure sometimes do not have the tools, ability, or unique knowledge that the amici possess. Whereas different amici, especially if they are international organizations with experience and expertise, can offer a different point of view or help from a legal point of view (for example, present a legal opinion that reviews the law from a comparative point of view) or even from a factual point of view to the arbitrators.[56] Thirdly, the intervention of amici in international arbitration procedures may affect the institutional regime of international institutions and cause a more transparent and visible activity of the arbitration procedure.[57] Sometimes, the media coverage that the amici receive leads

[54] Van Harten (2007). Transnational see in general: Dispute Management (TDM) 4.5. Kingsbury and Schill (2009), pp. 9–46.

[55] Graham (2012), pp. 6–7.

[56] For example, in the case of Biwater Gauff (Tanz.) Ltd. v. United Republic of Tanzania, ICSID Case No. ARB/05/22, Award, ¶ 359 (July 24, 2008), the respondent noted that the "amici" "approach[ed] the issues in this case with interests, expertise and perspectives that have been demonstrated to materially differ from those of the two contending parties, and as such have provided a useful contribution to these proceedings."

[57] Kawharu (2007), pp. 2–3.

to a public discussion of issues that the amici are trying to influence, thereby increasing public criticism of procedures that are sometimes done secretly.[58]

Even in these institutions, the Amicus Curiae practice is used as a deliberative practice by which various third parties (such as rights organizations or commercial companies) are allowed to present their position before the arbitration courts.[59] One of the paradigmatic examples of the involvement of amici in commercial arbitrations is the *Suez* case.[60] In this regard, the ICSID arbitral tribunal accepted in 2005 the request of several international non-governmental organizations to submit a brief as amici. The ICSID pointed out that the dispute involved questions that deal not only with the commercial interests of the parties to the arbitration but also with public issues. The tribunal indicated that before the decision is given in arbitration, it is appropriate to hear the perspectives and viewpoints of other parties who may be affected by the ruling.

As international arbitrations became more common and politically, ecologically, socially, and economically significant, various interest groups demanded that their voices and interests be reflected in arbitration proceedings. In this way, the scope of the "amicus phenomenon" is deepening every year at the same time and following the increase in the scope of international commercial arbitrations around the world.[61]

6.5.1 World Trade Organization

The World Trade Organization (WTO) has embraced the amicus, not without hesitation, in both the Dispute Settlement Body and the Appellate Body procedures.[62] The authority to accept amicus briefs in WTO arbitrations was discussed for the first time in 2000 in two precedent decisions, *Hot-Rolled Lead* and *Asbestos*.[63] In both cases, requests from amici to submit a written position were submitted

---

[58] Graham (2012), pp. 6–10. While the arguments in favor of the involvement of third parties are mainly voiced by non-governmental public organizations, the main arguments against "the adoption of the "amicus" are mostly voiced by developing countries, investors, and capitalists.

[59] De Brabandere (2011).

[60] Suez, Sociedad General de Aguas de Barcelona, S.A.and Vivendi Universal, S.A. v. Argentine Republic, ICSID Case No. ARB/03/19 (formerly Aguas Argentinas, S.A., Suez, Sociedad General de Aguas de Barcelona, S.A.and Vivendi Universal, S.A. v. Argentine Re Order in Response to a Petition for Transparency and Participation as *Amicus Curiae* (May 19, 2005), 21 ICSID Rev. 342 (2006).

[61] Ortino (2009), pp. 301, 316.

[62] World Trade Org. [WTO], Working Procedures for Appellate Review, r. 24, WTO Doc. WT/AB/WP/6 (Aug. 16, 2010); Robbins (2003), p. 317.

[63] U.S. – Imposition of Countervailing Duties on Certain & Bismuth Carbon Steel Prods. Originating in the U.K., Appellate Body Report, Hot-Rolled Lead WTO Doc. WT/DS138/AB/R (May 10, 2000); Eur. Cmtys. – Measures Affecting Asbestos and -Containing Prods., 40 I.L.M. 1193 (WTO Appellate Body 2001).

to the organization's appeals court. In the *Hot-Rolled Lead* case, it was the brief of the steel industries, while in *Asbestos*, it was environmental NGOs. Although the parties to the arbitration claimed that the dispute resolution panel had no authority to receive the brief, the Appellate Body determined that it was authorized to receive brief from third parties, noting that:

> We believe that we have the legal authority under the DSU to accept and consider Amicus Curiae briefs in an appeal in which we find it pertinent and useful to do so.[64]

Various issues that have arisen over the years in connection with the desire of amici to present their position in arbitration proceedings prompted the organization's institutions to reform the dispute resolution mechanisms and establish rules on the subject in 2010. Since then, joining amici in arbitration proceedings has become almost routine.[65] Of all the international institutions that have adopted the practice of Amicus Curiae interventions in recent years, the acceptance of the amicus practice in the World Trade Organization is an issue that is still in dispute and debate among the member states of the organization. The main concern is that of developing countries who fear a devaluation of their power and status in the World Trade Organization due to the participation of non-governmental organizations as amici (such as environmental quality organizations), and therefore, they try to thwart the adoption of the Amicus Curiae institution in the organization's arbitration mechanisms.[66]

Until the late 1990s Amicus Curiae participation was a non-issue in WTO dispute settlement. The Appellate Body and panels had received—and routinely rejected—submissions by non-state actors to serve as amici by pointing to the strict intergovernmental nature of the dispute settlement system.[67] The panels' reasoning was artificial in so far as select private actors strongly influenced the initiation and conduct of proceedings to the extent that, at times, they were considered the "real" parties to a dispute. But, over the years, panels and the Appellate Body have repeatedly confirmed their authority to admit Amicus Curiae briefs.

The WTO's Dispute Settlement Understanding (DSU) does not explicitly provide the dispute panels or the Appellate Body AB with the authority to receive and use amicus submissions. However, a panel addressed whether or not it had the authority to accept and consider an Amicus Curiae submission in 1998 after receiving two briefs from environmental groups in connection with the US–Shrimp dispute. The

[64] Hot-Rolled Lead (2003), para 42.

[65] Rule 24 of the Working Procedures for Appellate Review (2013); Bartholomeusz (2005), pp. 209, 236.

[66] Robbins (2003), p. 317. See also Gao (2006).

[67] 144 These cases were: European Communities – Measures Concerning Meat and Meat Products (Hormones) (hereinafter: EC–Hormones), Report of the Panel, adopted on 13 February 1998, WT/DS26/AB/R, WT/DS48/AB/R; United States – Standards for Reformulated and Conventional Gasoline (hereinafter: US–Gaso-line), Report of the Panel, adopted on 20 May 1996, WT/DS2/R and WT/DS4/R. See Marceau and Stilwell (2001), pp. 157–158; Charnovitz (2000), p. 182, FN 52; Factual Background Note to the General Council Special Meeting on 22 November 2000, referred to by Steger (2002), p. 438.

panel found it did not have the authority to consider such briefs because they were unsolicited. The panel's understanding was that while Article 13 of the DSU permitted panels to seek information and technical advice, such information had to be requested by the panel. Thus, "accepting non-requested information from non-governmental sources would be, in our opinion, incompatible with the provisions of the DSU." However, the panel did allow for amici to be attached to parties' submissions for consideration, which the United States had done with the two briefs. Later, when the dispute was appealed, the AB disagreed with the panel's findings, opting for a broader interpretation of Article 13. It found that:

> [a] panel has the discretionary authority either to accept and consider or to reject information and advice submitted to it, whether requested by the panel or not. The fact that a panel may motu proprio have initiated the request for information does not, by itself, bind the panel to accept and consider the information which is actually submitted.

In addition, the AB affirmed that the panel was entitled to consider the amicus, which the United States had appended to its own submissions. This decision, however, left unresolved whether the AB could accept and consider an amicus submission on its own.[68]

In the period between 1995 and 2014, there were 201 panel and 129 Appellate Body reports that were adopted. To date, unsolicited Amicus Curiae submissions have been received in 23 panel and in 19 Appellate Body proceedings, respectively.

To conclude, the WTO suggests that there is generally a high threshold to be met before an amicus brief is accepted and considered by the WTO DSM. It also reveals that the most controversial aspect of the DSM's work, legal interpretation, is largely unaffected by non-state actor involvement. To date, Amicus Curiae submissions have only been expressly considered on the basis of the factual information provided. But, the acceptance and consideration of an amicus is quite exceptional and conditional on satisfying both the political and legal constraints faced by the panels and AB. The high threshold for access, in terms of actually being included in how a legal dispute is adjudicated, means that the formal ability to access the panels and the AB rarely translates into participation. Thus, for the proponent of non-state actors' involvement, amicus access holds limited promise for participation.[69]

6.5.2 NAFTA

NAFTA does not contain any express provisions permitting Amicus Curiae submissions. While the Free Trade Commission (FTC) is authorized to issue binding interpretations, the 2003 FTC Statement on non-disputing party participation (FTC Statement) is nonbinding. Given the lack of consent from the claimants and the

[68] Squatrito (2017), Macrory, Appleton and Plummer (2005), pp. 1433–1435.

[69] Cambridge University Press (2017).

non-binding FTC Statement, the Tribunal must not allow Amicus Curiae participation in arbitrations.[70]

In *Methanex v. USA*, the Amicus Curiae was denied access to case documents following the parties' confidentiality order, given that it had no exceptional standing under the NAFTA or the UNCITRAL Arbitration Rules. The tribunal left open the question of whether Article 25(4) of the 1976 UNCITRAL Arbitration Rules implied a duty of confidentiality for all written submissions, as alleged by the claimant, because the parties had agreed on a confidentiality order. Admittedly, the tribunal was in a delicate situation. In their Article 1128 NAFTA submissions, the other NAFTA member states held contrary views on the issue.[71]

In arbitration procedures conducted within the NAFTA agreement (The North American Free Trade Agreement), the joining of an amicus was allowed for the first time in the 2000s. In the *Methanex* case from 2001, which dealt with the ban on the production of methanol gas, a non-governmental organization requested to join the proceedings as an amicus. Despite the parties' opposition, the NAFTA Dispute Settlement Panel has determined that it has enabled the authority to accept amicus briefs from third parties.[72] In justifying its decision, the tribunal stated that:

> There is undoubtedly public interest in this arbitration. The substantive issues extend far beyond those raised by the usual transnational arbitration between commercial parties... The public interest in this arbitration arises from its subject matter...[73]

In the United Parcel Service of America arbitration, the panel reiterated this position and noted that it is authorized to receive written briefs from amici even though they are not a formal party to the arbitration.[74] These decisions made it possible in the following years to accept dozens of amicus briefs from various groups and enabled the procedural anchoring of the amicus practice.[75] Accordingly, in 2003, the organization published a statement on ways of joining third parties as amici in arbitration proceedings (FTC Statement).[76] Based on this statement, the OECD published a

---

[70] Procedural Order No. 2 on Amicus Curiae and Non-Disputing Party Participation (2019).

[71] Mexico heavily opposed the opening of the proceedings to the public, while Canada supported full disclosure and announced that it would bring the issues to the attention of the NAFTA member states to regulate the issue of Amicus Curiae participation as a matter of urgency. Id paras. 9–10.

[72] Methanex Corp. v. United States, Decision on Petitions from Third Persons to Intervene as "Amici Curiae" (NAFTA Arb. Jan. 15, 2001); Barton Legum (2005).

[73] Methanex Corp. v. United States, Decision on Petitions from Third Persons to Intervene as "Amici Curiae" (NAFTA Arb. Jan. 15, 2001); para 49. The tribunal added that its authority to add "amici" to arbitration proceedings derives from the power of the rules of the United Nations Commission on International Commercial Law. Contrary to the request of the "amicus" in the case, the tribunal determined that the public interest can be fulfilled through the Submission of a written brief and that there is no need for the "amicus" to argue orally before them.

[74] United Parcel Serv. of Am., Inc. v. Canada, Decision on Petitions for Intervention and Participation as Amici Curiae (NAFTA Arb. Oct. 17, 2001).

[75] See for example Glamis Gold Ltd. v. United States, 48 I.L.M. 1038, 1041 (NAFTA Arb. 2009).

[76] NAFTA rules: Statement of the Free Trade Commission on Non-Disputing Party Participation (Oct. 7, 2003), http://www.state.gov/documents/organization/38791.pdf, are essentially similar to the rules of the Canadian judicial system. See also VanDuzer (2007), pp. 681–709.

report which called on the organization's members to allow for a more extensive intervention of third parties in arbitrations between investors and countries. The organization stated: "Members of the Investment Committee generally share the view that especially insofar as proceedings raise important issues of public interest, it may also be desirable to allow third-party participation, subject, however, to clear and specific guidelines."[77]

6.5.3 International Center for Settlement of Investment Disputes

The Amicus Curiae phenomenon has also been observed to have entered into the International Center for Settlement of Investment Disputes starting in 2005. In the *Aguas del Tunari* case that dealt with the dispute between Bolivia and the Netherlands, non-governmental public organizations requested to join the process and present their position as amici.[78] They claimed that at stake are public interests that the official litigants do not represent. The arbitration court did express its appreciation to the organizations but rejected the request for lack of authority.[79] In the next case discussed, the *Suez* case, the ICSID arbitrators determined that the tribunal has the authority to add amici to the proceedings.[80]

They received the brief of five international non-governmental organizations and noted that the conflict involved questions that deal with human rights and public issues, and therefore, it is appropriate to hear additional perspectives that enrich the information of the arbitrators and allow them to examine the broad implications of the issue.[81] In the decisions that were made afterward, criteria were determined by which it is possible to join as an "amicus." These were: the importance of the issue and the suitability of a third party to act as an "amicus,"[82] the background of the applicant who wished to be an Amicus Curiae, his expertise, his professional experience, and his contribution to the settlement of the conflict.[83] In 2006, these tests and other procedures were collected, edited, and published publicly. These rules stated, for example, that when the tribunal considers whether to accept such a

---

[77] Org. for Econ. Co-operation & Dev. [OECD], *Transparency and Third Party Participation in Investor-State Dispute Settlement Procedures: Statement by the OECD Investment Committee* (OECD Working Papers on Int'l Dev. No. 2005/01, 2005).

[78] Aguas del Tunari (2005), p. 450.

[79] Ibid, at p. 575. The tribunal noted that despite its sympathy for the request, it lacked the authority to allow it.

[80] Suez, Sociedad General de Aguas de Barcelona, S.A.and Vivendi Universal, S.A. v. Argentine Republic, ICSID Case No. ARB/03/19.

[81] Ibid.

[82] Ibid.

[83] Aguas Provinciales de Santa Fe S.A. v. Arg. Republic, ICSID Case No. ARB/03/17, Order in Response to a Petition for Participation as Amicus Curiae, 33–34 (Mar. 17, 2006).

brief, it must take into account several considerations. The tribunal must first consider the extent of the brief's potential contribution to resolving the dispute. It must also take into account the applicant's unique knowledge or insight that differs from those of the formal parties. Furthermore, the brief must refer to the issue that is within the scope of the dispute between the parties and present the interest that the applicant has in the procedure. The brief also must not prejudice or complicate the ongoing proceedings. The two official litigants who are in the arbitration procedure will be allowed to respond or refer to the brief submitted in their case.

In the decisions made in the following years, various tribunals added additional rules drawn mainly from American jurisprudence. For example, it was determined that the request to join as an Amicus Curiae must include the connections the applicant has with one of the official parties in the arbitration. The applicant must also disclose whether he directly or indirectly received financial or other support from one of the parties involved in the arbitration process. Moreover, the applicant must define what interest he has in the arbitration procedure as well as explain why the tribunal should permit him to submit a brief as an amicus.[84]

The procedural position of amici curiae is naturally weaker than that of parties to the dispute. Amici, therefore, lack the full procedural rights of disputing parties, such as commencement or withdrawal of arbitration or appointment of the tribunal. Mostly, amici are only allowed to file written submissions and do not participate in oral hearings, nor do they have some form of access to the documents of the arbitral proceedings.[85] However, there is a growing tendency to allow amici participation in oral hearings or having specific oral hearings to clarify the written submissions[86] or some form of access to documents,[87] largely after consulting with the disputing parties.[88] Lastly, it is worth mentioning that amici usually bear their costs.

[84] ICSID Arbitration Rules (2006), r. 37. For more see Biwater Gauff (Tanz.) Ltd. v. United Republic of Tanzania, ICSID Case No. ARB/05/22, Procedural Order No. 5, 55 (Feb. 2, 2007), 22 ICSID Rev. 217, 231 (2007); Pac Rim Cayman LLC v. Republic of El Sal., ICSID Case No. ARB/09/12, Decision on Respondent's Preliminary Objections under CAFTA Articles 10.20.4 and 10.20.5, ¶ 50 (Aug. 2, 2010); Commerce Grp. Corp. v. Republic of El Sal., ICSID Case No. ARB/09/17, Award, ¶ 39 (Mar. 14, 2011).

[85] See, for example, Rule 37(2) ICSID Arbitration Rules, Article 10.26(1) Korea-New Zealand FTA; Article 34 Benin-Canada BIT or Article 9.23(3) CPTPP only each mentioning written submissions; see for denied participation in oral hearings, for example, UPS v Canada (n 4); Chevron Corp and Texaco Petroleum Corp v The Republic of Ecuador (n 43); Bernhard von Pezold and others v Zimbabwe, ICSID Case No ARB/10/15, Procedural Order No 2 (26 June 2012).

[86] See, for example, Article 29.7 SIAC Investment Arbitration Rules; Article 3(7)(ii) SCC Arbitration Rules Appendix III; Annex C III.(8) and I. Canada-Latvia BIT; Article 33 and Annex–VI (9) Burkina Faso - Canada BIT; Annex B.III. and I. Canada – Czech BIT.

[87] See, for example, Article 3(3) UNCITRAL Transparency Rules; Article 29.8 SIAC Investment Arbitration Rules; Article 3(6) SCC Arbitration Rules Appendix III; Annex C III.(8) and I. Canada-Latvia BIT; Annex B.III. and I. Canada – Czech BIT; Aguas del Tunari SA v The Republic of Bolivia, ICSID Case No ARB/02/3, Petition (29 August 2002); Electrabel SA v Hungary, Procedural Order No 4, ICSID Case No ARB/07/19, 28th April 2009.

[88] See to the different forms of Amicus Curiae participation, Ishikawa (2010), paras. 8–30.

Furthermore, there is some tendency for cost orders against amici for additional procedural costs associated with their participation based on the general tribunal power to allocate costs[89] or special provisions,[90] which can serve to deter or mitigate unnecessary amicus submissions or procedural abuses by amici.[91]

6.6 Summary

The second major development of the Amicus Curiae phenomenon took place in international law, both in procedures related to public law and international commercial issues. Until the eighties of the twentieth century, the attitude of the international courts towards the wishes of third parties to express their position in ongoing proceedings was not sympathetic. On the other hand, starting in the 1990s, international tribunals, led by the European Court of Human Rights, gradually changed their approach and began to accept requests from amici, mainly international non-governmental organizations, to express their position in ongoing legal proceedings. The change in the trend about Amicus Curiae was characterized, among other things, by softening court orders towards requests from interest groups to present their position in ongoing proceedings, an increase in the number of entities that were not formal parties that were allowed to participate in the proceedings, the number of amici in each proceeding, and the possibility to argue orally before the courts.

At the same time, various international commercial organizations have adopted the practice of Amicus Curiae when there is a consistent increase in the number of briefs submitted and the number of organizations involved in the submission of briefs. Dispute settlement institutions frequently cite briefs of amici in their decisions. The change in trend is rooted in the understanding that commercial disputes discussed within the framework of international institutions encompass not only commercial interests but also fundamental issues of human rights, environmental quality, cultural heritage, and critical issues which the formal parties to arbitration are not interested in or are unable to present in the proceedings but should be examined before a decision is made in their case.[92]

[89] See, for example, Article 61(2) ICSID Convention; Article 42(1) UNCITRAL Rules; critical, Bjorklund, "The Emerging Civilization of Investment Arbitration" (2009) 113 Penn St L Rev 1269, 1293.

[90] See, for example, Article 3(10) SCC Arbitration Rules Appendix III.

[91] See, hereto (2007), p. 217; see also, Gómez (2012).

[92] Steger (2002), pp. 419, 447. See also Howse et al. (2013), para. 13 ('The preliminary submissions in this brief are aimed at correcting the misleading and incomplete manner in which Canada has characterized the objectives of the measures at iIe in this dispute...').

References

Aguas del Tunari SA (2005) v. Republic of Bol., ICSID Case No. ARB/02/3, decision on respondent's objections to jurisdiction (Oct. 21, 2005). ICSID Rev 20:450

Aguas Provinciales de Santa Fe SA (2006) v. Arg. Republic, ICSID Case No. ARB/03/17, Order in Response to a Petition for Participation as Amicus Curiae, 33–34 (Mar. 17, 2006)

Alexander A (2022) SSRN: critical analysis on third-party intervention before the international court of justice. https://papers.ssrn.com/sol3/papers.cfm?abstract_id=4107651

Alexander A, Shouvik KG (2022) Critical analysis on third-party intervention before the international court of justice (May 12) https://ssrn.com/abstract=4107651

Bartholomeusz L (2005) The Amicus Curiae before international courts and tribunals. Non-State Actors Int Law 5(209):236

Batura J (2023) The objective friends of the court – new insights into the role of third parties before the European Court of Human Rights. EJIL: Talk April 19

Charnovitz S (2000) Opening the WTO to nongovernmental interests. Fordham Int Law J 24:182

De Brabandere E (2011) NGOs and the "Public Interest": the legality and rationale of Amicus Curiae interventions in international economic and investment disputes. Chicago J Int Law 12: 85

Dolidze A (2015) Bridging comparative and international law: Amicus Curiae participation as a vertical legal transplant. Eur J Int Law 26:851

Frigessi di Rattalma M (2005) NGOs Before the European Court of Human Rights: beyond Amicus Curiae participation? In: Treves T et al (eds) Civil society, international courts and compliance bodies 57. T.M.C. Asser Press, p 131(320)

Gao HS (2006) Amicus Curiae in WTO dispute settlement: theory and practice. China Rights Forum 1:51

Gómez KF (2012) LLM perspective, rethinking the role of Amicus Curiae in international investment arbitration: how to draw the line favorably for the public interest. Fordham Int Law J 35: 510

Graham C (2012) Advocates for Int'l Dev., A "How To" guide to Amicus Curiae & international investment arbitrations 6–7 (Feb. 29)

Hereto R (2007) Opening the investment arbitration process: at what cost, for what benefit? In: Hoffman R, Tams CJ (eds) The international convention on the settlement of investment disputes (ICSID): taking stock after 40 years. Nomos, p 217

Hodson L (2011) NGOS and the struggle for human rights in Europe 52

Howse R et al (2013) Written submission of non-party amici curiae in EC-Seals. 11 February 2013, para. 13

Interights (1997) The Practice and Effectiveness of Submitting Amicus Curiae Briefs by NGOs in cases before international human rights treaty bodies and tribunals: notes on the example of the European court of human rights

Ishikawa T (2010) Third party participation in investment treaty arbitration. Int Comput Law Q 59(373):393

Juaristi FJR (2014) The amicus curiae in the inter-American Court of human rights (1982–2013)

Kawharu A (2007) Public participation and transparency in investment arbitration: recent developments and future challenges. IHLRes 2:2–3

Kingsbury B, Schill S (2009) "Investor-state arbitration as governance: fair and equitable treatment, proportionality and the emerging global administrative law." NYU School of Law, Public Law Research Paper 09-46

Land, Island & Maritime Frontier Dispute (El Sal. V. Hond.), Application to Intervene, Judgment, 1990 I.C.J. 92 (Sept. 13)

Lester A (1988) Amici curiae: third-party interventions before the European Court of human rights. In: Matscher F, Petzold H (eds) Protecting human rights: the European dimension, vol 341

Leach P (2011) Taking a case to the European Court of Human Rights. Oxford University Press

Mackenzie R (2005) The Amicus Curiae in international courts: toward common procedural approaches. In: Treves T et al. (eds) Civil society, international courts and compliance bodies. pp 295, 296

Macrory PFJ, Appleton AE, Plummer MG (2005) The World Trade Organization: legal, economic and political analysis. Springer, pp 1433–1435

Mahoney P (1983) Developments in the procedure of the European Court of Human Rights: the revised rules of the court. Yearb Eur Law 3:146

Mahoney P (2005) Commentaire. In: Hélène Ruiz Fabri, Jean-Marc Sorel (eds) Le tiers à l'instance devant les juridictions internationales pp 151, 155

Marceau G, Stilwell M (2001) Practical suggestions for amicus curiae briefs be- fore WTO adjudicating bodies. J Int Econ Law 4:157–158

Matscher F (1980) Überlegungen über die Einführung der "Interpretationsintervention" im Verfahren vor dem Europäischen Gerichtshof für Menschenrechte. In: Miehsler H (ed) Ius Humanitatis – Festschrift für Alfred Verdross zum 90. Geburtstag, Berlin, p 539

Mayer H (2011) NGO standing and influence in regional human rights courts and commissions. Brook J Int Law 36:911

Metcalfe E (2009) To assist the court: third party interventions in the UK, p 1

Mónica P 2005 NGOs and the Inter-American court of human rights. In: Treves T et al (eds) Civil society, international courts and compliance bodies. Asser Press, pp 47, 55–56

Mowbray A (2005) The creativity of the European Court of Human Rights. Human Rights Law Rev 5(1):57–79

Ortino F (2009) The impact of Amicus Curiae briefs in the settlement of trade and investment disputes. In: Meessen KM (ed) Economic law as an economic good. Sellier, pp 301, 316

Padilla D (1993) The Inter-American commission on humans rights of the organization of American states: a case study. Am Univ J Int Law Policy 9:95, 111

Palchetti P (2002) Opening the international court of justice to third states: intervention and beyond. Max Planck Yearb United Nations Law 6:139

Robbins J (2003) Recent developments, false friends: Amicus Curiae and procedural discretion in WTO appeals under the hot-rolled lead/asbestos doctrine. Harv Int Law J 44:317

Shelton D (1994) The participation of nongovernmental organizations in international judicial proceedings. Am J Int Law 88(611):637

Squatrito T (2017) Amicus Curiae briefs in the WTO DSM: good or bad news for non-state actor involvement? Published online by Cambridge University Press, https://doi.org/10.1017/S1474745617000052

Steger D (2002) Amicus Curiae: participant or friend? – the WTO and NAFTA experience. In: van Bogdandy A (ed) European integration and international co-ordination – studies in transnational economic law in honor of Claus-Dieter Ehlermann, The Hague, pp 419, 447

Umbricht G (2001) An "Amicus Curiae brief" on Amicus Curiae briefs at the WTO. J Int Econ Law 4:791

Van den Eynde L (2013) An empirical look at the Amicus Curiae practice of human rights NGOs before the European Court of Human Rights. Neth Q Human Rights 31(3):271–313

Van Harten G (2007) Investment treaty arbitration and public law-a return to the gay nineties? Transnational see in general: Dispute Management (TDM) 4.5

Wiik A (2018) Amicus Curiae before international courts and tribunals. Nomos Verlagsgesellschaft mbH & Co. KG

Williams SJ, Palmer E (2016) Civil society and Amicus Curiae interventions in the international criminal law. In: Williams SJ, Woolaver H (eds) JUTA pp 40–46

Woolaver H (2016) International Judicial Monitor: The Role of Amicus Curiae Submissions at International Criminal Tribunals. http://www.judicialmonitor.org/spring2016/specialreport2.html#_ftn2

Chapter 7
The Civil Law

The Amicus Curiae phenomenon has also spread to the continental legal system, primarily in Europe and Latin America, certain African countries (such as Uganda,[1] Ethiopia,[2] and Namibia[3]), and parts of Asia (such as South Korea[4] or Thailand[5]). While Amicus Curiae was not an inherent part of the legal systems in most these countries until the last decade of the twentieth century, following the adoption of the use of Amicus Curiae in international law, the practice began to be included in most European and Latin American countries in the past fifteen years. Primarily, the introduction of Amicus Curiae into these countries has been expressed through the submission of Amicus Curiae briefs in ongoing proceedings. The reception of the Amicus Curiae practice into the continental legal system and the change in approach towards the intervention of third parties has been enabled by two central avenues; both by formal legislation and by informal incorporation of this practice into the judicial system.[6] Professor Shelton aptly described this as:

> [T]he position of France and other civil law countries is to grant broad intervention rights. Associations and organizations concerned with the environment or human rights participate in cases as intervenors, serving the same purpose as amici in common law countries.[7]

---

[1] Kasirye (2012); Mubangizi and Mbazira (2012), pp. 199–200.

[2] Badwaza (2011).

[3] Hinson and Hubbard (2012), pp. 574.

[4] For example, Brief of the International Trademark Association as Amicus Curiae, Prefel S.A. v. Jae Ik Choi (S. Kor. S. Ct. July 23, 2002), available at http://www.inta.org/Advocacy/Documents/INTAPrefelChoi.pdf.

[5] For example, Amicus Brief of ARTICLE 19, Pub. Prosecutor, Office of the Attorney Gen. v. Pruksakasemsuk (Apr. 24, 2012), available at http://www.article19.org/data/files/medialibrary/3075/12-04-30-LM-thailand.pdf.

[6] Kochevar (2013).

[7] Shelton (2013), p. 616.

S. Farber, *The Amicus Curiae Phenomenon*, Ius Gentium: Comparative Perspectives on Law and Justice 119, https://doi.org/10.1007/978-3-031-67225-5_7

The divergent approaches to amicus curiae in civil law and common law countries stem from the fundamental differences between these legal traditions. In common law systems, which rely heavily on case law and judicial precedents, the amicus curiae practice evolved organically as a means for courts to seek additional information and perspectives to aid in their decision-making process. The concept of allowing non-parties to contribute to legal proceedings aligned with the common law tradition of shaping legal norms through judicial interpretation.

Conversely, in civil law systems, which are primarily based on comprehensive legal codes and statutes, the role of courts has traditionally been more limited to interpreting and applying the law, rather than actively shaping it through judicial decisions. As a result, the concept of allowing non-parties to contribute to legal proceedings was initially foreign and viewed as unnecessary in many civil law jurisdictions, where the focus was on strict adherence to codified laws.

However, as courts in civil law countries began to assume a more active role in addressing complex societal issues and shaping legal norms, the need for diverse perspectives and specialized knowledge became more apparent. This shift in judicial function, coupled with the influence of international legal developments and the growing importance of public interest litigation, paved the way for the gradual adoption of amicus curiae practices in civil law systems.

7.1 Latin America

7.1.1 Brazil

No Latin American countries formally recognized the practice of Amicus Curiae until the late 1990s. In 1999, Brazil became the first Latin American country to allow the inclusion of Amicus Curiae in proceedings before its Constitutional Court.[8] Even before the formal possibility of submitting Amicus Curiae briefs in Brazil, there was a practice in which the Constitutional Court would accept briefs from state representatives as "quasi-friends of the court." We, therefore, see that establishing the Amicus Curiae role in 1999 evolved from a semi-official practice regarding state authorities. The actual innovation lies in the possibility of including non-governmental organizations (NGOs) as amici and codifying these rules into law. Regulations establish a set of rules under which the Supreme Court can approve the inclusion of amici in ongoing proceedings, considering factors such as the importance of the issue at hand and the expertise of the third party. Additionally,

[8]Medeiros (2008). I am grateful to Marco Velásquez-Ruiz from Osgoode University in Canada for assisting me with the translation of some of the articles Written in Spanish and Portuguese.

the rules determine that the Amicus Curiae brief must be submitted at the beginning of the hearing.[9]

7.1.2 Argentina

In addition to Brazil, other Latin American countries also now recognize Amicus Curiae. For example, the Supreme Court of Argentina has ruled that the conditions for the inclusion of Amicus Curiae are as follows: (a) the applicant must indicate the extent of their contribution to the proceedings; (b) disclosure of their connections with any formal parties involved; (c) the issue must have a public interest or broad collective significance.[10]

7.1.3 Colombia

Similarly, the Supreme Court of Colombia allows for the participation of third parties as amici. Lower courts in Colombia also allow third parties to intervene in proceedings as long as they demonstrate a "legitimate interest" in the case.[11] In matters of public interest, third parties are allowed to join the proceedings without specifically demonstrating a legitimate interest.[12]

7.1.4 Cost Rica and Peru

The Supreme Court of Costa Rica,[13] and the Constitutional Court of Peru,[14] explicitly recognized the practice of Amicus Curiae and established legal procedures for submitting briefs by third parties in proceedings conducted before them. In Argentina and Peru, the formal reception of Amicus Curiae in legal procedures created a semi-official practice where different amici, primarily governmental authorities, were allowed to present their positions informally. Furthermore, several Latin

[9] Codigo de Processo Civil [C.P.C.] [Brazil Civil Procedure Code]. See also: Correa-Ordoñez and Mandakovic (2014).

[10] Amigos del tribunal, Acordada No. 28/2004, July 20, 2004, 30455 B.O.

[11] See Código General Del Proceso [C.G.P.] art. 71.

[12] Ibid section 171.

[13] Regarding the general rules concerning administrative courts, see Código Procesal Contencioso Administrativo [C.P.C.A.] art. 13. For proceedings in civil litigation, refer to Código Procesal Civil [C.P.C.] art. 112.

[14] Reglamento Normativo del Tribunal Constitucional, Resolución Administrativa No. 095-2004-P/TC, Sept. 14, 2004, art. 13-A; Defensoría Del Pueblo (2009), 45–46.

American countries explicitly permitted the participation of amici, including NGOs, in ongoing proceedings since 2011. It should be noted that the change in the court's attitude towards interest groups' desires to present their position in South American countries is also deeply rooted in broad democratic and economic reforms conducted in most of these countries. These include modernization, changing governance methods, expanding the business sector, increasing transparency, globalization, democratization, and more.[15]

7.2 European Continental Countries

Recently, many European countries belonging to the continental legal system have adopted the institution of Amicus Curiae for the first time. This has included allowing the submission of briefs and institutionalizing the practice within their legal frameworks. These changes began in the late nineteen nineties, continuing in the first two decades of the twenty-first century.

Poland, for example, recognized the possibility for third parties to submit Amicus Curiae briefs to the Supreme Court in 1997. Following the Supreme Court's ruling, lower courts in Poland also adopted the option for third parties to submit Amicus Curiae briefs. For instance, the Helsinki Foundation for Human Rights (HFHR) frequently submits Amicus Curiae briefs to various courts in Poland on human rights issues. This practice is positively received and encouraged both by non-governmental organizations and the courts, inviting them to present their positions as amici.[16]

In 2016, the Constitutional Tribunal of Poland issued a ruling that clarified the conditions under which Amicus Curiae briefs can be submitted in Polish courts. The ruling stated that Amicus Curiae briefs can be submitted by any person or organization with a legitimate interest in the case's outcome. The brief must be submitted in writing and must be signed by the person or organization submitting it. The brief must also be limited to 10 pages in length.[17]

One of the legal areas where the procedure of Amicus Curiae is widely employed in Europe is European Union (EU) competition law. Under EU law, all state

[15] Wiarda (2004); Código Federal de Procedimientos Civiles, art. 598, Diario Oficial de la Federación [DOF] 24-02-1943, últimas reformas DOF 09-04-2012 (Mex.); Bazán (2009).

[16] For further information, please refer to Maciej Bernatt Opinion of the Friend of the Court (Amicus Curiae) as an Auxiliary Legal Institution in the Jurisprudence of Polish Courts], Łukasz Bojarski (2008) & also see: Maciej Bernatt (2012).

[17] Statement of the Constitutional Tribunal of Poland regarding the admissibility of the participation of third parties in proceedings before the Constitutional Tribunal, issued on 16 December 2016. For further reference, see: Klub Parlamentarny Lewica i Demokraci v. Trybunał Konstytucyjny, Constitutional Tribunal of Poland, Case No. K 19/17, 22 June 2018 & also see: K'ub Parlamentarny Kukiz'15 v. Trybunał Konstytucyjny, Constitutional Tribunal of Poland, Case No. K 20/17, 22 June 2018.

authorities responsible for competition regulations are authorized to submit Amicus Curiae briefs and present oral arguments before national courts within the EU.[18] As a result of this practice, numerous Amicus Curiae briefs have been filed with the Federal Supreme Court in Germany and with federal courts in Germany.[19]

Similarly, various types of Amicus Curiae briefs have been submitted in recent years to courts in Sweden,[20] Austria,[21] the Czech Republic,[22] Slovakia,[23] and Belgium.[24]

7.2.1 *Spain*

In 2018, the Spanish Supreme Court issued a ruling that clarified the conditions under which Amicus Curiae briefs can be submitted in Spanish courts. The ruling stated that Amicus Curiae briefs can be submitted by any person or organization with a legitimate interest in the case's outcome. The brief must be submitted in writing and must be signed by the person or organization submitting it. The brief must also be limited to 10 pages in length.

---

[18] *Commission Observations to National Courts (*Amicus Curiae *Observations, Article 15(3))*, Eur. Comm'n: Competition, http://ec.europa.eu/competition/court/antitrust_amicus_curiae.html (last visited Aug. 8, 2016).

[19] Bernardo Cortese (2013). In recent years, the Federal Constitutional Court of Germany has accepted Amicus Curiae briefs in a number of cases, including The 2018 Case of the Federal Constitutional Court of Germany v. the German Parliament: In this case, the Federal Constitutional Court of Germany accepted Amicus Curiae briefs from a number of organizations, including the German Bar Association and the German Association of Lawyers for Human Rights. The briefs argued that the German Parliament had erred in its decision to pass a law that restricted the right to freedom of expression. The Federal Constitutional Court ultimately struck down the law, but it did so in part by considering the arguments made by the amici curiae. See Amicus Curiae Briefs of the German Bar Association and the German Association of Lawyers for Human Rights in Case 1 BvR 276/17, Federal Constitutional Court of Germany, German Bar Association and German Association of Lawyers for Human Rights, 2018.

[20] Vikingsoda AB mot Soda-Club (CO2) SA, Soda-Club International B.V., Svea Hovrätt 2010-03-25 Ö 1561-10.

[21] Oberster Gerichtshof Dec. 5, 2011, 16 Ok 4/11.

[22] Amicus Curiae Brief by Twenty-Five Non-Governmental Orgs. & Acad. Insts., Ústavní soud, No. 3073/08 (Feb. 18, 2010), http://www.mdac.info/en/amicus-curiae-brief-czech-constitutional-court.

[23] Observation by Eur. Comm'n, E.-P. v. Slovak NCA (Slovk. Sup. Ct.) (Sept. 21, 2012), http://ec.europa.eu/competition/court/amicus_curiae_epslovak_sk.pdf.

[24] In 2012, the Belgian Competition Authority submitted an Amicus Curiae brief to the Court of Cassation in a case concerning the abuse of a dominant position by a telecommunications company. The Competition Authority argued that the company's conduct had harmed competition and consumers, and it urged the Court to find in favor of the plaintiffs. Belgian Competition Authority, Amicus Curiae Brief in the Case of N.V. Proximus v. Belgian Consumer Protection Association' Court of Cassation, 1st Civil Chamber, 13 December 2012.

The ruling also stated that the court is not required to consider the arguments made in an *Amicus Curiae* brief, but it may do so if it chooses. One of the famous cases is the 2019 Case of the *Supreme Court of Spain vs. the Spanish Anti-Monopoly Service*. In this case, the Supreme Court of Spain accepted an Amicus Curiae brief from the Spanish Bar Association, the association of lawyers in Spain. The Bar Association's brief argued that the lower court had erred in its decision to uphold a decision by the Spanish Anti-Monopoly Service to fine a company for violating antitrust laws. The Supreme Court ultimately upheld the lower court's decision, but it did so in part by considering the arguments made by the amici.[25]

Another famous case is when the Supreme Court of Spain accepted Amicus Curiae briefs from several organizations, including the Spanish Bar Association and the Spanish Association of Lawyers for Human Rights. The briefs argued that the Spanish government had erred in its decision to deport asylum seekers to a country where they would face persecution. The Supreme Court ultimately ordered the government to allow the asylum seekers to stay in Spain. The arguments made by the amici were influential in the Supreme Court's decision.[26]

7.2.2 *France*

One prominent example of the acceptance of Amicus Curiae in Europe is France, which adopted the institution of Amicus Curiae fairly early on, back in 1988. In a case dealing with lawyers' professional liability, the President of the Court of Appeals approached the President of the Paris Bar Association and requested their input as the "amicus." In the request for assistance, the court stated that the Bar Association was asked to provide information that would enrich the court's understanding of the issue without becoming an official party to the proceedings.[27]

In 1991, the French Court of Cassation recognized the procedure of Amicus Curiae for the first time, allowing third parties to submit their positions as amici in various opportunities. Examples include maternity fund agreements,[28] compensation for individuals infected with AIDS,[29] and criminal aspects of infanticide,[30] the

[25] Asociación Española de Abogados (AEA) v. Servicio de Defensa de la Competencia (SDC), Supreme Court of Spain, Case No. 252/2018, 10 December 2019.

[26] María de los Ángeles González Carreño v. Ministerio de Justicia, Supreme Court of Spain, Case No. 1263/2018, 17 July 2018.

[27] See Gaz. Pal (1988). Laurin; David W. Duncan (1994) (hereinafter: Duncan); Shelton (2013).

[28] See Cour de cassation ass. plén., May 31, 1991, Bull ass. plén. No. 4.

[29] See Cour d'appel Paris, Oct. 16, 1992, D. 1993, 172, note Y. Laurin.

[30] See Cour de cassation ass. plén., June 29, 2001, Bull. crim. 2001, No. 165.

characterization of life insurance policies' investments, and other cases.[31] Additionally, dozens of Amicus Curiae briefs have been submitted in recent years to different courts in France, such as the Commercial Court of Paris (Tribunal de Commerce de Paris).[32]

Additional powers have been granted more recently to the courts in France, expanding the possibilities of assistance by Amicus Curiae. For example, in 2010, the courts dealing with administrative matters were given the authority to invite anyone whose skills or knowledge could be helpful to the court to submit an Amicus Curiae brief on a relevant and pending issue. Additionally, the courts were empowered to allow non-participating third parties to present oral arguments.[33]

In 2014, the Cour de Cassation (the highest civil court in France) accepted an Amicus Curiae brief from the French Bar Association on whether the right to privacy includes the right to be forgotten. The case involved a man who had been convicted of a crime in 1999 and had served his sentence. He then requested that Google remove links to news articles about his conviction from its search results. Google refused, arguing that the reports were accurate and in the public interest.

The French Bar Association argued in its Amicus Curiae brief that the right to privacy includes the right to be forgotten. The association argued that the right to privacy is not absolute but must be balanced against other important rights, such as the right to freedom of expression. The association also argued that the right to be forgotten is particularly important in the digital age, where information can be quickly and permanently stored online.[34]

The decision recognizing the possibility of accepting Amicus Curiae briefs in France sparked a controversy that spread to other European judicial systems. One of the main arguments was that adopting this practice contradicted the continental legal system and was done without proper authority since the Parliament did not authorize the judiciary to include "amici" in proceedings that did not concern them. On the other hand, it is argued that the court's inherent authority allows them to receive relevant information, including Amicus Curiae briefs, to assist them in their work.[35]

There are two important points to note regarding the amicus in France. Firstly, in 2004, the French government issued a report on using Amicus Curiae briefs in France. The report concluded that the practice was beneficial and should be encouraged. The report also made several recommendations for improving the use of Amicus Curiae briefs in France. Secondly, in 2010, the French Parliament adopted a law that reformed the French judicial system. The law included a provision that allows the courts to accept *Amicus Curiae* briefs in certain cases.

---

[31] See Cour de cassation ch. mixte, Nov. 23, 2004, Bull. mixte 2004, No. 4.

[32] Cortese (2013) at 148. Additional examples: Commission Observations to National Courts.

[33] Décret 2010-164 du 22 février 2010 relatif aux compétences et au fonctionnement des juridictions administratives, p. 3325.

[34] Google France v. Louis Costeja González, Cour de cassation (10 May 2014).

[35] Duncan (1994), p. 450. See also Coslin and Lapillonne (2012), p. 14.

In his article "*L'Amicus Curiae devant les jurisdictions administratives françaises*" (2005), Jean-Philippe Derosier argues that the practice of allowing Amicus Curiae briefs in French administrative law is a positive development that can help to improve the quality of justice. He notes that it has become increasingly common in France in recent years. He also notes that the courts have generally been receptive to Amicus Curiae briefs, which have helped provide additional information and perspectives on complex legal issues. He concludes by calling on the French government to adopt legislation that formally allows Amicus Curiae briefs in administrative law.[36]

7.2.3 Germany

There is no specific legislation in Germany about Amicus Curiae briefs.[37] However, the practice is becoming increasingly common, and the courts are generally receptive to Amicus Curiae briefs. In 2009, the German government issued a report on the use of Amicus Curiae briefs in Germany. The report concluded that the practice was beneficial and should be encouraged. The information also made several recommendations for improving the use of Amicus Curiae briefs in Germany.[38] The relevant provisions are found in the German Code of Civil Procedure (*Zivilprozessordnung*) and the German Code of Criminal Procedure (*Strafprozessordnung*). These codes outline the requirements and procedures for submitting *Amicus Curiae* briefs, including the deadline for submission, the brief's content, and the court's discretion in considering such submissions.

There are several cases in which the German courts have accepted Amicus Curiae briefs. In one case, the *Bundesverfassungsgericht* (the Federal Constitutional Court of Germany) accepted an Amicus Curiae brief from the German government on whether the right to privacy includes the right to be forgotten.[39] In another case, the *Bundesgerichtshof* (the Federal Court of Justice of Germany) accepted an *Amicus Curiae* brief from the German Bar Association on whether the right to freedom of expression includes the right to post hate speech online.[40]

[36] Jean-Philippe Derosier (2005).

[37] 'Freund des gerichts' or 'Freund des Gerichts' in German legal terminology.

[38] Kühne (2015).

[39] Ibid.

[40] Bundesgerichtshof, Urteil vom 11.12.2019 – VI ZR 232/19.

7.2.4 *Additional Countries*

Another way Amicus Curiae is adopted in continental law relates to requests from organizations to submit Amicus Curiae briefs in courts that do not recognize Amicus Curiae and are "forced to align" with other countries that have already adopted this practice. This action is carried out due to the activities of non-governmental international organizations that submit Amicus Curiae briefs on various topics in almost all countries belonging to the continental legal system, whether they have recognized Amicus Curiae or not. This includes countries in Southeast Asia, such as South Korea[41] and Thailand,[42]

---

[41] For example, see the Brief of the International Trademark Association as Amicus Curiae (2002), p. 678. Furthermore, in 2014, the Constitutional Court of Korea accepted Amicus Curiae briefs from several organizations, including the International Commission of Jurists, Amnesty International, and the Friends World Committee for Consultation, in a case challenging the constitutionality of the country's mandatory military service law. The Court ultimately upheld the law, but it did so in part by considering the arguments made by the amici curiae. See Korea JoongAng Daily (2014). In 2020, the Constitutional Court of Korea accepted Amicus Curiae briefs from several organizations, including Greenpeace Korea and the Korea Federation for Environmental Movements, in a case challenging the constitutionality of the government's plan to build a new nuclear power plant. See the Korea Herald (2020).

[42] Amicus Curiae briefs are not explicitly provided for in Thai law. However, in recent years, the Constitutional Court of Thailand has accepted Amicus Curiae briefs in a number of cases, including The 2017 Case of the Constitutional Court of Thailand v. the National Anti-Corruption Commission: In this case, the Constitutional Court of Thailand accepted an Amicus Curiae brief from the Association for the Protection of Children's Rights of Thailand, an NGO that works to protect the rights of children in Thailand. The Association's brief argued that the lower court had erred in its decision to dismiss the Constitutional Court's challenge to the constitutionality of a law that allowed the National Anti-Corruption Commission to investigate and prosecute children. The Constitutional Court ultimately upheld the lower court's decision, but it did so in part by considering the arguments made by the amici curiae.

regions in Russia,[43] and ends in the central region of Sub-Saharan Africa (such as Rwanda,[44] Kenya,[45] and Ethiopia[46]).

It is also important to note that, similar to developments in Latin America, the change in approach by courts towards the desires of interest groups to present their positions is deeply rooted in structural, democratic, and broad economic reforms that have taken place in these countries. These reforms include modernization, expansion of the business sector, the information revolution, increasing democratization, and other profound social processes.[47] In this way, international organizations "force"

---

[43] For example, in the case of Richemont International S.A. v. Russian Patent & Trademark Office, No. A40-73286/10-143-625 (Moscow Arbitrazh Court, Dec. 20, 2011), an amicus brief was filed by the International Trademark Association. You can find the brief at http://www.inta.org/Advocacy/Documents/INTARichemontRospatent.pdf. In Russia, Amicus Curiae briefs are not explicitly provided for in the law. However, in recent years, the Supreme Court of Russia has accepted Amicus Curiae briefs in several cases. One notable example is the 2019 case of the Supreme Court of Russia v. the Russian Anti-Monopoly Service. In this case, the Supreme Court accepted an Amicus Curiae brief from the Russian Bar Association, which argued against a decision by the Russian Anti-Monopoly Service. While the Supreme Court ultimately upheld the lower court's decision, it considered the arguments presented in the Amicus Curiae brief.

[44] Amicus Curiae briefs are not explicitly provided for in Rwandan law. However, in recent years, the Supreme Court of Rwanda has accepted Amicus Curiae briefs in several cases, including: (1) The 2018 Case of Agnes Nkusi v. Saidat Mukakibire: In this case, the Supreme Court of Rwanda accepted an Amicus Curiae brief from the Centre for Human Rights-Rwanda, an NGO that promotes human right' in Rwanda. The Centre's brief argued that the lower court had erred in its decision to uphold the conviction of Ms. Nkusi, who had been convicted of defaming a government official. The Supreme Court ultimately overturned the lower court's decision and acquitted Ms. Nkusi. (2) The 2022 Case of The Republic of Rwanda v. Ildephonse Hategekimana: In this case, the Supreme Court of Rwanda accepted an Amicus Curiae brief from the Kigali Bar Association, the association of lawyers in Rwanda. The Bar Association's brief argued that the lower court had erred in its decision to extradite Mr. Hategekimana to the International Criminal Tribunal for Rwanda (ICTR), which was trying him for war crimes and crimes against humanity. The Supreme Court ultimately upheld the lower court's decision, but it did so in part by considering the arguments made by the amici curiae. The use of Amicus Curiae briefs is becoming increasingly common in Rwandan courts as judges recognize the value of hearing from various perspectives on complex legal issues.

[45] Viljoen and Abebe (2014), pp. 22–44.

[46] For example, The 2020 National Election Postponement Case: In 2020, the Council of Constitutional Inquiry (CCI) accepted Amicus Curiae briefs from a number of organizations, including the Ethiopian Human Rights Commission, the Ethiopian Lawyers for Human Rights and Democracy, and the Ethiopian Women Lawyers Association, in a case challenging the constitutionality of the government's decision to postpone the 2020 national elections. The CCI ultimately upheld the government's decision, but it did so in part by considering the arguments made by the amici curiae. The 2018 State of Emergency Case: In 2018, the Federal Supreme Court of Ethiopia accepted Amicus Curiae briefs from a number of organizations, including the Ethiopian Human Rights Commission, the Ethiopian Lawyers for Human Rights and Democracy, and the Ethiopian Women Lawyers Association, in a case challenging the constitutionality of the government's decision to declare a state of emergency. The Federal Supreme Court ultimately upheld the government's decision, but it did so in part by considering the arguments made by the amici curiae.

[47] For example, the Amicus Curiae Brief of ARTICLE 19, In re Uwimana Nkusi, No. RP 0082/10/HC/KIG (S. Ct. Rwanda Oct. 24, 2011), can be found at http://www.article19.org/data/files/

courts to adopt the practice of Amicus Curiae, formally or partially. Often, even if a request to present a position as an Amicus Curiae is rejected, the content of the position is transmitted to the courts, and this information is used formally or informally.

7.3 Initial Outline for Developing Law in Continental Legal Systems

7.3.1 General

The practice of Amicus Curiae in countries belonging to the continental legal system is pragmatic and considers each case's unique circumstances. However, compared to other systems worldwide, rules and guidelines for the acceptance of amicus briefs are generally considered partial, insufficiently detailed, and, in some cases, disorderly. This is due to several reasons. Firstly, many issues that have been addressed and organized in other countries have not been discussed in most of these countries yet, such as the "duty of candor" that amici should fulfill before joining the proceedings or limitations on the scope of briefs.[48] Secondly, the development of rules related to Amicus Curiae currently depends directly on the initiative of the party approaching the court, formally or as an amicus, and their capabilities. As a result, the rules developed so far on the topic of Amicus Curiae are sporadic rather than systematic.

Thirdly, the litigants, through their various claims and appeals, direct and determine the rules regarding Amicus Curiae. Therefore, the judicial system responds to the issues brought before it and does not proactively initiate steps to improve and refine the situation, as has been done in other parts of the world regarding Amicus Curiae. For example, the United States Supreme Court has changed its rules on the matter several times, with initiatives of its own, in 1937, 1949, 1954, 1967, 1990, and 1997. Fourthly, without clear and grounded criteria, there is a concern that the court's policy regarding Amicus Curiae may lack uniformity.

We may speculate that the formal regulation of the topic will lead to increased use of Amicus Curiae by different interest groups. In the following pages, I will address several issues that need to be addressed concerning *Amicus Curiae* in these countries. The list of topics I will present is not exhaustive, nor can it be comprehensive due to reasons that will be apparent. My goal is modest and aims to draw attention to fundamental legal issues that require in-depth analysis and determination by the authorized bodies in each country.

---

medialibrary/2805/Amicus-Nkusi-and-Mukakibibi-English-submitted.pdf. For a description of the development of interest groups in non-liberal democracies, see Herbst (2001); Russian Civil Society: A Critical Assessment (Alfred B. Evans et al, 2006).

[48] Larsen (2014).

The normative examination of the various issues to be discussed below should be based on a series of fundamental assumptions and related issues concerning the Amicus Curiae and its role. These include the nature of the entities interested in joining as amici; and the relationship between the inclusion of amici and the management of the legal process. Other factors to be considered include the desired relief sought in the proceedings and the character and wishes of the formal parties to the proceedings. From the perspective of those seeking to be amici, several key issues should be examined, such as:

a. How does the information presented by the amici assist the work of the courts? Usually, third-party interveners have opinions or positions on ongoing proceedings. However, more than 'opinions' is needed when it comes to legal proceedings, with unique expert knowledge usually being required. The question is: what tangible value does the Amicus Curiae bring to the court beyond the information presented by formal litigants to aid its work?
b. Is the entity seeking to present its position as an Amicus Curiae suitable to do so? Is it an experienced and professional body? From the perspective of the amici, it is essential to determine whether joining as an Amicus Curiae serves its interests (association, society, academic institution, etc.). Are there more suitable third-party entities who could join as amici? Does the case in which the request for inclusion as an Amicus Curiae is made have significant importance and potential impact?
c. Other questions to consider include: What are the potential Amicus Curiae involvement costs? Does the contribution the entity offers outweigh the process's potential drawbacks? This assessment should not only consider direct financial costs (such as legal expenses) but also, for example, the risk that, as a result of the Amicus Curiae participation, the court's decision may be less favorable (in the view of the Amicus Curiae) than if it had not participated as an Amicus Curiae. Could joining as an amicus harm the desired outcome in the eyes of the Amicus Curiae? Is there a risk that the seeking organization's reputation will be tarnished due to an undesirable court decision in which it participated as an *Amicus Curiae* (which could lead, for example, to a decrease in donations, loss of members, etc.)? Is the entity seeking to be an amicus prepared to deal with negative publicity associated with its inclusion as an Amicus Curiae?

Another series of questions related to the regulation of the Amicus Curiae focuses on the court's considerations when deciding whether to accept an Amicus Curiae request to join the proceedings. The formulation that includes this examination should, in my view, strike a balance between the aspiration for the most accurate and complete decision-making and the efficiency of the process. I would suggest that this formulation be defined through a series of guiding principles, including:

(1) Denial of requests from amici that duplicate or replicate the formal parties' positions.

    In contrast, permission may be granted for an Amicus Curiae to join ongoing proceedings in the following cases:

(2) When a particular formal party is not adequately represented or not represented at all, and the amici seek to present the legal arguments on their behalf (similar to the classic amicus role, as described above).
(3) When the Amicus Curiae can identify a direct and tangible interest that may be harmed if not presented to the court (similar to the interests of an intervener but without turning them into a formal party).
(4) When the Amicus Curiae possesses vital information outside the hands of the formal parties or that the formal parties cannot present (due to lack of knowledge or other reasons).
(5) When the information presented by the Amicus Curiae is necessary for the purpose of "doing justice."[49]

In light of these principles the criteria outlined in the next sections should be considered.

7.3.2 Criteria for Including "Amicus Curiae": General

It can be argued that the contribution of the amicus's submission to the court should be the central criterion for the courts to consider, taking into account the general circumstances of the issue, the nature of the requesting party to join as an Amicus Curiae, and the potential impact on the parties' rights.[50] These criteria should be maintained in countries that have not explicitly regulated the amicus role. Similar to the general principles of the U.S. Supreme Court,[51] the Canadian Supreme Court,[52] and the ICSID Arbitral Tribunals,[53] a threshold test should be added. The amicus submission should only be accepted if the information presented is "distinct from the parties' positions, useful, and relevant to the court's work." In other words, the courts should ensure, as a threshold requirement, that entities seeking to join as amici present arguments that differ from the formal parties' arguments and that these arguments are only approved if they contribute to the clarification of the proceedings.

[49] Please see 223 F.3d 615 (7th Cir. 2000).

[50] For example, see the NAFTA regulations, page 665. This is also the law in federal courts in the United States. See Federal Rules of Appellate Procedure, Rule 29.

[51] SUP. CT. R. 37.1. The guiding principle states: An Amicus Curiae brief that brings to the attention of the court relevant matter not already brought to its attention by the parties may be of considerable help to the Court. An Amicus Curiae brief that does not serve this purpose burdens the court, and its filing is not favored.

[52] Regarding the case of Reference re Workers' Comp. Act, p. 341.

[53] ICSID Arbitration Rules (2006), r. 37.

7.3.3 *Supplementary Facets on the Parameters for the Inclusion of "Amicus Curiae"*

7.3.3.1 Transparency and Disclosure

In the interest of fairness and transparency, it is necessary to ensure that the Amicus Curiae fully discloses its sources and its social, ideological, or economic connections with the formal parties. The principles of disclosure developed worldwide have been based on accumulated experience from tens of thousands of briefs submitted to judicial forums emphasize complete transparency. These principles apply not only in the United States[54] but also in other countries. In the case of *Philip Morris*, the Massachusetts court noted in this context that: "Briefs of *Amicus Curiae* are intended to represent the views of non-parties; they are not intended as vehicles for parties or their counsel to make additional arguments beyond those that fit within the page constraints of their briefs."[55]

For example, starting in 2006, the International Centre for Settlement of Investment Disputes (ICSID) Arbitration Rules has developed rules on this matter. These rules state, among other things, that the request submitted by an Amicus Curiae should include a detailed disclosure of the organization's connections with any of the parties to the arbitration, as well as full disclosure regarding whether the applicant has received direct or indirect financial support or any other form of support from any of the parties to the arbitration.[56] Similarly, in Arizona, since 2014, the courts require applicants seeking to be amici to fulfill specific requirements, "[to] Identify every person or entity, other than the Amicus Curiae, its members, or its counsel, who made a monetary contribution to the preparation or submission of the brief."[57] Furthermore, in Arizona, it is stipulated that the attorneys representing the formal parties shall not assist in drafting the Amicus Curiae briefs.[58] In many states in the United States (such as Maryland, Minnesota, West Virginia, and Texas), there are similar rules on disclosure requirements for Amicus Curiae, resembling those in Arizona.[59] In states with no statutory disclosure rules for Amicus Curiae, the courts supplement it through case law.[60]

---

[54] SUP. CT. R. 37.6.

[55] Aspinall v. Philip Morris Cos., Inc., 813 N.E.2d 476, 480–81, n.8 (Mass. 2004).

[56] Please see Biwater Gauff, Procedural Order No. 5, (2007) *supra* note 741, at page 231.

[57] ARIZ. R. CIV. APP. P. 16.

[58] Title ("[c]ounsel for a party should not be permitted to write the amicus brief in whole or in part").

[59] See MD. R. 8-511(b)(1)(E); MINN. R. CIV. APP. P. 129.03; N.D. R. APP. P. 29(c)(4); TEX. R. APP. P. 11; W. VA. R. APP. P. 30(e)(5).

[60] Please see the court's remarks regarding Phillip Morris, Aspinall v. Philip Morris Cos., Inc., 813 N.E.2d 476, 480–81, n.8 (Mass. 2004), at page 480, para. 8 ("A full and honest disclosure of the interest of amici is crucial to the fairness and integrity of the appellate process").

Based on the experience accumulated in the surveyed countries, it is essential to establish principles of disclosure in countries using continental legal systems now developing criteria for approval of amicus briefs submitted to their courts. These principles will assist judges in adequately assessing the amicus brief placed before them, as there is no equivalent to a neutral brief compared to one funded, assisted, or "invited" by one of the formal parties.[61] Similarly, an amicus with a close connection to one of the parties is not comparable to a neutral *amicus* who sheds light and contributes unique perspectives to the court.[62] These principles will also help prevent the misleading impression that when many public organizations support a specific advocate, public opinion favors them. Meanwhile, these amici were "invited" or had their brief written by the "inviting" party, merely submitting the brief to the court to generate public support for their position. In other words, principles of disclosure may provide judges with a better perspective on the quality of information presented by the "amici," and therefore, it is appropriate, in my view, to establish these principles.

7.3.3.2 Credibility of the Brief

The misuse of research methods lacking scientific basis or being scientifically questionable is not unique to amicus briefs but can also occur in the briefs of formal parties. However, the phenomenon is more pronounced concerning amici curiae, who seemingly impress themselves by presenting arguments that formal parties would not. This is mainly due to the characteristics of amici, who are not subject to court sanctions, and the fact that they are third parties with less obligation to the process.[63] In my opinion, it is advisable to encourage the presentation of research from various fields of knowledge by amici curiae. Nevertheless, judges should be aware that amici may present research in a manner that is convenient to them or with information that is in some way exaggerated to serve their own purposes for the benefit of their cause. In judicial systems that utilize information from the social science field, there is a call to implement a procedural mechanism, such as an external expert, to evaluate amicus briefs, ensuring that they present social research in a more scientific and concise way. Another possible approach is the establishment of independent research institutions alongside the courts to assist the court in

[61] Rustad and Koenig (1993), pp.157–158.

[62] Sometimes it involves making "unpleasant" arguments that the formal party prefers someone else to do on their behalf, so that if things don't go well, it doesn't reflect directly on them but rather on the "amicus." Another example of continuing arguments through "amici" is when the court limits the number of pages for briefs. In such cases, official parties may turn to "amici" to continue their argument within the court's guidelines.

[63] Rustad and Koenig (1993), pp. 157–158.

assessing such briefs.[64] It is crucial for judges who receive amicus briefs to be aware of this and critically examine the research accompanying amici curiae briefs.[65]

7.3.3.3 Clarity of Submissions

Currently, in most civil law jurisdictions, there needs to be more clarity and uniformity regarding how submissions are presented. Some are submitted without argumentation, while others are submitted with complete argumentation even before a decision regarding the joinder has been made. Some submissions are considered separately and in the presence of the parties, but this is not always the case. Given that the issue is somewhat "unregulated," lawyers who submit joinder requests may make "minor improvements" based on the assumption that even if the joinder request is not officially accepted, the position expressed in the brief may be in the court's judgment.

It is not appropriate for the court to examine the request for a joinder and the brief simultaneously, as this may affect the court's decision on whether to accept the request and, in other cases, the decision itself, even if the request is rejected. Moreover, combining the joinder request with the brief may lead the court to stumble, for example, by providing confidential or misleading information that could influence the court's judgment. Therefore, it is necessary to establish a rule that separates the joinder request from the submission of the brief, where the joinder request should include a brief description of the proposed information and the existing interests in the proceedings.[66]

7.3.3.4 Legal Considerations Regarding the Involvement of "Amici"

In most Western countries, the possibility of joining as an Amicus Curiae in a legal proceeding is generally limited to significant or appellate cases with a specific avenue for incorporating amici in lower-profile cases with broader legal implications. However, there are countries (like Israel) where requests for Amicus Curiae participation can be submitted in almost all legal proceedings, including small claims courts.[67]

---

[64] Ibid, on pages 158–161; Faigman (1989), p. 1081 ("The legal relevance of social science research simply cannot be divorced from its scientific credibility").

[65] As mentioned, Prof. Larsen (Larsen (2014), p. 1757) warned against court rulings that cite information from amici curiae briefs and rely on them as facts without scientific credibility. She suggested that amici curiae should provide detailed scientific explanations about the methods and techniques used (including criticisms of the presented information, if applicable) upon which the brief relies. In this context, see also the concerns raised in Dwyer (2023).

[66] See, for example, Rules of the Supreme Court of Canada, SOR/2002-156, r 57(1).

[67] Neruzini case, Small Claims Court 8518-03-09 Neruzin v Kovner (Nevo 24.11.2009) in section 588. In this case, the Cat Lovers Association of Israel requested to join a small claims court lawsuit

In my opinion, third parties who can offer diverse perspectives and viewpoints on legal proceedings based on efficiency and proper policy considerations may be present in nearly every case. However, it is advisable to carefully consider and limit the inclusion of amici in relatively high-profile cases, such as the Supreme Court, constitutional courts, or appellate courts that focus primarily on legal issues without factual evidence.

Furthermore, the central issues for which amici seek to present their arguments are typically deliberated in high-profile cases, making their inclusion unnecessary in lower-profile cases. However, in cases where amici seek to present particular crucial information essential for clarifying the proceedings, it may be appropriate to consider including them since the appellate process generally does not address this aspect (which is an exception). In other words, alongside the general limitation, it is appropriate to leave judicial discretion to allow the inclusion of amici in exceptional cases.

The primary consideration for these judgments should be when the amicus possesses vital information that is not available to the formal parties or when the formal parties are unable to present it to the court (either due to lack of knowledge or other reasons). Additionally, when the presented information is required for the sake of "doing justice." Moreover, it may be appropriate to consider referring parties who do not meet these criteria to multi-party mediation under the auspices of the court, involving relevant parties who perceive themselves as applicable to the decision-making process. Such mediation can have a public nature, and the resulting agreement may be published without disclosing names, thus reinforcing the public norm.

7.3.3.5 Presentation of Factual Arguments

In most judicial systems worldwide, it is usual for amici to adhere to the factual record established before the court, and, just in exceptional cases, they are not allowed to add arguments regarding the accurate record. This practice is followed, for example, in the courts of Canada, New Zealand, and South Africa.[68] An exception to presenting new factual information by amici arises when it involves crucial facts that complement points not presented to the court (such as scientific data) in a way that the presented information may prevent reliance on exclusive sources of knowledge.[69] As mentioned above, the primary role of an amicus is to provide perspective, interest, or expertise that the court should hear. Therefore, I

---

as an Amicus Curiae. However, the court ruled that granting the association's request would effectively mean that the defendant or its claims, represented by legal counsel, would be addressed. Therefore, the court treated the request as a request for representation in the case and denied it.

[68] See, for example, New Zealand Fire Service Commission v Ivamy (1995) 8 PRNZ 632 at 634 (New Zealand); concerning Clark (2005), p. 38 (Canada). Also, refer to the customary rules of the Supreme Court (Rule 16A) in South Africa.

[69] See *Children's Inst. v. Presiding Officer of the Children's Court* [2012] ZACC 25, (2013) 2 SA 620., where the Constitutional Court of South Africa held that lower courts are allowed to consider

believe it is advisable to adhere as much as possible to the established factual record presented by the formal parties to minimize any potential harm to them.

7.3.3.6 The Format of the Brief

Many judicial systems restrict the length of an amicus brief to a specific number of words or pages. For instance, it is common practice for the Supreme Court in the United States, Canada, and international arbitration tribunals such as ICSID to limit the length of the brief to twenty pages.[70] In other parts of the United States (such as Kentucky or Missouri), the allowed length for amicus briefs is fifteen pages.[71] On the other hand, some states in the United States permit a longer length. For example, in Maine, the maximum length for an amicus brief is fifty pages,[72] and in Wyoming, it is thirty-five pages.[73] The federal appellate courts have established the principle that the length of the brief should be at most half the length allowed for the formal parties' briefs.[74] Similarly, some states, such as Nebraska and Iowa, have adopted this approach[75] (limiting the length of an "amicus" brief to half the length allowed for the formal parties). In contrast, other places impose restrictions based on word count. For example, the New York Court of Appeals has set the limit at 7,000 words (half the maximum length allowed for the formal parties' briefs).[76] The U.S. Supreme Court limits amicus briefs to approximately 9000 words, while the formal parties' briefs are limited to 15,000 words.[77] Additionally, it is prevailing practice for the brief to open with a table of contents specifying its content and its main arguments.

Countries that have not yet regulated the issue of the length of the brief should consider doing so. Alternatively, the length of the brief could be determined by reference to the existing limitations on the formal parties' briefs, as determined by the court. Additionally, to streamline the court's proceedings, it is desirable for the brief's submission to include detailed content.

---

statistical evidence regarding the expected impact of a judgment on the well-being of children, based on considerations of justice.

[70] Rules of Procedure for Arbitration Proceedings (Arbitration Rules), Rule 37. Despite the rules stipulating that the length of the memorial shall not exceed twenty pages, courts may allow deviations from this limitation if they find it appropriate. See Murray (1994), p. 256.

[71] KY. R. CIV. P. 76.12; MISS. R. APP. P. 29(b).

[72] ME. R. APP. P. 9(e)(1).

[73] WYO. R. APP. P. 7.12(d). Regarding City of Fairmont v. Pitrolo Pontiac-Cadillac Co., 308 S. E.2d 527, 539–40 (W. Va. 1983), the court critically examined the length of the memoranda submitted by the "amici" and noted that "one of the memoranda was certified by the Clerk of [the] Court as weighing one and three-eighths pounds."

[74] FED. R. APP. P. 29(d).

[75] IOWA R. APP. P. 6.906(3); NEV. R. APP. P. 29(e.).

[76] N.Y. CT. APP. R. 500.11. See also: Stashenko (2016), http://www.newyorklawjournal.com/id=1202760161078.

[77] SUP. CT. R. 33.1(g).

7.3.3.7 Right to Oral Argument

Although the historical origin of the amicus lies in oral argumentation, some judicial systems, like England and the European Court of Justice, have become more flexible in considering requests for oral argument by amici.[78] However, it is preferable to prioritize written arguments and reserve oral arguments for exceptional cases. Different judicial systems outright prohibit oral arguments by amici.[79] I believe the right to oral argument by amici should be minimized to the essential minimum, as oral argument tends to blur the necessary distinction between an amicus and a formal advocate. Moreover, the right to oral argument by an amicus may burden the proceedings more than a written brief. For example, the United States Supreme Court has held that a request for oral argument by an amicus may be made with the parties' consent or if the court grants such permission. In any case, the request must be filed within seven days of the submission of the brief.[80]

Even if amici are granted the right to oral argument, allocating a predetermined time for such arguments is crucial. For instance, in Canada, the limit for oral arguments by third parties is at least fifteen minutes.[81] Another common rule is that if multiple amici are authorized to present oral arguments, they must divide the allocated time among themselves, shortening the time for each party seeking oral arguments. Additionally, in many jurisdictions, the time granted for oral argument by an amicus is reduced compared to the formal parties supported by the amicus. Finally, some judicial systems have a practice of granting oral arguments specifically for political reasons rather than non-governmental public interests or private entities.[82]

I believe that the right to oral argument by amici should be preserved only in exceptional cases[83] and that the leading right of an amicus should be the written argument. Experience shows that in most cases, except for remarkable ones, the public interest can be served by submitting a written brief, and there is no need for amici to present oral arguments unless it is a unique matter.

---

[78] Or the words of Lord Hoffman in the case of E, E.v. Chief Constable of the Royal Ulster Constabulary [2008] UKHL 66, [2], [2009] 1 AC 536, 542 (appeal taken from Eng.) at p. 542 (para. 2). The European Court of Justice has also changed its approach, and the new rules of the court from 2011 explicitly provide for the option of oral argument by third parties. This is also the case with regard to the general principles of international criminal law. Int'l Crim. Ct., Rules of Procedure and Evidence, r. 103(1).

[79] ARK. SUP. CT. R. 4-6(b) ("Amici Curiae attorneys will not be permitted to participate in oral arguments").

[80] SUP. CT. R. 37.3.

[81] Crane and Brown (2007), p. 253. In contrast, in the House of Lords, it was customary for the average duration of oral argument by third parties to range from half an hour to an hour.

[82] Stern et al. (2002), p. 684.

[83] Alaska R. APP. P. 212(9) states that in the Alaska Court of Appeals, for example, "A motion of an Amicus Curiae to participate in the oral argument will be granted only for extraordinary reasons."

7.3.3.8 Consent of the Parties

In specific judicial systems, a party can act as an amicus if both formal parties agree to it. In such cases, a court decision is not required (as is the case, for example, in the federal system in the United States or South Africa).[84] In contrast, in other judicial systems such as the Supreme Court of Canada (except in cases of a request for intervention by the government's legal adviser), New Zealand, or the International Criminal Court in The Hague, the court's consent is required in any case. This is even if both formal parties agree to the request for intervention.[85] In a small number of states in the United States (such as Texas, Georgia, and Pennsylvania), it is possible to submit an Amicus Curiae brief without obtaining the consent of the parties or court approval, but the courts have the authority to reject the Amicus Curiae briefs of amici according to their discretion.[86]

It is appropriate to empower the courts to control the judicial process effectively and the allocated time and not merely rely on the parties' consent.[87] Therefore, in my view, even if an agreement is reached between the parties regarding the addition of amici, there is still an obligation to submit a preliminary request to the court to join as an amicus (preferably after the parties have expressed their opinion on the request) and leave the final discretion in the hands of the court.

7.3.3.9 Costs Imposed on Amici

There are judicial systems where costs can be awarded against amici in cases where they abuse their power for harm or their argument is frivolous or vexatious.[88] As mentioned, in response to the increasing presence of third parties in England and their impact on the process and the formal litigants, the Criminal Justice and Courts Act 2015[89] was enacted in England. The Act establishes rules for awarding costs against interveners in proceedings before administrative courts and the Court of Appeal of England and Wales. The new regime for expenses granting to interveners aims to prevent interveners' misuse of the process and to guide their behavior to

---

[84] Rule 16(1) of the Practice Directions of the Supreme Court of Appeal in South Africa, (High Court Case 519).

[85] Bryden (1987). See also International Criminal Court, Rules of Procedure and Evidence, Rule 103(1) (International Criminal Court); *Beneficial Owners of Whangaruru Whakaturia No. 4 v. Warin* [2009]. (Case 503, paragraph 19, New Zealand).

[86] GA. SUP. CT. R. 23; PA. R. APP. P. 531(a); TEX. R. APP. P. 11.

[87] There is also a general authority to impose sanctions on legal documents that do not comply with the required legal standards. See Federal Rules of Civil Procedure, Rule 11.

[88] See, for example, the case of S. China Strategic Ltd., [1997] H.K.L.R.D. 131 (C.F.I). If the court invites an "amicus" to assist in its work, it is customary for the state treasury to cover their expenses. Additionally, the court has the authority to impose the costs of the "amicus" on one of the formal parties.

[89] Criminal Justice and Courts Act 2015.

assist the court in the public interest they sought to join. As mentioned above in Sect. 5.3, the new law sets out a range of cases in which the court can award costs against third parties intervening in proceedings. "(a) an intervener has behaved unreasonably, or (b) has in effect taken on a role as one of the main parties to the dispute; or (c) an intervention is not of significant assistance to the court, or (d) relates in significant part to matters which are not necessary for the court to consider."[90]

However, imposing costs on an amicus is a relatively rare occurrence exercised only on rare occasions.[91] Due to this, in specific methods, there exists a practice where when a third party (primarily an intervenor but sometimes an amicus) approaches the parties and requests their consent to present their position to the court, they also request that no costs be imposed on them. Another approach is to seek prior approval from the court (in a request to join as a third party) that no charges be imposed.[92]

In my opinion, to encourage the involvement of amici in proceedings, it is appropriate not to impose costs on them except in the most exceptional cases.[93] The knowledge that various interest groups, especially NGOs, can submit amicus briefs without incurring financial costs encourages these groups to submit amicus briefs.[94] There is a concern that the imposition of the expenses on amici will deter them from participating in court proceedings. For example, in the case of *S*, which dealt with taking fingerprints and DNA samples from detained individuals, the Supreme Court allowed an NGO (Liberty) to submit a written position as an intervenor. The state's attorneys turned to the court and requested costs imposed on the organization, ultimately leading to the position's withdrawal.[95] On the other hand, it is advisable to preserve the right to charge exceptional costs in cases where

---

[90] Criminal Justice and Courts Act 2015 p. 11. Non-governmental social bodies criticized this legislation, arguing that it would discourage other non-governmental organizations from assisting the courts by joining as third parties in the proceedings.

[91] For example, "*In re Debs*" case (1895), the United States Supreme Court imposed a fine on the Amicus Curiae who had filed an unauthorized brief in the case. The court found that the brief contained improper statements and arguments and ordered the amicus to pay a $500 fine. In the case of "In re Amoco Cadiz" (1981), the United States Court of Appeals for the Fifth Circuit imposed sanctions on an Amicus Curiae for filing a brief that was deemed to be "frivolous" and "misleading." The court ordered the amicus to pay the opposing party's legal costs. In the case of "Troxel v. Granville" (2000), the United States Supreme Court imposed sanctions on an amicus curia for filing a brief that contained improper arguments and misrepresentations. The court ordered the amicus to pay a $500 fine.

[92] See also Supreme Court Rules 2009, SI 2009/1603, r46(3).

[93] In the case of "Marriage of McCallum" (Cal. App. 1985), the California Court of Appeals imposed sanctions on an Amicus Curiae for filing a brief that contained unfounded accusations and unsupported legal arguments. The court ordered the amicus to pay the opposing party's legal costs.

[94] Collins (2008).

[95] R (S) v. Chief Constable of S. Yorkshire Police [2004] UKHL 39, [2004] 1 WLR 2196 (HL) 2204 (appeal taken from Eng.). Ultimately, the European Court of Human Right' adopted the organization's position and determined that in the circumstances of the judgment, there was a 'violation of the citizens' privacy. S. v. United Kingdom, 2008-V Eur. Ct. H.R. 167.

amicus submissions are frivolous or vexatious and would burden and disrupt the judicial process.

Another question to consider is whether and under what circumstances there is a place in Israel to impose a filing fee on requests from third parties as amici. For example, in the Supreme Court of England, a third party (primarily intervenors) seeking to present their position must pay a filing fee of 800 pounds.[96] However, when a non-profit organization requests, the Registrar of the Court has the authority to exempt or reduce the fee.[97] It is important to emphasize that imposing a filing fee on "interveners" is the exception rather than the rule. In most countries surveyed above, there are no filing fees for intervenors, and costs for amici are minimal.

7.3.3.10 Costs in Favor of Amici Curiae

Another question is whether and in what circumstances costs can be awarded in favor of amici. Let me provide an example from Israel. In a Jerusalem court case,[98] the matter was a long-standing operation of strip clubs in the stock exchange area. The local committee sought to change the area and initiated a plan introducing additional uses such as student housing, protected housing, and hotels alongside the existing businesses. The question discussed in the proceedings was whether a city development plan initiated in the area allows for the continued operation of adult entertainment businesses. A women's rights organization joined the appeal as an Amicus Curiae and argued that the permissible uses in the proposed plan should not include adult entertainment due to its harm to women. The court, relying on the position of the amicus, ruled that the appropriate interpretation of the plan does not include the option to conduct adult entertainment businesses in the area. As for costs, the court held that due to the committee's lack of sufficient clarification and failure to present the whole picture, the Amicus Curiae should be compensated for their expenses.

Similarly, in this case, the essential components of the judgment were written based on information and arguments presented exclusively by the amici and not by the formal litigants. When a judgment heavily relies on the input of the amicus, while the formal parties have made little contribution to the judgment, it may be appropriate to consider awarding costs in their favor.

[96] Supreme Court Fees Order 2009, SI 2009/2131, as amended by Supreme Court Fees (Amendment) Order 2011, SI 2011/1737.

[97] Supreme Court Fees Order 2009, SI 2009/2131, as amended by Supreme Court Fees (Amendment) Order 2011, SI 2011/1737.

[98] Administrative Decision (Tel Aviv) 8707-07-15, Ramat Gan Local Planning and Building Committee, Jerusalem District (August 28, 2017).

7.3.3.11 Stage of the Third-Party Intervention

What is the appropriate stage for an Amicus Curiae to join the court proceedings? Different jurisdictions have different rules regarding the timing of the submission of amici. In certain courts worldwide (such as in England), the requirement is to file the intervention request "at the earliest opportunity" it becomes available.[99] In some states in the United States, it is specified that Amicus Curiae briefs should be filed by the formal party's deadline for support.[100] In the United States Supreme Court, for example, within seven days from the formal party's filing deadline that the amicus supports.[101] In California, within 30 days after all formal parties have filed their briefs.[102] In Kansas, Amicus Curiae briefs should be filed at least 30 days before the oral hearing in court.[103] In Nebraska, it is determined that amici must submit their briefs by 20 days before the oral hearing.[104] In Washington, it is determined that amici must submit their briefs by 45 days before the oral hearing.[105] In addition, in the United States Supreme Court, for example, the amicus is responsible for ensuring that all parties know their intention to file a brief at least ten days before the deadline for submitting it to the court.[106]

Considering the concern for the burden on the judicial process, it is advisable to establish a clear rule regarding the stage at which an Amicus Curiae brief can be filed. It is recommended to install a rule stating that Amicus Curiae briefs should be filed after the formal parties have submitted their briefs to the court. Alternatively, as described above, the brief should be submitted several days before the oral hearing.[107] In this way, the amici can examine their arguments and their contribution to the proceedings (e.g., whether they duplicate the positions of the formal parties). At the same time, at this stage, the courts can assess the impact of the brief on the proceedings and the work of the courts, among other things, about the formal parties' briefs.

---

[99] In the Constitutional Court of South Africa, for example, if the parties have not set a time limit for filing the response, the response must be filed no later than five days from the date of filing the appellant's arguments or five days from the date on which the respondent was supposed to file its arguments in writing. See Rules of the Constitutional Court 2003, Rule 10, Government Notice R165 of Government Gazette 25726 (October 31, 2003).

[100] ILL. SUP. CT. R. 345(b); IND. R. APP. P. 41(b); IOWA R. APP. P. 6.906(1); LA. SUP. CT. R. 7(12); MASS. R. APP. P. 17; MO. SUP. CT. R. 84.05(f)(2); N.H. SUP. CT. R. 30(1); N.C. APP. R. 28(i); OKLA. SUP. CT. R. 1.12(d)(1); PA. R. APP. P. 531(a)(1).

[101] SUP. CT. R. 37.3(a).

[102] CAL. R. CT. 8.520(f).

[103] KAN. SUP. CT. R. 6.06(b)(1).

[104] NEB. CT. R. 2-109(A)(4).

[105] WASH. R. APP. P. 10.2(f).

[106] SUP. CT. R. 37.2.

[107] On the other hand, there are cases where the courts allow the formal parties to respond to the submissions of the "Amicus Curiae," and in such cases, the significance of the deadline for filling the submissions of the "Amicus Curiae" is diminished.

7.3.3.12 Appeals by Amici Curiae

Despite the historical origin of allowing the Amicus Curiae to join proceedings as a "favor" granted by the court, the question arises as to how to treat the rejection of an amicus's request and whether it gives a right of appeal or a process of reconsideration by the court. For comparison, the rules of the United Kingdom Supreme Court and the Queen's Bench Division provide that a public body wishing to submit an Amicus Curiae brief in the public interest, as well as any person who was involved as a third party in the lower court, is entitled "as of right" to join the proceedings in the higher court.[108]

In contrast, in the *Nat'l Org. for Women* case, Judge Richard Posner determined about appeals by amici seeking to submit an Amicus Curiae brief that was rejected in the lower court, that the question of whether to grant a third party the authority to submit an Amicus Curiae brief is a matter of grace and not an acquired right.[109] There is no correct formulation on the subject, but it is vital to adhere to a general principle and avoid leaving the matter to sporadic judgments that sometimes create a lack of coherence. Needless to say, as a third party, an amicus lacks standing and does not have the right to challenge the outcome of the judgment given by the formal parties. As a general rule, the role of the amicus ends (legally) after submitting the brief.

7.3.3.13 Advocacy Rights of Amici

What rights should be granted to amici? In certain places around the world, amici have extensive powers. For example, a "Litigating Amicus" has the right to cross-examine witnesses, conduct counter-investigations, respond to written submissions of opposing parties, and more. Can one of the formal parties or other amici be authorized to investigate the "amicus" based on the information presented? It seems appropriate to preserve the uniqueness of the amicus's role in presenting written arguments (and, in exceptional cases, oral arguments) rather than allowing any further adversarial rights. It should be established that the amicus's right is limited to submitting a brief corresponding to presenting their position to the court. However, there may be exceptions where the court may seek oral clarifications regarding the brief. In such cases, the amici may be invited to a determined hearing, and if necessary, the brief's authors may be requested to provide various clarifications.

[108] Judicial Committee (Appellate Jurisdiction) Rules Order 2009, SI 2009/224, r 27(1).

[109] National Organization for Women, Inc. v. Scheidler, 510 U.S. 249 (1994).

7.4 Summary

The third central development of the Amicus Curiae phenomenon occurred in Continental law in Europe, Latin America, and parts of Asia and Africa. Most Continental legal systems have adopted the use of "amici" in their domestic law over the past fifteen years and have gradually allowed the submission of Amicus Curiae briefs in ongoing proceedings.

The inclusion of the practice of Amicus Curiae into the Continental legal system and the change in attitudes towards the intervention of third parties occurred in two main ways; through legislation and through the informal integration of this practice into the judicial system. No Latin American country had recognized the practice of Amicus Curiae before the late 1990s. In 1999, Brazil became the first Latin American country to allow the inclusion of amici in proceedings before its Constitutional Court. Subsequently, other Latin American countries explicitly permitted the participation of amici in judicial proceedings. Similarly, European countries belonging to the Continental system have adopted the institution of the Amicus Curiae and have allowed the submission of amicus briefs by amici into their legal orders. Sometimes, the adoption of the amicus is driven by requests from NGOs to submit amicus briefs in judicial systems that do not recognize the Amicus Curiae institution and a desire to align with other countries that have already accepted this practice.

In this way, countries such as South Korea, Thailand, and Rwanda have adopted the amicus. In contrast to the "Amicus Curiae phenomenon" in common law countries (primarily the United States), the significance of the amicus in Continental law is not determined by the number of amici relative to the number of proceedings initiated or the range of bodies employing the amicus or the branches of law in which amici participate. Its significance lies in the fact that it has been incorporated de facto into a legal system that previously considered this practice foreign and unnecessary.

Developing the Amicus Curiae practice in Continental law was not self-evident because the Continental legal system grants extensive powers to state representatives to intervene in the name of the public interest in state-related cases. In addition, this legal system provides judges with procedural tools to obtain the necessary information for the process, which to some extent fulfills the role of the amicus and seemingly obviates the need for it. The adoption of the amicus in Continental law teaches us that the existing judicial procedures are not necessarily sufficient and that additional tools are required for the judicial role to understand and learn the interests and desires of third parties.

In the second part of this book, we have seen how the "Amicus Curiae phenomenon" has developed more or less simultaneously in three different legal systems: Common Law, Continental Law, and International Law. These parallel developments along three different axes influenced each other and shared certain similarities. Generally, the development of the "Amicus Curiae phenomenon" worldwide followed a common pattern: initially, courts held an approach that excluded third-party participation in ongoing proceedings. The resistance to hearing the interests of third parties is rooted in various reasons, ranging from long-standing judicial tradition to arguments concerning the burden on the proceedings and concerns about harming the interests of formal parties. At a certain stage, usually starting from the 1990s and the beginning of the 2000s, but sometimes even earlier, this judicial attitude "softened." Therefore, a more flexible approach emerged in its place and took into significant consideration the desires of third parties to present their position to the courts on issues that impact their lives or well-being.

The change in trend is characterized, among other things, by a favorable interpretation and flexible legal procedures towards requests from interest groups to present their positions in ongoing proceedings; an increase in the number of non-formal parties allowed to participate in the proceedings (especially non-governmental bodies), and their ability to argue orally and be actively involved in court proceedings. Once the amicus is adopted, either formally (as in most common law countries) or partially or through a "leap" by force (as in some Latin American countries), there exists in certain countries a sort of "anticipation" of the phenomenon of amicus, manifested primarily in a significant increase in the number of amicus briefs submitted to almost all possible courts by tens of thousands of different interest groups.

In addition to the relative increase in the number of amicus briefs submitted, there is generally growth and diversification in the range of topics in which amicus briefs are presented to the courts (the term "amicus" is used in almost all areas of law). The types of judicial opinions to which amicus briefs are submitted also expand when amici join nearly all possible tribunals. Furthermore, the number of *amici* in "mega-cases" has grown in certain countries. In some cases (such as the right to abortion or health insurance), hundreds of amici representing thousands of different and diverse interest groups join a single case.

These changes are not limited to the courts but have also influenced other processes. For example, there is extensive coverage in the media, popular literature, blogs, search engines on the internet, and content-sharing platforms. Academic literature addressing the amicus and its impact on the courts' decision-making processes has also grown. A new specialization in legal practice has been created – the "Amicus Coordinator," who is responsible for coordinating and vetting all *amicus* briefs submitted in support of a specific position to avoid repetition. New courtrooms with unique seating arrangements for *amici* have been planned and built, even if they are not formal parties to the proceedings.

We have also seen how the role of the Amicus Curiae varies in different countries and legal systems. Even within the same legal system, there are differences among countries that adopt the same legal system and in the use of the amicus. In most common law countries, the Amicus Curiae is considered a third party with a more neutral and impartial character, invited by the courts to present briefs to assist them in their work (third parties with any interest in the proceedings utilize the mechanism of "intervention"). In contrast, in the United States, the Amicus Curiae serves as a third party that functions as a kind of lobbyist, actively supporting a particular position presented by one of the formal litigants. The phenomenon of Amicus Curiae is not uniform across all common-law countries. In some countries (such as the United States), its influence is particularly prominent, and its implications for the work of the courts are extensive. In contrast, the amicus is insignificant in other countries (such as Australia or New Zealand). Compared to the Amicus Curiae in common law, the importance of the amicus in civil law lies primarily in its integration into the practice and legal systems of a legal system that was previously unfamiliar with it.

References

Badwaza YM (2011) Public interest litigation as practiced by South African human rights ngos: any lessons for Ethiopia?

Bernatt M (2008) Opinia przyjaciela sądu jako pomocnicza instytucja prawna w orzecnictwie sądów polskich. In: Bojarski Ł (ed) 2 Sprawny Sąd Zbiór Dobrych Praktyk 184

Bernatt M (2012) Can the right to be heard be respected without access to information about the proceedings? Deficiencies of national competition procedure. Yearb Antitrust Reg Stud 5(6):91

China Strategic Ltd., [1997] H.K.L.R.D. 131 (C.F.I)

Collins PM Jr (2008) Friends of the supreme court: interest groups and judicial decision making

Correa-Ordoñez A, Mandakovic S (2014) A guide to filing Amicus Curiae Briefs in Latin America (Latin Am. Subcomm., INTA Int'l Amicus Comm. Oct. 15)

Cortese B (2013) Defining the role of courts and administrative bodies in private enforcement in Europe: United in diversity? In: Cortese B (ed) EU competition law: between public and private enforcement, p 145

Coslin C, Lapillonne D (2012) France and the concept of Amicus Curiae: what lies ahead? Paris Int Litigat Bull 4:14

Crane BA, Brown HS (2007) Supreme Court of Canada practice. Thomson Reuters Canada, p 253

Duncan DW (1994) A little tour in France: surrogate motherhood and amici curiae in the French legal system. Western State Univ Law Rev 21:447

Dwyer JG (2023) Faux advocacy in amicus practice. Pepperdine L Rev 50:633–718

Faigman DL (1989) To have and have not: assessing the value of social science to the law as science and policy. Emory Law J 35:1005–1095

Herbst J (2001) Political liberalization in Africa after ten years. Comp Polit 33:357; Russian Civil Society: A Critical Assessment (Evans Jr. AB, Henry LA, McIntosh Sundstrom L (eds) 2006)

Hinson Z, Hubbard D (2012) Access to justice in namibia: proposals for improving public access to courts: *amicus curiae* participation

Jean-Philippe D (2005) L'amicus curiae devant les juridictions administratives françaises, revue du droit public et de la science politique en france et à l'étranger

Kasirye A (2012) Uganda law society report of Ad Hoc committee on the reform of the civil procedure rules

Kochevar S (2013) Comment, Amici Curiae in civil law jurisdictions. Yale Law J 122:1653

Kühne U (2015) Amicus Curiae: richterliche informationsbeschaffung durch beteiligung dritter, vol 110. Mohr Siebeck

Larsen AO (2014) The trouble with amicus facts. Va Law Rev 100:1757–1818

Medeiros DB (2008) Amicus Curiae: a panorama of the third collaborator. Revista DA Esmarn 7: 279

Mubangizi JC, Mbazira C (2012) Constructing the amicus curiae procedure in human rights litigation: what can uganda learn from South Africa, 16 L. Democr Dev 199:200

Murray C (1994) Litigating in the public interest: intervention and the amicus curiae. 10 S Afr J Hum RTS 240:242

Rustad M, Koenig T (1993) The supreme court and junk social science: selective distortion in amicus briefs. 72 Ncl Rev 91:157–158

Shelton D (1994) The participation of nongovernmental organizations in international judicial proceedings, 88 AM. J Int Law 611:637
Stashenko J (2016) Court of appeals limits length of briefs. New York Law J June 16. http://www.newyorklawjournal.com/id=1202760161078
Stern RL, Gressman E, Shapiro SM, Geller KS (2002). Supreme court practice: for practice in the supreme court of the united states 684 (8th ed.).
Viljoen F, Abebe AK (2014) Amicus curiae participation before regional human rights bodies in Africa. 58 J Afr Law 22:24
Wiarda H (ed) (2004) Authoritarianism and Corporatism in Latin America – Revisited

Part III
The "Amicus Curiae Phenomenon": Causes, Explanations, and Meaning

Introduction

In recent decades, significant developments have occurred in most countries worldwide, as well as in the institutions of international law, regarding the use of the Amicus Curiae practice. These diverse developments, which we have referred to as the "Amicus Curiae phenomenon," include not only the reception and adoption of the "amicus" by various judicial systems and institutions around the world but also a significant increase in the amount of "amicus" brief submitted to the courts. There has also been an increase in the numbers and diversity of interest groups and non-governmental public organizations involved in the submission of briefs. Furthermore, the "amicus" briefs are submitted in an increasing variety of topics. These briefs concern diverse areas of law and are submitted to a growing variety of judicial courts.

The "Amicus Curiae phenomenon" has taken place without significant opposition, and has been accepted smoothly, and has taken root around the world. Today, it seems that the main focus of public, academic, and legal debate is no longer concerned either with whether to adopt or reject the practice of the "amicus," or with questions about limiting this right. Instead, discussion now center on how this mechanism can be improved and optimized within the work of the courts.[1]

---

[1] See, for example: Melinda S. Kollross,10 Tips for Securing Beneficial Amicus Support on Appeal, Federation of Defense & Corporate Counsel (Fall 2020). https://www.clausen.com/10-tips-for-securing-beneficial-amicus-support-on-appeal/. UNESCO launches practical guide for Amicus Curiae interventions in freedom of expression cases. https://www.unesco.org/en/articles/unesco-launches-practical-guide-amicus-curiae-interventions-f"eedom-expression-cases. "Expert Q&A on Best Practices for Amicus Briefing" https://www.sullcrom.com/files/upload/LIT_AugSep16_OfNote-Amicus.pdf. "7 Tips For Writing an Effective Amicus Brief," https://www.obwbip.com/04D540/assets/files/News/7-Tips-For-Writing-An-Eff"ctive-Amicus-Brief.pdf. "Tips for District Court Amicus Brief Success" - https://www.gibsondunn.com/wp-content/uploads/2020/12/Shapiro-Crain-LeSavage-Tips-for-District-Court-Amicus-Brief-Success-New-York-Law-Journal-12-23-2020.pdf.

The main questions discussed in this section are: how did a legal institution created hundreds of years ago gain so much momentum and become so widely recognized as a valuable asset in recent decades? What caused this phenomenon to gain momentum worldwide in recent decades—in common, continental, and international law? Why does it occur in these dimensions, and how can it be explained? What does this phenomenon mean, and what does it teach us about modern law and the role of the modern judicial system?

The thesis developed here is that the "Amicus Curiae phenomenon" is closely related to changes in the perception of the role and work style of the courts since the 1980s and 1990s. In recent decades, there has been a significant and continuous increase in the importance of the judicial system in society. As judicial systems have become increasingly aware of their role in shaping society in general, they also become more involved in shaping the lives of its individuals. As part of this trend, there is a growing reliance on the courts and legal procedures for the settlement and treatment of a wide variety of issues, many of which were not previously discussed in the courts.[2]

As a result of the significant involvement of the courts in the public sphere, several substantive and procedural changes are taking place in the work of the courts, such as the adoption of new work methods and new forms of discussion. Many public legal discussions turn from "classical" legal conflicts on who has a legal right to broader discussions that raise topical, value-based, and economic issues that concern a wider public. These discussions often use various fields of opinion and legal sources (literature, history, economics, and more).[3]

In terms of the form of the discussion, new working methods are adopted for the "management of the trial," such as active negotiations between the parties under the auspices of the court or mediation attempts under the leadership and management of

[2]Hirschl R (2006) The New Constitutionalism and the Judicialization of Pure Politics Worldwide. Fordham Law Rev. 75:721; Tate CN and Vallinder T (eds) 1995 The Global Expansion of Judicial Power; Hirschl, R (2004) Towards Juristocracy: The Origins and Consequences of the New Constitutionalism; Sieder et al (2005) The Judicialization of Politics in Latin America; Hirschl R (2008) The judicialization of mega-politics and the rise of political courts. Annu. Rev. Polit. Sci. 11: 93–118. Shapiro M and Stone Sweet A (2002) On law, politics, and judicialization. Oxford University Press; Jacob H et al. (1996) Courts, law, and politics in comparative perspective. Yale University Press.

[3]The diversity of the interdisciplinary content of the judicial system is related to several developments known as "law and...". They are, of course, related to the development of the "sociological approach to law," which called for an understanding of the overall social environment in which the law operates and the concept that social interests influence the law and the judicial system. The change in the sources of law is also related to other trends, such as the rise of the "law and economy" movement, within which the judicial function was given the content of solving problems according to economic principles. In addition, this change is also related to the "law and psychology" phenomenon, where the interrelationships between the law, the judiciary, and the decision-making mechanism of the judicial system and psychological research are examined. Belinda Brooks-Gordon & Michael Freeman (2006); Posner RA (2006), The Role of the Judge in the Twenty-First Century. B.U. L. Rev 86:1049; Kronman A (1988), Jurisprudential Responses to Legal Realism. Cornell Law Rev. 73:335.

the courts. New procedural grounds are created with specific remedies that are flexible and adapted to modern reality. Proceedings may also be conducted outside the court, being "under the supervision" of the court and subject to its inspection.[4] There has also been a change in the participants in the proceedings, with special procedures now being included, such as class actions, derivative suits, and "public petitions." In all of these, there is a shift from procedures involving individual "players" to procedures that involve the cooperation of many "players." These include, in addition to the formal parties, professional experts, representatives of professions (such as the bar association or the accounting association), NGOs, and diverse interest groups.

One of the main results of these changes is that courts worldwide have adopted and perfected another practice, which is at the same time also a factor of these changes: the Amicus Curiae. The amicus practice is one of the changes in the work of the courts, and it integrates with, and at the same time is influenced by, a variety of other procedures that are reshaping the work of the courts.

[4] It is important to note that this is a global trend and is prevalent in almost all countries of the world. The claim is that judges have become case managers and abandoned their traditional role as Judith Resnik first raised judges in her seminal 1982 article. Resnik J (1982) Managerial judges. Harv. Law Rev. 96: 374. See also: Donald EE (1986) Managerial judging and the evolution of procedure. U. Chi. Law Rev. 53:306. Langer, M (2005) The rise of managerial judging in international criminal law. The American Journal of comparative law 53.4: 835–909. Wolff, TB. (2012) Managerial judging and substantive law. Wash. UL Rev. 90:1027.

Chapter 8
The Changes That Took Place in the Judicial System

Since the 1980s, there have been significant changes in the judicial procedure in countries using varied judicial systems all around the world. There have been changes to content, performance, and the way in which judicial procedures are conducted. In the last three decades, it has been possible to identify a significant increase in the courts' awareness of their modern role and the involvement and centrality of the judicial system in society.[1] This increase in the involvement of the courts is still occurring in many countries in the industrialized world, including those with different legal traditions and even with diverse governance methods.[2] These

[1] Schultz (1998). Naturally, examining all the judicial systems in the Western world is impossible. Therefore, the focus is on general trends and developments of the law.

[2] Sweet (2000). Many researchers place these changes mainly from the 1980s. However, some believe this phenomenon has been going on for a longer time, starting in the early seventies and even before. For example, Martin Shapiro showed that as early as the 1960s and 1970s, democratic regimes treated the courts as "political actors." For example, in Germany and Italy after World War II, "judicial review" was introduced into the constitution to protect democracy. In France, in the 1960s, the Constitutional Council was an authority to review the legality of the laws of the Assembly of Representatives, and its functions have expanded over the years. See, for example, Shapiro (1986), pp. 1–64. As early as 1971, Mauro Cappelletti described a first wave of "constitutional revolutions" that swept the Western world first at the end of World War I when one after the other countries that differed in their social fabric, their culture, their economic structure, and their geopolitical situation all adopted the assumption of constitutional law as supreme, with interpretations made through the institution of the courts being entrusted with its protection. See also Cappelletti (1971). Cappelletti described the gradual and consistent transition of countries around the world towards the adoption of constitutions—and especially the adoption of the institution of judicial review—as a desirable process. The second wave he described took place from the end of World War II. Conventions regarding human rights or economic conventions regarding trade are key examples. During this period, the concept was established according to which norms of international treaty regimes (such as the European Court of Human Rights or the Inter-American Court of Human Rights) and international organizations (such as the European Union) could serve as a basis for a supreme law with constitutional status in state law. The third wave of democratization that took place mainly between 1974–1991 included the countries of Eastern Europe after the fall of the Berlin Wall, Latin America, and parts of Africa further strengthened the rule of law.

S. Farber, *The Amicus Curiae Phenomenon*, Ius Gentium: Comparative Perspectives on Law and Justice 119, https://doi.org/10.1007/978-3-031-67225-5_8

changes in the functioning and importance of the judicial system in recent decades are numerous and concern many issues. For convenience, the discussion will be divided into two: changes in substance that mainly relate to the perception of the judicial role and changes in form that mainly relate to the development of new forms of discussion or the improvement of existing forms of discussion.

Obviously, the division between substance and form is not dichotomous, and substance changes are often intertwined with procedural changes, and vice versa. In addition, while saying changes in the judicial procedure, I mean to mainly describe changes "within" the judicial system and less changes in similar or parallel procedures such as alternative dispute resolution procedures.[3]

8.1 Significant Changes

One of the noticeable changes in many countries in the world, mainly since the 1980s but sometimes even earlier, is a significant increase in the involvement of the judicial system in society. One by one, countries that are different from each other in their social texture, culture, economic structure, and geopolitical situation adopted the premise that the courts must protect human and civil rights as well as the government's relations with the citizens. In a short period, in historical terms, the abnormal and the extraordinary became normal and normative.[4]

A series of political, constitutional, and economic processes changed the face of the globe and significantly deepened the courts' powers and their involvement in society. Countries such as Spain (1978), Portugal (1982), and Greece (1975) transitioned from dictatorial regimes to democratic systems of government.[5]

Cappelletti's writing also marks later debates, such as the debate on constitutional pluralism. The theoretical framework sketched made it possible to see, and try to explain and evaluate, the simultaneous existence of different, similar, and sometimes overlapping constitutional orders. See Huntington (1991). Gardbaum wishes to add to this narrative the development of another constitutional model in the 1980s and 1990s in Canada, New Zealand, and Great Britain. This model is reflected in the British doctrine of the supremacy of Parliament and the French doctrine, according to which the legislature is the supreme expression of the people's general will. Gardbaum (2014), pp. 613–640.

[3] See also Shapiro (1993), pp. 37–64. Shapiro claimed that despite the common perception that the courts are "very different" from alternative legal procedures, judges often function similarly to the way arbitrators or mediators function and adopt working practices that suit their work. This description demonstrates, among other things, that the modern judicial procedure is different from the judicial procedure in the past, and it requires different skills than those required to fulfill the role in the past. See also Perlman (2009).

[4] Gardbaum (2014), p. 285 [Gardbaum argues that while the growth of judicial review has challenged the traditional model of legislative supremacy, it has also helped to promote constitutionalism and protect individual rights in established democracies].

[5] Ackerman (1997), pp. 778–779 Ackerman, showed that In the wake of the Cold War, many countries that were once ruled by authoritarian regimes have adopted new constitutions that

Similarly, it was possible to stand for processes in Belgium in 1988.[6] The fall of the Berlin Wall in 1989 symbolizes the transition of implementing democratic constitutional regimes in Eastern Europe and a natural strengthening of the courts to act in the social sphere.[7] The fall of communism and the transition to democracy led to the adoption of new constitutions and the establishment of "functioning" and strong courts (relatively speaking, compared to the preceding period) in the countries that belonged to the Soviet bloc.[8] Poland adopted judicial review as part of the legislation of 1985, Hungary established a constitutional court in 1989,[9] and similar processes took place in the Slovak Republic (1991), Czech Republic (1993), Lithuania (1992), Estonia (1993), Bulgaria (1991), and Romania (1991).[10]

Another central arena of changes that dramatically affected the strengthening of the courts is Asia, where judicial changes (that is, that expanded the powers of the courts and their involvement in society) can be observed in Indonesia, Thailand, South Korea, Taiwan, and Mongolia from the mid-1980s onward. Dramatic changes also occurred in South Africa in the 1990s, with a new constitution and regime change in 1997.[11]

This gradual change is reflected mainly in the growing reliance on the courts to regulate and handle various issues, some of which were not previously regulated in the judicial system. Courts are requested, and sometimes "forced" by society to resolve a wide variety of issues—religious freedoms, equal rights, telecommunications and communication in general, public policy related to criminal justice, high-tech and more traditional technology, housing, ethics, health, foreign relations,

establish democratic governments. This trend has been particularly pronounced in Eastern Europe and Africa].

[6] In Belgium, the process took place in two main phases: in 1988, the constitution was changed, and judicial review was made possible regarding violating some of the rights in the Bill of Rights in the constitution, and in 2003, this review was extended to all rights. See Gardbaum (2014), p. 285.

[7] Lustig and Weiler (2018), pp. 315–372. [The authors note that while judicial review has become more common in recent decades, there is still significant variation in how it is practiced around the world].

[8] Holmes and Sunstein (1995), pp. 275–306. [The authors provide several case studies of constitutional revision in Eastern Europe, including Poland, Hungary, and the former Czechoslovakia. They argue that constitutional revision is a highly political process that involves a range of actors, including politicians, judges, interest groups, and ordinary citizens].

[9] Gardbaum (2014), p. 285. [Discussion of the Hungarian issue, and counter-reactions].

[10] Schwartz (2000) The struggle for constitutional justice in post-communist Europe. University of Chicago Press. [Schwartz argues that while progress has been made in establishing constitutional justice in post-communist Europe, there is still much work to be done to ensure that these institutions are effective and sustainable over the long term]. See also: Durski and Toniatti (2015).

[11] It is understood that the dates on which a constitution or an institution for judicial review was adopted are not necessarily reliable markers of legalization processes and should be treated with due caution. These processes are complicated, complex, and not necessarily stable. However, it is difficult to ignore the trend towards the growing adoption of a constitutional model that includes the institution of judicial review since the second half of the twentieth century. Ginsburg (2008).

taxation, homeland security, education, family, immigration, and the environment.[12]

Sometimes, the courts focus on something other than the essential aspects of the issue but instead on its procedural elements. In this way, courts worldwide supervise various fields closely and require the application of multiple norms during the decision-making processes, such as correctness of procedures, fairness, justice, equal opportunities, transparency, and reasonableness.[13]

The legal sphere dominated relationships, leading to the courts taking an interest in cultural issues, including popular culture, cultural customs, and social conflicts. As a result, some of these issues were transferred to judicial decisions. In general, social groups use extra-judicial tools of discourse, being based on customs compromises and reach decisions without involving courts decisions. One of the claims is that when these extra-judicial processes function properly, helped by institutions of various kinds (for example, the home committee, the workplace, the party, the government), which function satisfactorily, the use of the law is an exceptional case. When they do not function properly, there is a growing need for a qualified mediator—the judicial system.[14]

The penetration of law into many areas of life has also led to an increase in the exposure of law and courts in the media (for example, there is interest in senior lawyers and senior judges in the gossip sections; there is an increase in movies and series dealing with the law) and the infiltration of legal terms into high profile speeches even in non-legal contexts ("balances," "proportionality" or "reasonableness").[15]

The trend of relying on judicial systems even brings the courts to deal with political issues and core disputes of companies and regimes when they must intervene in macroeconomic planning, national dilemmas, and constitutive problems at the level of national and collective identity. Topics such as Germany's place in the European Union, transitional justice in Latin American countries and post-communist Europe, the secular nature of Turkey, the political future of the Province of Quebec within the Canadian Federation, decisions on symbols and religious dress in Europe, withdrawal from the European Union (Brexit), the definition of Israel as a "Jewish and democratic" country—were all "framed" into legal rubrics and became

[12] Hirschl (2008), Tate and Vallinder (1995), Hirschl (2004) and Sieder et al. (2005).

[13] In Israel, for example, Mautner (2005), pp. 7–8 insisted on expanding the scope of the court's judicial review of the actions of the executive authority and subordinating various administrative bodies to the review of the judicial system—the president, the prime minister, the attorney general, and the state auditor.

[14] Indeed, in recent years we have witnessed growing need for the courts' mediation and decision-making in settling issues based on custom and cultural systems (for example, in the field of labor relations). See, for example, López (2006).

[15] For example: 1. Beyond a reasonable doubt: This standard is used in criminal trials to determine guilt, requiring that the evidence presented is so strong that there is no reasonable doubt about the defendant's guilt. Outside the legal context, it's often used to emphasize certainty or conviction about something. 2. Due process: In the legal context, it refers to the fair treatment and procedural rights given to individuals involved in legal proceedings. Outside the law, it's sometimes used to emphasize the importance of fairness or following proper procedures.

an object of discussion in judicial systems.[16] The hidden dimension behind the strengthening of the courts is a belief—overt or hidden—in courts, constitutional or otherwise, supreme or ordinary, supra-state or state-based, as institutions that effectively maintain and enforce the legal nature of entities.

Critics argue that this trend poses constitutional challenges, as decisions on such matters should ideally be made by elected officials, representing the people. Additionally, there's a contention that judges lack adequate tools to address these issues, and it's unclear why the judicial system is deemed the appropriate venue for clarifying and resolving such questions. However, it's widely recognized, albeit often implicitly, that this trend is supported by stakeholders or political interest groups who fear public backlash against the political system. Consequently, judicial systems worldwide are increasingly becoming integral in shaping the national identity and policies of many countries.[17]

Since the 1980s (and possibly even earlier), the concerns about strengthening the courts' power have received diverse solutions. However, despite the challenges inherent in these difficulties, strengthening the courts' authority and expanding judicial review has become a fait accompli. The decision of the European Court of Justice in the case of Les Verts, in which the court defined the institution of judicial review as a necessary element in the definition of the rule of law, is one of the explicit expressions of this.[18] The influence of judicial review, and courts in general, has developed far beyond the state level. The world experienced an "explosion" of developments of the legal order between countries and beyond countries in various configurations of international regimes—regional and global, bilateral, and multilateral—when this system was created and evolved from a liberal ethos.[19]

Expanding the judicial authority and discussing various state courts and international tribunals brought about a self-strengthening of the courts.[20] Stone Sweet claimed in connection with constitutional law that: "As the constitutional law expands to more and more policy areas, and as it becomes 'thicker' in each domain

[16] Judith Goldstein et al. (2001). Ran Hirschel described this process as "Juristocracy." Hirschl (2004), pp. 222–223.

[17] For a broader criticism of the woman questioning the wisdom of widespread use of litigation in the courts, see Foucault (1997); Unger (1976); Scheingold (2004), pp. 170–99; Derrida (2001).

[18] Case 294/83 Parti Ecologiste Les Verts v. European Parliament [1986] ECR 1339, at 4 para. 23: "[T]he European Economic Community is a community based on the rule of law, inasmuch as neither the Member States nor its institutions can avoid a review of the question whether the measures adopted by them are in conformity with the basic constitutional charter, the Treaty."

[19] Cappelletti (1971). It is important to note that Cappelletti's wave theories paint a picture of certain developments with rough brushstrokes. Other periods in the twentieth century also knew a vibrant constitutional paradise. The period between the world wars, for example, was a period of fascinating flowering in the constitutional tradition of the institution of judicial review in Europe. Countries in Latin America also underwent constitutional changes during this period, including Mexico and Brazil. Deener (1952), pp. Other countries also received a constitution during this period: Iraq, Turkey, China, and the Philippines.

[20] For criticism that the strengthening of the courts is a tactic of organized minorities to maintain their grip on the value and political agenda, see: Elster (1995), pp. 364; Ginsburg (2002).

(more dense, technical, and differentiated), so do the grounds for constitutional debate. The process tends to reproduce itself."[21]

In this way, courts have become an important forum, and in some cases the primary or exclusive forum, for clarifying public, economic, and social issues. Any issue in the public or private sphere may receive legal expression and be discussed in some judicial system. The result of this process is the transformation of judicial systems in the world into an integral and essential part both on the public level (such as in the mechanism for determining identity and national policy)[22] and on the personal level.

The increasing reliance on the judicial system occurs not only at the state level but also at the supra-state level, with the establishment of international courts (such as the European Court of Human Rights or the Inter-American Court of Human Rights) with broad and sometimes exclusive powers to deal with Human Rights issues, labor law, environmental quality, administrative issues, and monetary issues.[23] As part of this trend, the concept is established that norms of international institutions, such as the European Court of Human Rights or the European Court of Justice, serve as a basis for a supreme court with constitutional status also in the state law. Following this, state and international courts establish their status as significant societal institutions.[24]

A complex global regulatory framework, including international tribunals, has emerged to address growing interdependence in areas such as security, environmental protection, finance, telecommunications, trade, and services. Local and state systems struggle to cope with these challenges, leading to the expansion of global governance. Transnational regulatory bodies now wield significant power, shifting decision-making on key social policies from local to international realms.t.[25] International law is no longer governed exclusively by treaties concluded between countries, approved by their houses of representatives, thereby becoming their game's binding rules. International regulation includes hundreds of international and regional organizations, functional or identity-based, that produce legal rules, laws, and regulators.[26]

In most cases, the state can also violate the international obligation, and the result is a remedy at the international level. This ensures that the center of gravity shifts to the state and the state's courts, which are required to realize, enforce, and interpret

[21] Stone Sweet (2002), pp. 77, 95.

[22] Hirschl (2004), pp. 222–223; Shapiro (1993), pp. 37–64.

[23] Slaughter (2000) (demonstration of these processes in the World Trade Organization and the NAFTA organization).

[24] Christoffersen and Madsen (2011); Hillebrecht (2014), pp. 1100–1123.

[25] Kumm (2004), pp. 907–931. According to Article 46 of the Vienna Convention on Treaty Law, 1969, a contradictory rule in national law does not justify a violation of international law; International rule prevails in conflict. Peters (2006), pp. 579–610.

[26] Weiler (2020), pp. 3. Krisch and Kingsbury (2006), pp. 1–13.

international law obligations.[27] International law is constitutional in its self-perception as supreme law but realizes its constitutional status through the state. Therefore, the key players are the international tribunals and the state courts.[28] Their relatively high accessibility strengthens their power compared to international tribunals. The habit of obeying them and their established ability to enforce their decisions makes them the most relevant and effective enforcement agents of international law.[29]

The bottom line of these fundamental changes is that state and sub-state judicial systems specialized for their role, involved, and approved proposals in the state and supra-state decision-making processes.

8.2 Procedural Changes

Following the essential changes in the judicial procedure, and primarily as a result of these, changes took place in court hearings. These deliberative changes included, among other things, the following processes: the increased flexibility of the judicial procedure; opening it to different audiences (additional actors); and the development of new work methods (practices) designed to create necessary adjustments to the work of the courts against the background of the change in their role and changing needs. The new practices are naturally different, but their common denominator is the understanding that the legal reality is becoming more complex and complicated; the existing judicial tools are not optimal and, therefore, must be adapted to the dynamic and changing reality.[30] The use of amici and the increase in the involvement of third parties in judicial proceedings is a consequence of the changes in the work of the courts. At the same time, the practice of using amici also contributes to other forms of discussion involved in reshaping the work of the courts.

8.2.1 The Court As an "Umbrella Organization" for Managing Conflicts

In recent decades, courts have adopted a practice known as "rolling procedures," where they encourage parties to reach agreements through negotiations and

---

[27] Weiler (2020), pp. 3. [to complete the picture, Weiler argues that international law is facing a crisis of legitimacy due to the lack of democratic accountability in global governance structures. He suggests that international law needs to be reformed.

[28] Benvenisti and Downs (2009).

[29] Ibid.

[30] Epp (1998) and Hauser (2008). Also see Young (2002). [Young also argues that the term "judicial activism" is a pejorative term that is used to delegitimize the decisions of courts that conservatives disagree with].

meetings, closely monitored by the court, rather than rendering binary judgments. This approach allows for more flexible resolution of disputes without requiring rigid judicial decisions, and can often lead to quicker and more efficient proceedings.[31]

Courts now act as overseers of the dispute resolution process, facilitating negotiations and agreements between parties rather than rendering rigid judicial decisions. This flexible approach enables efficient conflict resolution but departs from the court's traditional role of adjudicating disputes strictly based on law. By closely monitoring proceedings and guiding negotiations, courts have adopted a supervisory role akin to administrative procedures, departing from their classic function of deciding cases per legal standards.[32]

At the foundation of this judicial conduct is the assumption that the issues brought to the courts are complex and have significant broad implications; a binary decision on these issues is not the appropriate social outcome, and therefore, it is fair to strive for another solution.[33] The courts, thus, operate differently from the classic judicial procedure, sometimes in a way that reminds us of our perceptions of alternative dispute resolution procedures (ADR).[34]

The tendency of the courts to accept fewer decisions is also related to the institutional and economic constraints of the legal system, with this tendency being called by many "The Vanishing Trial." "The Vanishing Trial" describes a trend based on extensive research conducted in the federal courts in the United States starting in the 1980s by Galanter.[35] He showed that, although the number of lawsuits filed in the federal courts has not decreased since the 1980s, the number of cases that ended in a detailed verdict has reduced by 60%.[36] Studies done worldwide show that the vast majority of lawsuits opened in the last decade in the court systems are not resolved in a step-by-step adversarial litigation process and do not end in a detailed and reasoned verdict.[37]

The prevailing adjudication in these systems reflects judicial conduct that strives to formulate an agreed solution and create arrangements between the parties instead of issuing a judicial decision. The trend of the reduction in the number of detailed judgments given by the courts is also related to several other factors, such as the deletion of lawsuits due to mediation arrangements made outside the court system or compromises and negotiations made between the parties during the proceedings.[38]

The decline in written judgments, coupled with the increased use of alternative dispute resolution procedures both within and outside the judicial system, has

[31] Petersen (2013), Baar (1992) and Perlman (2009).

[32] Resnik (1982), p. 374.

[33] Resnik (1982), p. 374.

[34] Shapiro (1993), pp. 37–64; Perlman (2009).

[35] Galanter (2004), p. 459.

[36] See also Ackerman (2006), p. 165; Resnik (2006), p. 1101; Burns (2012), p. 893.

[37] Stipanowich (2004), pp. 843–912.

[38] Fulton Hora and Stalcup (2008).

amplified the significance of amicus curiae. As substantive cases increasingly involve amici briefs rather than concluding with judgments, amici play a more pivotal role in shaping court rulings. Moreover, the reduction in verdicts primarily affects lower courts, while amici tend to focus on influential, high-impact cases heard in higher courts aligned with their advocacy interests. Therefore, amicus participation gains prominence as an avenue to inform judicial decision-making in consequential proceedings.

8.2.2 The Development of New Courts: "Problem-Solving" Courts, "Therapeutic Courts," and "Community Courts"

Another change is the emergence of "problem-solving" or "therapeutic" courts, rooted in the "therapeutic jurisprudence" movement.[39] These specialized courts aim to achieve positive therapeutic outcomes by expanding the law's application beyond formalistic questions to address needs, goals, feelings and relationships at individual and systemic levels. This comprehensive approach supports changes in legal procedures and the roles of lawyers and judges. While distinct from procedural changes in traditional courts, the development of problem-solving courts reflects the broader trend of adapting judicial processes to address complex societal issues more holistically.[40]

Problem-solving and therapeutic courts take a comprehensive approach by broadly examining conflict elements and stages to craft solutions addressing disputants' needs and interests holistically. Similar to alternative dispute resolution, they deal with deep-rooted social issues. This aligns with the amicus curiae's role of providing empathetic perspectives and giving voice to affected parties.[41]

Likewise, community courts aim to rehabilitate offenders by addressing the socioeconomic roots of criminality through cooperative rehabilitation programs supervised by the court, social services, and community actors. This systematic approach replaces punitive sentences.[42] The development of these specialized court models reflects the judicial system's endeavor to adopt more holistic, therapeutic practices understanding disputants' contexts beyond strict formalistic legal

[39] Perlman (2009).

[40] Goldberg (2005); Daicoff (2011), pp. 7, 18–21.

[41] Elliott (1986), pp. 306, 309.; Rabinovitch-Eini (2010).

[42] Wexler (2008), p. 17 [the article provides an overview of the development of therapeutic jurisprudence over the past two decades and its application in various areas of law, including mental health law, disability law, and criminal law]. Wexler (2000), pp. 125.

questions. The amicus curiae shares this spirit of expanding voices and viewpoints informing judicial decision-making.[43]

8.2.3 *Using the Tools of Communication to Convey Messages*

Another recent change in how the courts work and conduct is the media use by the courts or someone on their behalf to promote policies on current issues or inform the public of various rulings.[44] Gies and Bybee pointed to the strengthening of the ties between the media and the courts in recent years: unlike in the past, in many countries, the set of court spokespeople works to transmit proactive information both on the overt and covert levels (for example: "not to be quoted" conversations with journalists which present the "behind the scenes" of controversial decisions).

Davis described the relationship between the courts and the media as a "hesitant dance." He meant that judges serve as leaders and even shape the dance steps with the reporters covering their work. Although they avoid being interviewed officially due to the limited access to their connection with the media, they control the specialized messages about them.[45] This is a relatively new action strategy on the part of the judiciary. The possible explanation for this is the desire of the courts to convey messages to the public and its elected officials, and not only to the legal community; on the other hand, this channel reflects the company's interest in this information and expresses the company's recognition of the influence of the courts on it.[46]

The coverage of the trial and the commentary accompanying it have also changed in recent years beyond a concise report on court rulings. The journalists express their opinion on every procedure step and criticize the judges personally. In addition, lawyers from the private market also engaged in activities in the media arena to influence public opinion. Sometimes, the lawyers become "spokesmen for their clients." These trends are described as "Mediatization," i.e., an overall process of social change resulting from the spread of the media, its penetration into the heart of politics, and it is becoming a central player in public life.[47]

---

[43] McCoy (2003), pp. 1513; Berman and Feinblatt (2015); Winick (2002), pp. 1055. In general, see: Collins (2020), p. 1573.

[44] Sauvageau et al. (2006), p. 14; Malleson (1999), p. 182; Gies (2008), pp. 108–109. Malleson and Geis both showed the connections between the increase in judicial activism and media use.

[45] Davis (1994).

[46] On the strengthening of the ties between the media and the judicial process, see, Gies (2008), pp. 108–109.

[47] Bybee (2007); Strömbäk and Esser (2014), pp. 3–28. [Strömbäck and Esser also discuss the role of the media in shaping political agendas, influencing public opinion, and mediating political communication between citizens and political actors.

8.2.4 *Creating New Grounds and Flexible Remedies That Adapted to the Dynamic Reality*

8.2.4.1 Ripeness Doctrine

Another change in the work of the courts is the refinement or creation of new causes and remedies which help the courts in their role. Often, the basis of the flexibility of procedural arrangements is the consideration of promoting systemic efficiency. For example, we can see increasing use of the doctrine of "maturity" in legal proceedings (Ripeness Doctrine).[48] The grounds of ripeness allows the courts to decide that the decision on the issue placed before them will be accepted at a later stage, if at all, and this is due to the absence of a complete set of facts that is essential for rendering a judicial decision (i.e., the parties did not exhaust the procedures available to them before turning to the court). The apparent purpose of the maturity requirement is to delay the judicial review, but at the same time, it allows the courts to convey a message to the auditees that they are "expected" to act differently so that the defect is removed.[49]

Similarly, it is possible to see increasing use of legal grounds that allow the courts to avoid, according to their discretion, deciding on issues that they do not wish to rule on since there is a lack of material data to form a legal decision or because the petition is theoretical or premature.[50] Sometimes, the opposition to discussing the issues in general, while requiring the petitioners to turn to separate petitions, is explained as arising from the essence of the judicial role, which requires discussing each case with a complete factual infrastructure.[51]

8.2.4.2 "Proportionality" and "Reasonableness" Grounds

Another key development adopted by many courts worldwide are the legal grounds of "reasonableness" and "proportionality," allowing greater judicial scrutiny over constitutional rights and administrative actions. The reasonableness test requires authorities to properly balance relevant interests when infringing rights, even with

---

[48] Franklin (2009), pp. 689–692.

[49] Nichol (1987), pp. 153–183. Ferejohn and Kramer (2002), p. 962. [The paper explores various mechanisms for institutionalizing judicial restraint, including the development of norms and practices within the judiciary, as well as the role of external actors such as the legislature and the public in promoting and ensuring judicial restraint].

[50] Nichol (1987), pp. 153–183; Fallon Jr Richard (2011), p. 915.

[51] Barak-Erez (2006), p. 540; Floren (2001), p. 1107. On the requirement of maturity as a strategic tool for directing the behavior of petitioners, see: Franklin (2008), p. 689. See also Eskridge Jr (2004), p. 1279.

legal authorization. The proportionality test demands governmental means be carefully tailored and not exceed what's necessary to achieve stated goals.[52]

Developed almost exclusively by courts themselves, these tests transformed their role from merely policing authorities' adherence to granted powers to substantially supervising how those powers are exercised. No longer limited to reviewing excess of authority or rights violations, courts can now scrutinize the substance and justifications behind rights infringements.[53] These grounds provide practical tools enabling courts to exercise control over rights interpretations and administrative decisions through balancing tests and proportionality analyses. Their widespread adoption reflects courts' evolving efforts to expand their review powers and assert a more robust checking function on government overreach.[54]

8.2.4.3 The Purposive Interpretation

Simultaneously with the development of these grounds, the concept that emphasizes the purpose of the text became even more substantial. The "purposive interpretation" model, which focuses on the meaning of the norm inherent in the text, has become a dominant and sometimes controlling method of interpretation in many courts worldwide. The transition from the formalist interpretative concept to the purposive interpretation approach gave the courts dealing with interpretation relatively large flexibility and room for maneuver in the work of interpretation. This flexibility is reflected in the type of considerations they are allowed to consider in the interpretation process and the relative weight given to each of these considerations. This concept did not come to the world at once, too, but is the result of various developments in the law.

[52] Cohn (2010), pp. 583–629; Le Sueur (2005), pp. 32–51. Webber (2010), pp. 179–202; Bendor and Segal (2002), p. 683.

[53] The reasonableness and proportionality tests are justified according to the culture of justification in that they make the authority provide us with proper justifications. Mattias Kumm speaks in this context about the proportionality tests as producing a "Socratic contestation" of the state's action. When the courts ask the state to show that they correctly balanced the various considerations and did not harm the individual beyond what was required, they enter into a dialogue with the legislator whose goal is to make him clarify to himself and us, what the considerations were behind the legislation, and whether they provided sufficient justification for harming the individual. The method is called Socratic because it is similar to how Socrates made his interlocutors reveal the assumptions behind their positions and their contradictions. Kumm (2010), p. 141.

[54] Kumm (2010).

8.2.4.4 The Doctrine of Relative Nullity

Another example that describes the changes in the discussion in recent years is the growing adoption of the "relative nullity" doctrine in many courts worldwide.[55] According to the doctrine of relative nullity, an action that violates the law will not be considered void as long as its final result has not changed from that which would have occurred if the action had been performed lawfully. One of the classic examples of the use of this doctrine is the right of a hearing. According to the doctrine of relative nullity, in a case where a hearing was not held despite such an obligation in law, it is examined on its merits whether there are claims that would have been heard at the hearing that would have influenced the decision. If the claims could have an effect—the administrative decision will be annulled, and if they could not have an effect—the decision will not be annulled.

Until the adoption of the doctrine of relative nullity, two traditional models ruled: the first, the doctrine of absolute nullity, according to which the legality of the action is examined regardless of its results, and if an action was performed in violation of the law, then it is null and void from the moment it was performed.[56] The second is the doctrine of losses, according to which the governmental action is valid if a court has not canceled it. In other words, the operation is not automatically void but can be undonc.[57]

In contrast, the "theory of relative nullity" (or the relative result) recognizes the existence of judicial discretion regarding the results of a defective action, including the possibility of authorizing a defective action.[58] Unlike the traditional remedies, this device allows the courts to consider a series of circumstances that are not only related to the petitioner but also the nature of the defective action, and the importance of the violated right, including the presumed harm to third parties. The main advantage of the relative nullity doctrine over the other models is expressed in the flexibility in exercising the courts' discretion. This advantage is also the main disadvantage of the doctrine, as it creates uncertainty.[59]

To summarize this point, Judicial systems worldwide have evolved mechanisms and discussion formats to address new and intricate issues more flexibly. This adaptation varies based on court type, necessary changes, each country's normative system, and the extent of flexibility within the legal framework. While not all courts have fully embraced these practices, there's a general trend towards adaptation in recent decades, aligning with the dynamic and evolving reality.

---

[55] Scalise Jr (2013), p. 663.

[56] Wade (1967), pp. 499–526.

[57] Some believed that the difference between the doctrine of relative nullity and the doctrine of losses is more in theory and less in practice, for example, Barak, A Commentary in Law 3, p. 720–730.

[58] See Treacy (2023).

[59] Adams (2017), pp. 289–310. [He also argues that the standard theory fails to take into account the fact that public law is also a system of rules that are designed to protect the rights of individuals.

8.2.5 Expanding the Use of the "Balances" Doctrine

Another change in the work of the courts is related to the expansion of the use of the balancing doctrine.[60] The doctrine of balance is based on an image of the scales.[61] According to this image, when the court is required to make a judicial decision, it must identify the conflicting rights, assess their relative weight, and balance them.[62] The use of the theory of balances was also prevalent in the past, and in constitutional law in particular when, according to different approaches, balance is at the center of judicial action (such as the balance between the individual's rights and the interests of the society at large). However, starting in the late 1970s (and in the United States even earlier), the theory of balances began to be widely used in many courts around the world,[63] to the point that it is difficult to describe a case law (and in constitutional law in particular) that does not use it. In general, it is possible to point to a trend of spreading the work of balancing the work of the courts in many countries and even in international institutions such as the European Court of Human Rights and the World Trade Organization.[64] In all of them, balancing is seen as central and fundamental to judicial action.

There are several justifications for expanding the use of balancing work. First, balancing work is essential in polarized and divided societies because it guarantees that no party will find itself "outside" of balance, and its position will not be eliminated. Second, the balance is seen as pragmatic because it focuses on the results of the judicial decision and examines its advantages versus its disadvantages. Third, the balance promotes the rational construction of judicial discretion and the values of transparency and responsibility in judicial action.[65]

8.2.6 Changes in the Form of Reasoning

At the same time as, and following on from, the involvement of the courts in new, complex areas of law, there is an increasing understanding that in certain regions, judges do not decide, and sometimes cannot decide, only according to internal legal

---

[60] Bomhoff (2008a), p. 555. Pildes (2001), p. 179.

[61] See Curtis and Resnik (1987), pp. 1727. Curtis and Resnik analyze the images and icons commonly used to depict justice, such as the scales, blindfolded Lady Justice, and the courthouse. The authors argue that visual representations of justice play a crucial role in shaping societal perceptions and expectations of the legal system.

[62] Barak (2004), p. 262 ("You cannot balance if you do not have scales, and there is no use of scales unless the relative weight of the conflicting values is determined").

[63] Porat (2009), p. 349.

[64] Stone Sweet and Mathews (2008), pp. 68–149. In Germany, for example, the balancing act is considered at the center of the constitutional legal system. Bomhoff (2008a, b).

[65] See Coffin (1988); Henkin (1978), pp. 1022.

sources. Thus, they involve other areas of knowledge in their decisions. In complex issues with vast implications, the products of judicial systems in the world are decided and reasoned based on information and doctrines from various fields of thought such as sociology, psychology, criminology, environmental quality, geography, economics, philosophy, literature, technology, data science, and natural science.[66] Procaccia described it as: "The science of law is an open science... The most striking hint of the unreality of law as a separate scientific discipline is in abundance in the last generation of new branches of practice, called interdisciplinary..."[67]

Judgments given in recent decades around the world in many areas of law move away from the classic style of "dry" and formal legal decision-making. When it comes to judgments that deal with new, public, controversial, complex, or sensitive issues, the judges act in a different way from in "classic" decisions when they seek to explain and convince the readers (the litigants, their attorneys, and the public) of the rightness of their decision. Hence, they often use different areas of thought and disciplines to justify their approach.[68]

These rulings incorporate non-legal sources of information and extensive discussions on how the judgment applies to other affected groups. Judges are seen as representatives of the public, obligated to provide a thorough and understandable explanation of their decisions, especially to those impacted by them. Moreover, public expectations have shifted towards requiring judicial reasoning rooted in sociology or science rather than mere common sense or decency. Consequently, judgments across different legal domains now encompass a wider theoretical scope, delving into philosophical, economic, security, theological, environmental, and sociological perspectives to clarify and develop legal norms.[69]

One of the effects of this phenomenon is making the judgments more theoretical, which leads to a significant increase in the portion devoted to legal theories and, accordingly, an increase in the average length of the judgments.[70] The process of expanding the areas of knowledge discussed in legal frameworks and deepening the interdisciplinary content takes place in almost the entire industrialized world—The United States, Canada, Germany, Great Britain, New Zealand, Australia, India,

[66] For a description of the phenomenon in different countries see Petersen (2013).

[67] Procaccia (1990), pp. 9–10.

[68] See, for example, Holder and Harrison (2003), Ward (1995), Gardiner et al. (2012), Kapardis (2009) and Cooter and Ulen (1988).

[69] Following the "justification culture" that has brought a strike to most of the judicial systems in the world, every governmental action is bound by a well-founded rational justification. Zamir (2010), pp. 153–157; Dyzenhaus et al. (2001), pp. 5, 29.

[70] Petersen (2013). See, for example, also: Campbell Pearson and Wade (2013). For the connection between the lengthening of judgments and a decrease in public confidence in the United States courts, see Black and Spriggs II (2008), p. 621.

South Africa, Latin American countries, former Eastern Bloc countries, and international courts and arbitrations.[71]

8.2.7 Turning the Traditional Procedure into a Multi-Participant Procedure and Expanding the Legal Standing Right

Another significant change in the judicial procedure, in which the practice of the Amicus Curiae is a central factor, is the transformation of the "classic" bilateral procedure (plaintiff-defendant, petitioner-respondent, accuser-accused) into a multilateral and multidimensional procedure. Within the framework of the new model, the courts hear and express not only the positions and wishes of the formal parties but also other parties who have a say and wish to influence the decision-making processes concerning their environment and lives. In recent decades, third parties such as rights organizations, giant corporations, non-profit institutions, and private individuals have become central players in the judicial process, sometimes an integral part. Moreover, in cases where the public has a position on the matter, the number, scope, and, in many cases—influence—of third parties who are allowed to intervene in the procedure exceed the formal parties.

For example, in recent decades, the rules of legal standing have been changed in many countries (as mentioned in the changes required according to each country) to allow more parties to enter the court gates. Generally, in the past, the concept that prevailed was that the person who submits his petition to the court should show, before the clarification of the allegations, that he has a direct interest in the subject matter of the petition. He had to prove why he and no one else was entitled to have the court hear his petition.[72]

---

[71] Petersen (2013). Huneeus (2015), pp. 89–92. The interdisciplinary nature of judicial reasoning has been influenced by several prominent intellectual movements that emerged in recent decades. These include the sociological approach to law, which highlights the interconnectedness between societal interests and legal frameworks. Additionally, the law and economics movement advocates for applying economic principles to legal problem-solving, while law and psychology explore the intersection between legal processes and psychological research. Legal realism suggests that judges use law as a means to implement desired social policies and values through strategic interpretation. Furthermore, there has been a shift away from rigid formalism towards a more flexible and informal approach to judicial procedures. These movements collectively challenge traditional views of law as an isolated discipline and encourage courts to adopt contextualized, policy-oriented reasoning that considers sociological, economic, psychological, and ethical factors. This interdisciplinary expansion reflects law's growing integration with other disciplines to address the complexities of modern societies. Belinda Brooks-Gordon and Michael Freeman (2006); Posner (2006); Kronman (1988), p. 335.

[72] See, for example, HCJ 90/49 Nochimovski v. Minister of Justice (1949); HCJ 40/70 Becker v. Minister of Defense.(1970).

This idea of a public petitioner originates from the *Actio Popularis* institution of Roman law, according to which any public member (*quivis ex populo*) can initiate legal proceedings in favor of the public interest. An impressive development in legal standing and "opening the doors of the court" in an exceptionally liberal manner took place in Israel even more strongly, starting from the 1980s.[73] Similarly, the Indian Supreme Court expanded the traditional standing rules according to which only those personally harmed could seek judicial relief and allowed public interest litigation. The Supreme Court of Canada has also expanded the right to stand recently. In a series of critical judgments, the Canadian court ruled that when it comes to general legislation aimed at the public, a public petition must be allowed out of fear that without it, the examination of minor matters will be prevented.[74] Starting in 2012, in the well-known *SWUAV* case, the Canadian court significantly softened the tests of the right to stand and opened its doors to the public petitioner.[75]

Similarly, in England, the birthplace of the doctrine of the right to legal standing, the concept was initially discussed only in case law, which expressed contradictory trends. For a long time, the discussion of the right and its conditions was tied to the relief the petitioner requested in each case.[76] Over the years, the English court adopted a relatively liberal interpretation of "interest" that justifies granting a right to stand and even allowed third-sector organizations to represent general interests.[77] The Human Rights Act, enacted in 1998 to incorporate the European Convention on Human Rights into English law, must also be added to the standing model. This adoption has since allowed any British citizen to petition in a British court against any violation of a right from the treaty by the government.[78] Similar changes (albeit more limited) that expanded the possibility of third parties entering the court gates occurred in other countries (such as Australia and South Africa), including continental Europe.[79]

Generally, the change in approach to the question of the right to legal standing is attributed to a broader shift in the court's perception of the definition of its role. While according to the traditional approach, the role of the court is to act as an

[73] Segev (2006), pp. 505–506. Mautner (2005), pp. 7–8.

[74] Thorson v. Attorney General of Canada, 1974 CanLII 6 (SCC), [1975] 1 SCR 138; Nova Scotia Board of Censors v. McNeil, [1976] 2 S.C.R. 265.

[75] Canada (Attorney General) v. Downtown Eastside Sex Workers United Against Violence Society, 2012 SCC 45 (CanLII), [2012] 2 SCR 524.

[76] Loveland (2009).

[77] Eliantionio et al. (2012), pp. 60–63.

[78] Eliantionio et al. (2012), pp. 65–67. They show that since the Human Rights Act legislation adopted the Convention, in practice, into common law, there is a question regarding the relationship between the limited right to stand under Article 34 of the Convention and the broader right to stand defined in the Courts Senior Act. It needs to be clarified whether the provisions of the Convention on the subject of a Convention constitute a negative arrangement that prevents those entitled to compliance according to the English test from submitting petitions for infringement of their rights enumerated in the Convention.

[79] Eliantionio et al. (2012), pp. 60–63; van Wolferen (2016), pp. 914–930; Mqingwana (2012).

arbitrator in disputes between individuals and between the individual and the government authorities, the courts' new vision is that its role is broader and includes a concern for the rule of law in general matters as well.[80]

In recent decades, we've witnessed substantial changes in both the substance and procedures of the judicial process, reflecting courts' evolving understanding of their societal role. Materially, there's a growing reliance on courts and legal procedures to regulate a wide array of issues, extending beyond their previous scope. This increased involvement is evident across diverse legal traditions and governance models. In terms of procedural changes, new work styles have been adopted, including supervised negotiations and novel deliberative practices within court hearings. Additionally, new legal grounds and remedies have been introduced, while existing ones have been refined. Moreover, there's been a shift from traditional legal disputes to public debates that reflect contemporary societal values and economic concerns, drawing on diverse opinions and legal sources. Participants in legal proceedings have also experienced a transition, moving from disputes involving only formal parties to proceedings involving numerous stakeholders. Behind these changes lies the recognition that many issues under discussion are not solely the concern of two conflicting parties but also involve other stakeholders seeking involvement in decision-making processes.

8.3 The Main Explanations for the Changes in the Judicial System

The extensive involvement of the courts in society and the substantive and procedural changes associated with their growing importance is rooted in two central processes: the first is the expansion of the powers of the modern state (some also call it the "Activist State").[81] The second is the increasing complexity of modern societies demographically, technologically, ecologically, pedagogically, industrially, environmentally, and economically. It is evident that besides the expansion of state powers and the growing complexity of modern societies, there are other

[80] Along with the changes in the judicial system, significant changes have occurred in the behavior of executive and legislative authorities. These changes encompass heightened involvement of lobbyists in public decision-making, weakening governance within certain executive bodies, the emergence of private legislation, alterations in the powers and duties of elected officials, frequent changes in election methods, dynamic adjustments to the "rules of the game," the surge of populist movements, and the growing influence of media on both executive and legislative branches. See, for example: Thomas and Hrebenar (2008), pp. 1–14; Andeweg (2005), pp. 491, 494; McKay (2013); Berman (2021), pp. 71–88. [Berman argues that there is no single cause of populism, but rather a complex set of factors that have contributed to its rise. These factors include economic inequality, social and cultural change, and the decline of trust in mainstream institutions].

[81] Habermas (1986); Ackerman (1983); Klijn and Koppenjan (2000), pp. 109, 115.

explanations for the changes in the judicial system in recent decades.[82] The starting point for our discussion is the "Amicus Curiae phenomenon" and its meaning in judicial systems that in many countries have undergone a significant revolution in recent decades in their role, nature and form of their work, and ways of conducting themselves. These changes simultaneously affect and are affected by the "amicus phenomenon."

8.3.1 The Expansion of Modern State Powers

The first cause of the significant involvement of the courts and the changes in their work is the expansion of the state's administrative powers. The law of the country touches a citizen in almost all areas of his life, from the moment of his birth until his death. It consists of dozens of areas of law and knowledge that branch into thousands of different sub-areas: health, construction, education, housing, food, immigration, business licensing, environmental protection, transportation, burial, welfare services, employment, and the like. Modern law "touches" the citizen, to one degree or another, in almost every aspect of his life through an extensive labyrinth of regulation.[83]

Through its laws and regulations, the "interventionist" state accompanies every man every day of his life, from the moment he gets out of bed, hour after hour. The electricity he turns on, the television he watches, the food he eats, the school he sends his children to, the road he drives on—on each of these, and on other products and services that accompany him in his daily routine, the mark of the public administration is imprinted. It is the one who supplies it, supervises its production, sets its

[82]For example, an inevitable response to the systemic need to adopt standard and uniform legal norms in an era of economic market consolidation; the tendency of political institutions to transfer difficult decisions to the courts because of the electorate; various sociological transformations in modern society as a whole which has become litigious; The increased activity of various interest groups which caused a growing demand for legal decisions of all kinds and increasing use of lobbies, lobbying, and interest groups as part of the "politics of rights.", Tate and Vallinder (1995); Shapiro (1993); Kenneth M. Holland (1991); Kramer (2004); Waldron (1998), pp. 335; Posner (2005), pp. 32, 32–54.

[83]For expansion, see Teubner (1983), p. 239. [Teubner argues that the rise of reflexive law is a response to the increasing complexity and uncertainty of modern society. In a world where social problems are increasingly complex and interconnected, it is no longer possible for law to simply prescribe solutions from above. Instead, law must become more reflexive, allowing for the participation of all stakeholders in the regulatory process].

There are many answers to the question of what regulation is. I rely on the Faur, according to which regulation is "any administrative legislation (regulations, procedures, standards, guidelines, and orders) that shapes or establishes different individuals, groups or organizations within the regulatory body, and outside of it." Levi-Faur and David (2011); McLean (2004).

price, requires it with a license, imposes a tax on it, or regulates it in some other way.[84]

Since almost all developed countries are interventionists, even if they do not officially define themselves as such, which intervene in social questions, the law and, accordingly, the judicial system becomes an integral part of this intervention.[85] It is understood that as the state's intervention in the citizen's day-to-day life grows, the power, centrality, and significance of the law and the courts grow and deepen.[86]

The expansion of the state's powers also affects the power and status of the legal advisors of the government authorities in the governmental decision-making processes. The expansion of the areas brought to the decision of the legal advisors of the state authorities results from the fact that various state decisions are expected to be attacked in the courts. Therefore, the opinion of the legal advisors is requested regarding the possibility that these decisions will be invalidated.

The growth of state law, and as a result, the growth of the court, is linked and closely related to the increase in the centrality and influence of non-governmental organizations on the creation of law and its interpretation in the last three decades in national and international legal arenas.[87] NGOs specialize in "translating" public matters into formal legal frameworks, which have become the subject of discussion in judicial systems. Just for the record, in the United States today, there are over one and a half million non-governmental organizations[88]; in Russia—about three hundred thousand[89]; in India—over two million non-governmental organizations[90]; the number of international organizations that are not affiliated with any country and operate in international arenas only (such as: "Amnesty," "International Federation for Human Rights" (FIDH) or "Greenpeace") is over 40,000.[91]

In recent decades, NGOs have become essential and sometimes exclusive players in many fields, including human and civil rights struggles.[92] NGOs deal with various goals—environmental, political, security, and social (such as poverty reduction), legal advocacy, assistance with medical needs (supply of medical equipment such as wheelchairs), immigration, fighting terrorism, ecological, freedom of information,

[84] Roberts (2020), pp. 391–401. See also: Abel and Sementelli (2002), pp. 253–278.

[85] See Symposium (1983), pp. 1083; Unger (1976); Lewis (2019), pp. 767–789.

[86] Stivers (2008), pp. 53–56.

[87] Shelton (1994); Smith et al. (1998) [Smith, Pagnucco, and Lopez examine the activities and strategies employed by transnational human rights NGOs in their efforts to address human rights violations on an international scale].

[88] U.S. Dep't of State, Fact Sheet: Non-Governmental Organizations (NGOs) in the United States (Jan. 12, 2012).

[89] Rodriguez (2008).

[90] ArchnaShukla, *First Official Estimate: An NGO for Every 400 People in India*, Indian Express, July 7, 2010, http://archive.indianexpress.com/news/first-official-estimate-an-ngo-for-every-400-people-in-india/643302.

[91] The exact answer to "How many international non-governmental organizations are there in the world?" is complex and depends on the criteria used to define these organizations.

[92] Reimann (2006).

and human rights. They do this in various ways: demonstrations, protests, documentation of human rights violations, information services for citizens, providing legal aid to the underprivileged, and lobbying policymakers.

On the international level, today, almost no international diplomatic conference convenes for the formulation of international treaties or for a substantial discussion of global issues without international organizations that will participate in formal advisory roles or with the status of observers. The literature that deals with this phenomenon in international law tends to focus not only on the increase in the number of international organizations but on their significant influence on the most crucial global decision-making processes. These organizations have themselves become constitutional mechanisms that assist in the transformation of the international order into a constitutional order.[93] Some scholars propose to refer to central international organizations even as constituents of constitutional order.[94]

Some attribute the strengthening of the power of NGOs and their influence on law design partly to privatization, a pervasive vision in the Western world. Many countries are privatizing services and powers previously provided by the public: health services, education, welfare, policing, and incarceration powers.[95] This phenomenon has contributed to the increase in the power of non-governmental public organizations and their ability to influence the law as those who fulfill many functions that were until now in the hands of the state (air pollution, the capital market, the war on terrorism, online trade and more).[96]

It's crucial to understand that privatization and globalization don't eliminate state involvement but redefine its role. Privatization increases the need for regulation to safeguard public interests. International regulations also shape state actions. While regulations don't replace state norms, they significantly limit state discretion. For instance, trade agreements may prohibit discrimination. Regulatory impacts can be achieved through economic incentives or mechanisms like shaming. Despite reduced direct service provision, state intervention through regulation expands.[97]

The "private" business world is never conducted in a vacuum but operates within a public sphere involving governmental powers and regulatory roles.[98] In any case,

---

[93] Charnovitz (1997) and Collins Jr (2008).

[94] Jackson (2001), pp. 67–78. Fassbender (2009). [He offers insights into the Charter's legal and normative framework and its significance in promoting peace, human rights, and global governance].

[95] Benvenisti (2014). See, in general, the following writing dealing with the subject: Yarrow and George (1986), pp. 323–364; Mason and Cody (2013); Rizvi (2016); Maarse (2006), pp. 981–1014.

[96] Sometimes these organizations are called CSOs (Civil Society Organizations). Terry L. Anderson and Peter J. Hill (1996); Dickinson (2006), pp. 383, 385 (A fascinating description of the privatization of US security and foreign policy powers). Barak-Erez (2017), pp. 533–551.

[97] Pestoff (1992), pp. 21–45; Roitman (2017).

[98] Waters (2001). For the effects of globalization on access to law, see Shapiro (1993), pp. 37–64. Shapiro discusses how globalization has led to the proliferation of international legal institutions and frameworks, such as treaties, conventions, and organizations, which govern various aspects of global governance and cooperation.

the influence of non-governmental organizations on the state and supra-state decision-making processes will continue to increase. The phenomenon of the flourishing of the NGOs and their influence on the changes in the courts can only be understood against the background of profound transformations that have taken place in culture, politics, economics, law, and society worldwide.[99]

8.3.2 *The Complexity of the Law*

The second major factor in the changes in the conduct of the courts is the increasing complexity of modern societies. This, in turn, has led to a greater complexity of the law and made it richer, more varied, and with increased content. This phenomenon will be called: the "complexity of the law." The complexity of the law is a direct consequence of the increasing complexity of modern societies demographically,[100] occupationally, pedagogically,[101] economically, environmentally,[102] and technologically, which brings the law and the court new challenges and new legal issues to its door.

Of course, it is impossible to discuss all the changes human society has experienced in recent decades. Only a few of these processes will be demonstrated, which in turn affect the expansion of modern law (and, accordingly, the involvement of third parties in legal proceedings).

Occupationally, significant changes have occurred across various sectors, directly influencing legal frameworks. These changes include longer working hours, decreased tenure at one workplace, declining power of worker organizations, rising retirement ages, and increased reliance on outsourcing and subcontractors. These

---

[99]There are even hundreds of non-governmental organizations whose job is to sort and name the number of non-governmental organizations worldwide at any given moment. Regarding international non-governmental organizations, the research and popular literature dealing with these transformations often give them postmodern labels such as global governance or globalization. In practice, these terms are vague and have different interpretations. Charnovitz (1997); Jens Steffek and Kristina Hahn (2010).

[100]Demographically, expert forecasts predict a consistent growth of the world's population, and the expectation is about 10.5 billion people by the year 2050. Another analysis conducted by a team of researchers from the University of Washington showed that the world's population may reach 11 billion people by the end of the century. Univ. of Wash., *World Population Could Be Nearly 11 Billion by 2100*, ScienceDaily (June 13, 2013), http://www.sciencedaily.com/releases/2013/06/130613111942.htm; Dep't of Econ. & Soc. Affairs, Population Div., *World Population Prospects: The 2012 Revision*, U.N. Doc. ST/ESA/SER.A/345 (2013).

[101]Pedagogically, as the Western educational paradigm moves away from rigid standards toward a focus on meaningful learning experiences, new challenges emerge for legal frameworks. This shift grants educators greater autonomy in shaping teaching and learning processes, prioritizing impactful learning outcomes over prescriptive teaching methods. This transition underscores the importance of transformative learning experiences and the rights of teachers in educational practices. See Kuusilehto-Awale and Lahtero (2014) and Volansky (2010).

[102]Chang and Turner (2019), pp. 503–509.

shifts have heightened job instability, resulting in increased workloads, multitasking, and the need for diverse skills among employees. Additionally, there's been a decrease in the proportion of full-time permanent positions. The COVID-19 pandemic further catalyzed changes, with many individuals transitioning to remote work, either partially or entirely, altering traditional workplace dynamics.[103]

From an economic point of view, it is possible to point to a significant increase in the scope of international trade, liberalization of currency trade, profound changes in the data communication processes of the stock exchanges, the expansion of the scope of giant corporations, the mobility of factories between different countries, and a decrease in the ability of central banks in other countries to influence the local currency.[104]

Technologically, the judicial system grapples with emerging fields propelled by rapid technological advancements, necessitating responses to new and intricate issues. Innovations in computers, the internet, copyright, the metaverse, digital information, and networks fuel social, economic, and political transformations.[105] Online activities encompass various aspects of daily life, from financial transactions to social interactions, culture consumption, job searches, and service orders. Some argue that technological progress not only shapes but also redefines human activity.[106]

Every day, courts face new legal challenges stemming from rapid technological advancements. However, addressing these complex changes requires more than just one-time legal solutions. The pace and scale of technological evolution demand a fresh approach, prompting courts to reconsider existing legal tools and adapt them to emerging realities.[107] The courts must know how to react to these changes, but at the same time, the response should be informed, rooted in the existing legal tradition, and justified in itself.[108]

The environmental changes also bring new challenges and new legal issues to the door of the courts. Many new problems have arisen or intensified during the last few decades, all of which force the courts to develop ways of managing those cases involving environmental issues. A partial list of the many and diverse issues includes problems associated with changes in air quality, pollution, ecological damage, destruction of animal habitats, gas discoveries, deforestation, protection of wild animals, discharge of pollutants into water sources, radiation damage as a result of mobile phones or wireless transmissions, the treatment of solid waste and its effect

---

[103] See Papadopoulos et al. (2010); Newfarmer and Sztajerowska (2012), pp. 7–73. Hite and McDonald (2020), pp. 427–437. Ratten (2020), pp. 503–516.

[104] Cohn and Hira (2020) and Balaam and Dillman (2015).

[105] Haber (2023). Available at SSRN: https://ssrn.com/abstract=4400281.

[106] Brownsword and Goodwin (2012) and Elkin-Koren and Birnhak (2011).

[107] For example, is it permissible to disclose details of anonymous Internet surfers, and how? When can surfing the Internet constitute consent to a valid contract? How is the liability of Internet service providers for defamation spread by surfers assessed? Elkin-Koren and Birnhak (2011), p. 13; Susskind (2018).

[108] Tidmarsh (1992); 76 Fordham L. Rev. 2 (2007).

on the soil and food, noise hazards, global warming[109] and severe meteorological and geological disturbances that have afflicted the world (earthquakes, volcanic eruptions, hurricanes, floods, droughts, forest fires).[110]

The swift environmental and technological shifts demand that the law and courts swiftly adapt by developing and enforcing a range of legal measures. This entails a diligent and careful approach to address the evolving landscape effectively. The extensive involvement of courts across all facets of life has led to the diversification of legal content and the emergence of new branches and disciplines. Consequently, the judicial system grapples with a broad spectrum of novel issues and areas of expertise, including internet gaming, cyber laws, advanced technology regulations, telecommunications, renewable energy, space laws, bioethics, climate change legislation, and environmental compliance and privacy laws, among others.[111]

Even relatively traditional areas of law such as contract law, family law, or tax law have become more complex in recent decades due to the increased complexity of economic and social arrangements involving dynamic regulation of new areas of activities, all requiring novel legal sub-specialties. These relate to ever more complex tax aspects of mergers and acquisitions and various new fields of finance developed in the twenty-first century, including derivatives, issuances, private allocations of capital, and planning of the holdings structure.[112] In brief, in many countries around the world, due to the development of various social arrangements related to the fact that life has become more complex, today's legal norms have greater depth and breadth than before.

Another example of the growing complexity of law can be found in the development of international law. In recent decades, tribunals that deal with international law must become familiar with increasing volumes of diverse and complex legal material touching upon and including: international treaties, state law, local cultural customs, general principles of international law, decisions of various international organizations, decisions of international and state tribunals, and extensive legal and social literature. Increasingly complex diverse areas of international law are, in many cases, renewed or implemented through a continuous interaction between political and legal processes.[113]

---

[109] Diffenbaugh and Burke (2019), pp. 9808–9813.

[110] Bodansky et al. (2017), Simlinger et al. (2019) and Setzer and Vanhala (2019).

[111] An example that helps to identify the expansion and diversity of sources of law in our lives are websites of law firms from which it is possible to argue about various "new" and modern legal fields. See, for example, the diverse and detailed areas of practice on the websites of the largest law firms in the world for 2023: Kirkland & Ellis, Latham & Watkins, DLA Piper, Baker McKenzie, Skadden, Arps, Slate, Meagher & Flom LLP and Affiliates, Dentons, Clifford Chance, Allen & Overy LLP.

[112] For example, Miller and Curry (2009), pp. 839–864.

[113] Stone Sweet and Brunell (1998) [Stone Sweet and Brunell analyze how the European Court of Justice (ECJ) and the Commission of the European Communities (now the European Commission) have played crucial roles in shaping the supranational constitution of the European Community].

As mentioned above, the two factors—the expansion of the state's powers and the growing complexity of modern societies—are not the only factors capable of explaining the changes in the judicial system. They fit into a whole set of changes in systemic perceptions. One of them is a change in the judges' own minds regarding their role and powers and regarding what society expects of them and their role.[114] This change of mind-set stems partly from a political concept according to which, in a democracy, natural access to justice must be allowed and a legal solution provided to all strata of the populace (such as people experiencing poverty, women, or members of minorities).[115] The more and more groups in society participate in society and the economy, and the more there is equality or at least a call for equality, the more the court is aware that it must provide a legal answer to the issues required.

The complexity of the trial can, of course, also be explained through additional explanations such as an increase in the level of crime, a growing awareness among the public of their rights (consumer rights, economic rights, and the like), an increase in the level of media coverage of the trial (fraud and deception by companies, violence by institutions, exorbitant prices), the accumulation of private property and the development of a competitive economy.[116] It is enough if we start from the premise that the world of law has changed beyond recognition in recent years. These changes pose new challenges to the courts; challenges, which, as will be expanded below, the amici seek to fulfill, at least in part.

References

Abel CF, Sementelli A (2002) Power, emancipation and the administrative state. Admin Theory Praxis 24(2):253–278

Ackerman BA (1983) Foreword: law in an activist state. Yale Law J 92:1083

Ackerman B (1997) The rise of world constitutionalism. Va Law Rev 771-797:778–779

Ackerman RM (2006) Vanishing trial, vanishing community? The potential effect of the vanishing trial on America's social capital. J Disp Resol:165

Adams T (2017) The standard theory of administrative unlawfulness. Camb Law J 76(2):289–310

Andeweg RB (2005) The Netherlands: the sanctity of proportionality. In: Gallagher M, Mitchel P (eds) The politics of electoral systems, p 491, 494

[114]Robinson (2009). See also Perlman (2010).

[115]Francioni and Francesco (2007) [see especially the third part exploring the challenges to access to justice and the measures that can be taken to overcome these challenges]. See also Genn (2012). [Genn delves into the various approaches and perspectives on civil justice, examining the role of traditional court systems and the challenges they face in providing effective and accessible justice].

[116]For a general description of these trends, see Harari (2014, 2016). The complexity of trials can also be explained through additional explanations such as an increase in the level of crime, a growing awareness among the public of its rights (consumer rights, economic rights, etc.), an increase in the level of media coverage of trials (fraud and fraud by companies, violence by institutions, exorbitant prices), the accumulation of private property and the development of a competitive economy.

ArchnaShukla, *First Official Estimate: An NGO for Every 400 People in India*, Indian Express, July 7, 2010. http://archive.indianexpress.com/news/first-official-estimate-an-ngo-for-every-400-people-in-india/643302
Baar C (1992) Social action litigation in India: the operation and limits of the World's Most active judiciary. In: Jackson DW, Tate CN (eds) Comparative judicial review and public policy, p 77
Balaam DN, Dillman B (2015) Introduction to international political economy. Routledge, Milton Park
Barak A (2004) Judge in a Democratic Society, at p. 262 (2004)
Barak, A Commentary in Law 3, at pp. 720–730
Barak-Erez D (2006) Israel: the security barrier—between international law, constitutional law and domestic judicial review. Int J Const Law 4:540
Barak-Erez D (2017) Three questions of privatization. In: *Comparative administrative law*. Edward Elgar Publishing, Cheltenham, pp 533–551
Bendor AL, Segal Z (2002) Constitutionalism and trust 683
Benvenisti E (2014) The law of global governance. Brill, Leiden
Benvenisti E, Downs GW (2009) National Courts, domestic democracy and the evolution of international law. Eur J Int Law 20:59
Berman S (2021) The causes of populism in the west. Annu Rev Polit Sci 24:71–88
Berman G, Feinblatt J (2015) Good courts: the case for problem-solving justice, vol 8. Quid Pro Books
Black RC, Spriggs JF II (2008) An empirical analysis of the length of U.S. Supreme Court opinions. Hous Law Rev 45:621
Bodansky D, Brunnée J, Rajamani L (2017) International climate change law. Oxford University Press, Oxford
Bomhoff J (2008a) Balancing, the global and the local judicial balancing as a problematic topic in comparative (constitutional) law. Hast Int Comp Law Rev 31:555
Bomhoff J (2008b) Luth's 50th anniversary: some comparative observations on the German foundations of judicial balancing. German Law J 9:121
Brownsword R, Goodwin M (2012) Law and the Technologies of the Twenty-first Century: text and materials. Cambridge University Press, Cambridge
Burns RP (2012) Advocacy in the era of the vanishing trial. Univ Kan Law Rev 61:893
Bybee KJ (2007) Bench press: the collision of courts, politics, and the media
Cappelletti M (1971) Judicial review in the contemporary World
Chang CC, Turner BL (2019) Ecological succession in a changing world. J Ecol 107(2):503–509
Charnovitz S (1997) Two centuries of participation: NGOs and international governance. Mich J Int Law 18:281–282
Christoffersen J, Madsen MR (eds) (2011) The European court of human rights between law and politics. Oxford University Press, Oxford
Coffin FM (1988) Judicial balancing: the protean scales of justice. NY Univ Law Rev 63:1
Cohn M (2010) Legal transplant chronicles: the evolution of unreasonableness and proportionality review of the administration in the United Kingdom. Am J Comp Law 58(3):583–629
Cohn TH, Hira A (2020) Global political economy: theory and practice. Routledge, Milton Park
Collins PM (2008) Friends of the Supreme Court: Interest groups and judicial decision making
Collins ER (2020) The problem of problem-solving courts. UC Davis Law Rev 54(2020):1573
Cooter, Ulen T (1988) Law and economics
Curtis DE, Resnik J (1987) Images of justice. Yale Law J 96:1727
Daicoff S (2011) The future of the legal profession. Monash Univ Law Rev 37(1):7, 18–7, 21
Davis R (1994) Decisions and images: the Supreme Court and the press
Deener D (1952) Judicial review in modern constitutional systems. Am Polit Sci Rev 46(4): 1079–1099
Derrida J (2001) Force of Law, in Acts of Religion 228 (Gil Anidjar ed.,2002)
Dickinson LA (2006) Public law values in a privatized world. Yale J Int Law 31:383, 385

Diffenbaugh NS, Burke M (2019) Global warming has increased global economic inequality. Proc Natl Acad Sci 116(20):9808–9813
Durski W, Toniatti R (2015) Central and eastern European constitutionalism a quarter century after the fall of the Berlin Wall: introduction to the symposium. Int J Const Law 13:119
Dyzenhaus D, Hunt M, Taggart M (2001) The principle of legality in administrative law: internationalisation and Constitutionalisation. Oxford Univ Commonwealth Law J 1:5, 29
Eliantionio M, Backes C, Rhee van CH, Spronken TNBM, Berlee A (2012) Standing up for your right(s) in Europe - a comparative study on legal standing (locus Standi) before the EU and member states' courts. Policy Department for Citizen's Rights and Constitutional Affairs, European Parliament. https://doi.org/10.2861/10624
Elkin-Koren N, Birnhak M (2011) *Introduction: Law and Information Technology*. In: Elkin-Koren N, Birnhak M (eds) Legal Network: Law and Information Technology Rev, vol 11
Elliott DE (1986) Managerial judging and the evolution of procedure. Univ Chicago Law Rev 53: 306, 309
Elster J (1995) Forces and mechanisms in the constitution-making process. Duke Law J 45:364
Epp CR (1998) The rights revolution: lawyers, activists, and Supreme Courts in comparative perspective
Eskridge WN Jr (2004) Pluralism and distrust: how courts can support democracy by lowering the stakes of politics. Yale Law J 114:1279
Evaluating Transnational NGOs: Legitimacy, Accountability, Representation (Jens Steffek & Kristina Hahn eds., 2010)
Fallon Jr Richard H (2011) Fact and fiction about facial challenges. Calif Law Rev 99:915
Fassbender B (2009) The United Nations charter as the constitution of the international community. Brill, Leiden
Ferejohn JA, Kramer LD (2002) Independent judges, dependent judiciary: Institutionalizing judicial restraint. NY Univ Law Rev 77:962
Floren D (2001) Pre-enforcement ripeness doctrine: the fitness of hardship. Or Law Rev 80:1107
Foucault M (1997) The politics of truth (Sylvère Lotringer ed.)
Francioni F (ed) (2007) Access to justice as a human right. Oxford University Press, Oxford
Franklin DL (2008) Looking through both ends of the telescope: facial challenges and the Roberts court. Hastings Const Law Q 36:689
Franklin DL (2009) Looking through both ends of the telescope: facial challenges and the Roberts court. Hastings Const Law Q 36:689–692
Fulton Hora P, Stalcup T (2008) Drug treatment courts in the twenty-first century: the evolution of the revolution in problem-solving courts. Ga Law Rev 42:717
Galanter M (2004) The vanishing trial: an examination of trials and related matters in federal and state courts. J Emp Legal Stud 1:459
Gardbaum S (2014) Are strong constitutional courts always a good thing for new democracies. Colum J Transnatl Law 53:285
Gardiner S et al (2012) Sports law. Routledge, Milton Park
Genn H (2012) What is civil justice for-reform, ADR, and access to justice. Yale J Law Human 24: 397
Gies L (2008) Law and the media: the future of an uneasy relationship 108–09
Ginsburg T (2002) Economic analysis and the design of constitutional courts. Theoretical Inquiries Law 3:1
Ginsburg T (2008) Constitutional courts in East Asia: understanding variation. J Comp 3
Goldberg S (2005) Nat'l judicial inst., judging for the 21st century: a problem-solving approach
Haber E (26 March 2023) The criminal metaverse. Indiana Law Journal, Forthcoming, https://ssrn.com/abstract=4400281
Habermas J (1986) Law as medium and law as institution, in dilemmas of law in the welfare state 203 (Gunther Teubner ed.)
Harari YN (2014) Sapiens: a brief history of humankind. Random House, New York
Harari YN (2016) Homo Deus: a brief history of tomorrow. Random House, New York

Hauser SE (2008) Predatory lending, passive judicial activism, and the duty to Decide. NC Law Rev 86:1501
Henkin L (1978) Infallibility under law: constitutional balancing. Colum Law Rev 78:1022
Hillebrecht C (2014) The power of human rights tribunals: compliance with the European court of human rights and domestic policy change. Eur J Int Rel 20(4):1100–1123
Hirschl R (2004) Towards juristocracy: the origins and consequences of the new constitutionalism
Hirschl R (2008) The judicialization of mega-politics and the rise of political courts. Annu Rev Polit Sci 11:93–118
Hite LM, McDonald KS (2020) Careers after COVID-19: challenges and changes. Hum Resour Dev Int 23(4):427–437
Holder J, Harrison C (2003) Law and geography
Holmes S, Sunstein CR (1995) The politics of constitutional revision in Eastern Europe. In: Levinson (ed) Responding to imperfection. Princeton University Press, Princeton, pp 275–306
Huneeus A (2015) Introduction to symposium on the constitutionalization of international law in Latin America. Am J Int Law 109:89–92
Huntington SP (1991) The third wave: democratization in the late twentieth century
Jackson JH (2001) The WTO 'constitution' and proposed reforms: seven 'mantras' revisited. J Int Econ Law 4(1):67–78
Kenneth MH (ed) (1991) Judicial activism in comparative perspective
Kapardis A (2009) Psychology and law: a critical introduction. Cambridge University Press, Cambridge
Klijn EH, Koppenjan J (2000) Interactive decision making and representative democracy: institutional collisions and solutions. In: van Haffen O, Kickert W, Thomassen J (eds) Governance in modern society, p 109, 115
Kramer LD (2004) The people themselves: popular constitutionalism and judicial review
Krisch N, Kingsbury B (2006) Introduction: global governance and global administrative law in the international legal order. Eur J Int Law 17(1):1–13
Kronman A (1988) Jurisprudential responses to legal realism. Cornell Law Rev 73:335
Kumm M (2004) The legitimacy of international law: a constitutionalist framework of analysis. Eur J Int Law 15(5):907–931
Kumm M (2010) The idea of Socratic contestation and the right to justification: the point of rights-based proportionality review. Law Ethics Human Rights 4:141
Kuusilehto-Awale L, Lahtero T (2014) Finnish case of basic education for all—with quality learning outcomes. J Educ Res:6
Law And Psychology (Belinda Brooks-Gordon & Michael Freeman eds., 2006)
Le Sueur A (2005) The rise and ruin of unreasonableness? Judic Rev 10(1):32–51
Legalization and World Politics (Judith Goldstein et al. eds., 2001)
Levi-Faur D (2011) The Odyssey of the regulatory state—episode one: the rescue of the welfare state, Jerusalem Papers in Regulation & Governance, Paper No. 39, November
Lewis DE (2019) Deconstructing the administrative state. J Polit 81(3):767–789
López J (2006) International labour law and judicialization of legal systems in a multi-level legal context: rethinking immigration, presentation at cornell university, ILR School, International Programs (Oct. 17, 2006)
Loveland I (2009) Constitutional law, administrative law, and human rights: a critical introduction, 5th edn, pp 543–544
Lustig D, Weiler JHH (2018) Judicial review in the contemporary world—retrospective and prospective. Int J Constitutional Law 16(2):315–372
Maarse H (2006) The privatization of health care in Europe: an eight-country analysis. J Health Polit Policy Law 31(5):981–1014
Malleson K (1999) The new judiciary: the effects of expansion and activism 182
Mason C (2013) International growth trends in prison privatization. Sentencing Project, Washington DC
Mautner M (2005) Judicial activism—evaluation. Ali Mishpat Rev 4:7–8

McCoy C (2003) The politics of problem-solving: An overview of the origins and development of therapeutic courts. Am Crim L Rev 40:1513
McKay D (2013) American politics and society (8th ed. 2013)
McLean I (2004) The history of regulation in the United Kingdom: three case studies in search of a theory. In: Jordana J, Levi-Faur D (eds) The politics of regulation: institutions and regulatory reforms for the age of governance. Edward Elgar, Cheltenham
Miller B, Curry B (2009) Expertise, experience, and ideology on specialized courts: the case of the court of appeals for the Federal Circuit. Law Soc Rev 43(4):839–864
Mqingwana B (2012) An analysis of locus standi in public interest litigation with specific reference to environmental law: a comparative study between the law of South Africa and the law of the United States of America. Diss. University of Pretoria
Newfarmer R, Sztajerowska M (2012) Trade and employment in a fast-changing world. Policy Priorities Int Trade Jobs:7–73
Nichol GR (1987) Ripeness and the constitution. Univ Chic Law Rev 54(1):153–183
Papadopoulos G et al (2010) Occupational and public health and safety in a changing work environment: an integrated approach for risk assessment and prevention. Safety Sci 48:943
Perlman C (2009) The new judge? Transformations and challenges in the judicial role at the beginning of the 21st century, in the Light of the ADR (Alternative Dispute Resolution) Movement and the Therapeutic Jurisprudence Movement (Thesis for the Doctor of Philosophy–degree, Bar-Ilan University - Faculty of Law)
Perlman K (2010) The role of the therapeutic judge and his reference to ideas from the school of legal realism. Legal Studies Rev 26:415
Pestoff VA (1992) Third sector and co-operative services—an alternative to privatization. J Consum Policy 15(1):21–45
Peters A (2006) Compensatory constitutionalism: the function and potential of fundamental international norms and structures. Leiden J Int Law 19(3):579–610
Petersen N (2013) Avoiding the common-wisdom fallacy: the role of social sciences in constitutional adjudication. Int J Const Law 11:294
Pildes RH (2001) The structural conception of rights and judicial balancing. Rev Const Stud 6:179
Porat I (2009) Sixty years of balance: on the transition from secondary balance to essential balance in the ruling of the supreme court. Law Bus Rev 10:349
Posner RA (2005) The supreme court: 2004 term—forward: a political court. Harv Law Rev 119: 32–54
Posner RA (2006) see *supra* note 54
Procaccia U (1990) Judgment Bubbles. Laws Rev 9:9–10
Rabinovitch-Eini A (2010) Courts solve problems and the problem of responsibility: lessons from the institutionalization of the mediation procedure. Law Stud Rev 26:51
Ratten V (2020) Coronavirus (covid-19) and entrepreneurship: changing life and work landscape. J Small Bus Entrep 32(5):503–516
Reimann KD (2006) A view from the top: international politics, norms and the worldwide growth of NGOs. Int Stud Q 50:45–67
Resnik J (1982) Managerial judges. Harv Law Rev 96:374
Resnik J (2006) Whither and whether adjudication? Boston Univ Law Rev 86:1101
Rizvi F (2016) Privatization in education: Trends and consequences
Roberts A (2020) Should we defend the administrative state? Public Adm Rev 80(3):391–401
Robinson P (2009) Settlement conference judge—legal lion or problem solving lamb: an empirical documentation of judicial settlement conference practices and techniques. Am J Trial Advoc 33: 113–165
Rodriguez A (May 7 2008) *Hobbled NGOs Wary of Medvedev*, Chi. Trib., http://articles.chicagotribune.com/2008-05-07/news/0805060608
Roitman Y (2017) Administrative law in the era of the regulatory state. Law Government Rev 18: 219
Sauvageau F, Schneiderman D, Taras D (2006) The Last Word 14

Scalise RJ Jr (2013) Rethinking the doctrine of nullity. Louisiana Law Rev 74:663
Scheingold SA (2004) The politics of rights 170–99 (2nd ed.)
Schultz DA (1998) Leveraging the law: using the courts to achieve social change
Schwartz H (2000) The struggle for constitutional justice in post-communist Europe. University of Chicago Press, Chicago
Segev Y (2006) Commentaries on the right of the traditional right of standing, The Advocate Rev
Setzer J, Vanhala LC (2019) Climate change litigation: a review of research on courts and litigants in climate governance. Wiley Interdiscip Rev Clim Chang 10(3):e580
Shapiro M (1986) Courts: a comparative and political analysis 1–64
Shapiro M (1993) The globalization of law. Indiana J Glob Legal Stud 1(1):37–64
Shelton D (1994) The participation of nongovernmental organizations in international judicial proceedings. Am J Int Law 88:611–637
Sieder et al (2005) The judicialization of politics in Latin America
Simlinger F, Mayer B (2019) Legal responses to climate change induced loss and damage: concepts, methods and policy options. In: Mechler, Surminski (eds) Loss and damage from climate change, pp 179–203
Slaughter AM (2000) Judicial globalization. Va J Int Law 40:1103
Smith J, Pagnucco R, with George A. Lopez (1998) Globalizing human rights: the work of transnational human rights NGOs in the 1990s. Human Rights Q 20:379
Stipanowich TJ (2004) ADR and the "vanishing trial": the growth and impact of "alternative dispute resolution.". J Empir Leg Stud 1(3):843–912
Stivers C (2008) The significance of the administrative state. Public Adm Rev 68(1):53–56
Stone Sweet A (2002) Constitutional courts and parliamentary democracy. West Eur Politics 77:95
Stone Sweet A, Brunell TL (1998) Constructing a supranational constitution: dispute resolution and governance in the European Community. Am Policy Sci Rev 92:63
Stone Sweet A, Mathews J (2008) Proportionality balancing and global constitutionalism. Colum J Transnat Law 47:68–149
Strömbäk J, Esser F (2014) Mediatization of politics: towards a theoretical framework. In: Mediatization of politics: understanding the transformation of Western democracies, pp 3–28
Susskind J (2018) Future politics: living together in a world transformed by tech. Oxford University Press, Oxford
Sweet AS (2000) Governing with judges: constitutional politics in Europe
Symposium (1983) The legacy of the new Deal problems and possibilities in the administrative state. Yale Law J 92:1083
Tate CN, Vallinder T (1995) The global expansion of judicial power
Teubner G (1983) Substantive and reflexive elements in modern law. Law Soc Rev 17:239
The Privatization Process: A Worldwide Perspective (Terry L. Anderson & Peter J. Hill eds., 1996)
Thomas CS, Hrebenar RJ (2008) Understanding interest groups, lobbying and lobbyists in developing democracies. J Public Aff Int J 8(1–2):1–14
Tidmarsh J (1992) Unattainable justice: the form of complex litigation and the limits of judicial power. Geo Wash Law Rev 60:1683
Treacy E (2023) The nullity doctrine. Va Law Rev 109(6):1331
Unger RM (1976) Law in modern society: towards a criticism of social theory
van Wolferen M (2016) The limits to the CJEU's interpretation of locus Standi, a theoretical framework. J Contemp Eur Res 12(4):914–930
Volansky A (2010) *Israel, in* international encyclopedia of education 618 (Penelope Peterson et al. gen. eds., 3d ed.)
Wade HWR (1967) Unlawful administrative action—void or voidable. Law Q Rev 83(4):499–526
Wade CP (2013) Clarity in the Court of Appeal: measuring the readability of judgments. *Bachelor thesis, law, University of Otago*
Waldron J (1998) Judicial review and the conditions of democracy. J Political Philos 6:335
Ward I (1995) Law and literature: possibilities and perspectives. Cambridge University Press, Cambridge

Waters M (2001) Globalization (2d ed.)
Webber GCN (2010) Proportionality, balancing, and the cult of constitutional rights scholarship. Can J Law Juris 23(1):179–202
Weiler JHH (2020) The geology of international law-governance, democracy and legitimacy. Rev Derecho del Estado 46:3
Wexler D (2000) Therapeutic jurisprudence: an overview. TM Cooley Law Rev 17:125
Wexler DB (2008) Two decades of therapeutic jurisprudence. Touro Law Rev 24:17
Winick BJ (2002) Therapeutic jurisprudence and problem-solving courts. Fordham Urban Law J 30:1055
Yarrow G (1986) Privatization in theory and practice. Econ Policy 1(2):323–364
Young EA (2002) Judicial activism and conservative politics. Univ Colo Law Rev 73:1139
Zamir Y (2010) The administrative authority, at p. 153–157 (2nd new ed.)

Chapter 9
The Changes in the Judicial System and the "Amicus Phenomenon"

One of the main results of the widespread changes in the work of the courts, which is also in part a cause of them, is that courts worldwide have adopted or included the practice of the "Amicus Curiae." Against the background of the changes that took place in the courts and their causes, it is possible to understand why many judicial systems—in Europe, Asia, Latin America, and Africa; as well as international courts and international arbitration institutions—adopted the "amicus" for the first time and began to use it extensively. Furthermore, other judicial systems worldwide, primarily: the United States, Canada, Australia, and South Africa—have significantly increased the use of Amicus Curiae. The dynamic social and legal reality and the consciousness regarding the role of the courts in society necessitated adjustments in the work of the courts, and the Amicus Curiae practice may help to bridge the gaps developed in these areas for two interrelated reasons, as will be detailed below.

9.1 The Institutional Explanation of the "Amicus Phenomenon"

9.1.1 The Court's Need for Additional Information

Due to the expansion of state and supra-state law and the process of increasing legal complexity, the courts, who are not experts in each new, rapidly developing field, need to be advised by more capable experts in some of the areas of opinion brought to them. The courts do not control all the existing legal subspecialties and, of course, cannot control the ever-increasing numbers of new subspecialities that continually arrive, one step ahead of them. They also often are not knowledgeable in related relevant areas that are not purely legal matters. The expertise of judges, that for which they are appointed to their position, is their specialization in the legal

S. Farber, *The Amicus Curiae Phenomenon*, Ius Gentium: Comparative Perspectives on Law and Justice 119, https://doi.org/10.1007/978-3-031-67225-5_9

profession.[1] They are not sociologists, psychologists, criminologists, economists, environmental and natural science experts, or philosophers. They are jurists appointed to the position of judge. Even the broadest education they have acquired cannot simultaneously provide a deep understanding of many fields.[2]

To fulfill their current judicial role successfully and in order to deal effectively with the diverse and complex content that confronts them, judges need rich and broad information, including, where relevant, access to different points of view. In order to make fully informed decisions, judges will often need information that is not necessarily the property of the formal parties in the discussion. That is to say, they need external information from third parties that is relevant to the specific occurrence that is the subject of the litigation and information that helps formulate the appropriate legal policy.[3] Sometimes, they need information that the formal parties do not wish to present to them because it harms their interests or because they are unable[4] or it is simply not in their interest (such as in cases where third parties who are not parties to the proceedings seek to show how the ruling may affect them, even though they are not a formal part of the proceedings).[5]

The institution of Amicus Curiae plays an important part in supplying expert information. A judicial system that has increased its involvement in the design of society and that deals with new and dynamic areas of law based on additional areas of opinion needs various amici to help it in its role. These amici can be academics,[6] governmental or non-governmental public organizations (such as human rights organizations, quality preservation organizations, and the environment), or members of a profession (such as the Bar Association, the Chamber of Accountants, or the

---

[1] Cheng (2008), p. 519. [Cheng critically examines the idea that judges are capable of handling a wide range of legal issues and argues that specialization is more prevalent and beneficial in judicial decision-making].

[2] See Mouttotos (2020), pp. 99–130; See also Dillon (2018) https://escholarship.org/uc/item/5tj3q025.

[3] Spriggs and Wahlbeck (1997). [The authors conclude that amicus briefs can play an important role in the Supreme Court decision-making process. They argue that amicus briefs can help the Court to make better decisions by providing them with valuable information and by helping them to anticipate the impact of their decisions].

[4] Steger (2002), pp. 419, 447. See also Howse et al. (2013), para. 13 ('The preliminary submissions in this brief are aimed at correcting the misleading and incomplete manner in which Canada has characterized the objectives of the measures at issue in this dispute...').

[5] See Glamis v. USA (19 August 2005), pp. 3–4. The tribe stated that its goal was to ensure that the tribunal would fully take into account the 'sensitive and serious nature of indigenous sacred areas' and that it would address issues such as the value of the area's cultural and environmental resources, the authorization process for the mine, the regulatory framework for mining, as well as the legal framework for the protection of indigenous sacred places under national and international law.

[6] Collins showed that a joint memo of academics has a better chance of being cited in the judgments. For example, in *Regents of the University of California v. Bakke*, 438 U.S. 265 (1978) (affirmative action), Judge Powell relied on the information in a joint brief written by the Harvard, Columbia, Stanford, and Pennsylvania universities deans. See Collins Jr (2004), p. 827. See, for example, Amicus Project Practicum https://www.swlaw.edu/experiential-learning/practicum-programs/amicus-project-practicum.

Chamber of Engineers). The amici assist the courts discussing a long series of social issues and diverse areas of opinion, some of which have not been discussed before, based on varied and new sources. They provide expert information and offer broad or different points of view from those presented by the formal parties. The United States Supreme Court Judge, Stephen Breyer, insisted on this when he called on the American public and various interest groups to submit an Amicus Curiae brief to help the judges in their work:

> [Amicus] briefs play an important role in educating the judges on potentially relevant technical matters, helping to make us not experts, but moderately educated lay persons, and that education helps to improve the quality of our decisions.[7]

Similarly, former Australian Supreme Court Judge, Michael Kirby, pointed out that the work of modern courts entails dealing with social issues and determining social policy, which should consider diverse perspectives and interests other than those of the formal parties. He suggested that the courts would be assisted by amici in accepting all the existing social options and determining the appropriate legal policy. Regarding *the Breckler* case, Kirby said:

> In many proceedings, especially in recent years, [the High] Court has granted leave to governmental and non-governmental organizations to make submissions as *amici curiae* where their interests have suggested a capacity to provide submissions from a specialised viewpoint, an industry perspective or in the public interest.

He added that the social role of the Supreme Court in Australia requires that in the appropriate cases it will assist "amici:"

> Once this Court became the final court of appeal for Australia and recognised that its function involved more than the declaration of indisputable, pre-ordained law, it was necessary to adapt the Court's procedures to permit assistance to be had in some cases from a wider range of interests than those conventionally received.[8]

The former president of the Canadian Supreme Court, Bora Laskin, expressed a similarly positive view about the role of amici in helping the courts through presenting supplemental social information that formal parties did not present. In a long series of judgments that came out under the hand of Judge Laskin, the possibility of third parties presenting their points of view in ongoing proceedings was developed and expanded. Judge Leskin allowed interest groups to join as amici quite liberally when the judgments he wrote institutionalized the participation of third parties in legal proceedings in Canada. They confirmed the assumption that to fulfill their current role successfully, courts need additional types of information

---

[7] Breyer (1998). Justice Breyer repeatedly reiterated this position and emphasized that "amici" help the courts fulfill their current societal role. He emphasized the importance of the public's involvement in social life, though, among other things, appeals to the courts. Breyer (2005, 2015). Justice Breyer also holds the record for citations of "amicus" memos when, between 2014–2015, he cited memos in 63 percent of his judgments. See Franze and Anderson (2015). For examples of "amicus" memos whose influence on the verdict was decisive, see also Ennis (1984).

[8] *A-G (Cth) v Breckler* (1999) 197 CLR 83, [103].

(social, economic, security, environmental), which need to be submitted in "amicus briefs" supplementing the presentations of the formal parties.[9]

The shifts in the work of the courts sharpened their understanding that the information presented to them never presents a complete, consistent, and coherent picture of the situation. Therefore, the courts need different types of information from third parties.[10] The work of the courts has always been based on facts and evidence presented to the courts, which is then considered in judicial deliberations through accepted behavior patterns of the courts. However, aside from all of this, due to the complexity of the law and the expanding occupation of the courts in additional areas of knowledge, the weight of required knowledge has increased, so increasing the necessity of receiving input from third parties with specialized knowledge in all areas of life.[11] From the courts' point of view, the combination of these insights, namely the understanding that the information presented to the courts is incomplete and there is a growing need for knowledge, explains the "amicus phenomenon."

The question of how judges process the information contained in the numerous amici briefs they receive, especially in high-profile cases that may attract dozens of briefs, is an important one. While it is unlikely that the justices themselves read every amicus brief in full, evidence suggests that either the justices, their law clerks, or both, do pay attention to the information contained in at least some of these briefs.[12] According to a survey of state high court justices and clerks, amicus briefs are generally perceived as useful in helping the court sort out policy considerations and

[9]We can assume a connection between the "amicus" phenomenon and the judicial activity of specific judges since the way judicial systems operate is influenced, among other things, by the views and the personal experience of judges serving within these systems. When making a legal decision, the judges have many conflicting legal sources. Therefore, the judge's unique personality and life experience are reflected in judicial decisions. In this way, it is possible to note in particular the contribution of the President of the Supreme Court in the United States, Earl Warren, to the development of the "amicus" institution in the United States, the contribution of Judge Michael Kirby to the development of the "amicus" institution in Australia, the contribution of the President of the Supreme Court, Bora Laskin for the development of the "amicus" institution in Canada, and finally the contribution of the President of the Israeli Supreme Court Aharon Barak to the adoption of the "amicus" in Israel.

[10]Spriggs and Wahlbeck (1997) and Smith et al. (1998).

[11]See also Floridi (2010). In essence, Floridi's position is that the information age has blurred the boundary between man and the information environment, or as he calls it: the infosphere. During the information revolution, man became increasingly dependent on the digital information environment, starting with communication and information (email and search engines) and ending with the needs of business, culture, law, everyday life, and entertainment. As a result, the grip of the infosphere deepened on human life, and his dependence on it increased. As much as he adopted and accepted the information environment as an integral part of his daily life, he also led it to surround and influence his human existence. In this way, the infosphere is perceived as inseparable from human life to the point of creating a symbiotic relationship between the two. For Floridi's approach, the dynamics of information, i.e., the changing nature of information environments and the life cycle of information, is too complex for the existing ethical theories, and it raises the need for a new broad ethical framework that can answer its various aspects. See also his later writing on the matter: Floridi (2013).

[12]Flango et al. (2006), pp. 180–190.

access social science research and data that the parties themselves may not provide. The justices and clerks indicated a desire for better coordination and consolidation of amicus briefs to avoid repetition and focus the information on new, relevant content. This suggests that while not every brief is read in full, court staff make efforts to identify and focus on the most relevant and informative briefs.

Furthermore, research on US Supreme Court clerks demonstrates that the ideological composition of a justice's group of clerks can measurably influence the direction of the justice's votes, likely through clerks discussing cases with their justice and bringing different perspectives and information to the table. Justices have also been shown to directly cite or reference information from amicus briefs in their opinions, indicating that at least some of this information does factor into their decision-making.[13] So while justices may not personally read every brief, information from amici appears to reach the justices through their clerks and to shape judicial choices in measurable ways. The role of clerks in filtering, focusing on, and transmitting key information from amici to their justices helps explain how the court processes the large volume of briefs it receives.

The supplementary and additional information presented by amici helps the courts learn the overall complexity of the issue, together with the broad implications for parties who are not claimants, The amici also help locate a variety of possible solutions to the issue with a forward-looking view. Such complementary and broad information, in particular in areas that judicial systems have not dealt with in the past and do not have sufficient expertise with or understanding of, expands the courts' perspectives so that they learn of factual claims that are unfamiliar to them, social claims from different perspectives or legal claims in principle that help in formulating the appropriate legal policy.

The judges may believe that amici can contribute to the minimization of judicial errors by allowing them to receive extensive social knowledge found by entities not part of the formal judicial process. In this way, the information presented by amici may prevent reliance on limited or exclusive sources of knowledge from those with power and interests.

While the advent of the internet and legal search engines has undoubtedly made it easier for judges and clerks to access a vast array of legal information, the role of amici curiae remains crucial in providing courts with diverse perspectives, specialized knowledge, and real-world insights that are often necessary to fully understand the broader implications of their decisions.

Even with digital legal databases at their disposal, courts still need the unique viewpoints and expertise that amici curiae can offer. These third-party contributions often include scientific or technical expertise, data-driven analyses, or practical insights from industry professionals that may not be readily available through traditional legal research alone. By providing this specialized knowledge and empirical evidence, amicus briefs can offer courts a deeper understanding of the social,

[13] Kromphardt (2015), pp. 277–304. In this matter, see also: Black and Boyd (2012), pp. 147–173; Black et al. (2014), pp. 98, 75.

economic, and policy considerations that are relevant to the case but may fall outside the legal expertise of the court or the strategic interests of the formal parties.

In essence, while legal search engines have revolutionized access to legal information, they cannot replace the valuable role that amici curiae play in supplying courts with the diverse viewpoints, real-world knowledge, and broader implications that are crucial for informed decision-making, particularly in cases with significant societal impact.

As noted, the information presented by amici is unique and utterly different from the information presented to the courts by expert witnesses. That is because while the role of the expert witness is to discuss, under testimony, the meaning of the facts presented to the court from a professional perspective, the role of the amicus is to add a perspective, interest, or expertise that he thinks should be heard before the court.[14]

When the courts are busy shaping the public and private space of the citizen with a forward-looking view and not only in individual conflicts, their awareness of the general implications of their choices on broad populations who are not necessarily represented in court intensifies and increases because almost every decision in a dispute affects or may affect third parties and various interest groups which are not directly part of the formal dispute.

This judicial approach requires openness to receiving different points of view from other parties who are not directly involved in the formal dispute and may be affected by the court's judgments. The "amicus phenomenon" makes it clear that modern law cannot be satisfied with the existing legal tools. Modern courts involved in shaping society need different amici who help them understand not only different types of information not presented by the formal parties but also a variety of potential consequences to their decisions. These consequences include the social (for example, interpersonal relations or the quality of life),[15] political,[16] ecological,[17] security, cultural (such as: changing norms, values, and beliefs that shape the consciousness of the individuals and the society in which they live) and economic (for example, taxation or job security)[18] effects that the judicial decisions have on a broad sphere of influence as well as on the parties involved in a particular dispute.

---

[14] For a detailed account of distinctions between the "amicus" and an expert witness, see Sect. 2.3.

[15] Spriggs and Wahlbeck (1997).

[16] See, for example, Mclauchlan (2005).

[17] See for example: Stoknes, Per Espen. What we think about when we try not to think about global warming: Toward a new psychology of climate action. Chelsea Green Publishing (Stoknes 2015), [explores the psychological barriers that hinder effective climate action and proposes strategies for overcoming them]. See also Berrang-Ford et al. (2011), pp. 25–33 [examines the concept of adaptation to climate change and assesses the extent to which societies are effectively adapting to the challenges posed by a changing climate].

[18] See for example Economics Professors Amicus Brief in Rambus v. FTC. In this case, the Federal Trade Commission (FTC) is challenging Rambus, a technology company, for allegedly engaging in anticompetitive conduct. Amici curiae, a group of economics professors, filed a brief in support of the FTC. The brief argues that Rambus's conduct has harmed competition and consumers, and that the FTC should be allowed to take action to prevent future harm. Source: https://www.ftc.gov/sites/default/files/documents/cases/2004/04/040415scholarsamicusbrief.pdf. See also: Economists

The attention of the courts involved in shaping the state and its societal values is not only directed backward toward the past but also forwards toward the future. Today's focus of the courts on the issues brought before them is more prospective than retrospective, and the amici support this because every decision in a dispute affects, or may affect, third parties who are not directly part of the formal dispute.

This is how Judge Aharon Barak explained it in his book "Judge in a Democratic Society," describing the court's current role and the desired attitude to the Amicus Curiae practice. Barak insisted that the court wants to know "what happened" in the specific case and "what will happen," for example, whether the law will be changed or the court will accept or reject a particular petition. He noted that-

> For this purpose, he must receive information about the considerations of legal policy that lie at the foundation of the old and new law. He must accept "legislative" and "social" facts... He requests that a factual foundation be laid before him, allowing him to make a rational decision on the various social options presented to him.[19]

The practice of Amicus Curiae fulfills this function. Against the background of the deep involvement of the courts in society, amici help the courts to understand the social, political, ecological, and economic consequences that a judicial decision between two parties has in a broader circle of individuals, various interest groups, and on the public.

The formal content of Amicus Curiae briefs is not limited to information about the broad implications of the court's ruling. An emphasis is also placed on the actual submission of the brief and the interest groups behind the submission. Since judges also tend to consider public opinion (especially in cases with public resonance, but not only), they treat the Amicus Curiae brief that is presented to them as a kind of "barometer" that helps them understand the expected consequences of their decision.[20] Through the briefs of amici, the judges "feel" the public pulse because the amici reflect a more comprehensive range of opinions than those presented by the formal parties.[21]

Here are some examples that may illustrate what is stated above. In a matter that dealt with the conservation of deserts in Tasmania, the Tasmanian government supported the construction of an electric dam in its state. In contrast, the Australian government opposed it for reasons of land conservation. The Supreme Court of Australia allowed various amici to discuss the broad implications of the

---

Amicus Brief in Dobbs v. Jackson Women's Health Organization. This brief was filed by over 150 economists and researchers in support of abortion rights. The brief argues that overturning Roe would have a negative impact on women's economic security, education, and health. The brief also argues that overturning Roe would disproportionately harm low-income women and women of color. Source: https://reproductiverights.org/economists-amicus-brief-in-dobbs-v-jackson-womens-health/.

[19] Barak (2004). Aharon Barak expanded on some of these things in his book Barak (2009). Barak relies, among other things, on the approach of the former president of the Supreme Court of Canada, Antonio Lamer, to the role of the "amicus." Lamer (1994).

[20] Garcia (2008).

[21] Salzman et al. (2011); Collins Jr (2004), pp. 807–832. Collins Jr (2018), pp. 219–237.

issue due to awareness of the issue's ecological, economic, and political implications.[22] Another example: In the case of *Quinn's Supermarket*, the Supreme Court of Ireland invited the Chief Rabbi of Ireland as an Amicus Curiae to receive a religious review of the matter and to learn the expected consequences of the judgment for the Orthodox Jews in Ireland.[23]

Another example concerns the Earth Law Center Organization (ELC), which deals with transforming the law to recognize, honor, and protect nature's inherent rights to exist, thrive, and evolve. The organization submits dozens of amicus briefs to various courts worldwide to defend environmental rights. Since 2018, ELC has innovated a program to submit amicus briefs to protect the Rights of Nature and human environmental rights worldwide, focusing on Latin America. The Earth Law Center joined an amicus brief in Washington State supporting youth plaintiffs' challenges to state policies causing and contributing to climate change.[24] Similarly, amicus briefs were filed to the Constitutional Court of Ecuador at Mining concessions within a biodiverse and protected Andean cloud forest.[25] In another example, the Earth Law Center filed an amicus brief in the District Court, State of Oaxaca, Mexico, regarding Extreme pollution in two rivers.[26]

Additional examples that express the growing awareness of the courts of the overall consequences of their choices and the use of the practice of Amicus Curiae as a response to this need can be found in recent decades in many other judicial systems around the world. This is seen in the common law countries,[27] in the European Court of Human Rights,[28] in the Court of Human Rights of Latin America,[29] in international arbitration proceedings and in particular in the World Trade Organization[30] and the International Criminal Court,[31] and state courts in Latin America (Argentina,

---

[22] *Commonwealth v Tasmania* (1983) 158 CLR 1, p. 50–51.

[23] Quinn's Supermarket Ltd. v. Att'y Gen. [1972] IR 1, 16.

[24] Aji P. et al. v. State of Washington, (No. 99564-8). the Center for Environmental Law & Policy led the amicus brief.

[25] Constitutional Court of Ecuador Case No. 1149-19-JP.

[26] TRIBUNAL COLEGIADO DEL CENTRO AUXILIAR DE LA SÉPTIMA REGIÓN EN ACAPULCO, GUERRERO. The organization submitted briefs to courts in many countries in Latin America: Mexico, Ecuador, Argentina, and Colombia.

[27] *Reference re Secession of Quebec* [1998] 2 S.C.R. 217. *Hoffmann v. S. Afr. Airways* 2001 (1) SA 1 (CC) (South Africa); *Zaoui v. Superintendent, Auckland Central Remand Prison* [2004] NZSC 22. (New Zealand); YL v. Birmingham City Council [2007] UKHL 27, [2008] 1 AC 95 (England); *Project Blue Sky v. Austl Broad Auth* (1998) 194 CLR 355 (Australia); S v. Zemburuka (1) 2003 NR 112 (HC) (Namibia).

[28] Chahal v. United Kingdom, 1996-V Eur. Ct. H.R. 1831, for example, Amnesty International, Aire Centre, Liberty Justice.

[29] Pinto (2005), pp. 55–56.

[30] U.S.—Imposition of Countervailing Duties on Certain Hot-Rolled Lead & Bismuth Carbon Steel Prods. Originating in the U.K., Appellate Body Report, WTO Doc. WT/DS138/AB/R (May 10, 2000); Eur. Cmtys.—Measures Affecting Asbestos and Asbestos-Containing Prods., 40 I.L.M. 1193 (WTO Appellate Body 2001).

[31] Shelton (1994).

Brazil, Colombia, and Ecuador).[32] The words of the dispute settlement body of the NAFTA organization regarding the *Methanex* case sum up this issue nicely:

> There is undoubtedly public interest in this arbitration. The substantive issues extend far beyond those raised by the usual transnational arbitration between commercial parties... The public interest in this arbitration arises from its subject-matter...[33]

9.1.1.1 Brandeis Brief

The increase in the use of Amicus Curiae is related to the openness of the courts to the various types of information they are willing and interested in receiving from parties to litigation or from third parties. The jurist and judge Louis Brandeis was the pioneering jurist who first used social facts (rather than "classical" legal claims as was customary at the time) to persuade the court.[34]

In the precedent case *Muller v. Oregon* from 1908, the lawyer Brandeis used studies from the field of social science to prove that women's strenuous work harmed their health.[35] He submitted to the court a document which covered sociological information that supported his claim that labor laws should be adapted for working women.[36] The court accepted the brief presented to it by Brandeis, noted that the social information presented to it significantly updated the court, and emphasized that the information presented to it raised -

> A widespread belief that a woman's physical structure and the functions she performs in consequence justifies special legislation.[37]

The "Brandeis Brief," as it was later called, or "the brief authored by Brandeis," was a precedent example, which in the following years and even more so nowadays, became extremely popular in many judicial systems around the world for the use of

---

[32] Bazán (2009), pp. 310, 310–312. Bazán examines the history and evolution of Amicus Curiae in different legal systems and analyzes its role in promoting transparency and accountability in the judicial process.

[33] Methanex Corp. v. United States, Decision on Petitions from Third Persons to Intervene as "Amici Curiae" (NAFTA Arb. Jan. 15, 2001), par. 49. Contrary to the "amicus" request in the case, the tribunal determined that the public interest could be fulfilled by submitting a written brief and that there was no need for the "amici" to argue orally.

[34] For more on the character of Brandeis, see Urofsky (2009) and Rosen (2016).

[35] Muller v. Oregon 208 U.S. 412 (1908). The brief was compiled with his sister-in-law, a researcher of labor law in the United States and head of the National Consumers League in the United States, lawyer Josephine Clara Goldmark.

[36] For a feminist reading of this judgment, see Becker (1986). [The article also analyzes the evolution of laws related to women's reproductive rights, from the landmark case Muller v. Oregon to the emergence of fetal vulnerability policies].

[37] Ibid. For a description of Brandeis' activity in court, see Klebanow and Jonas (2003). Brandeis argued that public service and political commitment are central components of the lawyers' identity.

knowledge from the field of social sciences and the humanities through the submission of an amicus brief on sensitive, new or precedent issues.[38]

One of the famous cases in which this technique was used is *Brown v. Board of Education*, where the United States Supreme Court's decision was based on an amicus brief which presented psychological and sociological information that proved that racial segregation instilled a sense of social inferiority among non-white citizens.[39] Similarly, many precedential judgments in American history and worldwide were based on social information presented to the courts by amici.[40] In precedent cases in the history of the United States, the social information presented in the amicus briefs served as a significant, and sometimes the only, factor in the court's decision-making processes.

This was the case in judgments that dealt, for example, with possibly limiting the right to perform abortions,[41] the right to die,[42] freedom of speech,[43] gay and lesbian rights,[44] and mandatory health insurance reform.[45] It was also the case in judgements dealing with a long list of other issues, including: same-sex marriage,[46] climate

[38] Johnson (2005). For the dangers of using these types of information, see Rustad and Koenig (1993), pp. 91, 157–58.

[39] Brown v. Bd. of Educ., 347 U.S. 483 (1954). In total, the American Civil Rights Association submitted six "amici" memoranda in this case. As detailed in the chapter on the United States, the use of "amicus" in the United States started early compared to other countries in the Anglo-Saxon system. The "amicus" was recognized in the United States as early as 1823. However, until the 1970s, its use was relatively few (less than 10%), while starting from the 1970s, there was an increase in the use of "amicus." However, even though the judgment was considered revolutionary, Gerald Rosenberg showed, from a constitutional point of view, that it did not cause a significant social change in the southern countries but only after the enactment of the civil rights law. Rosenberg (2008).

[40] Spriggs and Wahlbeck (1997), p. 372. Similar memos were also submitted in Browder v. Gayle, 142 F. Supp. 707 (M.D. Ala. 1956), which was issued against the background of the Montgomery bus boycott and the conviction of Rosa Parks for refusing to give up her seat on the bus to a white person, and in Loving v. Virginia, 388 U.S. 1 (1967), In which the Supreme Court struck down a Virginia state law that prohibited interracial marriage.

[41] Webster v. Reproductive Health Services, 74 Judicature 261, 262

In this petition that dealt with the constitutionality of reducing the possibility of performing abortions, more than 80 "amicus" briefs were attached, representing more than 420 different organizations on both sides of the issue. The court accepted all 80 briefs submitted to it (except one) and, in its precedential decision, cited from 12 briefs submitted to it. The Webster case is one of the high points of the participation of non-governmental public organizations in the decision-making process of the Supreme Court, and it raised questions among various public organizations related to litigation tactics. Kolbert (1989), p. 262.

[42] Cruzan v. Dir., Mo. Dep't of Health, 497 U.S. 261 (1990).

[43] Pac. Gas & Elec. Co. v. Pub. Utils. Comm'n of Cal., 475 U.S. 1 (1986).

[44] Romer v. Evans, 517 U.S. 620 (1996).

[45] Nat'l Fed'n of Indep. Bus. v. Sebelius, 132 S. Ct. 2566 (2012).

[46] Obergefell v. Hodges, 576 U.S. 644 (2015).

change,[47] election propaganda,[48] the right to bear arms,[49] protection against discrimination because of sexual or gender identity,[50] or the right to receiving an artificial abortion.[51] Although formally, the amici are seemingly secondary players to the original litigants, in practice, the power they hold and the influence they bring to bear on the decision-making processes of the courts are highly significant.

The institutional explanation also offers insights into the rapid development of the "amicus phenomenon" in international courts in recent years. As mentioned above, starting in the 1990s, various international organizations were allowed, for the first time, and contrary to decades of judicial tradition, to intervene as amici in the proceedings conducted in various international courts. This was the case in a long line of precedent and founding judgments of international courts and institutions, and in particular in the European Court of Human Rights. Examples of issues covered in these judgements include: in illegal wiretapping, in defining the limits of freedom of expression, in prisoner's rights, in extradition laws, in immigration laws and the violation of religious sentiments.[52] This was also the case with the unique international criminal tribunals established to investigate the crimes committed in Yugoslavia, Rwanda, and Sierra Leone.[53] Also, international courts need to receive social, legal, or comparative information that the formal parties do not provide due to incapacity, lack of relevance to the matter, or fear of harming their interests.[54]

While on the one hand, the courts need amici who supply them with additional information from diverse perspectives, various amici also have their own agendas. The courts are thus not the only beneficiaries of the amicus briefs. Amici coming mainly from various international NGOs (such as Amnesty, Greenpeace, International Federation for Human Rights, ActionAid, Human Rights Watch, Doctors Without Borders, and thousands of other international organizations) use the process of supplying amicus briefs to gain publicity and influence international public policy

---

[47] Massachusetts v. Environmental Protection Agency, 549 U.S. 497 (2007).

[48] Citizens United v. FEC, 588 U.S. 310 (2010).

[49] District of Columbia v. Heller, 554 U.S. 570 (2008). New York State Rifle & Pistol Association Inc. v. Bruen, 141 S. Ct. 2304 (2022).

[50] Bostock v. Clayton County, 590 U.S. (2020).

[51] Thomas E. Dobbs, State Health Officer of the Mississippi Department of Health, et al. v. Jackson Women's Health Organization, et al. 2022.

[52] Laura Van den Eynde (2103); Soering v. United Kingdom, 161 Eur. Ct. H.R. (ser. A) (1989).

[53] Gómez (2012).

[54] To complete the picture, it should be noted that the practice of using "amicus" in international criminal law is not without criticism. First, it is argued that receiving briefs from "amici" harms the defendant's interest in the fairness of the criminal procedure. This approach becomes valid if the "amici" wish to support the prosecution's position, which is seen as having excess power over the defense. Second, the international criminal courts did not explicitly define the role of the "amicus." In three different international criminal tribunals, the "amicus" served in several different positions, and it is not clear what the role of the "amicus" is in these institutions. Razzaque (2001), pp. 169–200.

in accordance with their own perspectives. In doing this, they also provide essential information—a review of comparative law, security, political, environmental, historical, economic, and demographic reviews of what is happening in conflict zones to various courts.

Sometimes, amici may ask to present "social facts" or alternative facts to the courts that were not presented by the official claimants and that were not available to the court because they did not appear in the pleadings of the authorized parties.[55] In other cases, they ask to present authentic documentation of the victims' or potential victims' testimonies (for example, how establishing a factory in a particular area will lead to the contamination of water sources hundreds of kilometers away from the factory area).

In these diverse ways, the amici help the courts to fulfill their role (i.e., to reach a correct and just legal decision). However, this help also earns the amici certain gains, as they try to influence the courts to accept their point of view and unique perspectives. This is a tango dance. In other words, the court's need for complete and detailed knowledge about the particular issue also requires additional and different perspectives and positions. This distillation is an opening for third parties to influence the court decision-making processes through their roles as amici.[56]

The "amicus phenomenon" that is now gaining momentum in the countries of continental law, particularly in Latin America, also illustrates the growing awareness of the courts of the consequences of their judgments on audiences who are not directly involved in the proceedings.[57] As discussed in detail above, in France, in contrast with their a judicial tradition that recognized the amicus practice but did not adopt it,[58] the French Supreme Court has, in recent years, received dozens of amici briefs that presented the overall social implications of many issues in particular cases. These issues have wide ranging implications for various groups when dealing with matters such as surrogacy agreements, compensation for AIDS patients, euthanasia, prosecution for killing a fetus, in characterizing investments of life insurance policies, and other issues.[59] This is also the case in most Latin American and

---

[55] See, for example, Amicus Curiae brief of the Law Society of England and Wales in the case R (on the application of Miller) v. Secretary of State for Exiting the European Union (2017) [UK]. Amicus Curiae brief of the People's Union for Civil Liberties in the case Suresh Kumar Koushal v. Naz Foundation (2009) [India]. Amicus Curiae brief of the Federal Public Defender's Office in the case Ação Direta de Inconstitucionalidade 4.357 (2012) [Brazil]. Amicus Curiae brief of the Legal Resources Centre in the case Minister of Health v. Treatment Action Campaign (2002) [South Africa].

[56] For a description of different types of appearances by "amici" in international criminal courts, see Williams and Woolaver (2006) [The author called the tribunals to be more open to accepting amicus briefs, and on amici curiae to file briefs that are well-informed and helpful to the tribunals].

[57] See Kochevar (2013).

[58] As detailed above, see the detailed discussion in Sect. 7.2.2.

[59] Cour de cassation ass. plén (1991), Bull ass. plén. No. 4. For expansion, see Duncan (1994), p. 450.; Coslin and Lapillonne (2012).

European countries.[60] However, this legal development is relatively surprising since, as mentioned above, continental law provides its judges procedural tools that fulfill, to a certain extent, the role of the amicus and seemingly eliminates the necessity of the procedures of submitting amicus briefs in this legal system.[61]

The adoption of Amicus Curiae in Continental law countries and its increasing use in European and Latin American courts demonstrates that the existing legal procedures are insufficient. This indicates that additional tools are needed to enable the judicial role of fully understanding the interests and desires of third parties to an acceptable level. The complex legal reality and the deep involvement of the courts in shaping society means that even courts that operated in the past without "amici" now need them to present them with the general implications of court rulings on affected groups and are interested in learning more details from third parties with appropriate knowledge and additional points of view.

Generally, the 1980s and 1990s, and perhaps even earlier,[62] were a turning point in the functioning of many courts worldwide and their social involvement.[63] These were significant changes in their scope and in the content they dealt with related to deep processes that took place in those years in society, economy, and politics. At the basis of these changes in the courts' functioning was the courts' awareness of their roles as public policy designers and the perception that the courts must play a central role in creating applicable law in the country. As a result of this new dominance in society, the style of judgments changed, and the sources of law varied.[64] In addition, judgments began to be decided based on information and

[60] See for example Argentina: Amicus Curiae brief of the Center for Legal and Social Studies in the case of Mendoza v. Argentina (2006). Brazil—Amicus Curiae brief of the Federal Public Defender's Office in the case of Ação Direta de Inconstitucionalidade 4.277 (2012). Colombia—Amicus Curiae brief of the Colombian Constitutional Court in the case of Sentencia C-228/15 (2015). Mexico—Amicus Curiae brief of the National Human Rights Commission in the case of Amparo en revisi6n 101/2011 (2012).

[61] Langbein (1985) and David and Brierley (1978).

[62] See Cappelletti (1971) who described the global trends in the 1970s.

[63] Some have labeled this dominance "judicial activism." Judicial activism is a term that began to take shape in the literature dealing with the judgment of the American Supreme Court. This term has diverse definitions, and many researchers have given it a different meaning. One of the accepted approaches to this term is the approach of Canon (1982) Who set six parameters for the examination of judicial activism in the field of public law: the extent to which the court is willing to cancel policy lines established in democratic procedures; the degree of change in the existing law; the extent to which the judge interprets a text contrary to the intention of its creator or its clear language; The extent to which the court determines the policy, and is not reduced to maintaining the democratic process; The extent to which the court determines the policy itself, or leaves its determination to the government or an individual; and the extent to which the judicial decision replaces the considerations of other authorities in the same matter. For this matter, see also: Kmiec (2004). Young (2002) [the article also concludes that the concept of judicial activism is often used as a political tool rather than a legal principle].

[64] See in general—Holland (1991).

doctrines from extra-legal fields of opinion, such as sociology,[65] geography,[66] economics,[67] philosophy,[68] communication,[69] criminology,[70] and psychology.[71]

Giving amici the opportunity to present their point of view by submitting a brief fits well with the change in the perception of the role of the courts. The courts are not experts and are not expected to be experts in various fields. Therefore, the courts in the modern and complex world need different amici who will present external information that is not only relevant to the specific case but information that will help to formulate legal policy on the matter. Since the courts have increased their involvement in shaping society, they need amici to assist them in decision-making by presenting different or broader perspectives than those presented by the formal

[65] For example, In the case of Atala Riffo et al. v Chile (2012), a group of sociologists filed an Amicus Curiae brief arguing that the Chilean government's ban on same-sex marriage was discriminatory and violated the rights of same-sex couples. The brief cited research showing that same-sex couples are just as capable of forming stable and loving relationships as opposite-sex couples and that same-sex marriage has a positive impact on the well-being of same-sex couples and their children.

[66] For example, in 2016, the European Court of Justice (ECJ) heard a case concerning the definition of "geographical indications" for food products. The ECJ invited a number of amici curiae to submit briefs on the case, including the International Association of Agricultural Economists (IAAE), the International Geographical Union (IGU), and the World Trade Organization (WTO). These amici curiae briefs provided the ECJ with information on the economic and social importance of geographical indications, as well as on the legal principles governing their protection.

[67] For example, Amicus Brief of the European Commission in Support of Respondents in the case of C-441/14, Associação Nacional de Empresas Chinesas v. Autoridade Tributária e Aduaneira. This brief was submitted to the Court of Justice of the European Union (CJEU) in a case concerning the application of EU law on state aid to Chinese companies. The European Commission argued that the measures at issue in the case constituted illegal state aid and should be prohibited.

[68] See the case of Obergefell v. Hodges (2015), the American Philosophical Association filed an Amicus Curiae brief arguing that the right to same-sex marriage is a fundamental right protected by the Constitution. The brief cited philosophical arguments about the nature of marriage and the right to equal protection.

[69] In 2017, the European Court of Justice (ECJ) heard a case about the right to be forgotten. The case was brought by a Spanish man who wanted Google to remove links to a news article about a property auction that he had defaulted on. A number of organizations, including the European Publishers Council (EPC), submitted amicus briefs to the court arguing that the right to be forgotten would have a chilling effect on freedom of expression.

[70] For example, in 2020, the Supreme Court of India heard a case about the constitutionality of the death penalty. The case was brought by a man who had been sentenced to death for murder. A number of organizations, including the National Law University Delhi (NLU Delhi), submitted amicus briefs to the court arguing that the death penalty is cruel, inhuman, and degrading punishment and that its use violates the Constitution of India.

[71] See for example Atkins v. Virginia. Amicus Brief: A brief of the American Psychological Association, American Psychiatric Association, and National Alliance on Mental Illness as Amici Curiae in Support of the Petitioner (https://www.apa.org/about/offices/ogc/amicus/atkins-virginia.pdf). See also: Fisher v. University of Texas at Austin (2013). Amicus Brief: Brief of the American Educational Research Association, American Psychological Association, and National Association of School Psychologists as Amici Curiae in Support of Respondents (https://www.apa.org/about/offices/ogc/amicus/fisher-university-texas.pdf).

parties. The role of the amici, according to the former President of the Supreme Court of Israel, Prof. Aharon Barak, is to "assist the court in formulating positions and rulings that faithfully reflect the variety of situations and problems in the particular issue that arose."[72]

Throughout the developments described here, we have seen that the "Amicus Curiae phenomenon" is a consequence of the perception of the role of the courts in which they not only influence public policy but are also well aware of the effects of their judgments and understand how their rulings will affect society, the economy, and the public. The social, political, and economic processes that took place in the last decades (as described above) resulted in the courts needing third parties to help them understand the overall consequences that each judicial decision has in a broader circle of individuals. The courts became more interested in the question "what will happen" if the law is changed or if they will accept or reject a particular petition. Therefore, they more and more frequently have asked to receive information about the considerations of the legal policy that lay at the foundation of the law, requesting that a broad factual infrastructure be placed before them, allowing them to make a rational decision on the various social options presented to them.[73]

9.1.1.2 Intra-State Institutional Factors

The desire of the courts to use amici to obtain complementary knowledge and broad general implications is also related to the wave of "constitutional revolutions" that have occurred in recent decades around the world, which increased the involvement of the courts in society and as a result, increased the need for the involvement of amici. As discussed above, in the 1980s and 1990s, drafting new constitutions boomed among post-authoritarian (authoritarian) countries that, included 85 constitutions introduced between 1989 and 1999.[74]

The series of political and constitutional processes underway in various countries around the world significantly deepened the court's power and its involvement in society in these countries. Some of these countries, like Spain, Portugal, and Greece,

---

[72] The State of Israel vs. Kozali 19.10.1985, 349/84 at p. 554.

[73] For example, in *Koffman* Case, 3471/07 Tel Aviv, (published in Nevo 12.3.2007) the District Court in Israel accepted the request to join the Association of Journalists as an "amicus" in a case that had a vast impact on the press institution and stated that: the applicant united among its ranks 1300 journalists who naturally have an interest in the results of the proceedings, because of its effect on the extent of the copyrights they have in their works. Moreover, this is a precedent decision with far-reaching implications. Since this is not a routine issue, it is precisely in this kind of procedure that it is essential to receive the position of entities such as the applicant who has the power to assist the court in clarifying the disputes and illuminate the issue from another angle. See also Obergefell v. Hodges, 576 U.S. 644. (2015)., in which state restrictions on same-sex marriage were found unconstitutional by the Supreme Court.

[74] Derbyshire and Derbyshire (1996).

went from dictatorial regimes to democratic government systems.[75] The fall of the Berlin Wall in 1989 and the transition to democracy led to the adoption of new constitutions and the establishment of "functioning" and strong courts (relatively speaking, compared to the period before it) in the countries that belonged to the Soviet bloc: Poland, Slovakia, the Czech Republic, Lithuania, Estonia, Bulgaria, and Romania.[76] Similarly, significant constitutional and legal processes that expanded the powers of the courts took place in various parts of Asia, Indonesia, Thailand, South Korea, Taiwan, and Mongolia from the mid-1980s onwards.[77]

For example, a significant landmark in Canada's "Amicus Curiae phenomenon" lies in adopting the Bill of Rights in 1983. The adoption of the Charter marked a change in the Canadian constitutional concept. It resulted in an increased preoccupation by the Canadian courts with the interpretation of the Constitution and Human Rights.[78] Following the Bill of Rights adoption, the Canadian Supreme Court began to be directly involved in shaping the society since it was also authorized to declare legislation as void if it did not conform to the principles outlined in the Charter. The new starting point of the courts in Canada assumed that the new judicial role of the courts would require them to receive more extensive information about the social effects of the court judgments, information that is not necessarily in the possession of judges, necessitating help from amici.[79] Indeed, studies show that in the years following the enactment of the Canadian Charter, third parties, mainly various NGOs, "shifted" their attention from the political arena to the legal arena by joining trial proceedings as intervenors or as amici. This is thanks to the adoption of liberal rules by the courts, which were often introduced thanks to pressure brought by these amici.[80]

Similarly, a constitutional process that affected the "Amicus Curiae phenomenon" in England was adopting the Human Rights Act of England in 1998.[81] Despite England being a nation with a long tradition of protecting human rights, it does not have a written constitution that protects these rights. The English Human Rights Act annexed lengthy sections of the European Convention on Human Rights into state

[75] Ackerman (1997), pp. 778–779.

[76] Holmes and Sunstein (1995), pp. 275–306 [The authors provide 1 case studies of constitutional revision in Eastern Europe. They argue that constitutional revision is a highly political process that involves a range of actors, including politicians, judges, interest groups, and ordinary citizens].

[77] The Judicialization of Politics in Asia Björn Dressel (2012); Dressel (2014), pp. 259–278. See also: Dressel and Mietzner (2012), pp. 391–414.

[78] Canadian Charter of Rights and Freedoms, Part I of the Constitution Act, 1982, *being* Schedule B to the Canada Act, c 11 (U.K.). In addition, in 1988, following the recommendations of parliamentary committees, Canada adopted a law anchoring its commitment to multiculturalism: Canadian Multiculturalism Act, R.S.C., 1985, c 24 (fourth Supp.). During the 1990s, most of the provinces in Canada adopted legislation in this vein, for example: The Manitoba Multiculturalism Act, C.C.S. M., c M223.

[79] Brodie (1992).

[80] Ibid; Nevitte (1996) and Choudhry and Hunter (2003).

[81] Clayton et al. (2000) and Dickson (2013).

legislation and, to a large extent, reshaped the relationship between citizens and government systems.[82] The law includes, for example, the right to life, the right to a fair trial, the prohibition of torture, the right to privacy, freedom of thought, conscience, and religion, freedom of expression, freedom of association, and the right to marry.[83]

The Human Rights Act led to a considerable increase in the courts' involvement in English society and its influence on citizens' lives. With the law's adoption, the courts increasingly dealt with public and social policy. Therefore, they needed to accept the general implications and social information presented to them by various amici.[84]

A constitutional process that contributed to the growth of the "Amicus Curiae phenomenon" in South Africa was the adoption of the Constitution in 1996. The enactment of the Constitution and the establishment of the Constitutional Court changed the perception of the judiciary's role and its involvement in South African society, as occurred in other countries undergoing changes in their constitution or adopting a constitution for the first time. As a result, as with the other countries already mentioned, amici began to be involved in ongoing proceedings. The South African Constitution was adopted as an antithesis to the apartheid-era Constitution, which was unusually restrictive for a country that pretended to be a democracy. Unlike other constitutions, the South African Constitution explicitly enshrines social and economic rights such as the right to housing, the right to health, the right to food, the right to water, the right to social security, and the right to education. The Constitution of South Africa states, for example, that if an unjustified

[82]Human Rights Act 1998, c. 42. It seems that this change is the most significant in British constitutional law since the Bill of Rights was issued in 1688 (Bill of Rights 1688, 1 W. & M. Sess. 2, c. 2).

[83]The law does not authorize the courts to invalidate a law of the Parliament. However, at the same time, the law gives the courts new powers that allow them to determine that a particular law is inconsistent with the European Convention. The law authorizes the courts to examine whether a particular law is compatible with the rights outlined in the convention and to declare "incompatibility" if such is found ("declaration of incompatibility"). In such a case, the judges may recommend that the Parliament reconsider the impugned law. Following the political norms used in Great Britain, such a recommendation is seen as binding and results in a law change by the Parliament.

[84]The Lord Chancellor described it well when he pointed out that in light of the Human Rights Act, the "amicus" must be adopted in the rules of the English judicial system: "So it appears to me, as at present advised... that our courts will be ready to permit amicus written briefs from non-governmental organisations; that is to say briefs, but not to treat them as full parties." 24 Nov. 1997, Parl Deb HL (2007) col. 833 (Lord Irvine). The public criticism was not long in coming: It was claimed that the judges had become part of the political arena even though they were not elected to do so. It is further argued that court judges have become policymakers even though they do not pass judgment on their actions, unlike the politicians elected by the public. King (2001) pp. 54–55, 59–61, 71–73, 95–96.

violation of a right is found, the element of the violation, the whole or part of the law, will be considered null and void.[85]

As happened in Canada and England after the adoption of the constitution, and since the courts began to influence public policy to a larger extent, there has been a significant increase in the rate of individuals and interest groups joining the courts, in particular the Constitutional Court, as amici who sought to influence the decision-making processes of the courts by presenting their positions.[86]

Constitutional processes that led to a significant increase in the "Amicus Curiae phenomenon" took place not only in England, South Africa, and Canada but also in other countries such as Ireland,[87] Hong Kong,[88] Namibia,[89] India,[90] New Zealand,[91] and other European countries (Malta, Czech Republic, Sweden, Netherlands, Poland, Belgium)[92] and Latin America.[93] In these countries, internal constitutional changes also resulted in the judicial systems becoming more involved in determining the values in society and, correspondingly, resulted in the courts' focus becoming more prospective than retrospective.

---

[85] du Plessis (1999) [The article evaluates the approach of the South African Constitutional Court to constitutional interpretation].

[86] The process of accepting the constitution was also accompanied by a broad media review which intensified the public's involvement. The South African Constituent Assembly deliberations were broadcast live, and the public listened to these broadcasts. In addition, the text of the proposed constitution was distributed to the public. It made accessible the possibility of the "small" citizen and interest groups to join constitutional procedures conducted as "amici."

[87] O'Brien (2004).

[88] These processes include for example the enactment of the Hong Kong Bill of Rights Ordinance, (1991) Cap. 383, the Hong Kong residency debate, the enactment of China's national security law in Hong Kong, the outlawing of human rights organizations in Hong Kong. Murray (1994), p. 244.

[89] Namibia gained its independence from South Africa in 1990. The Namibian Constitution (Namib. Const.) is a modern constitution that was given after gaining independence and it grants a broad set of individual rights. The first case in which the joining of "amici" is discussed is *Zemburuka* Case, S v. Zemburuka (1) 2003 NR 112 (HC) (Namibia), that discussed a constitutional question about the powers of the general prosecution. The Supreme Court was aware of this issue's political and social implications and therefore summoned as "amici" the President of the State, the Attorney General, and the Acting Deputy Attorney General. The court emphasized that this summons was made by the inherent authority of the court and stated at p. 117 that it "Frequently invites or appoints counsel as *Amicus Curiae* to represent an undefended appellant despite the absence of statutory authority to do so." Hinson and Hubbard (2012).

[90] Such as democratization processes, the fight against corruption, or the integration of women in politics. Sundaram vs Unknown on 15 December 2000. See also Supreme Court Rules, 2013, Gazette of India: Extraordinary, Order IV para. 1(a) (May 29, 2014).

[91] Such as the adoption of the Charter of Human Rights in 1990, the establishment of the Supreme Court in 2004, and the taking of powers from the Queen's Council (Privy Council of the United Kingdom). Clark (2005). *Beneficial Owners of Whangaruru Whakaturia No. 4 v. Warin* [2009].

[92] See the footnotes of the discussion in the previous chapter about European countries.

[93] See, see footnote 1154; Malloy (1976), Sieder et al. (2005).

9.1.2 The Amici As a Social "Barometer"

Another institutional explanation for the increase in the "Amicus Curiae phenomenon" is not necessarily related to the content of the information transmitted to the courts but to the social role that the amici play. In addition to the various types of information that are transmitted to the courts through "amici" (legal, social, historical, theological, literary, factual, or technical information) and information that presents broad implications of a particular case, the brief from "amici" constitute for some judges a kind of a "social barometer" for the public's position on that case.[94] Kearney and Merrill (2000) argued, for example, that it is possible that the role of amici is not limited to presenting information but that the presence of the amici, as incorporated interest groups, creates pressure on the judges to accept the position that the interest group advances.[95]

This approach of "broadcasting" and conveying messages to the court on the part of interest groups about the desired result assumes that judges tend not to stray too far from the public consensus, that they are attentive to the public's positions, as mentioned above, and that they give considerable importance to the positions of interest groups, especially if they are highly influential interest groups.[96] In other words, the information about the broad implications of the court's judgment is more comprehensive than just the formal content of the brief. The emphasis is placed on the identity and influence of the interest groups behind the submission.

As a rule, courts act according to the accepted narratives and according to the state ideology that shapes the boundaries to their activities. In addition, the courts must consider institutional constraints, which arise from possible modes of response of bodies such as the government, the legislative authority, the public, or the security forces. Since in certain matters, especially if they are issues with a significant public dimension, judges tend to consider public opinion more than in ordinary disputes. They then may look at the amicus briefs that are presented to them as social "barometers" that help them better understand the expected consequences of their decision. This is because the amicus briefs reflect a more comprehensive range of opinions than those presented by the formal parties.[97]

Empirical studies show that some judges do not carefully read the briefs presented to them (often due to the enormous length of a brief that may contain a total of

[94] Collins Jr (2004), pp. 814–815. Many studies emphasize that a dominant component in these processes originates from "responsiveness to social demand," which increased in part due to the efforts of interest groups to achieve through the courts what is impossible to achieve in the legislative and executive authorities. See, for example also, in Zannoti (1995) and Hirschl (2006).

[95] Kearney and Merrill (2000), p. 785 ("Affected Groups Hypothesis"). See also: The 15 Biggest NGOs in the World, located in https://www.humanrightscareers.com/issues/biggest-ngos-in-the-world/. The article lists a series of non-governmental organizations spread across dozens of countries, with thousands of volunteers and huge budgets. For example, Save the Children, Doctors without Borders, World Vision, Amnesty International, ActionAid International, Plan International.

[96] Heller (1984).

[97] Collins Jr (2004), pp. 807–832.

thousands of pages) but rather skim through the headings and key points of the brief in a superficial manner. They do this to understand the general "spirit of the information" that is written in the brief and to understand which NGOs, individuals, politicians, companies, and key interest groups have a "special interest" or a "strong interest" in the judgment. The judges conclude or try to infer from the title of the brief, and entities behind the brief, what the expected consequences and aftereffects may be from the expected judgement after superficially skimming through the submitted materials, and then also try to gauge the future intentions of the groups that submitted the brief.[98]

The judge's examination of the brief files, often with the help of a legal assistant who prepares a summary of those interest groups with an interest in the case for the judge, provides the court with essential information regarding the various interest groups that may be affected by the judgment (directly or indirectly), and which organizations and pressure groups are involved in the particular case.[99] A review of the summary also provides the court with information or well-founded hypotheses on the question of which interest groups may continue to be involved in the issue if the court's judgment does not coincide with their worldview—in the media, in government, in the legislative authority, and other legal proceedings. These briefs also help the courts understand a series of questions that need to be made known to the formal parties or that the formal parties need to be willing to assist in the matter.

One of the questions that may preoccupy the judges in connection with this is whether interest groups affected by the court's judgment will support the judgment, providing assistance "in spirit" in further legal proceedings or vice versa?[100] Will the media be involved in the issue, and if so—in what way will the issue be covered?[101] Will unsatisfied interest groups try to overturn the court's judgment in different ways? In other words, occasionally, the importance of the brief is not limited to the arguments written in it, but to the understanding of the courts that their judgments and their social choices have consequences for different interest

[98] See, for example, Simard (2008), pp. 669.

[99] See Collins Jr (2018), ("there is evidence in the US Supreme Court that amicus briefs are triaged by law clerks, thus indicating that not all (or even most) amicus briefs are read by judges. [discusses how interest groups and other entities use amicus briefs to attempt to influence judicial outcomes while attending to organizational maintenance concerns].

[100] Studies conducted in the United States found evidence of general support for the courts based on a pool of positive feelings towards the courts despite the interviewees' disagreement with controversial decisions. The institutional support provides a "backbone" that allows the courts to intervene even in sensitive social disputes. Friedman (2003). [Friedman argues that popular constitutionalism is mediated by a number of institutions, including the media, interest groups, and the legal academy. These institutions help to shape the public's understanding of the Constitution and to transmit that understanding to the courts.

[101] In the 1960s and 1970s, critical legal studies (Critical Legal Studies) took shape simultaneously with the rise of social protest movements. These approaches believed, among other things, that the opinion of the judges, given their professional and political future, shapes their judicial decisions. See, for example: Macey (1994).

groups, In these cases, the Amicus Curiae practice helps the courts to "feel" and better understand these potential consequences.

Studies that examined the effect of Amicus Curiae briefs on United States federal judges (Circuit Courts and District Courts) confirm this. These studies confirm that amicus briefs help judges better understand the expected general consequences of their judgments.[102] One study showed that the judges welcome briefs that draw their attention to the social, environmental, or other consequences related to the verdict. On the other hand, the judges expressed displeasure with amici, who spread their ideological doctrine, and they believe that these briefs are unnecessary.[103]

At the same time as the court's growing awareness of the lateral consequences for third parties, and while the understanding that the amici help to feel society's pulse, the courts also began to be aware of various manipulations that some so called "amici" could exert on them through their briefs. The first court to recognize this was the American Supreme Court, which, as a procedural step designed to identify the nature and quality of the brief, formulated procedural rules under which an obligation was imposed on "potential amici" to disclose the relationship between them and the formal parties to the procedure as well as to reveal the identity of the entities that participated in financing the submission of the brief or its writing.[104] For example, in the case of *Philip Morris*, the court in Massachusetts stated in this context that: "Briefs of Amicus Curiae are intended to represent the views of non-parties; they are not intended as vehicles for parties or their counsel to make additional arguments beyond those that fit within the page constraints of their briefs."[105]

It can be estimated that the origin of these requirements is the desire of the judges who read the brief to evaluate it correctly.[106] Another possible explanation for these rules is that the official litigants may manipulate the court by inviting many so-called "amici" to support their position. The courts may get the mistaken impression that when many public organizations join in favor of a particular claimant—the public opinion supports him, while these "amici" were actually "invited" by a formal party, or a claimant wrote the formal brief, and they were only instructed to submit the brief to create a "supportive atmosphere."[107]

Following these concerns, many courts have begun to develop regulations on this matter. For example, starting in 2006, the ICSID arbitration panel formulated rules that state, among other things, that the request submitted by an Amicus Curiae must include details of the relationships that the organization has with one of the parties to

[102] Simard (2008), pp. 669.

[103] Simard (2008), p. 692.

[104] As mentioned above, various judicial systems have adopted similar procedural rules—in South Africa, Australia, Canada, and international courts.

[105] Aspinall v. Philip Morris Cos., Inc., 813 N.E.2d 476, 480–81, n.8 (Mass. 2004).

[106] For example, see New York Times article "Seeking Facts, Justices Settle for What Briefs Tell Them." The article reports that Justice Antonin Scalia criticized the court's acceptance of data found in amicus briefs. The article also mentions that some amicus briefs are careful and valuable, citing peer-reviewed studies and noting contrary evidence, while others cite more questionable materials.

[107] See Rustad and Koenig (1993), pp. 157–158; Larsen (2014).

the arbitration, as well as full disclosure as to whether the applicant directly or indirectly received financial or other support from one of the parties to the arbitration process.[108]

Similarly, the courts in Arizona required, starting in 2014, from bodies or individuals applying to submit amicus briefs "[to] Identify every person or entity, other than the Amicus Curiae, its members, or its counsel, who made a monetary contribution to the preparation or submission of the brief."[109] Beyond that, it was determined in Arizona that the lawyers of the formal parties would not assist in writing the brief of the "amici."[110]

In many states in the United States (such as Maryland, Minnesota, West Virginia, and Texas), there are due diligence rules for amici in wording like that existing in Arizona.[111] In other states, where due diligence rules for Amicus Curiae are not regulated in legislation, the courts complete it in their judgments.[112]

9.1.3 Democratization of the Judicial Procedure

From the courts' perspective, there is another explanation for adopting the Amicus Curiae practice. According to this explanation, which I call "the democratic factor," the institutional legitimacy of the courts is strengthened through the Amicus Curiae, and at the same time, the amici bring a more significant commitment of the public to the government by being part of the procedure, even if their position was not accepted. This occurs through the extension of the public's participation in the courts. The submission of the amicus briefs is a means to an end, with the end being the expansion of the public's participation in the courts' procedures, thus establishing the public institutional legitimacy. This, in turn makes it appear to be in the interests of the public to expand the courts' influence on the public's environment and on wider elements of its life.[113]

---

[108] See *Biwater Gauff* (2007), p. 231.

[109] Ariz. R. Civ. App. P. 16.

[110] Ibid ("[c]ounsel for a party should not be permitted to write the amicus brief in whole or in part").

[111] See Md. R. 8–511(b)(1)(E); Minn. R. Civ. App. P. 129.03; N.D. R. App. P. 29(c)(4); Tex. R. App. P. 11; W. Va. R. App. P. 30(e)(5).

[112] Philip Morris Brands Sàrl, Philip Morris Products S.A. and Abal Hermanos S.A. v. Oriental Republic of Uruguay, ICSID Case No. ARB/10/7 (2016) ("A full and honest disclosure of the interest of amici is crucial to the fairness and integrity of the appellate process").

[113] As will also be detailed later, the possible critical position towards this explanation would be that the expansion of public participation through the "amicus" and the establishment of public legitimacy neutralize pockets of opposition to the court in the sense that the "amici" are a "fig leaf" that gives legitimacy to the verdicts.

The status of the courts in the eyes of the public and how the public relates to the courts and their verdicts are key elements in the strength and importance of the courts in a democratic country.[114]

The legitimacy of adjudication is generally seen to depend on two pillars: selecting an impartial, independent, and knowledgeable adjudicator and creating an adequate procedure that permits the participation of all those affected by a decision.[115]

In 2008, the Association of American Judges (AJA) published a position paper regarding proper judicial conduct in the United States and Canadian court systems. The AJA's position paper is based, among other things, on Tom Tyler's research regarding the difference between how judges see the judicial process and how the public understands it.[116]

There is a difference between the point of view of decision-makers, who are focused on the fairness of their decision, and the point of view of the parties, who focus on the fairness of how these decisions were made, and the experience in court. This means that people are willing to accept a loss in a trial if the results were achieved fairly from their standpoint. Moreover, parties in court who appreciate and value the conduct of the judicial process will translate this into an appreciation of the legal system and the country as a whole.[117] The judicial procedure, according to the position paper of the AJA, as it is perceived by the parties in court, and the judicial task required for understanding its construction is made up of four central components:

(1) *"Giving a voice"*—people want to be allowed to state their position directly, in their own words, before decisions are made in their case. The opportunity to

[114]For example, studies in the United States indicate decreasing public trust in all social institutions, including the courts and law enforcement. Shaw and Brannan (2009). In general, in most democratic countries, there is a continuous erosion of public trust in political actors and state institutions. (e.g. in Ireland, Germany, Italy, Sweden, Japan, Great Britain, Belgium, Denmark, Iceland, Netherlands). It is interesting to note that despite the public's disapproval of the political system, there is no visible erosion in the citizens' commitment to democratic norms. These studies show that the commitment to democracy increased. In other words, the decline is focused on the institutions' functioning level and not on the democratic principles themselves. See also Torcal and Montero (2006). See Kingsbury and Schill (2009) (Signs of the legitimacy crisis in investment arbitration are seen in the withdrawal of several Latin American states such as Bolivia and Venezuela from investment treaties and the ICSID Convention); Van Duzer (2007); See also: Chinkin and Mackenzie (2002).

[115](Howse argues that at a minimum level it suffices to establish publicity so that those affected can understand how they are affected and on what basis the outcome was achieved.) Howse (2001).

[116]Tyler (2004, 2006).

[117]See also Tyler's other writing on this subject in which he emphasized some elements of deliberative justice. Tyler and Bies (1990).

express their point of view and the feeling that the courts have seriously considered their claims positively affects their experience in court.[118]

(2) Neutrality—neutrality is built from the consistent application of legal rules and transparency of how the decision was made and what the reasons were that led to its acceptance.
(3) Respectful attitude—matter-of-fact and polite treatment of the parties.
(4) Trust in authority—when a person feels that the judge listens to him, is aware of the case, and discusses his case thoughtfully, he develops trust in the system and does not believe it acts with bias or bias.[119]

That is, from the point of view of the courts, listening to the legal or social position presented by amici who represent different segments of the public, even without the court agreeing to the position itself, strengthens the court's institutional legitimacy because the very willingness of the court to listen to the arguments of the amici shows appreciation on the part of the court for these people. Positive experiences of being taken into consideration during a trial creates in the amici and other groups a more outstanding obligation to respect the judgments. Listening to the position presented by amici, even without accepting their position, is an expression of the fact that the court represents the political and cultural conventions of the cultural community within which it functions and that it gives each party and each person in society, even if they are not a formal part, their "day" in court and their ability to influence their own lives. In this way, the practice of Amicus Curiae ensures that even those who ultimately "lose" in the process, in the sense that the court did not accept their position—feel that their voice was heard and that they had a part in the process that led to the design of the decision and its implementation.[120]

[118]See for example The Supreme Court of Ohio's publication "Ensuring the Right to be Heard: Procedural Fairness for Self-Represented Litigants" which discusses the ethical obligation and duty of judicial officers to ensure that parties are respected and feel that their voice is heard, which is essential for fairness to be perceived.

[119]The interest and consideration or lack of interest and consideration for their case before the judge. It is interesting to note that the image of the goddess of justice, Themis, depicted as a blindfolded woman holding scales in one hand and a sword in the other, faithfully represents the aspiration to a system of value judgment: the sword symbolizes the power and the ability to implement judicial decisions. The scales represent the value of fair weighing between the parties' arguments and their rights. The blindfold is intended to emphasize the judicial neutrality and impartiality of the judge towards the parties appearing before him. See Tyler (1988).

[120]For the purpose of this discussion, I want to make a distinction between two concepts—public trust and institutional legitimacy. The public's trust in the courts is based on many parameters, mainly: the moral-ethical level of the judges, their integrity, the degree of equality for litigants, the extent to which the judges listen to the parties, the efficiency of the judges and the absence of judicial torture. That is, public trust in the courts depends mainly on the courts' personal, procedural, and organizational characteristics. On the other hand, the institutional legitimacy of the courts is expressed in the degree of respect and obedience of the public and its elected officials to judicial decisions. Public trust is a necessary condition for the institutional legitimacy of the courts, but it is not a sufficient condition. Institutional legitimacy also depends on the nature of the decision and judicial reasoning and the widespread perception in the public about the status and powers of the courts. The lack of public legitimacy of the court is not necessarily because the public believes that

Allowing a third party to participate in the discussion by expressing his point of view, his position, or his story is of great importance in strengthening the legitimacy of the courts,[121] particularly during a period when there is a specific decrease in the legitimacy of the courts. The feeling that the judge seriously considered the claims, "voices," and stories of audiences other than the formal litigants (amici) has a positive effect that strengthens trust in the judicial system and its products and leads to a moral commitment on the part of these groups to respect the verdicts.

This is doubly true when the court to which the amicus brief was submitted later quotes from the brief submitted by the amici. In these cases, the amici feel that the court has legitimized their activity and that their presence in the court is essential and justified.[122] The more the court decision is seen as legitimate and open to all positions, the more likely the public will respect and follow it. When social movements express their position as amici, they accept the legitimacy of the courts as an axiom.

The practice of Amicus Curiae allows the parties whom the legal process touches in some way to express their point of view, thus giving them a sense of self-worth, procedural justice, and commitment to the process, and respect for the decision made.[123] The Amicus Curiae practice also presents the judicial system as one that allows any party and any interested person, even if he is not a formal part of the procedure but has some connection to it, to "get his day in court" and try to influence the judicial decision.[124]

There is reason to believe that the "Amicus phenomenon" is also related to therapeutic judicial conduct since, in this conduct, an emphasis is placed on empathic behavior, understanding the point of view of the disputants, and giving a voice to the disputants.[125] Other prominent examples of the adoption of Amicus Curiae as a deliberative practice that increases democratic values of legitimacy and commitment to decisions can also be seen in NAFTA,[126] the World Trade

---

the judges are not legitimate or that the judges did not consider substantive considerations but because the public believes that the court's ruling does not rise to the same scale as its values and priorities.

[121] See Susan J. Pharr and Robert D. Putnam (2000); Van Duzer (2007).

[122] For public trust and procedural justice see Warren (2000), see Tarr (2003); Howse (2003), pp. 496–497.

[123] Brynat (2001), p. 99; To a large extent, it is a mutual cultural acquisition, see also O'Connor and Epstein (1981).

[124] Della Noce (1999). The article questions whether and how ideology affects mediator practice and argues that mediators must be able to empathize with parties in order to understand their perspectives and help them reach a mutually beneficial agreement.

[125] Giving proper respect to a person as an autonomous being requires us to hear his claims and provide him with an opportunity to change his decision when an act harms him. The use of "amicus" partially satisfies this need when they allow the individual to impose on other authorities to hear any person who may be harmed by their action and allow him to present his claims. Eylon and Harel (2006).

[126] Van Duzer (2007), p. 709.

Organization,[127] in ICSID,[128] in Latin American countries (Peru, Mexico, Colombia, Argentina),[129] in Israel,[130] and Africa (South Africa, Ethiopia, and Namibia).[131]

In other words, on the one hand, the courts receive factual or social information from different groups in society, but at the same time, they give them a partnership, or a sense of collaboration, in the decision-making processes that affect their lives. Even if, in practice, there is no actual basis for the information presented by the amici, the court's mere acceptance of the briefs presents the court as a body that rules by the social, cultural, and political norms of the society in which it serves. It also conveys the message that the court's ruling is objective and based on broad, professionally organized information presented to it from various entities with a range of viewpoints.[132] In this sense, the amicus is a "democratic" factor that, on the one hand, increases public participation in the legal process and, at the same time, transforms judicial institutions that are based on hierarchy and authority into more open, attentive, and participatory institutions.[133]

Accepting the Amicus Curiae institution in modern law is one of the practices adopted by the court to expand the participation of different members of the public whose trust in the courts has weakened. On the one hand, as stated, it enables the court to receive information and perspectives from other entities related to the ongoing process. On the other hand, this also allows the court to establish institutional legitimacy and enables broader sections of society to commit to its decisions. Social diversity, often accompanied by value diversity, challenges institutional legitimacy. When social diversity divides society and polarizes factions, the challenge to institutional legitimacy becomes more acute. The use of "amicus" to broaden the inclusion of individual citizens and groups of people from a variety of backgrounds with diverse identities, so enabling these people to have a perception of taking part in decision-making, can be a powerful instrument for establishing legitimacy.[134]

---

[127] Ortino (2009), p. 316.

[128] Graham (2012).

[129] Medeiros (2008) and Bazán (2009).

[130] See entry The Center for the Exercise of Medical Rights Ltd. v. The Israel Bar Association, Paragraph 2 of Judge Amit's judgment (June 25, 2014). Judge Amit noted about the requests of several organizations ("The Civil Rights Association," "Tamura - the Legal Center for the Prevention of Discrimination") to express their position in the process as "friendship" on behalf of needy populations: "When I came to discuss this case, I thought that real weight should be attached to their position of the social organizations, as a 'friend of the court,' who in his capacity can offer the court a point of view that is hidden from our eyes and serve as a mouthpiece for a large segment of the population."

[131] Hinson and Hubbard (2012).

[132] Duncan Jr. (1999) and Gramberger (2001).

[133] Bobbio (1987). In his book, Bobbio outlines the changing nature and image of modern democracy. He argued that the future of democracy depends on the ability of democratic institutions to adapt to changing circumstances and to respond to the needs of citizens.

[134] Williams (2000) and Halpin (2006).

Accepting amici into the courts and paying attention to their briefs, giving weight to the information they bring to the court, made the courts seem like professional bodies that do not pass judgements solely based on a subjective worldview or on partial information. The amici enhance the courts image as being professional bodies who pass judgements appropriate to the cultural and political nature of the society in which they serve. They also cultivate the court's acceptance within diverse elements of society as a body whose rulings are objective and well-founded and based on a broad, professional, and diverse information that was presented to them through various parties.[135] Providing a platform for expressing the positions of different groups with different opinions enabled the courts to gain the image of being institutions who initiate contact with all types of populations, are attentive to their needs and opinions, and increased the moral obligation on the part of interest groups to accept the court's decisions.[136]

The fascinating process of recognizing the Amicus Curiae practice in many countries around the globe and deepening the use of amici shows that these developments are not coincidences but rather a clear trend to change the "old" rules about the courts' status and allow many groups and individual citizens to enter the courthouse gates and voice their position. The explanation for adopting different ways to allow third parties to present their position in many countries is closely related to the new worldview of the court about its role in society.[137] Presumably, the recognition of amici can be considered a purely procedural matter since recognizing an amicus does not mean accepting the position presented to the court or even considering this position. However, it is clear that accepting an amicus means increasing the involvement of the courts in shaping society.

9.1.4 *The Policy Diffusion*

The global spread of amicus curiae briefs can be also better understood through the lens of policy diffusion theory, which explains how policy choices in one jurisdiction influence those made in others.[138] Several mechanisms of policy diffusion are at play in the case of amicus curiae. First, policymakers learn from the perceived effectiveness of amicus briefs in shaping legal discourse and judicial decisions in

[135] Duncan Jr. (1999), p. 169. [While the article does not specifically discuss Amicus Curiae participation, it provides valuable insights into the importance of promoting participation and ensuring that all stakeholders have a voice in the public hearing process].

[136] The fact that the "amicus" serves as an additional channel for establishing legitimacy is not a negative thing since the legitimacy that the judiciary receives from the citizens is one of the cornerstones of the courts. Because public trust in the judiciary is one of the most valuable assets that this authority has. Lack of trust in the judiciary is the beginning of the end of society. See also Barak (1965).

[137] Barak (2002).

[138] Simmons et al. (2006), pp. 781—810.

other jurisdictions. Second, competition among jurisdictions to enhance their legal systems and demonstrate their progressiveness could have spurred the uptake of amicus practices. Third, transnational networks of legal experts and international organizations have played a crucial role in promoting amicus briefs as a global best practice.[139]

Furthermore, the diffusion of amicus curiae briefs can be seen as a form of institutional isomorphism, whereby countries adopt similar structures and practices to gain legitimacy and conform to international norms. The global spread of democratic values, human rights, and the rule of law has created a conducive environment for the acceptance of amicus briefs as a means of enhancing participatory justice and transparency in legal proceedings. This trend is particularly evident in post-authoritarian and post-conflict societies, where the adoption of amicus curiae practices is often part of broader efforts to strengthen the rule of law and promote public participation in governance.

While policy diffusion theory offers a compelling framework for understanding the proliferation of amicus curiae briefs, it is important to recognize the complex interplay of domestic and international factors that shape the adoption and adaptation of this legal instrument in different contexts.[140] The specific contours of amicus participation, such as the rules governing submission, the types of entities allowed to file briefs, and the weight accorded to amicus arguments, may vary across jurisdictions based on their unique legal traditions, political systems, and societal needs. Moreover, the effective implementation of amicus curiae practices may be hindered by resource constraints, lack of awareness among potential amici, and resistance from some judicial actors.

In addition to the explanations provided in this book, such as the courts' need for additional information and expertise in complex cases, the desire of courts to enhance their legitimacy through greater public participation, and the increasing activism of NGOs and other civil society actors, policy diffusion theory provides a complementary perspective on the rapid and widespread adoption of amicus curiae practices worldwide. By highlighting the interdependence of policy choices across jurisdictions and the various mechanisms through which policies spread, this theory sheds light on the broader global context in which the amicus curiae phenomenon has unfolded. Future research could further explore how policy diffusion interacts with the domestic drivers of amicus curiae adoption and how this interplay shapes the form and function of amicus participation in different legal systems.

[139] Haas (1992).

[140] Dolowitz et al. (2000). See also Stone (2012).

9.2 The Social Factor of the "Amicus Phenomenon"

Another explanation for the global "Amicus Curiae phenomenon" is social. This concept has been introduced in various places in the previous section but will be expanded upon here. Courts are interested in receiving complementary information from amici and different perspectives in complex and new areas of opinion to understand their rulings' implications better and formulate an appropriate legal policy. However, there are other factors besides the institutional factor. The courts' need for amici is equaled by the desire of the various amici to influence society through submitting amicus briefs to the courts. That is, the practice of the amicus plays a significant role in opening the law's doors to greater influence and involvement of society in the decisions made by the judicial system. The use of Amicus Curiae constitutes another significant channel of civic participation in public life by interest groups in society alongside existing tools such as direct discussion with policymakers or indirect influence through political parties or public opinion.

Not only does the practice of the amicus allow a more significant involvement of the public in the decision-making processes of the courts (such as presenting all the information relevant to the issue and reducing judicial errors based on partial information or a missing social image), but the submission of amicus briefs by interest groups or citizens, constitutes to a large extent the exercise of their right to shape their lives and well-being.[141]

A democratic view would argue that similar to the right to vote, which is the right to influence the elected authority, there is a right for third parties who are not a formal part of a litigation process to submit amicus briefs to the courts on issues that affect their lives and well-being. From a conceptual point of view, the "right" of third parties to be partners in decisions that affect their well-being by joining legal proceedings as amici, even if the proceedings do not directly concern them, is somewhat similar to the right of access to the courts and its justifications. This is a constitutional right of the first degree in most countries but differs from it in that there is no direct interest of an involved party.[142]

The use of "amicus" expands the freedom of expression because presenting arguments and viewpoints of third parties as amici is used not only to present a formal position to the court but also as a way to express positions and perspectives to the members of the group, to the decision-makers in other authorities (the legislative

[141] This principle is simply called "the basic democratic idea" or "the autonomy of the individual." This is in contrast to participation in elections, which is a partial framework for exercising a person's right to influence their well-being because it is indirect or gives a limited ability to influence the representatives' decisions. In any case, studies show that citizens do not believe in their ability to influence government policy. Many people do not believe in their ability to influence the political system. Disaffected Democracies, Nancy Perkins Spyke (1999).

[142] The roots of this right are deep within history Bill of Rights 1688, 1 W. & M. Sess. 2, c. 2; Petition of Right 1628, 3 Car. 1. c. 1; Magna Carta (1215; later enacted Magna Carta 1297, 25 Edw. 1, c. 9); Andrews (1999), p. 557; Lawson and Seidman (1999). On the social and cultural justifications see Friedman (1978).

and executive bodies) and the entire public. Social movements and interest groups, in their part as amici, use court proceedings, or the possibility of appealing to them, to promote their goals of changing social orders.[143]

For example, the pro-communist newspaper (at the time) "The Daily Worker" in the 1960s called on United States citizens to submit amicus briefs directly to the judges who heard the *Lawson* case, which dealt with refusing to answer questions from a Senate committee about membership in the Communist Party.[144] In the eyes of the interest groups behind this call, the "amicus" was seen as a formal expression of a political struggle. Therefore, sending letters to sitting judges by citizens, which is tantamount to crossing red lines in the eyes of the legal community, was seen in their eyes as a proper and reasonable activity.

Also, dozens of amicus briefs were submitted to the court by dozens of citizens as part of the attempt to save the life of Willie McGee, an African-American sentenced to death in Mississippi, probably without having committed any wrongdoing on his part.[145] Similarly, dozens of citizens' amicus briefs were submitted to the courts to prevent the execution of the Rosenbergs, who were convicted of espionage and handing over American nuclear secrets to the Soviet Union.[146] Many personal amicus briefs were also submitted regarding the refusal of an American citizen of Japanese origin, Korematsu, to honor a presidential removal order issued against the population of Japanese citizens in the United States during World War II.[147] By the way, Korematsu himself submitted many amicus briefs on Human Rights issues during his lifetime, the most famous of which is a brief submitted in 2006 to the United States Supreme Court on the question of the legality of the detention of *al-Qaeda* detainees in the military prison in Guantanamo.[148]

---

[143] The difference between ordinary litigation in courts and legal social leadership is that ordinary litigation is focused on achieving a legal victory in a given legal case, (legal mobilization) Focused on achieving goals outside the walls of the court. Zemans (1983), pp. 690–703. Also see McCann (2008).

[144] Lawson v. United States, 176 F.2d 49 (D.C. Cir. 1949).

[145] Heard (2010).

[146] Ranzal (1953) and Roberts (2003).

[147] Korematsu v. United States, 323 U.S. 214 (1944).

[148] Hamdan v. Rumsfeld, 548 U.S. 557 (2006). In this famous case, amicus briefs were filed by two United States senators, John Kyl and Lindsey Graham. In another case dealing with the legality of detention at the military prison in Guantanamo, a brief was filed by retired federal judges who argued that the law violated the United States Constitution. Liptak (2006).

9.2.1 The "Amicus" As an Expression of Deliberative Democracy

Society's involvement in court proceedings by submitting amicus briefs can be explained as an expression of "deliberative democracy."[149] Deliberative democracy, also called "orderly democracy," is a significant current in the liberal thought of recent decades that seeks to deal with the difficulty of democratic life in a society that is run through representatives. It emphasizes the discourse, communication, and sharing process leading to the decision stage.

According to this theory, citizens are obliged to regulate their lives and well-being through public, open, and accessible discussion and to establish public institutions by hearing all the voices involved in the matter. Deliberative democracy considers the full participation of the various representatives in the discussion that precedes the decision to be the source of legitimacy for the final decision (which is usually a decision by representatives).[150] Deliberative democracy refers not only to the final result but to the procedure that leads to the final decision—a procedure based on discourse and hearing all the positions that may be relevant to the issue.[151]

Since the courts have become significant forums in the public decision-making processes, it is easier to understand the "Amicus Curiae phenomenon" and the active participation of citizens in planning the spheres within which their lives are conducted because the very participation is, in itself, a realization of the democratic idea.[152]

Recognizing the expression of the viewpoints of third parties as amici in international law is a good illustration of this. In international criminal proceedings, there is an ongoing trend whose purpose is to present to the courts the viewpoints of people involved in the proceedings and especially the voices of the victims beyond the "general" views of the public interest.[153] International crimes are crimes perpetrated against the international community, and the international community is

[149] This phrase was first used in Bessette (1980). Other scholars that have shaped this discussion are Ulster et al. (2004), p. 134; Estlund (1993).

[150] Leib's work is noteworthy, as it presents a practical method of integrating discussion between citizens within the existing framework of representative democracy. His plan is indeed based on the United States, but according to him its applicability is wider. Leib (2006). For a critique on Deliberative Democracy see Posner (2003).

[151] Elster (1998). For relevance to the courts as arenas that encourage deliberation see Zurn (2007), pp.163–84 [judicial review can be seen as a form of deliberative democracy, as it provides a forum for public deliberation and debate on important issues].

[152] Mansbridge (2006); Edwards (2017); Collins Jr (2004), pp. 807–832.

[153] For a deeper discussion on this theory see Farber (2019), pp. 235. [the article provides insights into the potential benefits of allowing crime victims organizations to participate as amici curiae in criminal trial courts. The article acknowledges that there may be concerns regarding harming the defendants' rights but argues that the addition of crime victim's organizations as Amici Curiae can provide valuable information to the court and help ensure that the interests of crime victims are taken into account in the criminal justice system].

interested in bringing criminals to justice. However, while the prosecutor's role is to reflect the public interest in the prosecution, certain decisions related to procedure management lead certain groups to feel that their interest needs to be adequately represented in the courts.[154] Amicus briefs submitted to international criminal courts ensures that the voices and perspectives of these groups, especially if they are the victims of the crime or vulnerable groups, will be heard in the courts, and their feelings will be adequately expressed.[155] Indeed, many international organizations authenticate the testimonies of victims or potential victims in conflict zones, intending to present them in the courts as Amicus Curiae briefs.[156]

Sometimes, political or social circumstances lead to the deprivation of different societal populations. These groups are usually characterized by a lack of representation in the governmental decision-making processes, which generally negatively affects and stigmatizes their status.[157] The expression of the positions of these groups as amici through submitting amicus briefs helps, to a certain extent, to change this perception.[158] Allowing third parties to take part in a judicial process that has some effect on them through the expression of their point of view has a positive impact on the element of society involved. They experience a degree of empowerment by being enabled to express their position on issues that affect lives, as well as their opinions of the courts. This, in turn, improves the image of the courts, which are perceived as professional bodies who consider the positions of all parties, including vulnerable and powerless groups, in the fabric of social and governmental life.

The courts' final decisions are usually better and more complete when all relevant viewpoints are considered and addressed. This is especially true regarding the point of view of disadvantaged minority communities whose voices are not heard in the public discourse and who are usually empowered by their position being heard.[159] The emphasis in this trend is the "flexibility" of the procedure that allows the

[154]The prosecutor at the court is an independent personality responsible for the investigation, the preparation of the indictments and the administration of the lawsuit. At the same time, the final decision regarding the filing of an indictment rests with the Pre-Trial Chamber. An important characteristic of the court is the status accorded to the victims of the crime within the criminal procedure. For example, the court established a "unit for witnesses and victims" as well as a victim compensation fund. Razzaque (2001).

[155]See more at Wiik (2018) and Bartholomeusz (2005), pp. 209, 236

[156]For example, in the case of The Prosecutor v. Germain Katanga, the ICC received Amicus Curiae briefs from a number of organizations, including HRW, Amnesty International, and the Coalition for the International Criminal Court. These briefs argued that the ICC should collect and preserve evidence of crimes committed against civilians in the Democratic Republic of the Congo. In the case of The Prosecutor v. Jean-Pierre Bemba Gombo, the ICC received Amicus Curiae briefs from a number of organizations, including HRW, Amnesty International, and the Coalition for the International Criminal Court. These briefs argued that the ICC should collect and preserve evidence of crimes committed against civilians in the Central African Republic.

[157]Duncan Jr. (1999).

[158]Quigley (1995).

[159]Kastellec and Lebo (2010) https://scholar.princeton.edu/sites/default/files/kastellec_racial_diversity_final_0.pdf.

participation of third parties and not necessarily on the outcome of the procedure. Even if, following a consideration of their merits, the arguments of the amici are rejected in the end, the opportunity given to interest groups to make their voices heard in court is a respectful approach, which allows them to influence the courts.[160]

Society's desire to influence the decision-making procedures consists of three interwoven layers that together drive and increase the global "Amicus Curiae phenomenon:" interest groups led by public, NGOs; the increase in numbers and strengthening role of lawyers; and economic considerations that encourage the use of "amici."

9.2.2 *The Economic Aspects of the "Amicus"*

The third social factor for the "Amicus Curiae phenomenon" is the economic factor. Society's desire to influence decisions that shape communal space through participation as amici also has financial aspects since the economics involved in working with amici incentivize their use. In general, writing an amicus brief and submitting it to the court involves (1) low costs and (2) low financial risks, which leads to a growth of the "Amicus Curiae phenomenon."[161]

First, from the point of view of the applicants to be amici, this process has low costs, certainly compared to other alternatives such as an independent petition or joining as a formal party to the procedure. Amici are not required to pay a procedure initiation fee or fees for other requests.[162] Moreover, amici are also not charged additional fees, such as an appeal fee imposed on the official litigants, since the formal parties pay the fees and the amicus only joins the procedure. The amici are not required to guarantee the expenses of other parties in the procedure and are exempt from the costs of the procedure (such as submitting pleadings to the court or confirming their delivery).

Furthermore, if the procedure to which the Amicus Curiae joined ends with a ruling on court costs—the formal party is the one who bears the burden, and the amicus does not bear these costs at all.[163] In judicial systems around the world, there

[160] This action also has a significant educational effect. As John Rawls explained, the role of a court is not merely "protective." Its role, in a certain sense, is being an example of "public reason," as it is required to express high morality. Also see, Baister (1997).

[161] Simpson and Vasaly (2004).

[162] With the exception of "interveners" in the English judicial system, and even then, in exceptional and special cases when the court registrar has the authority to reduce the expenses or cancel them entirely at his discretion. See for example Supreme Court Fees Order 2009, SI 2009/2131, sch. 2.

[163] Although in some places, there is a moral authority to impose legal costs on third parties (mostly, it is about imposing costs on "intervenors" who have a direct interest in the procedure, but costs can also be imposed on "amici"). However, the use of this authority is rare. In England, for example, since there is authority to impose costs on third parties, there is a kind of practice according to which when a potential third party addresses the parties and asks for their consent to submit a written

are several accepted methods for calculating court costs and how they are distributed between the litigants (such as: "equal division" or "the loser pays the winner's expenses"). Nevertheless, in any case, since the amici are not litigants in the formal sense, the legal expenses are not imposed on them. This circumstance means that the amici have no financial risks when submitting their briefs. Indeed, empirical studies have shown that the knowledge of various interest groups, particularly NGOs, that they can submit amicus briefs without risking financial costs encourages them to submit their position to the courts as amici.[164] This means that economic barriers that may prevent or make access to justice difficult in other cases do not exist in the practice of the "amicus."

Second, writing an amicus brief is relatively simple and straightforward. In terms of the brief's content, for the most part, the briefs rely on existing materials, data, and studies. There is no need to generate new information but to express an opinion or give a different interpretation or perspective regarding a particular issue.[165] It is often about collecting and presenting information to the court rather than creating new information or research, so the costs are relatively low. In addition, the brief-writing procedure is usually shorter than the other litigation alternatives, which require a significant investment of time. Within the framework of the brief, it is optional to refer to all the parties' arguments, refute them, contradict them, or confront them. An amicus may discuss one issue while the parties must address all the issues that arise in the case (such as special discussion issues for the procedure). All that is required from the point of view of the amicus is to compose a brief that presents his worldview or to provide information not presented by the formal parties concerning the issue that is being deliberated and elucidated in court, which is mainly based on existing knowledge.

Moreover, the brief is frequently written by ordinary citizens without the mediation of law firms, which also entails significant savings. In the United States, for example, it is common for private individuals to write briefs to the courts and seek to present their worldview on a particular issue.[166] For example, private citizens have written many briefs to the California Supreme Court on the issue of same-sex marriage.[167] In many cases, briefs from amici are free of charge (or at

---

position, he also asks them not to ask for legal costs to be imposed on him. That is, all the existing costs in the procedure that are imposed on the formal parties are not imposed on the "amici."

[164] Koshner (1998).

[165] For the problematics involved with this, see Rustad and Koenig (1993), pp. 91, 157–158. See also in this context the concerns raised in Dwyer (2022).

[166] See, for example Howse (2003). For example, Citizens United v. Federal Election Commission (2010). In this case, which dealt with campaign finance regulations, numerous private individuals filed amicus briefs expressing their opinions on the issue. See Abrams, Floyd (2015). Amicus brief on behalf of a group of constitutional scholars supporting the petitioner. Citizens United v. Federal Election Commission, 558 U.S. 310. (2015).

[167] See, for example, a brief from a San Francisco citizen to the California Supreme Court on same-sex marriage: Amicus Curiae Brief for Divine Queen Mariette Do-Nguyen, Lockyer v. City & County of San Francisco, 95 P.3d 459 (Cal. 2004) (No. S122923).

a relatively small cost) since students in legal clinics at universities and colleges write them.[168,169]

In addition, there is a common practice in which different interest groups come together to write a joint brief as they share the same values and the desire to save financial expenses.[170] It is also a common practice for small or "niche" NGOs, for economic considerations, to join in with the briefs submitted by large organizations that become a sort of umbrella organization, such as the Civil Rights Association. This is a relatively easy and cheap way, certainly compared to other legal alternatives, to increase efficiency and influence the court's decision-making process.[171]

The social factors related to society's desire to influence the court's decision-making processes also explain the "Amicus Curiae phenomenon" in most countries reviewed in the previous chapters. Due to the processes mentioned above, there is tremendous momentum both in the activity of NGOs and in the activity of lawyers in most countries who see the submission of amicus briefs as a potential means for advancing their goals in the legal scene.[172] In addition, many legal procedures

---

[168] See for example The Center's Civil Rights & Criminal Justice Advocacy, SEATTLE UNIV. SCH. OF LAW (2016), www.law.seattleu.edu/centers-and-institutes/korematsu-center/litigation/the-civil-rights-amicus-brief-project (last visited Oct. 16, 2019). Civil Rights Amicus Brief Project, SEATTLE UNIV. SCH. OF LAW (2016), www.law.seattleu.edu/centers-and-institutes/korematsu-center/litigation/the-civil-rights-amicus-brief-project. For example, in Fisher v. University of Texas at Austin (2016): (Affirmative action in college admissions), several university legal clinics filed amicus briefs. For instance, the Supreme Court Litigation Clinic at Stanford Law School submitted a brief on behalf of a group of leading social scientists, supporting the University of Texas at Austin's admissions policy. See: Stanford Law School Supreme Court Litigation Clinic. "Fisher v. University of Texas at Austin." Stanford Law School, www.law.stanford.edu/stanford-law-school-supreme-court-litigation-clinic/fisher-v-university-texas-austin.

[169] In light of this, it is no wonder that important social struggles are organized today by legal clinics in universities and colleges, and not by private individuals.

[170] In addition, writing a joint memo and submitting it to the court is an extensive platform for creating collaborations and coalitions between different organizations. The joint work on writing the memo and the meetings held to plan the strategy create working relationships between non-governmental organizations that work for public interests.

[171] When several organizations join together and voice a unified front, this may create a great impression on the court. At the same time, there is a difficulty in establishing a broad agreement on the content of the position to be presented, on the tactics and methods of operation of the united front. As I recall, the *Webster* case is one of the high points of the participation of non-governmental public organizations in the decision-making process of the Supreme Court, and it raised among various public organizations questions related to litigation tactics, where one of the key questions in this context is "which is a more effective strategy, to file as many individual briefs as possible or to gather a larger total number of cosponsoring organizations?". Behuniak-Long (1991), p. 262.

[172] Today, in most countries, the third sector is an integral part of the state services system. Some believe that the privatization processes in the world were made possible, among other things, due to the activities of non-governmental public organizations because by their very existence, they legitimized the existence of an alternative to the state, and secondly because they spurred the government sector to privatize more services. Be that as it may, there is no doubt that the changes in the judicial system, the intensification of the privatization processes, and the increase in the power of third-sector non-governmental public organizations are related to one another.

actively encourage the submission of "amicus" briefs. The willingness of the courts to intervene in issues that arouse public controversy planted the feeling among many interest groups and communities that it is possible, and perhaps even appropriate, to change the face of society through active participation in the judicial process, either as formal parties or as third parties (amici). Through the practice of the "amicus," groups that were absent from the legal process began to be more involved in the legal discourse and the determination of values in the country.

Furthermore, groups that participated in legal proceedings diversified the legal tools at their disposal and increased the frequency of using the "amicus" to promote their interests. The explanation for this is twofold. On the one hand, the courts have encouraged interest groups to participate in the legal process by using amici. On the other hand, interest groups that were interested in influencing the courts' decision-making processes took advantage of this opportunity and submitted their position to the court through amicus briefs, and on and on it goes.

As a result of the deep involvement of the courts in the public sphere in recent decades and since the law is becoming more complex and diversified, there is a continuous process of developing, perfecting, and adopting new working methods and forms of discussion designed to assist the courts. The "Amicus Curiae phenomenon" is one of the main results of these changes in the work of the courts, and to some extent, it is also a cause of them. These are cyclic processes. The practice of the "amicus" has been adopted and perfected in most countries and almost all international tribunals for two intertwined reasons—institutional and social.

Institutionally, from the point of view and the interests of the courts, the amici help the courts fulfill their current judicial role successfully by providing information that is not in the possession of the formal parties or that the formal parties do not wish to present to the courts. The diverse information that flows to the courts through the amici allows them to fulfill their current job—deciding disputes and bridging the gap between the law and the changing social reality. Sometimes, the arguments presented by amici do not update the courts regarding the broad overall implications of the issue or do not add information that the court needs. However, nevertheless, they are accepted because they serve as some conduit for receiving social information about the interest groups behind the issue and their future intentions.

From a social point of view, in recent years, almost all individuals who are determined to influence and shape their world through the courts use "amicus:" ordinary citizens, students in legal clinics, academics, professionals, politicians, commercial companies, journalists, and various rights organizations. In recent years, all of these individuals and groups have been using "amicus" in by submitting amicus briefs in small and large issues to influence their lives and their well-being.

Interest groups see the submission of amicus briefs as an action strategy, often the only one, to advance their goals. Submitting an amicus brief is seen as a stage whereby it can influence the shapers of public opinion, decision-makers, and other public bodies. The strengthening of the role of the lawyer from a social point of view, and in particular the increase in the number of lawyers engaged in promoting various public goals (ecological, security, economic, political), affects the "Amicus

Curiae phenomenon" since in their view the "amicus" is a successful tool for achieving their goals.

Furthermore, the economic aspects related to "amicus" encourage its use because writing a brief and submitting it to the court involves relatively low costs (for example, there are no legal fees, and the costs of the procedure are few) and low economic risks (there is no fear of costs being ordered). Socially, submitting an amicus brief has a dual role. On the one hand, it expands the basis of public participation in legal proceedings and thus establishes the institutional legitimacy of the courts. And on the other hand, it raises the influence of the public on its environment and life. It thus leads to a public obligation to respect the judgments, even though the public's position was not necessarily accepted. The reason for this is that even the people who "lose" in the end feel that their voices were heard in the judicial process and, that they got their "day in court," and that they had a part in the process that led to the shaping of the decision.

The "Amicus Curiae phenomenon" is essentially a consequence of the perception of the role of the courts in which they not only influence public policy but are also well aware of the consequences of their rulings. The courts became more interested in the question "what if" when the law is changed or when a particular petition is accepted or rejected by the court. Therefore, they were asked to receive information about the legal policy's considerations, allowing them to make a rational decision in the various social options presented to them.

The "Amicus Curiae phenomenon" generates profound changes in the law and the work of the courts as it is integrated into various procedures that reshape the work of the courts. The previous scenario, with a limited number of formal parties and a judge who decides between them, is considered, so to speak, the "old" world of litigation. In contrast, the "new world" becomes a multidimensional procedure consisting of formal parties of tens or hundreds of different amici. Using the "amicus" as a strategy to influence the courts' results simultaneously creates a significant change on several levels. The form of the discussion becomes multilateral for all its meanings. (For example, in some proceedings, most of the information presented to the courts is presented by third parties rather than by the formal parties). Secondly, a change in the conducting style of the judges and the parties in the courtrooms (and often, outside them: in demonstrations and the media).

Third, the creation and flexibility of legal procedures, sometimes "forced" on the courts, contrary to a judicial tradition that is hostile to the intervention of third parties (for example, in some Latin American countries) to consider additional interests other than those of the formal parties. Fourth, in conventional legal thinking, the judges are ready to accept new and diverse types of information (social sciences and the humanities and exact sciences), which are conveyed mainly by the various amici, and then take the data and information into consideration when making their decisions. Fifth, the "amicus" has caused a development towards in new type of process in decision making, which, like in litigation, becomes more similar to a public debate and open to the general public. From a formalist point of view, the Amicus Curiae is "all in all" a legal practice used after complying with specific rules. From a more profound observation, the "Amicus Curiae phenomenon" embodies wide-ranging in depth processes that have taken place in recent years in the perception of the role of the courts.

9.2.3 The Rise of Non-governmental Public Organizations

While the courts' desire or need to receive social information and different perspectives, various interest groups, primarily NGOs, see the submission of amicus briefs as a potential means for advancing their goals, as these briefs allow them to express their position and point of view in the legal arena. In recent decades, there has been a significant increase in the power and number of NGOs in national and international legal arenas.[173] In recent decades, many NGOs have become essential and sometimes exclusive players in many fields.[174] As mentioned, NGOs specialize in "translating" public matters into formal legal frameworks, which become the subject of discussion in judicial systems.[175] In recent decades, NGOs have become particularly active in human and civil rights struggles, where they may be seen as the most influential bodies acting in these spheres.[176] NGOs also deal with various environmental, political, and security goals as well as social agendas (such as reducing poverty, legal advocacy, assistance with medical needs, fighting terrorism, ecological issues, and the freedom of information). On the international level, these organizations also significantly influence the most crucial global decision-making processes (in formal advisory roles or as observers).[177]

Due to the increase in the power of the law and the courts, NGOs see the submission of amicus briefs as an effective tool—sometimes the only one—to advance their goals. In the eyes of some of these organizations, the "amicus" is seen as the formal end of a political and values struggle and as another stage where it is possible to influence the shapers of public opinion and the decision-makers in the various authorities, alongside other tools such as petitions, lobbying in parliament, protest demonstrations, and advertising in the media.

The intensive use of "amicus" on the part of NGOs, which began mainly in the mid-twentieth century in the United States, has in recent decades gone beyond the borders of the United States and has been copied to almost all countries of the world: in Canada, the United Kingdom, Australia, Ireland, the International Tribunal in The Hague and the Court for Human Rights, in the Human Rights Court of Latin America, in international criminal courts, in commercial arbitration proceedings, in the World Trade Organization, in NAFTA and Latin American countries

[173] Reimann (2006) and Charnovitz (1997); Evaluating Transnational NGOs, *supra* note 966.

[174] Charnovitz (1997) and Collins (2008).

[175] Smith et al. (1998).

[176] Reimann (2006). [The article argues that the growth of NGOs is due to a combination of factors, including the increasing importance of human rights and the spread of democratic norms].

[177] Charnovitz (1997) and Collins (2008).

(in particular, Brazil, Colombia, Uruguay, Peru, and Argentina[178]) and even in democratic countries with a limited, liberal culture (such as Russia, Eastern European countries, certain countries in Asia, and certain countries in Africa).[179]

Although several different interest groups (mainly railroad, oil, tobacco, and alcohol companies and, on the other hand—the American Labor Union) made use of Amicus Curiae briefs in the United States in the first half of the twentieth century, the use of this tool by NGOs, and in particular human rights organizations, is the one that led to widespread public attention and a significant development in the "Amicus Curiae phenomenon" in the United States and around the world.[180]

Critical Human Rights cases conducted in the twentieth century in the United States resulted in the submission of thousands of amicus briefs from hundreds of different Human Rights organizations and a significant increase in the use of this practice within legal proceedings. Throughout the twentieth century, there has been a substantial increase in the number of briefs submitted by various NGOs acting as amici to the Supreme Court in the United States, such as the American Civil Rights Association (ACLU), the American Jewish Congress (AJC), the organization for the advancement of black rights in the United States (NAACP), and the American Federation for Labor Rights (AFL).[181]

Throughout the twentieth century, collaborations between various NGOs were recorded regarding joining procedures conducted as amici. Despite differences in approaches between the various organizations, the legal strategy was the same, so the collaborations increased and intensified. Many ideological struggles found themselves in the courts, and for these organizations, this was a golden opportunity to present their ideological doctrine by presenting their position as amici.[182]

The entry of NGOs into the legal field through their massive use of the Amicus Curiae practice did not always go smoothly. Traditionally, an Amicus Curiae was a recognized jurist who usually had prior acquaintance with the judges. The roles of judges and attorneys in their relationships as amici were established under the auspices of their membership in a common professional guild or group based on a

---

[178] For example, The Inter-American Commission on Human Rights submitted an Amicus Curiae brief in the case of the Mapiripán Massacre before the Colombian Supreme Court. In this brief, the Inter-American Commission on Human Rights argued that the Colombian state had violated the human rights of the victims of the Mapiripán Massacre by failing to investigate and prosecute the perpetrators.

[179] As mentioned above, this development in civil society and the rise of non-governmental organizations that try to influence the decision-making processes is also related to broader changes that have taken place in these countries, which include democratization and economic changes Evans Jr. (2005).

[180] As stated above, in the case Ah How v. United States, 193 U.S. 65 (1904), a human rights organization called the "New York Chines Charitable and Benevolent Association" submitted an "amicus" brief on the first issue of the deportation of the Asian population from New York at the beginning of the twentieth century. See Krislov (1963), pp. 694–721.

[181] This was the case, for example, in cases dealing with the rights of African Americans to vote in local elections; on racial discrimination in law schools; and the right to avoid self-incrimination.

[182] See the study of Abi-Hassan et al. (2022) https://doi.org/10.7910/DVN/TOYNMH.

professional or personal relationship.[183] The amici of the judges were, at most, a limited guild of veteran and respected lawyers. Thus, the courts had difficulties in accepting that an NGO or other social organization could be accepted in this role and referred to as an "Amicus Curiae."

Accordingly, NGOs did not initially receive the independent status of amici, and the courts only granted the right to join proceedings by submitting amicus briefs to members of lawyers' organizations. They adhered to the principle that the laity could not be included among amici, who essentially were their professional colleagues. It can be assumed that judges felt uncomfortable adding amici when it could be concluded that the intention of these "amici" was not to help the judges reach a better informed judicial decision but rather to help one of the parties win the case and to do so even in a way with certain political connotations. In addition, it can be assumed that the court judges were uncomfortable with the laypeople bringing briefs to the court that could be regarded as seeking to correct the judges' legal errors publicly.[184]

The use by NGOs of the Amicus Curiae legal procedure also changed the courts' approach towards amici. As mentioned, following the involvement of NGOs, particularly Human Rights organizations, in the judicial proceedings and their attempts to influence the court's decision-making process by submitting Amicus Curiae briefs, the possibility of identifying them as a "classic amicus" which by definition meant a friend to the judge, became very blurred.[185]

The influence of public NGOs in adopting the Amicus Curiae practice in Latin American countries is particularly interesting. Public NGOs, especially Human Rights organizations, almost exclusively caused the adoption and institutionalization of the Amicus Curiae practice in Latin America. Various international organizations operating in Latin America submitted amicus briefs to state courts on a variety of issues—poverty, environmental quality, health, immigration, water and electricity supply, preservation of antiquities, corruption, and Human Rights, and brought

[183] See the description of Banner (2003), pp. 1790–1890. Also see Mohan (2010), pp. 352–374.

[184] As a result of this approach, the labeling in the judgments about the identity of the "amicus" is always recorded in the name of a lawyer. Only from the mid-twentieth century, court clerks began to list the NGO as an "Amicus Curiae" rather than their lawyer. Banner (2003), pp. 1790–1890.

[185] As mentioned, following the change in the role of the amicus, and in accordance with it, many courts in the world began to develop different procedures designed to question the amicus's actions and the motives behind them [such as: who financed them? What are their interests in the case] and more. An independent "amicus" brief is not similar to a brief written with the funding of one of the official litigants. There is a fear that the parties may manipulate and influence the court's decision-making by inviting many influential "amici." The court may get the mistaken impression that when many bodies support a particular litigant, then public opinion supports him, while these "amici" were "invited" or that their memo was written or financed by the "inviting" party. They were only instructed to submit the memo to generate public support of some sort in this position. Krislov (1963), pp. 694–721.

about the adoption of the Amicus Curiae practice in the courts, even though this practice was not accepted by local law.[186]

Although in most Latin American countries, third parties are not allowed to intervene in ongoing legal proceedings without the existence of a direct interest, the Amicus Curiae briefs of these organizations caused a legal and public discussion on the subject and eventually an official recognition of the Amicus Curiae institution. The most prominent examples are the successes of international organizations in submitting an amicus brief and influencing the legal situation in Brazil, Uruguay, Argentina, Mexico, and Peru through the use of the Latin American Court of Human Rights rulings in Costa Rica. The briefs submitted by various organizations caused the state courts to adopt this practice, sometimes "grudgingly" and sometimes contrary to the formal parties' positions in the procedure.[187]

In other words, in some Latin American countries, assertive NGOs ("pushy NGOs") were not only one of the reasons for the "Amicus Curiae phenomenon"[188] but, to a large extent, the main cause of this phenomenon. It is important to note that the very fact that many countries in Latin America or their agencies have themselves submitted "amicus" briefs to the United States Supreme Court and to other international institutions such as the World Trade Organization or the Latin American Court of Human Rights (which is heavily influenced by the legal systems of the European Court of Human Rights) also contributed to the adoption and increase of the "amicus phenomenon" in these countries.[189]

---

[186]For example, the organization Earth Law Center, which deals with transforming the law to recognize and protect Nature's inherent. The organization submitted dozens of briefs to various courts in Latin America in order to protect various environmental rights (air pollution, water sources, deforestation, etc.). Kochevar (2013).

[187]For example, In the case of "Atala Riffo and Daughters v. Chile" (2012), the Inter-American Court of Human Rights allowed several international organizations to file Amicus Curiae briefs. These organizations included the International Lesbian, Gay, Bisexual, Trans, and Intersex Association (ILGA), the International Commission of Jurists, and the International Association of Women Judges. The organizations argued that Chile's ban on same-sex relationships violated international human rights law In the case of "Gutiérrez-Soler v. México" (2006), the Inter-American Court of Human Rights allowed the Inter-American Commission on Human Rights to file an Amicus Curiae brief. The Commission argued that Mexico's criminalization of defamation violated the right to freedom of expression. In the case of "Juan Humberto Sánchez v. Honduras" (2011), the Inter-American Court of Human Rights allowed the Inter-American Commission on Human Rights to file an Amicus Curiae brief. The Commission argued that Honduras' imposition of a mandatory life sentence without parole violated international human rights law.

[188]As mentioned, it is likely that internal political democratic reforms and the adoption of constitutions among some Latin American countries strengthened this process. Also see Malloy (1976), Huneeus (2015) and Sieder et al. (2005).

[189]Bazán, V *La reglamentación de la figura del Amicus Curiae por la Corte Suprema de Justicia argentina*, 3 Revista Iberoamericana de Derecho Procesal Constitucional 3, 3–4 (Bazán 2005). Charnovitz. For example, in the case of "Bacardi & Company Ltd. v. Compañía Ron Bacardi S.A." (2001), the United States Supreme Court allowed the government of Venezuela to file an Amicus Curiae brief. Venezuela argued that the Bacardi company's use of the "Havana Club" trademark violated international law. In the case of "Cisneros v. Alpine Ridge Group" (2005), the United States Supreme Court allowed the government of Mexico to file an Amicus Curiae brief. Mexico

It is worth noting that the submission of amicus briefs by international NGOs in Latin American countries is not without criticism. One of the possible claims in this regard is that international NGOs are organizations with great resources, experience, and power. Therefore, they enjoy a notable advantage compared to the other formal litigants in the courts of developing countries. This gives them a significant advantage over the formal parties and harms their autonomy to conduct proceedings without the intervention of third parties in their case.[190]

Another criticism maintains that judges in state courts in Latin America who receive amicus briefs from international organizations that influence the international arena do not always have the skills and ability to correctly interpret or apply the brief in the efficient way presented to them by these organizations. Sometimes, judges in various countries in Latin America have an excessive appreciation for international organizations and praise their position over the position of the litigants, with these positions given a falsely high status, as seen in the "as seen and sanctified" examination.[191]

The use of amicus briefs by NGOs as a tool to promote their position is an essential landmark in developing the work of the courts and the judicial process in general.[192] Their use of the Amicus Curiae practice brought about not only specific changes in concrete rulings but also a significant change in the form of discussion, conventional legal thinking, and the nature of public litigation in the courts when this change was replicated and copied to other countries. Today, there is almost no procedure for discussing public policy without many amici expressing their positions through submitting amicus briefs. Often, judges are exposed to more materials from amici, both in quantity and quality, than those of the official parties.[193] For example, in the issue that dealt with same-sex marriage in the United States, hundreds of NGOs and various interest groups joined together and submitted 147 briefs that together covered thousands of pages.[194]

As long as a crucial case raises an important question, various NGOs from both sides of the fence appear in court and often express their position relatively loudly through the submission of an amicus brief accompanied by a great deal of public and

argued that the Alien Tort Statute, which allows foreign nationals to sue in United States courts for violations of international law, did not apply to the case. In the case of "United States v. Bond" (2014), the United States Supreme Court allowed the government of Colombia to file an Amicus Curiae brief. Colombia argued that the Chemical Weapons Convention did not authorize individual criminal liability under United States law for offenses related to chemical weapons.

[190] In this context, see also the difficulties presented by Larsen (2014). Also, see also the concerns raised in connection with the use of a friend in the following article- Dwyer (2022). [Dwyer argues that there is a growing problem with Amicus Curiae briefs that are filed by individuals or organizations who do not have a legitimate interest in the case and who are not truly advocating for the interests of the parties involved].

[191] Defensoría Del Pueblo (2009), pp. 45–46.

[192] Krislov (1963), pp. 694–721.

[193] Box-Steffensmeier et al. (2013), pp. 446–460.

[194] Obergefell v. Hodges, 576 U.S. 644. (2015).

media interest. Opposing groups generate further media attention, including conservative organizations vs. liberal organizations, "green" organizations vs. energy companies, workers' organizations vs. employers' organizations, capitalist organizations vs. socialist organizations, senior organizations vs. organizations of crime victims, rights organizations vs. commercial companies, etc. Outside the courts, citizens, demonstrators, and sign carriers sometimes stand to express support for the organizations that submitted the briefs.[195] The submission of amicus briefs by these organizations is thus often also accompanied by extensive media publicity. The media interview volunteers in the organizations and their representatives, explain their agendas, and try to convince the public and the courts to accept their positions.[196]

The use of the "amicus" by NGOs and the changes that occurred as a result of this use is an example of a broader and more comprehensive systemic change in the judicial process that is reflected in the style of conduct in the courtroom, in the use of social information presented in briefs (in the form of "Brandeis briefs"), in the understanding of the broad implications of modern law, and the adoption of new modes of action and forms of discussion.

9.2.4 The Growth of the Legal Profession and Legal Guilds

Legal Profession Guilds are organizations in the public sphere, concerned with strengthening the legal profession, especially from a social point of view, but also involved with the desire of members of the legal profession to influence the society in which they live. Guilds facilitate close cooperation between members of the legal profession in various endeavors, including the submission and coordination of amicus briefs. The rise of such guilds is also related to the tremendous growth in numbers of lawyers in the population. Due to a higher awareness of liberal rights closely related to capitalism, personal capital accumulation, industrialization, and economic development, the number of lawyers in industrialized countries has increased significantly in recent years. The growing number of lawyers in the world, and their organization into guilds, facilitating cooperation of increasing numbers of lawyers engaged in promoting various social and public goals (Cause Lawyering, or Public Interest Lawyering or Social Lawyering or Political

[195] Collins (2008); Songer and Sheehan (1993), pp. 339–354. for example, In Citizens United v. Federal Election Commission, the Supreme Court case that overturned limits on campaign spending, a number of organizations filed Amicus Curiae briefs in support of the plaintiffs. These organizations included the Cato Institute, the Competitive Enterprise Institute, and the Center for Responsive Politics. These organizations also protested outside the Supreme Court building on the day of the oral arguments. See Citizens United v. Federal Election Commission, 558 U.S. 310 (2010).

[196] Collins (2008).

Lawyering), contributes significantly to the growth and strengthening of the "Amicus Curiae phenomenon."[197]

For example, the number of lawyers in the United States has climbed in recent years to approximately 1300,000 when, in the United States as a whole, there is one lawyer for every 248 Americans.[198] In the state of New York itself, over 170,000 lawyers work in a population of about 19 million people (a lawyer for every 110 inhabitants, one of the highest density of lawyers per capita in a US District, after the District of Columbia where the Supreme Court is located, as would be expected).[199]

Further examples of the high numbers of lawyers per capita found in areas of the US in descending order of prevalence include Massachusetts, where 43,221 lawyers work in a population of about 6.8 million (one lawyer for about 158 people); Connecticut with one lawyer for every 166 people; Illinois, with one lawyer for every 203 people; New Jersey, with one lawyer for every 215 people and finally California, where there is one lawyer for every 234 people.[200] The increase in the number of lawyers in the District of Columbia, which, as mentioned, is the location of the Supreme Court, and as such is a phenomenon in its own right, is especially noticeable (one lawyer for every 13 people). In Europe, there has also been a sharp increase in lawyers per capita in recent years. For example, Spain currently has over 253,000 lawyers; in Italy, there are about 250,000; in Germany, about 165,000; in England and Wales, about 185,000 lawyers; in France—54,000 lawyers; and in Turkey—46,000.[201]

In countries around the world, in recent years, a significant increase in the number of lawyers has also been recorded, in line with the rise in the population. For example, about 571,000 lawyers work in Brazil today. However, there are other countries where the rate of increase in numbers of lawyers outgrows even the dramatic rate of population increase. For example, the number of lawyers in India today stands at over 1300,000—an increase of tens of percent in recent years compared to the population growth rate.[202] The same is true in Israel, where the number of lawyers in Israel is over 80,000, of which over 68,000 are active lawyers

[197] Hunter (1997).

[198] For the Distribution of lawyers by category see *Lawyers per Capita by State*, Last Gen X Am., lawschooltuitionbubble.wordpress.com/original-research-updated/lawyers-per-capita-by-state. Also see https://worldpopulationreview.com/country-rankings/lawyers-per-capita-by-country.

[199] Laroche (2009), p. 701.

[200] ABA National Lawyer Population Survey/U.S. Census Bureau.

[201] For the increase in the number of lawyers in Europe see Council of Bars & Law Soc'ys. of Eur., Lawyers' Statistics 2015, www.ccbe.eu/fileadmin/user_upload/NTCdocument/2015_Table_of_Lawyer1_1433140834.pdf.

[202] Kian (2013), www.legallyindia.com/201302183448/Bar-Bench-Litigation/rti-reveals-number-of-lawyers-india. See also https://worldpopulationreview.com/country-rankings/lawyers-per-capita-by-country.

(one lawyer for every 132 people).[203] According to studies, the leading countries in the world, according to the number of lawyers per capita, are Israel, the United States, Brazil, New Zealand, Italy, England, Spain, Germany, and France.[204]

As a rule, the number of lawyers in common law countries is more remarkable because their training leads them to see their occupation as general (hence, the "Amicus Curiae phenomenon" is also more pronounced in these countries). Moreover, the relative autonomy of the courts in common law countries allows fertile ground for lawyers dealing with social goals, as is the situation in the United States.[205] On the other hand, the courts in continental law countries have a role that is seen as limited and more technical.[206] Most courts in continental law countries do not tend to interfere in government policy as is done in courts in the Anglo-Saxon world. Therefore, the number of lawyers, including those dealing with social issues, is lower in continental law countries.

Furthermore, it is clear that in countries with liberal and democratic regimes, there are more diverse opportunities for public law. These countries allow lawyers to adopt different action strategies to attempt to bring about change in the social, economic, and political status quo. Conversely, in authoritarian countries or countries lacking democratic roots, these opportunities are relatively few. Often, these regimes are committed only to providing their citizens with minimal Human Rights; therefore, advocacy for public purposes is limited (such as protective custody).[207]

---

[203] While the average number of lawyers in the Council of Europe countries is 151.3 lawyers per 100,000 inhabitants, in Israel, the number of lawyers registered in the Bar Association (including lawyers who do not practice the profession) is much higher and stands at 636.9 lawyers per 100,000 inhabitants. In addition, according to the European Conference on the Efficiency of Justice report for 2012, the number of lawyers compressing the number of judges in the Council of Europe countries is, on average, 14.7, compared to 78.1 lawyers per judge in Israel. The report ranks Israel in 34th place out of 42 countries in the ratio of the number of judges to the size of the population... Zar-Gutman (2014).

[204] Eur. Comm'n for the Efficiency of Justice (CEPEJ), Report on "European Judicial Systems—Edition 2014 (2012 Data): Efficiency and Quality of Justice" (2014) (a report of an organ of the Council of Europe aimed at streamlining and improving legal procedures in its 24 member states); Harper (2013) (When there is a gap between the rate of growth in the population of lawyers and the rate of growth in the population, the supply of lawyers is expected to increase without the demand for lawyers' services increasing in a similar way); Garoupa (2014). See also William (2007).

[205] Shall and Crocker (2014), and Sarat and Scheingold (1998).

[206] Dainow (1966) in that context also see The Role of Lawyers in European Integration by R. Daniel Kelemen, published in the Journal of European Public Policy (2009). This article examines the role of lawyers in the process of European integration, and how their work has shaped the development of the European legal system. See also The Changing Role of Lawyers in the Continental Legal System by Francisco Reyes Villamizar, published in the International Journal of Law and Society (2017). This article discusses the changing role of lawyers in the continental legal system, including the impact of globalization, the rise of alternative dispute resolution mechanisms, and the changing demands of clients. See also Abel (1993). [The article provides a comparative analysis of the role of lawyers in the civil law tradition, with a focus on France, Germany, and Italy].

[207] Sarat and Sheingold (1998).

In any case, in the opinion of the lawyers, particularly those who promote social changes or the reallocation of power, resources, and wealth in society, using "amicus" is one of the accepted forms of law to promote various interests and create social changes.[208] Lawyers for social groups see the law as a space where different techniques are used for purposes much broader than questions of winning or losing specific litigation. In various legal contests, particularly those with the potential of "legal leadership," considering whether to be involved in an ongoing legal process does not only involve likelihood of victory. Sometimes, involvement in the process as an amicus can bring the represented group to public prominence and establish it in public opinion and public awareness, even sometimes at the cost of losing the specific litigation.[209]

Taking into account the frequent changes in the law, lawyers in various fields are not satisfied today with relying solely on customary practices to achieve an appropriate result for their clients. They also constantly search for additional, innovative practices like the "amicus" to promote the interests of their clients.'[210] Lawyers must know precisely what the courts need to know and want to hear and how to present the information in order to use this practice effectively. How, for example, should information be renewed beyond the existing information presented by the parties? How should the information be presented within the existing procedural limitations?[211] To assist lawyers in this task, a considerable amount of practical literature in the field has been written in recent years. This literature presents examples of effective briefs and gives tips and guidelines on how to write them.[212]

In addition, videos on the internet and content-sharing sites, mainly on YouTube, help lawyers, students, and even high school students write amicus briefs that will

[208] Trubek (1996). [The article explores the role of lawyers in social change and how their practices are embedded in social structures and relationships with clients].

[209] Meaning that leadership processes of using legal proceedings by social movements to exert public pressure on decision makers in a way that will encourage and incentivize political reforms. Ronen Shamir and Ziv (2001). On social-legal mobilization see McCann (1994).

[210] It is also possible that one of the reasons for using a "amicus" may be related to the competition between the lawyers in the conditions of a market "flooded" with lawyers.

[211] In addition, like any legal matter, lawyers dealing in the field must be familiar with the procedures related to "amicus" such as: submission deadlines, the length of the memo, the information that is allowed to be presented in the memo, the way of submission to the court, the manner of presenting the arguments in the memo and various limitations that apply to the memo.

[212] for example, see Farber (2015) biulawblog.blogspot.co.il/2015/06/blog-post.html; In the United States see *Brief Bank*, Innocence Network, http://innocencenetwork.org/briefbank; *United States*—Amicus Curiae *Briefs*, *Am. Law Sources On-line*, http://www.lawsource.com/also/usa.cgi?usb; Simpson and Vasaly (2004). The sites were last visited at (13/08/2023) Also see Melinda S. Kollross (2020). https://www.clausen.com/10-tips-for-securing-beneficial-amicus-support-on-appeal/. UNESCO launches practical guide for Amicus Curiae interventions in freedom of expression cases. https://www.unesco.org/en/articles/unesco-launches-practical-guide-amicus-curiae-interventions-freedom-expression-cases. "Expert Q&A on Best Practices for Amicus Briefing" https://www.sullcrom.com/files/upload/LIT_AugSep16_OfNote-Amicus.pdf. "7 Tips For Writing An Effective Amicus Brief." https://www.obwbip.com/04D540/assets/files/News/7-Tips-For-Writing-An-Effective-Amicus-Brief.pdf.

fall on attentive ears.[213] Many legal blogs also deal with writing briefs.[214] In the journal entitled "Amicus Curiae," published since 1997 by the School of Advanced Study, University of London, many articles and position papers are published which offer, among other things, ways to promote various social issues through the submission of amicus briefs.[215]

9.2.4.1 Amicus Coordinator

Finally, in the United States and recently in international institutions and other countries, interest groups hire a lawyer called an "Amicus Coordinator." This lawyer is tasked with coordinating the variety of arguments put forward by all the "amici" from the same side, and with making sure that the arguments do not repeat each other. It is important to organize the material well so that a unified front is presented to the court while avoiding unnecessary repetitions but maintaining the diverse terms of its claims too allow as many chances of success as possible.

The role of an Amicus Coordinator can vary depending on the context but generally involves managing the process of submitting Amicus Curiae briefs to courts. The Amicus Coordinator may identify potential amici, communicate with them about the case, and coordinate the drafting and submission of the briefs. They may also review and edit briefs before submitting them to the court.[216] It is important to note that Amicus Coordinators typically work behind the scenes, and their role may not always be explicitly mentioned in judgments.

The concept of the Amicus Coordinator exists mainly in "mega cases" where dozens of briefs from hundreds of different organizations are filed. For example, in the procedure that dealt with the right to abortion, the *Webster* case,[217] dozens of amicus briefs were submitted that represented over 420 different organizations from the entire spectrum of political opinion in the United States, which represented 5469 interest groups and private individuals: interest groups of liberals, African-

---

[213] For example. The use of videos on digital sites to raise awareness of civil rights and influence issues in legal proceedings has been very popular in recent years and thousands of videos can be found on various topics, mainly in India and Latin America. For example, searching for the words Amicus Curiae or Amicus Curiae tips on YouTube yields thousands of results. There are videos on the subject in a wide variety of languages.

[214] I emphasized the topic of blogs because recently their circulation is very high and some believe that legal blogs are to some extent the future of legal writing in the coming decades Caron (2006).

[215] In the introduction to the journal, it was stated why the name "Amicus Curiae" was chosen for the journal: "We chose the name Amicus Curiae—friend of the court—to give emphasis to our desire to promote legal research and scholarship which is relevant to and supportive of the administration of justice. It is our view that academia has much to offer the practice of law, and practitioners certainly have much they could contribute to the advancement of scholarship. Amicus Curiae will, we are sure, become an important vehicle for raising and exploring issues, primarily of a topical nature, which can then be taken further by the Society and Institute. Rider (1997).

[216] Litman (2018).

[217] Webster v. Reproductive Health Services, 74 Judicature 261, 262.

Americans, Civil Rights Associations, organizations that specialize in medical ethics, the umbrella organization of the churches in the United States, women's organizations, the Association of Physicians, the Association of Deans of Medical Schools in the United States.[218]In the "re Marriage Cases" (2008), which involved the legality of same-sex marriage in California, the court acknowledged the role of the Amicus Coordinator in managing the submission of Amicus Curiae briefs. The court's opinion mentioned the extensive briefing by amici and recognized the efforts of the Amicus Coordinator in coordinating the briefs.[219]

References

Abel RL (1993) The role of lawyers in the civil law tradition: a comparative study published in the Journal of Law and Society (1993)

Abi-Hassan S, Box-Steffensmeier J, Christenson D, Kaufman A, Libgober B (2022) Replication data for: the ideologies of Organized Interests & Amicus Curiae Briefs: large-scale, social network imputation of ideal points. Harv Dataverse V1. https://doi.org/10.7910/DVN/TOYNMH

Ackerman B (1997) The rise of world constitutionalism. Va Law Rev:771–797. (p. 778-779)

Andrews CR (1999) A right of access to court under the petition clause of the first amendment: defining the right. Ohio St Law J 60:557

Baister S (1997) The court as educator: the social courts system of the German democratic republic. J Legal History 18(2):47–90

Banner S (2003) The myth of the neutral amicus: American courts and their friends, 1790–1890, 20. Const Comment 111

Barak A (1965) In: Cohen CH, Zamir Y (eds) The supreme court and public trust selected writings volume 1. 2000

Barak A (2004) Judge in a democratic society, p 262

Barak A (2002) A judge on judging: the role of a supreme court in a democracy. Harv Law Rev 116: 19

Barak A (2009) The judge in a democracy. Princeton University Press, Princeton

Bartholomeusz L (2005) The amicus curiae before international courts and tribunals. Non-State Actors Int Law 5:209–236

Bazán V (2005) La reglamentación de la figura del Amicus Curiae por la Corte Suprema de Justicia Argentina. Revista Iberoamericana de Derecho Procesal Constitucional 3:3–4. Charnovitz

Bazán V (2009) En Torno al amicus curiae. Revista Oficial del Poder Judicial 3(301):310–12

Becker ME (1986) From Muller v. Oregon to fetal vulnerability policies. Univ Chicago Law Rev 53:1219

Behuniak-Long S (1991) Friendly fire: amici curiae and Webster v. reproductive health services. Judicature 74:261–262

[218]It is almost certain that the development of this new legal role is also related to a change in the perception of the modern legal profession as a profession that goes beyond the provision of purely legal services. In other words, a lawyer is not a legal technician, but his role is much broader.

[219]Case No. S147999 (2008), the California Supreme Court acknowledged the role of the Amicus Coordinator in managing the submission of Amicus Curiae briefs. The court's opinion mentioned the extensive briefing by amici and recognized the efforts of the Amicus Coordinator in coordinating the briefs.

Berrang-Ford L, Ford JD, Paterson J (2011) Are we adapting to climate change? Glob Environ Chang 21(1):25–33
Bessette J (1980) Deliberative democracy: the majority principle in republican government. In: Goldwin RA, Schambra WA (eds) How democratic is the constitution? vol 102
Black RC, Boyd CL (2012) The role of law clerks in the US Supreme Court's agenda-setting process. Am Politics Res 40(1):147–173
Black RC, Boyd CL, Bryan AC (2014) Revisiting the influence of Law Clerks on the US Supreme Court's agenda-setting process. Marq Law Rev 98:75
Bobbio N (1987) The future of democracy: a defence of the rules of the game. University of Minnesota Press, Minnesota
Box-Steffensmeier JM, Christenson DP, Hitt MP (2013) Quality over quantity: amici influence and judicial decision making. Am Polit Sci Rev 107(3):446–460
Breyer S (1998) The interdependence of science and law. Judicature 82:24, 26
Breyer S (2005) Active liberty: interpreting our democratic constitution
Breyer S (2015) The Court and the World American law and the new global realities
Brodie Ian (1992) Interest groups and the charter of rights and freedoms: interveners at the Supreme Court of Canada (unpublished M.A. thesis, University of Calgary)
Brynat S (2001) The five habits: building cross cultural competence in lawyers. Clinical Law Rev 8(33):99
Canon BC (1982) A framework for the analysis of judicial activism. In: Halpern SC, Lamb CM (eds) Supreme court activism and restraint, p 385
Cappelletti M (1971) Judicial review in the contemporary world
Caron PL (2006) Are scholars better bloggers? Bloggership: how blogs are transforming legal scholarship. Wash Univ Law Rev 84:1025
Charnovitz S (1997) Two centuries of participation: NGOs and international governance. Mich J Int Law 18:281–282
Cheng EK (2008) The myth of the generalist judge. Stans Law Rev 61, 519
Chinkin C, Mackenzie R (2002) International organizations as 'friends of the court,'. In: de Chazournes LB et al (eds) International organizations and international dispute settlement: trends and prospects, Ardsley, p 13
Choudhry S, Hunter CE (2003) Measuring judicial activism on the supreme court of Canada: a comment on Newfoundland (Treasury Board) v. NAPE. McGill Law J 48:525
Clayton R, Tomlinson H, George C (2000) The law of human rights, vol 2. Oxford University Press, Oxford
Collins PM (2008) Friends of the Supreme Court: interest groups and judicial decision making
Collins PM Jr (2004) Friends of the court: examining the influence of amicus curiae participation in United States supreme court litigation. Law Soc Rev 38(4):807–832
Collins PM Jr (2018) The use of amicus briefs. Ann Rev Law Soc Sci 14:219–237
Coslin C, Lapillonne D (2012) France and the concept of amicus curiae: what lies ahead? Paris Int Litig Bull 4:14
Dainow J (1966) The civil law and the common law: some points of comparison. Am J Comp Law 15
David R, Brierley JEC (1978) Major legal systems in the world today (2d ed.)
Della Noce DJ (1999) Seeing theory in practice: an analysis of empathy in mediation. Negot J 15(3): 271–301
Derbyshire JD, Derbyshire I (1996) Political systems of the World (2nd ed.)
Dickson B (2013) Human rights and the United Kingdom supreme court. Oxford University Press, Oxford
Dillon J (2018) Epistemic institutions: law's encounters with knowledge. D.phil dissertation. https://escholarship.org/uc/item/5tj3q025
Disaffected Democracies (Susan J. Pharr & Robert D. Putnam eds., 2000)

Disaffected Democracies, Nancy Perkins Spyke (1999) Public participation in environmental Decisionmaking at the new millennium: structuring new spheres of public influence. BC Environ Aff Law Rev 26:263, 266–263, 269
Dolowitz DP, Marsh D (2000) Learning from abroad: the role of policy transfer in contemporary policy-making. Governance 13(1):5–23
Dressel B (2014) Governance, courts and politics in Asia. J Contemp Asia 44(2):259–278
Dressel B, Mietzner (2012) A tale of two courts: the judicialization of electoral politics in Asia. Governance 25(3):391–414
du Plessis LM (1999) The evolution of constitutionalism and the emergence of a constitutional jurisprudence in South Africa: an evaluation of the south African constitutional Court's approach to constitutional interpretation. Sask Law Rev 62:299
Duncan (1994) A little tour in France: surrogate motherhood and amici curiae in the French legal system. West State Univ Law Rev 21:447
Duncan JC Jr (1999) Multicultural participation in the public hearing process: some theoretical, Pragmatical, and Analeptical considerations. Colum J Environ Law 24:169–248. on pp 186, 199
Dwyer JG (2022) Faux advocacy in amicus practice
Edwards LH (2017) Telling stories in the supreme court: voices briefs and the role of democracy in constitutional deliberation. Yale J Law Femin 29:29
Elster J (1998) Introduction to deliberative democracy 1 (Jon Elster ed., 1998)
Ennis BJ (1984) Effective amicus briefs. Cath Univ Law Rev 33:603
Estlund DM (1993) Who's afraid of deliberative democracy? On the strategic/deliberative dichotomy in recent constitutional jurisprudence. Tex Law Rev 71:1437
Evans AB Jr (2005) Russian Civil Society. In: White S, Gitelman Z, Sakwa R (eds) Developments in Russian politics, vol 6, p 96
Eylon Y, Harel A (2006) The right to judicial review. Va Law Rev 92(5):991–1022
Farber S (2015) How to be a good 'friend' of the court? On the agenda: sentences (1.6.2015) biulawblog.blogspot.co.il/2015/06/blog-post.html
Farber S (2019) Crime victims organizations as amici curiae in criminal trial courts: a new beginning. Wayne Law Rev 65:235
Flango VE, Bross DC, Corbally S (2006) Amicus Curiae Briefs: The Court's Perspective. Justice Syst J 27:180–190
Floridi L (2010) Information: a very short introduction
Floridi L (2013) The philosophy of information. Oxford University Press, Oxford
Franze AJ, Anderson RR (2015) *Record breaking term for Amicus Curiae in Supreme Court reflects new norm*, Natl Law J. http://www.nationallawjournal.com/supremecourtbrief/id=1202735095655
Friedman LM (1978) Access to Justice: Social and Historical Context. In: Cappelletti M, Weisner J (eds) 2 Access To Justice: Promising Institutions 3
Friedman B (2003) Mediated popular constitutionalism. Mich Law Rev 101:2596
Garcia RJ (2008) A democratic theory of amicus advocacy. Fla St Univ Law Rev 35:315
Garoupa N (2014) Globalization and deregulation of legal services. Int Rev L Econ 38:77
Glamis v. USA, Quechan Indian Nation Application for Leave to File a Non-Party Submission, 19 August 2005, pp. 3–4
Gómez KF (2012) LLM perspective, rethinking the role of amicus curiae in international investment arbitration: how to draw the line favorably for the public interest. Fordham Int Law J 35:510
Graham C (2012) Advocates for Int'l Dev., a "How To" guide to amicus curiae & international investment arbitrations, pp 6–7
Gramberger M (2001) Citizens as partners: OECD Handbook on Information, Consultation and Public Participation in Policy-Making
Halpin DR (2006) The participatory and democratic potential and practice of interest groups: between solidarity and representation. Public Adm 84(4):919–940
Harper SJ (2013) The lawyer bubble: a profession in crisis 14

Haas PM (1992) Introduction: epistemic communities and international policy coordination. Int Organ 46(1):1–35

Heard A (2010) The eyes of Willie McGee: a tragedy of race, sex, and secrets in the Jim crow south. Harper Collins, New York

Heller TC (1984) Structuralism and critique. Stand Law Rev 36:127

Hinson Z and Hubbard D (2012) Access to justice in Namibia: proposals for improving public access to courts: amicus curiae participation

Hirschl R (2006) The new constitutionalism and the judicialization of pure politics worldwide. Fordham Law Rev 75:721

Holland KM (ed) (1991) Judicial activism in comparative perspective. Springer, Cham

Holmes S, Sunstein CR (1995) "Twelve. The politics of constitutional revision in Eastern Europe." Responding to imperfection. Princeton University Press, Princeton, pp 275–306

Howse R (2001) Adjudicative legitimacy and treaty interpretation in international trade law: the early years of WTO jurisprudence. In: Weiler J (ed) The EU, the WTO and the NAFTA. Oxford Academic, Oxford

Howse R. Amicus Brief (2003) in European Communities-Trade Description of Sardines, Report of the Appellate Body, WT/DS231/AB/R,AB 2002–3, 6 September 2002

Howse R et al (2013) Written submission of non-party Amici Curiae in EC-seals, 11 February, para. 13

Huneeus A (2015) Introduction to symposium on the constitutionalization of international law in Latin America. Am J Int Law 109:89–92

Hunter ND (1997) Essay, lawyering for social justice. NY Univ Law Rev 72:1009

Johnson JW (2005) Brandeis brief. In: Hall K, in chief (eds) The Oxford companion to the supreme court of the United States, 2nd edn, p 100

Kastellec JP, Lebo MJ (2010) Racial diversity and judicial influence on appellate courts. Princeton University, Princeton. https://scholar.princeton.edu/sites/default/files/kastellec_racial_diversity_final_0.pdf

Kearney JD, Merrill TW (2000) The influence of amicus curiae briefs on the Supreme Court. Univ Pa Law Rev 148:743–855

Kian G (Feb. 18, 2013) *RTI Reveals: 1.3m Advocates; 1 in 300 Delhi-Ites a Lawyer; Maharashtra Lawyers 'Richest'; Jharkand, Assam, J&K Fastest*, Legally India , www.legallyindia.com/201302183448/Bar-Bench-Litigation/rti-reveals-number-of-lawyers-india

King A (2001) Does the United Kingdom Still Have a Constitution? 54–55, 59–61, 71–73, 95–96 (2001)

Kingsbury B, Schill S (2009) Investor-state arbitration as governance: fair and equitable treatment, proportionality and the emerging global administrative law. NYU School of Law, Public Law Research Paper, pp 09–46

Klebanow D, Jonas FL (2003) People's lawyers: crusaders for justice in American History 70–71

Kmiec KD (2004) The origin and current meanings of judicial activism. Calif Law Rev 92(5): 1441–1477

Kochevar S (2013) Comment, Amici curiae in civil law jurisdictions. Yale Law J 122:1653

Kolbert K (1989) The Webster amicus curiae briefs: perspectives on the abortion controversy and the role of the supreme court—introduction: did the Amici effort make a difference? Am J Law Med 15:153

Koshner AJ (1998) Solving the puzzle of interest. Group Litigation Greenwood Press, Santa Barbara, pp 7–11

Krislov S (1963) The amicus curiae brief: from friendship to advocacy. Yale Law J 72:694–721

Kromphardt CD (2015) US Supreme Court Law Clerks as Information Sources. J Law Courts 3: 277–304

Lamer A (1994) Canada's legal revolution: judging in the age of the charter of rights. Israel Law Rev 28:579

Langbein JH (1985) The German advantage in civil procedure. Univ Chicago Law Rev 52:823, 826, 833–823, 826, 839

Laroche M (2009) Is the New York State court of appeal still "Friendless?" an empirical study of amicus curiae participation. Alb Law Rev 72:701
Larsen AO (2014) The trouble with amicus facts. Va Law Rev 100:1757–1818
Lawson G, Seidman G (1999) Downsizing the right to petition. Nw. U L Rev 93:739, 740
Leib EJ (2006) Essay, Can direct democracy be made deliberative. Buff Law Rev 54:903, 904
Liptak A (2006) *Appeals Court rejects brief submitted by ex-judges*, N.Y. Times, Dec. 30, at A15
Litman LM (2018) An Introduction to the Amicus Curiae Brief. University of California, Davis Law Review
Macey JR (1994) Judicial preferences, public choice, and the rules of procedure. J Leg Stud 23:627
Malloy J (1976) Authoritarianism and Corporatism in Latin America
Mclauchlan JS (2005) Congressional participation as amicus curiae before the U.S. Supreme Court American legal institutions
Mansbridge J (2006) Conflict and self-interest in deliberation. In: Besson S, Martí JL (eds) Deliberative democracy and its discontents, vol 107
Medeiros DB (2008) Amicus curiae: a panorama of the third collaborator. Revista Da Esmarn 7:279
McCann MW (1994) Rights at work 48–91
McCann M (2008) Litigation and legal mobilization. In: Whittington K, Keleman D, Caldiera G (eds) The Oxford handbook of law and politics. Oxford University Press, Oxford, pp 522–540
Mohan SC (2010) The amicus curiae: friends no more? Singapore J Legal Stud 2:352–374
Mouttotos N (2020) Reform of civil procedure in Cyprus: delivering justice in a more efficient and timely way. Common Law World Rev 49(2):99–130
Murray C (1994) Litigating in the public interest: intervention and the amicus curiae. S Afr J Hum Rts 10(240):242
Nevitte N (1996) New politics, the charter and political participation. In: Bakvis H (ed) Representation, integration and political parties in Canada, vol 355
O'Connor K, Epstein L (1981) Amicus curiae participation in U.S. Supreme Court litigation: an appraisal of Hakman's "Folklore,". Law Soc Rev 16:311
O'Brien Z (2004) The courts make a new friend? amicus curiae jurisdiction in Ireland. Trinity C L Rev 7:5
Ortino F (2009) The impact of amicus curiae briefs in the settlement of trade and investment disputes. In: Meessen KM (ed) Economic law as an economic good, vol 301, p 316
Pinto M (2005) NGOs and the inter-American Court of human rights. In: Treves T et al (eds) Civil society, international courts and compliance bodies, vol 47, pp 55–56
Posner RA (2003) Law, pragmatism, and democracy 16–18
Quigley WP (1995) Reflections of community organizers: lawyering for empowerment of community organizations. Ohio Northern Univ Law Rev 21:455
Ranzal E (1953) Greenglass, in prison, vows to kin he told truth about Rosenbergs, N.Y. Times, Mar. 19, 1953, at 1
Razzaque J (2001) Changing role of friends of the court in the international courts and tribunals. Non-State Actors Int Law 1(3):169–200
Reimann KD (2006) A view from the top: international politics, norms and the worldwide growth of NGOs. Int Stud Q 50:45–67
Rider B (1997) Bringing the profession together. Amicus Curiae 1
Roberts S (2003) The brother: the untold story of the rosenberg case 11
Rosen J (2016) Louis D. Brandeis: American prophet. Yale University Press, New Haven
Rosenberg GN (2008) The hollow Hope: can courts bring about social change? 2nd edn. The University of Chicago Press, Chicago
Rustad M, Koenig T (1993) The Supreme Court and junk social science: selective distortion in amicus briefs. NCL Rev 72(91):157–158
Salzman R, Williams CJ, Calvin BT (2011) The determinants of the number of amicus briefs filed before the U.S. Supreme Court, 1953–2001. Just Sys J 32:293, 294–293, 295

Sarat AD, Scheingold SA (1998) Cause lawyering and the reproduction of professional authority: an introduction. In: Sarat A, Scheingold S (eds) Cause lawyering: political commitments and professional responsibilities, vol 3
Shelton D (1994) The participation of nongovernmental organizations in international judicial proceedings. Am J Int Law 88(611):637
Shall A, Crocker HD (2014) Cause lawyering. Ann Rev Law Soc Sci 10:301–320
Shamir R, Ziv N (2001) State-oriented and community-oriented lawyering for a cause. In: Sarat A, Scheingold S (eds) Cause lawyering and the state in a global era, vol 287
Shaw GM, Brannan KE (2009) Confidence in law enforcement. Pub Opinion Q 73:199
Sieder R et al (2005) The judicialization of politics in Latin America
Simard LS (2008) An empirical study of amici curiae in Federal Court: a fine balance of access, efficiency, and Adversarialism. Rev Litig 27:669. (referring to Grutter v. Bollinger, 539 U.S. 306 (2003)
Simmons BA, Dobbin F, Garrett G (2006) Introduction: The International Diffusion of Liberalism. Int Organ 60(4):781–810
Simpson RW, Vasaly MR (2004) The Amicus brief: how to be a good friend of the court (2nd Ed.)
Smith J, Pagnucco R, Lopez GA (1998) Globalizing human rights: the work of transnational human rights NGOs in the 1990s. Human Rights Q 20(2):379–412
Songer DR, Sheehan RS (1993) Interest group success in the courts: amicus participation in the Supreme Court. Polit Res Q 46(2):339–354
Spriggs JF, Wahlbeck PJ (1997) Amicus curiae and the role of information at the Supreme Court. Polit Res Q 50(2):365–386
Steger D (2002) Amicus Curiae: participant or friend?—The WTO and NAFTA experience. In: Bogdandy AV (ed) European integration and international co-ordination—studies in transnational economic law in honour of Claus-Dieter Ehlermann, The Hague, p 419, 447
Stoknes PE (2015) What we think about when we try not to think about global warming: toward a new psychology of climate action. Chelsea Green Publishing, Vermont
Stone D (2012) Transfer and translation of policy. Policy Stud 33(6):483–499
Tarr GA (2003) Judicial process and judicial policymaking 233–43 (3d ed.)
The Judicialization of Politics in Asia (Björn Dressel ed., 2012)
The Role of Lawyers in European Integration by R. Daniel Kelemen, published in the Journal of European Public Policy (2009)
Torcal M, Montero JR (2006) Political disaffection in comparative perspective. Political disaffection in contemporary democracies. Routledge, Milton Park, pp 25–42
Trubek LG (1996) Embedded practices: lawyers, clients, and social change. Harv Civil Rights Civil Liberties Law Rev 31:415
Tyler TR (1988) What is procedural justice? Criteria used by citizens to assess the fairness of legal procedures. Law Soc Rev 22(1):103–135
Tyler TR (2004) Procedural justice. In: Sarat A (ed) The Blackwell companion to law and society, vol 435
Tyler TR (2006) Psychological perspectives on legitimacy and legitimation. Ann Rev Psychol 57: 375
Tyler R, Bies RJ (1990) Beyond formal procedures: the interpersonal context of procedural justice. In: Carroll J (ed) Applied social psychology and organizational settings, 2nd edn. 2015. Psychology Press, East Sussex, pp 77–98
Ulster J, Haberms J, Rawls J, Fishkin J, Gutman A, Thompson D (2004) Why deliberative democracy? 134
Urofsky MI (2009) Louis D. brandeis: a life. Schocken
Van Duzer JA (2007) Enhancing the procedural legitimacy of investor-state arbitration through transparency and amicus curiae participation. McGill Law J 52:681–709
Warren RK (2000) *Public trust and procedural justice*, Ct. Rev., Fall, at 12
Wiik A (2018) Amicus curiae before international courts and tribunals. Nomos Verlagsgesellschaft mbH & Co. KG

William D (2007) The globalization of the legal profession. Indiana J Global Legal Stud 14(1):1–3
Williams M (2000) The uneasy alliance of group representation and deliberative democracy. Citizenship Diverse Soc:124–154
Williams S, Woolaver H (2006) The role of the amicus curiae before international criminal tribunals. Int Crim Law Rev 6:151
Young EA (2002) Judicial activism and conservative politics. Univ Colo Law Rev 73:1139
Zannoti F (1995) The judicialization of judicial salary policy in Italy and the United States. The Global Expansion of Judicial Power. https://doi.org/10.18574/nyu/9780814770078.003.0014
Zar-Gutman L (2014) "The Effects of the Dramatic Increase in the Number of Lawyers" Law No. 51
Zemans FK (1983) Legal mobilization: the neglected role of the law in the political system. Am Polit Sci Rev 77(3):690–703
Zurn CF (2007) Deliberative democracy and the institutions of judicial review 163–84

Chapter 10
Summary and Conclusions

> The amicus has the power to speak to many audiences simultaneously. In the courtroom, it is the honest broker; in the public media, it is the educator; in academia, it is the scholarly analysis and historical perspective.[1]

10.1 Advantages and Disadvantages of the Use of Amicus Curiae: Interim Summary

Before concluding the book and examining the overall implications of adopting the Amicus Curiae practice and summarizing the influence of the Amicus Curiae phenomenon in the world, it is appropriate to prepare a brief and concise summary of the advantages and disadvantages of using the Amicus Curiae practice. These claims were scattered throughout the book and are now, for convenience, bound together.

10.1.1 Potential for the Most Complete and Correct Judicial Decision

Using the information presented by the Amicus Curiae mechanism may reduce judicial errors and lead to the best and most complete decision based on the broadest possible knowledge, taking into account that this, of course, is bound by the circumstances and institutional limitations within which the courts operate. "It is

[1] Strutin (2015), http://www.llrx.com/2015/04/amicus-curiae-information-in-the-service-of-justice.

S. Farber, *The Amicus Curiae Phenomenon*, Ius Gentium: Comparative Perspectives on Law and Justice 119, https://doi.org/10.1007/978-3-031-67225-5_10

for the honor of a court of justice to avoid error in their judgments," an English court ruled in 1656 about "amicus," and these words have not expired.[2]

The use of information—factual, legal, or social—presented by the amici has the potential to reduce possible errors in the decision-making process of the courts, which may have been derived from the interests of third parties having any bearing on the proceedings not having been heard or expressed in court.[3] The practice of the Amicus Curiae makes it possible to introduce into judicial systems extensive knowledge from various fields, adding additional information to that presented by the formal parties, from a wide range of third parties who have some interest in the proceeding.[4] Amici may make more principled arguments that have future broad implications rather than focusing only on the concrete arguments of the case. In this way, the amici may prevent the court from relying on exclusive (and sometimes erroneous) sources of knowledge presented to them by formal litigants without consideration of additional interests,[5] including those of third parties.[6] It can be assumed that the broader and more complete the information presented to the court, the lower the chance of error.[7] Using Amicus Curiae does not guarantee that a mistake will not be made in the judicial decision-making process, but it can certainly improve the situation. The assumption is that judges want to receive all the essential information, legal or factual, to properly and efficiently decide the case before them. The information presented in briefs, in terms of both quantity and content, primarily influences the content of the majority opinion rather than determining who wins or loses. This is understandable, as information is inherently nuanced, and opinions contain far more subtlety than the binary determination of whether to affirm or reverse the lower court's ruling. While the case outcome matters to the litigants and links to the opinion's content, it is the details within that opinion that generate the legal policies governing people's lives. Relevant information helps judges reduce uncertainty about how their preferences will map onto policy outcomes when rendering decisions. The repetition of information across briefs becomes its own signal for the Court to evaluate argument credibility amidst the increasing amount of information provided in each case. Sometimes, the role of amici may be expressed, not necessarily in presenting all the information but rather in directing the court to the most appropriate and accurate materials.[8]

If judges believe that the inclusion of third parties as amici (or interveners) may increase the chances of a more complete and better decision (of course, relatively speaking) by presenting new, significant information that has not been presented by the formal parties (either because they are unaware of it, are not interested in

[2]Protector v. Geering (1656), 145 Eng. Rep. 394, 394; Hardres 85, 85, 86.

[3]Spriggs and Wahlbeck (1997).

[4]See Johnson and Tuerk (2005), pp. 24.

[5]Umbricht (2001).

[6]Levine (2011).

[7]Schachter (2004), p. 111.

[8]Hazelton and Hinkle (2022).

presenting it, or are unable to do so), then they will incline to approve their request to join the process.[9]

10.1.2 The Amicus As a Generator of Influence on Court Rulings

The information presented by amici can influence the outcome of the judgment, depending on the position or perspective that the amicus wishes to promote. The question of how the Amicus Curiae practice affects decision-making processes is complex and inconclusive. Empirical studies claim that explicit references or quotations of the information presented by amici in judgments indicate that briefs submitted by amici influence judgments.[10] For example, in about a third of the rulings handed down from the mid-twentieth century to the 2000s by the U.-S. Supreme Court, the court referenced or referred in some way to the information presented to it in an amicus brief. This phenomenon has intensified in recent years.

In the years 2015 and 2016, about 54% of U.S. Supreme Court rulings included explicit references to information presented by amici.[11] Similarly, between 2010 and 2016, in about 50% of cases in which a verdict was handed down, the Supreme Court mentioned, quoted, or referred to information presented by amici.[12] Data showing extensive use of information presented by amici in court rulings can also be found in international courts such as the Latin American Human Rights Court[13]or the European Human Rights Court.[14]

This data supports the hypothesis that the courts were affected in some way by the amicus brief submitted to them, although it is impossible to determine precisely to what extent, in what way, and exactly how this was done. These studies admit that it is possible to dispute the extent to which an amicus brief affects the court, but its citation or mention indicates that the court did take the brief into account in some way.

However, extreme caution should be exercised with this criterion for several reasons. First, studies show that, sometimes, judges cite briefs submitted by amici on

---

[9] Alarie and Green (2010).

[10] Lynch (2004); Abramowicz and Colby (2009), pp. 965, 987 ("There has been no shortage of praise in the legal literature for the ability of amicus briefs to 'inform the court of implications of a decision'... [and] provide relevant factual information not offered by the parties").

[11] Franze & Anderson (2015).

[12] Collins et al. (2015). Between 2010 and 2016, Judge Ginzberg, in 45 percent of her rulings, referred to information presented to her by "amici." Justice Kennedy used information presented to him by amici in 42% of his rulings. (Sotmayor—40%; Roberts—40%; Breyer—39%; Kagan—35%; Alito—27%; Scalia—24%; Thomas—22%). Franze and Anderson (2015).

[13] Juaristi (2014).

[14] Van den Eyn, see also *supra* note 224. Lester et al. (1988) Protecting human rights: the European dimension—studies in honour of Gérard J. Wiarda, Cologne, p. 342.

both sides to present an equally objective picture of the situation. Judges may also quote from one or more amicus briefs in their rulings to show that the position of amici and the position of formal litigants are the same. On the other hand, sometimes judges let amici argue orally and therefore find no further need to address what they say in their ruling, and in other cases, judges do not want to quote specific briefs due to the public image of the particular organizations who submitted the briefs and the fear of public support for what is implied in their actions.[15]

In other words, citations of information submitted by amici can have different explanations besides having had an influence on the verdict. In any event, it is possible to dispute the extent to which an amicus brief affects the court, but its quotation or mention shows, with due caution, that the court took the brief into account, among other considerations.[16] The citations of the information presented by the amici show that it is helpful in the court's decision-making process.

Other studies rely on in-depth interviews with judges to prove the influence of amici on the work of the courts. For example, from Simard's research, an examination of amici joining United States federal courts shows that most federal judges (about 77% of judges in circuit courts and 82% of judges in district courts) believe that the amicus briefs submitted to them help them to better understand the general implications of court rulings on the interests of third parties.[17]

Another way of examining the influence of the Amicus Curiae on the work of the courts has to do with the "social information" that judges draw about the public sentiments of society through the amici. For some of the justices, the amicus briefs constitute a kind of "social barometer" of the public's position on the issue.[18] In some ways, the role of amici is not limited to presenting information, but rather the presence of certain amici, in some cases, as organized interest groups, creates pressure on judges to accept the position promoted by the interest group.[19]

This approach of interest groups "communicating" their desired outcome to the court is based on the assumption that judges tend not to stray too far from the public consensus, that they are attentive to the public's positions, and that they give considerable significance to the positions of interest groups, which is undoubtedly so in the case of influential interest groups. In other words, the courts accept briefs from amici not only because of the formal content of the brief that is supposed to assist them in their work but also because of the identity and influence of the interest

[15] Franze & Anderson (2016), Larsen and Devins (2016), Feldman (2016) and Lynch (2004).

[16] For a representative example, see U.S. Supreme Court Chief Justice John Roberts' reference to an "amicus" memo by a former White House adviser on alleged corruption by the Virginia governor. Coyle (2016).

[17] Simard (2008), pp. 669

[18] Collins Jr. (2004), pp. 807–832. Many studies emphasize that the most dominant component of these processes stems from the "response to social demand," which has increased, among other things, due to the efforts of interest groups to achieve through the courts what cannot be achieved in the legislative and executive branches. Zannoti (1995), https://doi.org/10.18574/nyu/9780814770078.003.0014.

[19] Kearney and Merrill (2000), pp. 743–855.

groups behind the submission. In some issues, especially if they are "volatile" or have a prominent public dimension, judges tend to take public opinion into account more than in ordinary disputes. In these cases, they may look at amicus briefs as a kind of social indicator that helps them to understand the expected consequences of their decision.[20]

10.1.3 Low Economic Costs

The economic parameters of the procedures involved in submitting amicus briefs may incentivize using an amicus. Firstly, using an amicus brief has lower costs than other alternatives, such as filing an independent petition or joining the proceedings as a formal party. Amici are not required to pay various fees (such as the fee for initiating a proceeding). In addition, amici are not charged additional fees since the formal parties pay the fees since the amicus only joins the proceedings. Other costs associated with the proceedings are also not imposed on them. Thus, for example, the amici are not required to guarantee other parties' expenses in the proceedings. In addition, if the proceeding joined by the amicus ends with an award of court costs, the formal party bears the burden, and the amicus is not exposed to these expenses.[21]

Secondly, writing an amicus brief is simpler and cheaper than the alternative of filing an alternative independent petition. The process of writing an amicus brief is usually shorter than other alternative forms of litigation, which require the investment of a great deal of time. In the framework of an amicus brief, there is no need to address, refute, contradict, or confront all of the parties' arguments. An amicus may discuss one issue while the parties must argue all the issues that arise in the case. Moreover, the brief is sometimes written by lay individuals or law students, which also involves savings.[22]

Furthermore, some of the procedural aspects affecting formal parties to the proceedings do not apply to amici, with the results of the proceeding not establishing an act of the court against the amici. A person who is not a party to the proceeding (the amicus) cannot claim estoppel in his favor, and estoppel cannot be asserted against him. Other estoppels, such as judicial estoppel or motives due to bad faith, also do not apply to the amicus.

---

[20] Collins Jr. (2004), pp. 807–832.

[21] Although in some places there is authority in principle to impose legal costs on third parties (for the most part, this is the imposition of costs on "interveners," but costs can also be imposed on "amici"). However, the use of this authority is rare.

[22] Fisher v. University of Texas at Austin (2016), United States v. Windsor (2013); *The Center's Civil Rights & Criminal Justice Advocacy*, Seattle Univ. Sch. of Law (2016), www.law.seattleu.edu/centers-and-institutes/korematsu-center/litigation/the-civil-rights-amicus-brief-project.

10.1.4 Cooperation and Strengthening Ties Between Social Organizations

Joining the process as amici submitting an amicus brief may be fertile ground for creating collaborations and strengthening working relationships between various social organizations. These collaborations enhance civil society and should be seen both as a means and as a worthy end in themselves. Collaborations between social organizations around joining legal proceedings as amici and creating coalitions of amici include a variety of modes of action: writing a joint brief on behalf of several social organizations, mutual brainstorming, work meetings, and ongoing consultations between representatives of the organizations regarding the arguments that should be staged in the court position. Sometimes, working relationships between organizations are expressed in their capacity as amici in the invention of existing legal materials, scientific or social studies, or in providing experts (for example: experts in environmental science or labor law) for the coalition partner organization.[23]

Sometimes, collaborations between social organizations regarding using the Amicus Curiae practice include building a joint action strategy for managing the process. An "invitation" for cooperation in connection with the submission of a supportive amicus brief does not exist only between public NGOs but also crosses sectors and occurs between state institutions and social organizations.

In addition, when several organizations join together and voice a united front in the court as a coalition of amici, they may create a more significant impression on the court and the public. At the same time, as noted, it isn't easy to establish broad agreement on the content of the position to be presented, on the tactics and modus operandi of the United Front.[24] In addition, not only is writing a joint amicus brief on the part of several entities likely to strengthen the power of the brief and may save the overall expenses of the amici, but it may also facilitate the work of the court, which will read and study fewer briefs, thus saving judicial time.

---

[23] In Israel, for example, in two cases related to privacy protection (hacking into an employee's email box; and a biometric attendance clock in the workplace), the Association for Civil Rights in Israel and *Kav LaOved* collaborated in writing an "amicus" brief to the court. On the one hand, the Association provided experts in the field of information privacy, and on the other hand, Kav LaOved provided the Association with expertise in labor law. See Labor Appeal (national) 90/08 Inbar–v. State of Israel - Commissioner for the Women's Labor Law (8.2.2011). Appeal of a national collective dispute 7541-04-14 New General Workers' Union South Triangle Region— Kalansawa Municipality (March 15, 2017).*s*.

[24] See the discussion above regarding Webster v. Reproductive Health Services, 74 Judicature 261, 262, which dealt with the right to an abortion.

10.1.5 Strengthening the Institutional Legitimacy of the Courts

Using Amicus Curiae may strengthen the institutional legitimacy of the courts by presenting the image of the courts as institutions that consider the public interest and are not isolated from the concerns of the general public. This, in turn, may lead to a more significant commitment on the part of members of the public to court rulings, which include amicus briefs as part of the process, even if a brief representing an individual's position was not accepted. Expanding public participation in the courts through the submission of an amicus brief is the result of an interaction between the interests of the courts in expanding the public's participation base in proceedings and thereby establishing its public and institutional legitimacy and the interests of members of the public[25] who wish to increase their influence on their environment and on all aspects of their lives.

As far as the courts are concerned, listening to the legal or social positions presented by amici representing different segments of the public, even without acceding to the position itself, may strengthen their institutional legitimacy because the very willingness of the courts to listen to the arguments of amici expresses appreciation on the part of the courts for the amici and creates a more significant commitment among them and other groups to respect the rulings.[26] Listening to the position presented by amici, even without accepting their position, is an expression of the fact that the court represents the political and cultural conventions of the cultural community in which it functions. The Amicus Curiae process thus underlines the commitment of the courts to give every interested person from all groups within society, even if they are not a formal party to the proceedings, their "day in court;" so giving them a sense of empowerment, stemming from being active participants in the decision-making processes that influence their lives. In this way, the amicus practice also ensures that even those who "lose" in the end feel that their voices are heard in the process that leading to shaping the courts' decisions and implementing them.[27]

The feeling that the judge seriously considered their "voices" and the stories of individuals and groups other than the formal litigants (amici) has a positive effect that strengthens trust in the judicial system and its rulings and leads to a moral

---

[25] Studies indicate a downward trend in public trust in the courts and law enforcement authorities. Shaw and Brannan (2009). In most democratic countries, there has been an erosion of public trust in political actors and state institutions. Disaffected Democracies (Susan J. Pharr and Robert D. Putnam (2000) (the study looked at Finland, Norway, Spain, France, United States, Canada, Ireland, Germany, Italy, Sweden, Japan, United Kingdom, Belgium, Denmark, Iceland, Netherlands). See also: Wolfrum (2008); Voßkuhle and Sydow (2002); Choudhury (2008), p. 775.

[26] See, for example, De Brabandere (2011).

[27] Blackaby and Richard (2010) ("Considering that public participation is at the heart of democratic processes, it is assumed that increased civil society participation will enhance the legitimacy and acceptance of the system).''

obligation on the part of these groups to respect the verdicts.[28] This is even more true when the court to which the brief was submitted did indeed quote from the brief submitted to it by the amici. In these situations, the amici feel that the court has legitimized their activities and that their presence in court is essential and justified. The greater extent to which the legitimacy of the courts' decisions is bolstered by these processes, demonstrating that they are "open" to all positions, the greater the chances are that the public will respect and act on them. When social movements express their position as amici, they accept legitimacy as an axiom of the courts.[29]

Apart from these considerations, the following points should also be considered, which take place mainly (but not only) in international arbitration proceedings:

Firstly, an amicus brief may help protect the public interest, especially in developing countries or in proceedings with significant power gaps, on various issues: human rights, the environment, labor rights, protection of local heritage, and the fight against corruption. The argument is that there are disputes in which there is no consideration whatsoever of certain essential issues, even though they are involved (either directly or indirectly) in the proceedings. In some cases, the amici are the only ones who are interested (or able) to present certain important and worthy issues which are not included within the commercial (and legitimate) interests of the formal parties. In light of this, that information presented by the amici, which has not been presented by the formal parties to the dispute, must be brought to the arbitrators' attention.[30]

Secondly, sometimes, the parties to the arbitration process do not have the tools, ability, or unique professional knowledge at the disposal of "amici." In contrast to the formal parties to the dispute, amici, especially if they are well-informed international organizations with well-researched scientific knowledge at their disposal, together with the experience and expertise in ways of presenting the information effectively, can offer a different perspective or assist arbitrators legally, factually, or technically.[31]

Thirdly, the intervention of amici in international arbitration proceedings affects the institutional regime of international institutions and leads to greater transparency and more democratic modes of action.[32] Furthermore, sometimes, the media coverage received by the amici leads to public discussion of issues that the formal parties

---

[28] See Warren (2000). For a description of the evolution of the problem of public trust in the U.S. court system. See Tarr (2003), pp. 233.

[29] Brynat (2001).

[30] Graham (2012), pp. 6–7.

[31] For example, Biwater Gauff (Tanz.) Ltd. v. United Republic of Tanzania, ICSID Case No. ARB/05/22, Procedural Order No. 5, ¶ 55 (Feb. 2, 2007), 22 ICSID Rev. 217, 231 (2007), "approach[ed] the issues in this case with interests, expertise and perspectives that have been demonstrated to materially differ from those of the two contending parties, and as such have provided a useful contribution to these proceedings."

[32] Kawharu (2007), pp. 2–3.

try to influence, thereby increasing public criticism of proceedings that are sometimes carried out in secret.[33]

10.1.6 Public Transparency

There are some claims that investment tribunals, and especially the WTO dispute settlement institutions, suffer from a lack of transparency in their proceedings and decision-making.[34] One of the benefits of having Amicus Curiae briefs in these courts is the transparency it produces. By allowing third-party individuals or organizations to provide information to the court, the court gains a broader perspective on the legal issues presented in the case. This, in turn, can help promote transparency in the legal system by ensuring that all relevant arguments and perspectives are considered before a decision is made.[35] The Amicus Curiae can help ensure that the court's decision is not based on incomplete or biased information but instead reflects a well-rounded understanding of the legal issues at hand.[36] For example, in several investment arbitration cases, Amicus Curiae applicants opined that their participation would "allay public disquiet as to the closed nature of arbitration proceedings."[37]

10.2 The Main Disadvantages of Using Amicus

10.2.1 Politicization of the Legal Process

One disadvantage of the Amicus Curiae practice is that its improper use may politicize the courts and turn them into an arena for promoting the political interests of competing groups. There is concern that some of the amici will copy political debates belonging to the legislative and executive branches, bringing them into the judiciary, so causing the judicial system to be perceived as an explicitly political

[33] Graham (2012), pp. 6–10. Naturally, while the arguments in favor of the involvement of third parties are mainly made by public NGOs, the main arguments against adopting the "amicus" are usually made by developing countries, investors, and financiers.

[34] McRae (2004), p. 12 ('Lack of transparency is a critical issue for the credibility of the WTO dispute settlement system.'). see Lacarte (2004), pp. 685–686.

[35] Brinkmann (2013); Kearney and Merrill (2000), pp. 743–855.

[36] Martin (2014), Johnson (2016) and Corbin (2017).

[37] Methanex v. USA, decision of the tribunal on petitions from third persons to intervene as 'amici curiae', 15 January 2001, para. 5. See vick p. 64.

arena.[38] In the United States, for example, one gets the impression that there is an attempt to influence the courts by recruiting amici: those who have many "amici" (more so when these are influential bodies) have a better chance of winning the case. For this reason, it is important to return to the traditional interpretation of the "classic amicus" and to determine that "amici" should only be allowed to join proceedings and submit briefs if the Amicus Curiae has new information that assists in the work of judging and has not been presented by the formal parties.[39]

10.2.2 Use of Amicus Curiae by Powerful Groups

Various studies, especially those conducted in the United States, have shown that in a significant number of the cases in which amicus briefs are submitted, the "amici" who join the proceedings are actually lobbyist interest groups that support powerful forces in society (for example, banks and giant corporations).[40] Sometimes, these are "amici" sent by the formal parties in sophisticated ways while complying with the legal rules to strengthen their arguments by presenting a public atmosphere favorable to their case as one of the formal litigants. In other words, there is concern that instead of promoting proper public values, the "amici" who participate in the proceedings (or those who are "hired" to misrepresent themselves as neutral amici when they are actually anything but neutral) actually support the positions of one of the formal litigants who may be commercial corporations in areas such as energy corporations, tobacco companies, large financial concerns, alcohol and firearms traders and manufacturers.[41] However, Morgan and Hazelton argue that 'even a brilliantly crafted brief submitted by those unfamiliar in the halls of the Supreme Court cannot fully compete with the elite attorneys and filers well known to the justices.' Their results suggest the resource advantage stems not just from the ability to produce high-quality briefs but also from 'the justices also know[ing] they can trust such attorneys since repeat players in the Supreme Court environment can't

[38] Anderson (2015), Some refer to U.S. judges as "black-robed politicians." In contrast, other scholars have pointed to an emphasis on the court's autonomy and its immunity to political pressure. Davis (1994).

[39] Jaffee v. Redmond, 518 U.S. 1, 35–36 (1996).

[40] There is a concern that these companies may have a specific agenda or interest that they are advocating for, which can lead to a perception of bias or lack of objectivity. For example, in the case of Citizens United v. Federal Election Commission, several oil and gas companies filed Amicus Curiae briefs arguing that campaign finance laws violated their free speech rights. Similarly, in the case of American Bankers Association v. National Credit Union Administration, the banking industry filed Amicus Curiae briefs arguing that a credit union regulatory rule was unlawful. Sachs and Revesz (2010).

[41] Wohl (1996) and Ward (2007).

afford to get caught misleading the Court.[42] Other scholars have suggested that the participation of corporations in Amicus Curiae briefs can undermine the legitimacy of the legal system and lead to a perception that justice is for sale to the highest bidder. In addition, some scholars have suggested that corporations' use of Amicus Curiae briefs can contribute to the "capture" of regulatory agencies, where these agencies become more responsive to the interests of the industries, they are meant to regulate rather than the public interest. This can lead to a situation where corporations have undue influence over regulatory policy, which can be detrimental to the environment, public health, and consumer protection.[43]

For example, Senator Sheldon Whitehouse has raised related concerns that wealthy, influential groups, particularly those aligned with conservative or Republican interests, have exploited the amicus process as a tool for coordinated judicial lobbying that undermines judicial independence and public trust. In his view, donor networks have funded extensive "amicus armadas" while also influencing judicial nominations, allowing them to potentially shape judicial outcomes through amicus influence without transparency around their funding sources. Whitehouse warns that such undisclosed amicus campaigns by monied interests could "weaken public faith in the courts and the foundations of our democracy." His central criticism highlights the need for robust disclosure requirements to promote accountability around significant amicus funders.[44]

A study conducted in the United States relating to the middle of the twentieth century found that commercial corporations and various professional groups that are collectively powerful interest groups submitted more than 58 percent of the amicus briefs submitted to the Supreme Court, while other organizations, such as consumer organizations or environmental organizations, submitted less than 42% of the amicus briefs.[45] On the other hand, the opposite criticism was voiced against the use of "amici," mainly in international courts (but not only) when it was argued that in international proceedings, the "amici" tend to be one-sided when they stand, almost automatically, on the side of the "underdog" taking the side of poor countries against strong countries or the side of weak parties against groups of investors and capitalists, regardless of the examination of the facts in their entirety.[46]

In other words, opening the doors to third parties to express their interests as amici in ongoing proceedings may serve the vital forces in the economy, which can better use an "amicus." Moreover, powerful interest groups will be able to relatively quickly "acquire" or send various "amici," who can influence the courts, depending on the interests of their senders. The ability of powerful economic actors to file amicus briefs can lead to a perception that the legal system is biased in favor of

[42] Hazelton and Hinkle (2022). Persuading the Supreme Court: The Significance of Briefs in Judicial Decision-Making. University Press of Kansas.

[43] Kagan (1991) and Sachs and Revesz (2010).

[44] Whitehouse (2021).

[45] Bradley and Gardner (1985), p. 91; Kearney and Merrill (2000).

[46] Mourre (2006), p. 266; Gruner (2003), p. 955; Hobér (2008), p. 155.

corporate interests rather than being impartial and fair to all parties involved. This can contribute to disillusionment and mistrust in the legal system, particularly among those who feel their voices are not being heard.[47]

10.2.3 Little Control Over the Legal Process

As mentioned repeatedly in the previous sections, Amicus Curiae has clear advantages (for example, low costs and a relatively low rate of risk about incurring additional legal expenses). At the same time, a person who chooses to participate in the process as an Amicus Curiae consciously decides to be a passive partner in the legal process (except in the case of the "litigating amicus," sometimes referred to as "Amicus Plus," but as stated, this mechanism is not common). Apart from presenting their position in writing, "classic amici" have no real ability to control the judicial process. The involvement of the amicus in the proceedings is usually limited to the submission of a written brief and relatively rarely includes oral arguments. The formal litigants are those who conduct the proceedings under the auspices of the court and can, at their discretion, decide to delete, reject, withdraw a petition, or compromise the proceeding without consulting the amici.

When a person or organization submits an amicus brief, they do not have direct control over the legal strategy or decision-making process of the formal parties involved in the case. This lack of control can limit their ability to shape the arguments or outcomes in a manner that aligns perfectly with their interests.[48]

10.2.4 Low Contribution to the Legal Process and the Fear of Harm to the Formal Parties

Another argument against third parties joining as amici is that some of them make no real contribution to the work of the courts. The argument is that the briefs submitted by many amici do not add any new vital information to the court. They often only replicate arguments made by formal litigants in different ways (such briefs which only repeat information already submitted to the proceedings are sometimes referred to as "me too briefs").

[47] In addition, "information flooding" on the part of "amici" may cause the courts to weed out the information that reaches them from the "amici" and leave only the information that is based and supported by expert opinions. This will give an advantage to strong groups and sectors that have the power to fund scientific opinions over weaker groups. Goldman (2011), pp. 907, 909–11; Larsen (2014).

[48] Hansen and Watson (2009), 86–106.

Moreover, some amici are liable to burden the courts with a great deal of information that is not only not essential to its work but also causes a corruption of the judicial process by diverting time and energy away from the relevant issues in a way that violates the parties' rights to an efficient and speedy process.[49] In other words, the possibility of submitting an amicus brief without clear procedural limitations (such as the test proposed below, according to which the brief may only be accepted if the information offered by the Amicus Curiae sheds new light on the proceedings by adding new, relevant data), may place a burden on the courts in the form of too many lengthy briefs. As stated, this may cause a substantial impairment of the efficiency of the judicial process and a violation of the procedural rights of the formal parties to an efficient process.

Submitting multiple amicus briefs can inundate the court with diverse perspectives and arguments. This influx of information may overload the court's capacity to thoroughly analyze and evaluate each brief, potentially compromising the quality and efficiency of the decision-making process.[50]

Moreover, when it comes to the use of an amicus in arbitration proceedings (or other proceedings whose common denominator is the consent of the parties to the outline of the proceeding), it should be remembered that an arbitration proceeding is by its nature a process of agreement conducted with free will between two parties, and therefore when a particular party does not wish to add amici to the arbitration process, it cannot be forced to take such a step because such coercion contradicts the rationale of the arbitration process.[51]

In other words, opponents to the participation of amici argue that this process can interfere with the formal parties' autonomy because it introduces external voices into a process designed to be consensual and confidential. They argue that allowing "amicus" submissions can disrupt the balance between the parties and may unduly influence the decision-making process of the arbitral tribunal.[52]

[49]Ramseyer and Rasmusen (2008). [Courts often have limited resources, including staff, time, and budget. The additional work associated with reviewing and considering amicus briefs can strain these limited resources, potentially affecting the court's ability to efficiently handle its overall caseload and delaying the resolution of cases].

[50]Nelson (2011), pp. 121–186.

[51]First Mexican 1128 Submission ¶ 5, United Parcel Serv. of Am., Inc. v. Canada (NAFTA Arb. June 11, 2001). In NAFTA's UPS arbitration, Mexico said it was "deeply troubled" by the addition of "amici" to the arbitration process, arguing that this development in procedural law was a risky move contrary to the organization's tradition. See also by Catherine A. Rogers Amicus Curiae Participation in International Commercial Arbitration International Journal of Procedural Law.

[52]de Arboleda and Yasmin (2013) http://renati.sunedu.gob.pe/handle/sunedu/881650. The article examines the participation of Amicus Curiae in investor-state arbitration. It analyzes the potential effects on the autonomy of the parties and the arbitral process, and discusses the various approaches and rules adopted by different arbitral institutions and tribunals.

10.2.5 Increasing Legal Process Costs

Another argument is that those briefs submitted by amici which do not assist in the work of the courts lead to an increase in the overall costs of the legal process.[53] As more amicus briefs are filed and the participation of interest groups balloons to unprecedented dimensions, the total costs involved in conducting proceedings may also increase in ways that become cumbersome to the process due to excessively lengthy time periods required to examine the briefs.[54]

In some of the proceedings, there is a concern that certain "amici" will flood the courts with non-essential information and materials that ultimately impair the ability of the courts to act quickly and efficiently.[55] Judge Richard Posner of the former Chicago Court of Appeals was one of the advocates of this criticism. He has ruled on several occasions that the "amicus" representation mechanism (as interpreted by most United States courts) has failed in its role to assist the courts. In his view, the "amici" hamper the work of the courts, making it more difficult while wasting valuable judicial time and increasing the costs of the legal process.[56]

Moreover, in arbitration proceedings joined by amici, it is further argued that the "amici" are not "true" friends of the court as they cause unnecessary delays in the arbitration process, which is intended to be short and efficient rather than turning to other courts, thereby increasing the costs imposed on the parties who tried in advance to avoid this by resorting to arbitration.[57] In other cases primarily related to arbitration proceedings, "amici" ask arbitrators to instruct the parties to provide them with commercial documents and materials that the parties to the dispute do not necessarily wish to hand over. In doing so, they impair the autonomy of the parties to conduct the arbitration as they want and increase the costs of the procedure.[58]

---

[53] Posner (1993), pp. 23–30.

[54] Flechtner (2013), pp.1211–1263. [examining the economic implications of amicus participation in international commercial arbitration within the United States]. See also Williamson (2010), pp. 491–518. It focuses on the relationship between costs and the involvement of Amicus Curiae in the Canadian legal system. The author conducts an empirical study to explore the impact of amicus participation on the overall costs of legal proceedings. The study examines the costs associated with Amicus Curiae participation in different types of cases, such as appellate litigation or constitutional matters, within the Canadian context.

[55] Goldman (2011), pp. 907, 909–11; Larsen (2014).

[56] Ryan v. Commodity Futures Trading Comm'n, 125 F.3d 1062, 1063 (seventh Cir. 1997) p. 1063; 223 F.3d 615 (seventh Cir. 2000).

[57] Sabater (2010), p. 51.

[58] Ishikawa (2010), p. 393.

10.2.6 Use of Unsubstantiated Research Methods

Another shortcoming of the Amicus Curiae practice is that some "modern amici" who participate in ongoing legal proceedings use research methods that are not scientifically based, meaning that the court cannot properly evaluate the information presented.[59] Caitlin E. Borgmann noted that "amicus briefs may be replete with dubious factual assertions that would never be admitted at trial."[60]

According to this criticism, judges should be aware that not all information presented by "modern amici" is reliable and well-founded. Indeed, the information they present may be excessive, inaccurate, or erroneous. For example, Rustad and Koenig argued that in light of the possibility of "amici" presenting information in an exaggerated or unreliable manner (a phenomenon known as "junk science"),[61] courts should appoint a professional expert to provide independent and critical advice regarding briefs containing various types of information. They suggested that these experts will examine briefs presented by amici in the social sciences and humanities (such as psychology, sociology, criminology, theology, and language).[62]

Another option proposed to counteract the fear of excessive information or misinformation presented by "modern amici" seeking to support formal litigants is the establishment of independent research institutes alongside the courts to help them correctly and accurately evaluate such briefs.[63]

Larsen agrees with this position, and she, too, has warned against judgments that quote information from amicus briefs and rely on them as indisputable facts, even though they are scientifically questionable. She wrote, "It is a mistake to conclude that the justices can easily tell which of these amici are real factual experts and which are not."). She suggested that a condition for submitting a brief in any field of research is that the "amici" present to the courts a detailed and comprehensive scientific explanation of the research methods and data analysis (and criticisms of the information presented, if any) relied upon in the brief.[64]

In recent years, large numbers of individuals and groups from diverse backgrounds in society who are highly concerned about issues affecting their world

---

[59] Collins et al. (2015). See also: Blake (2019). See also the concerns raised in Dwyer (2023).

[60] Borgmann (2013).

[61] This term took root in part thanks to Huber (1991) Huber argued that there is high-quality, well-established science and that there is "junk science"—idle and unacceptable science masquerading as real science.

[62] For recent use in the social sciences of an amicus's brief, and for an analysis of its use, see: Horn et al. (2020), pp. 449–476.

[63] Rustad and Koenig (1993), pp. 91, 157–58; See also, Faigman (1989), pp. 1005–1095.

[64] Larsen (2014). Larsen relies to some extent on the series of measures proposed by Huber (1991) To prevent abuse of legal process through idle science Cf. Larsen (2014), p. 1811–12 ("the Court could decline to accept any amicus brief filed with factual claims that are not backed up with an explanation of the methods used to discover them" or that are supported only with research reports that are not readily available to the court and other participants in the case, because they are unpublished.

have reached the courts by submitting an amicus brief. These include social organizations, professionals, academics, including university professors, law students involved in amicus clinics, private individuals, politicians, various interest groups, and commercial companies. As we have seen throughout the book, in general, using an amicus brief has several advantages and disadvantages, which I will recount in this summary. Beginning with the positive aspects from the perspective of the work courts, first and foremost, an overwhelming advantage of using Amicus Curiae is that the information submitted by amici may lead to a more accurate and complete legal decision that also considers the interests of third parties that may be affected by court rulings. Looking at advantages from the perspective of the amici, a second benefit is that Amicus Curiae is a tool that enables a diverse range of individuals and groups access the courts with the potential to influence their rulings in various areas that influence people's lives including ecological, economic, and social fields. From the perspective of both the courts and the amici, a third benefit of using Amicus Curiae is that it has low costs and financial risks for the amici and, when used properly, does not burden the courts with costly or lengthy procedures. From society's point of view, a fourth benefit is seen in that using Amicus Curiae increases cooperation between interest groups, NGOs, and various other groups in society and between the private and public sectors. These collaborations strengthen civil society and have great self-worth. Finally, a fifth benefit that has been discussed is that the amicus supports the institutional legitimacy of the courts because of the very willingness of the courts to listen to the arguments of various amici present, with this expressing an appreciation on the part of the courts for the amici which in turn creates a more significant commitment from various sectors of society to respect the court rulings.

Using the Amicus Curiae practice also has disadvantages. First of all, one of the serious concerns is that the amicus practice may turn the courts into political arenas. Secondly, it sometimes appears that massive use of the Amicus Curiae practice by interest groups and "powerful" corporations means the practice is "hijacked" by those having the means to pay for apparently neutral "amici" in a way that presents a misleading understanding of how widespread an opinion presented by them is in society. From the point of view of the amici themselves, using Amicus Curiae rather than joining a proceedings as a formal party has limitations, as amici have limited control over the legal process. A fourth disadvantage I have discussed is that lengthy amicus briefs may load the courts with irrelevant information or data that does not add anything new or useful for the courts' decisions. Furthermore, a fifth disadvantage has been seen in that misuse of "amicus" may lead to protracted proceedings and the potential infringement of the rights of formal litigants. Finally, it is important that the information in amicus briefs is only collected and analyzed using established scientific methods, with a sixth potential disadvantage being that the use of unsubstantiated research methods could mean that the information is invalid, and the "amicus" tool looses scientific credibility.

10.3 Book Summary

This book discusses the "Amicus Curiae phenomenon," which has now spread throughout the common law judicial system (Anglo-American) the continental judicial system (Romano-Germanic) and is widely used in international law. Within a short period, dozens of countries worldwide, including developing countries in Latin America, Africa, Asia, Eastern Europe, and most of the world's international institutions, adopted the Amicus Curiae practice one after the other. Countries that have already recognized the amicus in the past have significantly increased its use so that amici now appear in most courts.

The "Amicus Curiae phenomenon" is a multidimensional phenomenon with many facets. As we have seen, the first characteristic of the phenomenon is the adoption of the amicus practice in various countries worldwide that did not use this practice until about 30 years ago. A second characteristic is the diversity of the range of areas withing which amicus briefs are submitted to the courts, and thirdly, these briefs are also submitted in increasingly diverse types of judicial instances. An additional characteristic of the phenomenon is the increased number of briefs submitted in "mega cases" (such as affirmative action or same-sex marriage). A fifth and final characteristic of the phenomenon is the increase in the type, variety, and nature of entities that have begun to use Amicus Curiae to influence court rulings (such as private individuals, NGOs, professional bodies, corporations, and politicians).

The rise of the "Amicus Curiae phenomenon" has had widespread effects in the legal world beyond influencing particular judicial proceedings. First, and possibly most directly, there has been an increase in awareness of Amicus Curiae through its coverage in the media, popular literature, blogs, search engines on the Internet, and video content sharing sites. There has also been an increase in academic literature and academic research on the practice of amicus and its impact on the decision-making processes of the courts. The phenomenon has led to the opening of many clinics around the world that train students to submit a brief as amici on a variety of topics. This, in effect, has created a new area of expertise in the work of lawyers, with a novel role introduced of a lawyer with the title of "coordinator for submitting amicus briefs" who is responsible for coordinating and regulating all amicus briefs submitted in support of a particular position, Finally, the Amicus Curiae phenomenon has also had an impact on the planning and appearance of courtrooms, with unique seating provided for amici, even though they are not formal parties to the proceedings.

The book begins by describing the Amicus Curiae institution and then traces the transformations that have taken place in it from Roman law to the present day. It goes on to present a typology of the prototypes of the "amicus" (from the "classic amicus" to the "modern amicus") and notes the differences between the "amicus" and other third-party practices (such as the "intervener"). It then discusses the "Amicus Curiae phenomenon," in its various manifestations, and its expression in modern law. Later, the question of why the "Amicus Curiae phenomenon" grew so quickly, with the amicus practice becoming so popular in such a variety of countries and courts, is explored while attempting to explain its broad scope and depth.

Having discussed the various layers of the "Amicus Curiae phenomenon," each in its own right, and indeed their cumulative effect, it becomes evident that the "Amicus Curiae phenomenon" is indeed a central, topical, and significant phenomenon in judicial systems today. The rise of the "Amicus Curiae phenomenon" is one of the notable large-scale changes that have taken place within the work of the courts over the last three decades. Although formally amici are secondary actors to the original formal litigants, their centrality, power, and importance to the courts' decision-making processes are highly significant, often more so than the influence of the official litigants.

The "Amicus Curiae phenomenon" is deeply rooted in the processes that have taken place over the past three decades in the judicial system, including the changing perception of its role and its work style. To successfully fulfill their modern judicial role and deal with the diverse content of modern law, including many increasingly complex issues and questions relating to our rapidly changing world, the courts need to keep up to date with new developments, which involves accessing vast quantities of information, while also obtaining different perspectives that are not the domain of the formal parties at a hearing. Sometimes, they need information that the formal parties want to avoid presenting because it harms their interests, or they cannot present it. The dynamic legal reality requires adjustments in the work of the courts, and the Amicus Curiae is a procedural practice that helps bridge these gaps.

The diverse information that flows to the courts through the amici enables the courts to fulfill their obligation to do their work in a comprehensive manner—bridging the gap between the existing law and the changing social reality. When the courts are deeply involved in shaping the public and private spheres, their awareness of the diverse interests and the broad implications of their choices on society at large, including on diverse social groups, particularly those other than the formal parties to the proceedings, intensifies. This judicial policy requires openness to receive social information and different perspectives from other parties who are not directly part of any formal dispute yet may be affected by court rulings. The overall perspectives and insights conveyed to the courts through amici are, to a large extent, the "elixir" of law since they "connect" the law to society and its desires. The courts are aware of the "meta-legal" power of the Amicus Curiae that goes beyond providing information not presented to the courts by the parties.

Sometimes, the courts accept briefs from amici, even though they do not bring new information per se relating to the dispute, but because they serve as a conduit for conveying information about the public lobby and the interest groups behind the issue. The amicus briefs express the views of those bodies that will probably continue to operate in the public, legal, media, and political arenas if their position is not accepted. Therefore, the courts attach importance to briefs, even if they do not formally add significant new information. Instead, they serve as a kind of "social barometer" reflecting opinions relating to the overall implications of the issue (the "institutional factor").

The Amicus Curiae practice enables groups in society to have a greater influence over their lives and well-being because it is a window through which different interests and perspectives enter the legal system that have not entered it beforehand. For interest groups in society, submitting an amicus brief is an effective way to actively participate in shaping the decisions that affect their environment. They see the submission of an amicus brief as a strategy of action, often an exclusive one, for advancing their goals. In their eyes, the Amicus Curiae is perceived as a platform in which it is possible to influence public opinion and, directly or indirectly, decision-makers, along with other tools such as petitions, lobbying in the legislature, protest demonstrations, and advertising in the media. Sometimes, the amicus brief submitted by interest groups is not intended to attain an "immediate achievement" but rather to lead to broad and significant public processes later on, sometimes outside the courts. The social change in the role of lawyers and the growing number of lawyers in the world, and in particular the increase in the number of jurists engaged in promoting various public goals (social, ecological, security, economic, political), also affects the "Amicus Curiae phenomenon," since in their view the Amicus is a successful tool for achieving their goals.

In addition, the economic aspects related to the amicus practice incentivize its use because writing a brief and submitting it to the court involves low costs (no court fees, no proceeding costs) and low economic risks (no fear of awarding costs). In other words, financial barriers that prevent or delay access to justice do not exist in the amicus practice (the "social factor").

The "Amicus Curiae phenomenon" is the result of an interaction between the interests of the courts in expanding the public's participation base in proceedings and thereby establishing their institutional legitimacy and the interests of the people in a democratic society wish to increase their influence on their environment and their lives.

While acknowledging the global phenomenon of "Amicus Curiae," it is prudent to consider the insightful perspectives of Martin Shapiro (1993) on the globalization of law. Shapiro argues that despite shared themes and aspirations for uniformity across national legal systems, the process of globalization in law is complex and multifaceted. He suggests that true globalization of law, in the sense of a single set of legal rules governing the entire world, remains limited. Instead, the convergences and parallel developments in national legal systems often stem from shared needs and challenges, such as the distrust of bureaucratic discretion and the desire to protect individuals from powerful entities. However, Shapiro cautions against the uncritical adoption of American legal approaches and practices, as the U.S. legal system itself may exhibit excesses, such as excessive distrust of government and corporations, adversarial legalism, and an overabundance of lawyers and litigation. Shapiro's nuanced insights underscore the importance of recognizing both the convergences and the enduring national distinctiveness of legal systems worldwide.

The Amicus Curiae procedure makes the law accessible to diverse groups in society, enabling them to participate in the legal discourse. This process is an essential component in strengthening the legitimacy of the courts and leads to a commitment on the part of these groups to respect the rulings because even those who "lose" in the judicial process feel that their voice has been heard. Knowing that they have played a part in the process that led to the shaping of the decision enables them to understand it, and possibly stop acting against it, even if they do not support it. The more legitimate, balanced, and considered the decision made by the courts is perceived as being, and the more "open and considerate" it is to all public positions, even those representing these positions are not a formal part of the process but are only amici, the more likely it is that the public will respect the decision and accept it.

These institutional, social, and democratic processes also explain internal "Amicus Curiae phenomena" in many countries worldwide that have only begun to adopt "amicus" in recent years. The legal, constitutional, social, political, and economic processes that took place in countries around the world starting in the 1980s (sometimes a little earlier and sometimes later, depending, of course, on events in each country) led to the courts needing third parties to assist them not only in obtaining various types of information that the formal parties did not present but also in understanding the overall implications looking to the future that each judicial decision has on a broader circle of individuals.

Amicus Curiae is, therefore, a procedural practice that not only facilitates the receipt of information that the original parties to a legal proceeding did not provide but also expands the base of participation of additional sectors of society, thereby establishing public legitimacy for the courts' decision-making processes and creating commitment to their decisions.

The "Amicus Curiae phenomenon" brings about profound changes in law and the courts' work as it integrates into various processes that reshape the work of the courts. It has contributed to the fact that a judicial proceeding on a central issue in which there are a limited number of formal parties and a judge deciding the issue between them is considered the "old" world of litigation, while the "new world" becomes a multidimensional process composed of formal parties and dozens or even hundreds of different "amici." In recent years, many individuals from almost every group in society who want to influence and shape their world through the courts, use the Amicus Curiae practice. This includes ordinary citizens, students, academics, professional bodies, college professors, politicians, commercial companies, journalists, and rights organizations. Almost without exception, people from all of these backgrounds have been using the Amicus Curiae practice in recent years on issues large and small to influence their lives and well-being.

The use of Amicus Curiae as a strategy to influence the outcomes of the courts brings about a significant change not only in the form of discussion that becomes multilateral with all the accompanying implications (for example, in some proceedings, most of the information presented to the courts is presented by third parties rather than by the formal parties) but also in the style of conduct of judges and parties in the courtrooms (and often, outside of them: at demonstrations and in the media). The amicus has been influential in creating more flexible processes, in contrast with the older judicial tradition that was hostile to the intervention of third parties. It has prompted the courts to take into account interests other than those of the formal parties. In this way, Amicus Curiae has brought about a new era in which the prevalent legal thinking of judges is characterized by a willingness to accept new and varied types of information (such as sociology, criminology, anthropology, or exact sciences) and decide proceedings on the basis of this information transmitted to them by amici,"with this happening at a time when the nature of the litigation has become more polar, more divided and more vocal.

The idea embodied in the redesign that Amicus Curiae gives to the work of the courts is that many issues discussed in the courts are not necessarily the exclusive domain of the formal parties to the dispute but of the public in general and, indeed, of other parties affected by court rulings or those who wish to influence them.

Many modern judicial processes have political, ecological, security, social, and economic implications that are broader than the legitimate interests of formal litigants. Therefore, additional groups and individuals have the right to express their opinion on any procedure that can affect their lives and well-being. This is, in fact, a revival of the perception of litigation as a broad social process in which not only the formal parties are involved but also many other entities, including experts and professional consultants, as was the case in the past ("Iuris Consulti").

Amicus Curiae not only brings about a profound change in law and in the work of the courts, but at the same time, it also is indicative of the role of the courts in society and their worldview regarding the place of law in society. The courts' responses to the desire of amici to express their position in ongoing proceedings primarily reflect their perception of their own role. There is thus a strong correlation between the perception of the judicial role and the rise of the "Amicus Curiae phenomenon." In places where the courts have broad powers and deep involvement in society (such as the United States, Canada, or South Africa), we can see more active participation of amici, who will try to influence court policy and vice versa. Courts that are sympathetic to and welcome amicus interventions tend to view their own role more broadly than one simply defined by adjudicating disputes. These courts that are interested in accepting Amicus Curiae perspectives tend to be aware of their dominant role in shaping the law applicable in the country.

From a formal perspective, the amicus practice is "totally" and solely a legal procedure that is used after adhering to strict rules. However, from a deeper perspective, the amicus practice embodies extensive in-depth processes that have taken place in recent years in the perception of the role of the courts. The perspectives, positions, needs, interests, types of information, and insights conveyed to the courts through the amici expose the courts to a broader world, including fields of knowledge and disciplines that previously were foreign and unknown to them. The submission of well organized, relevant information enables the courts to decide complex and diverse issues in a better-informed manner, and in a more "open" way than was customary in the past. Recognizing an Amicus Curiae and opening the door to any individual who wishes to influence his life through the submission of an amicus brief means a change in the work of the courts and their increasing involvement in shaping society. The conclusion drawn from this depth examination of the processes involved in the increase in use of the Amicus Curiae practice and of the impact of this practice both on the work of the courts and on society, is that as a result of the rise of the "Amicus Curiae Phenomenon," the role of the courts in society is now broader than ever before.

References

Abramowicz M, Colby TB (2009) Notice and-comment judicial decision making. Univ Chicago Law Rev 76:965, 987

Alarie BRD, Green AJ (2010) Interventions at the Supreme Court of Canada: accuracy, affiliation and acceptance. Osgoode Hall Law J 48(3/4):381–410

Anderson HA (2015) Frenemies of the court: the many faces of amicus curiae. Univ Rich Law Rev 49:361

Blackaby N, Richard C (2010) Amicus curiae: a panacea for legitimacy in investment arbitration? In: Waibel M et al (eds) The backlash against investment arbitration: perceptions and reality, Alphen aan den Rijn, p 269

Blake WD (2019) Don't confuse me with the facts: the use and misuse of social science on the United States Supreme Court. Md Law Rev 79(216):252. at 252, 248

Borgmann CE (2013) Appellate review of social facts in constitutional rights cases. Calif Law Rev 101:1185, 1216

Bradley RC, Gardner P (1985) Underdogs, Upperdogs and the use of the amicus brief: trends and explanations. Justsys J 10:78, 91

Brinkmann TM (2013) Transparency and amicus curiae in supreme court decision making. J Law Courts 1(1):81–102

Brynat S (2001) The five habits: building cross cultural competence in lawyers. Clinical Law Rev 8 (33):99

Choudhury B (2008) Recapturing public power: is investment arbitration's engagement of the public interest contributing to the democratic deficit. Va J Transnational Law 41:775

Collins PM Jr (2004) Friends of the court: examining the influence of Amicus Curiae participation in United States Supreme Court litigation. Law Soc Rev 38(4):807–832

Collins PM Jr, Corley PC, Hamner J (2015) Influence of amicus curiae briefs on U.S. Supreme Court opinion content. Law Soc Rev 49:917

Corbin CR (2017) Amicus curiae and transparency in the Supreme Court. Ohio State Law J 78 (3):593–624

Coyle M (2016) Roberts singles out former white house counsel for 'Extraordinary' brief. ART. COM. http://www.law.com/supremecourtbrief/almID/1202756102813

Davis R (1994) Decisions and images: the Supreme Court and the press

de Arboleda C, Yasmin. (2013) Amicus curiae participation in investor-state arbitration: enhancing transparency and procedural legitimacy of investment dispute resolution. University of London, London. http://renati.sunedu.gob.pe/handle/sunedu/881650

De Brabandere E (2011) NGOs and the public interest—the legality and rationale of amicus curiae interventions in international economic and investment disputes. Chin J Int Law 12:85–113

Disaffected Democracies (Susan J. Pharr & Robert D. Putnam 2000)

Dwyer JG (2023) Faux Advocacy in Amicus Practice. Pepperdine L Rev 50:633–718

Faigman DL (1989) To have and have not: assessing the value of social science to the law as science and policy. Emory Law J 35:1005–1095

Feldman A (2016) The most effective friends of the court, empirical SCOTUS https://empiricalscotus.com/2016/05/11/themost-effective-friends-of-the-court

Flechtner HM (2013) The economic impact of amicus participation in U.S. international commercial arbitration. UC Davis Law Rev 47(4):1211–1263

Franze AJ, Anderson RR (2015) Record breaking term for amicus curiae in Supreme Court reflects new norm. Nat Law J. http://www.nationallawjournal.com/supremecourtbrief/id=1202735095655

Franze AJ, Anderson RR (2016) In unusual term, big year for amicus curiae at the Supreme Court. Nat Law J. https://www.apks.com/~/media/files/perspectives/publications/2016/09/in-unusual-term-big-year-for-amicus-curiae-at-thesupreme-court.pdf

Goldman P (2011) Note, Should the supreme court stop inviting amici curiae to defend abandoned lower court decisions? Stan Law Rev 63:907, 909–907, 911

Graham C (2012) Advocates for Int'l Dev., a "How To" guide to amicus curiae & international investment arbitrations, pp 6–7
Gruner M (2003) Accounting for the public interest in international arbitration. Columb J Transnational Law 41:955
Hansen W, Watson AH (2009) The role of amicus curiae briefs in the federal appellate courts. Just Syst J 30(1):86–106
Hazelton MLW, Hinkle RK (2022) Persuading the Supreme Court: The Significance of Briefs in Judicial Decision-Making. University Press of Kansas, Kansas
Hobér K (2008) Arbitration involving states. In: Newman L, Hill R (eds) The leading arbitrators' guide to international arbitration, New York, chapter 8, p 155
Horn CL et al (2020) Shaping educational policy through the courts: the use of social science research in amicus briefs in fisher I. Educ Policy 34(3):449–476
Huber PW (1991) Galileo's Revenge: Junk Science in the Courtroom
Ishikawa T (2010) Third party participation in investment treaty arbitration. Int Comp Law Q 59: 373, 393
Johnson TJ (2016) Amicus curiae participation in United States Supreme Court cases: a network analysis. Soc Networks 47:116–129
Johnson L, Tuerk E (2005) CIEL's experience in WTO dispute settlement: challenges and complexities from a practical point of view. In: Treves T et al (eds) Civil society, international courts and compliance bodies, The Hague, p 24
Juaristi FJR (2014) The amicus curiae in the inter-American Court of human rights (1982–2013)
Kagan A (1991) Adversarial legalism and American Government. J Policy Anal Manage 10(1):1–18
Kawharu A (2007) Public participation and transparency in investment arbitration: recent developments and future challenges. IHLRes 2:2–3
Kearney JD, Merrill TW (2000) The influence of amicus curiae briefs on the supreme court. Univ Pa Law Rev 148:743–855
Lacarte J (2004) Transparency, public debate and participation by NGOs in the WTO: a WTO perspective. J Int Econ Law 7:685–686
Larsen AO (2014) The trouble with amicus facts. Va Law Rev 100:1757–1818
Larsen AO, Devins N (2016) The amicus machine. Va Law Rev 102:1901
Lester A (1988) Amici curiae: third party interventions before the European court of human rights. In: Matscher F, Petzold H (eds) Protecting human rights: the European dimension—studies in honour of Gérard J. Wiarda, Cologne, p 342
Levine E (2011) Amicus curiae in international investment arbitration: the implications of an increase in third-party participation. Berkeley J Int Law 29(1):200–224
Lynch KJ (2004) Best friends? Supreme Court law clerks on effective amicus curiae briefs. JL Pol 20(33):46–56
Martin AD (2014) Strategic amici curiae and Supreme Court decision-making. Law Soc Rev 48 (3):527–562
McRae D (2004) What is the future of WTO dispute settlement? J Int Econ Law 7:12
Mourre A (2006) Are amici curiae the proper response to the public's concerns on transparency in investment arbitration? Law Practice Int Courts Tribunals 5:266
Nelson WE (2011) Taking interests into account: amicus curiae participation in Supreme Court litigation. Stanford Law Rev 63(5):121–186
Posner RA (1993) What do judges and justices maximize? (The same thing everybody else does). Sup Ct Econ Rev 3(1):23–30
Ramseyer JM, Rasmusen EB (2008) When are amicus curiae briefs unhelpful? Int Rev Law Econ 28(3):224–232
Rustad M, Koenig T (1993) The Supreme Court and junk social science: selective distortion in amicus briefs. NC Law Rev 72(91):157–158
Sabater A (2010) Towards transparency in arbitration (A cautious approach). Berkeley J Int Law Publicist 5(47):51

Sachs B, Revesz RL (2010) Corporate amicus briefs. Mich Law Rev 108(5):787–823
Schachter M (2004, 2004) The utility of pro bono representation of U.S.-based amicus curiae in non-U.S. and multi-national courts as a means of advancing the public interest. Fordham Int Law J 28:111
Shapiro M (1993) The globalization of law. Indiana J Glob Legal Stud 1(1):37–64
Shaw GM, Brannan KE (2009) Confidence in law enforcement. Public Opin Q 73:199
Simard LS (2008) An empirical study of amici curiae in Federal Court: a fine balance of access, efficiency, and Adversarialism. Rev Litig 27:669, (referring to Grutter v. Bollinger, 539 U.S. 306 (2003)
Spriggs JF, Wahlbeck PJ (1997) Amicus curiae and the role of information at the Supreme Court. Polit Res Q 50(2):365–386
Strutin K (2015) Amicus curiae: information in the Service of Justice. LLRX, http://www.llrx.com/2015/04/amicus-curiae-information-in-the-service-of-justice
Tarr GA (2003) Judicial process and judicial policymaking, 3rd edn, p 233–43
Umbricht G (2001) An "Amicus Curiae brief" on amicus curiae briefs at the WTO. J Int Econ Law 4:783
Voßkuhle A, Sydow G (2002) Die demokratische Legitimation des Richters. Juristische Zeitung 57
Ward SF (2007) Friends of the Court are friends of mine. ABA J 24(93):11
Warren RK (2000) Public trust and procedural justice. Ct Rev Fall 12
Whitehouse S (2021) A flood of judicial lobbying: amicus influence and funding transparency. Yale LJF 131:141
Williamson (2010) Costs and the participation of amicus curiae in Canada: an empirical study. Dalhousie Law J 33(2):491–518
Wohl A (1996) Friends with agendas. J ABA 82:11
Wolfrum R (2008) Legitimacy of international law from a legal perspective: some introductory considerations. In: Wolfrum R, Röben V (eds) Legitimacy in international law, Berlin
Zannoti F (1995) The judicialization of judicial salary policy in Italy and the United States. The global expansion of judicial power

SPRINGER NATURE

GPSR Compliance

The European Union's (EU) General Product Safety Regulation (GPSR) is a set of rules that requires consumer products to be safe and our obligations to ensure this.

If you have any concerns about our products, you can contact us on ProductSafety@springernature.com

In case Publisher is established outside the EU, the EU authorized representative is:

Springer Nature Customer Service Center GmbH
Europaplatz 3
69115 Heidelberg, Germany

The manufacturer's authorised representative in the EU is Springer Nature Customer Service Centre GmbH, Europaplatz 3, 69115 Heidelberg, Germany. If you have any concerns regarding our products, please contact ProductSafety@springernature.com

Printed and bound by CPI Group (UK) Ltd, Croydon, CR0 4YY
08/10/2026
02229827-0001